Early Church Records of Gloucester County New Jersey

Friends' Meeting House (built 1690), Haddonfield, N.J., c. 1842.

Compiled by
*Charlotte D. Meldrum
and John Pitts Launey*

HERITAGE BOOKS
2008

HERITAGE BOOKS
AN IMPRINT OF HERITAGE BOOKS, INC.

Books, CDs, and more—Worldwide

For our listing of thousands of titles see our website
at
www.HeritageBooks.com

Published 2008 by
HERITAGE BOOKS, INC.
Publishing Division
100 Railroad Ave. #104
Westminster, Maryland 21157

Copyright © 1995 Charlotte D. Meldrum
and John Pitts Launey

All rights reserved. No part of this book may be reproduced or transmitted in any form or by any means, electronic or mechanical, including photocopying, recording or by any information storage and retrieval system without written permission from the author, except for the inclusion of brief quotations in a review.

International Standard Book Numbers
Paperbound: 978-1-58549-347-0
Clothbound: 978-0-7884-7492-7

CONTENTS

Introduction v

Haddonfield Monthly Meeting
    Births and Deaths 1
    Deaths 28
    Marriage Certificates 33
    2nd Declarations of Marriage 64
    Going out in Marriage from minutes. 88
    Certificates of Removal (1681 - 1750) 93

Marriages of Gloucester Co. from court records of New Jersey 110

Moravian Register, West Jersey 1742-1794
    Births 116
    Receptions (Members) into the Congregation 136
    Marriages 139
    Deaths 141

Woodbury Monthly Meeting
    Births and Deaths 150
    Family Relationships from Minutes 171
    Marriages 178
    Minutes of Meeting 187

Congregation of the Episcopal Church of St. John 237

Register of St. Mary's Church, Colestown 240
    Subscribers 241

Index 243

OLD GLOUCESTER

Early Quakers

In late Fall 1677, the *Kent* took on Quaker passengers at Hull on the east coast of England. Known as the "Yorkshire Tenth," this group came mainly from Yorkshire, Nottinghamshire, and Derbyshire in northern England. The *Kent* set sail and proceeded south to London, where additional Friends were boarded. Known as the "London Tenth," these passengers came from Northamptonshire, the County of Northumberland, Oxfordshire, Buckinghamshire, and Berkshire, as well as London. After a voyage of six weeks, she sailed up the Delaware River with the tide and put to shore near the mouth of Raccoon Creek in Gloucester County. The Yorkshire Tenth turned north and decided to settle in the fertile region later known as Burlington County. By negotiations not specifically detailed in the record, they were able to convince the smaller London Tenth to leave Gloucester and join them.

HADDONFIELD MONTHLY MEETING

The few households that remained in Gloucester County joined together and requested permission from the Salem Quarterly Meeting to establish a Monthly Meeting in Newton Township. This was granted in 1686 and the Meeting was first known as Newton Monthly Meeting. In the 12th month, 1721/2, it was moved to the town of Haddonfield and renamed Haddonfield Monthly Meeting. As good land became scarce and more expensive in Burlington County to the north and Salem County to the south, expansion increased into Gloucester County. In addition, large numbers of new arrivals from all parts of England, Ireland, and Wales found the cheaper, more abundant land in Gloucester County to their liking. Eventually, the population increased to the point that a northern portion of Gloucester County, including Haddonfield, was partitioned and renamed Camden County. This gave rise to the informal term "Old Gloucester" when referencing its previous boundaries.

WOODBURY MONTHLY MEETING

By 1782, Haddonfield Monthly Meeting increased in membership to the point that division became necessary. After three years of discussion and planning, Woodbury Monthly Meeting was established by the authority of the Salem Quarterly Meeting at the request of

Haddonfield Monthly Meeting. The verge, or service area, designated for Woodbury included Haddonfield members residing in Deptford Township and portions of the townships of Upper Greenwich, Upper Woolwich, and Lower Gloucester, including the Town of Gloucester. The first Monthly Meeting was held in the Town of Woodbury, Deptford Township, on the 11th day of the first month, 1785.

SOCIETY OF FRIENDS (QUAKERS)

The Religious Society of Friends, frequently known as the Quaker movement, began in England during the 1650s primarily due to the dedication, inspiration, and leadership of a simple, Yorkshire tailor named George Fox. The movement took its members from the ranks of the Church of England that grew dissatisfied with its corrupt and often politically motivated leaders and doctrine. The motivation to abandon land and position in England and begin again in the Jerseys was supplied by the persecution of a Puritan dominated government and an intolerant crown.

Friends saw a fundamental evil in the use of repetitive ritual and ceremony and created a society carefully avoiding these practices. Rather than wedding ceremonies, public marriages were held in private homes or meeting houses. Rather than funeral services, memorial essays were carefully and lovingly composed and read to the membership at Monthly Meetings. Baptisms and the sacrament known as the Lord's Supper in other denominations were not practiced. The child of two Quaker parents was accepted as a member by birthright. It was important, therefore, to keep meticulously accurate records of births, marriages, disownments, and reinstatements.

Every meeting had two copies of the *Book of Discipline*, one each for the Men's and Women's Meetings. This volume specified in detail how Friends must conduct their daily affairs. Many forms of diversion and entertainment common in those days were forbidden, including horse racing, betting, games of chance, hawking, and fox hunting. Alcohol was not forbidden, but drinking to excess or frequenting "houses of diversion" were causes for discipline.

The *Book of Discipline* also specified the procedure to be followed in an orderly marriage. At a Monthly Meeting, the couple would announce their intentions to marry for the first time. If one of the two young people was not a Friend, he or she was told the procedure necessary to request membership. If both were already members, they were instructed to bring letters of consent from their parents, or bring the consenting parents, to the next meeting. If one was a member of a different Monthly Meeting, which was often the case, he or she was instructed to also bring a "certificate of clearness to marry" from that Meeting. This letter would specify his or her freedom from engagements or other marriages. Next, a committee of two or more were appointed to interview the couple, their parents, and acquaintances to determine if any objection existed to the marriage.

At a subsequent Monthly Meeting, usually the next one, the couple again appeared and announced their continued intentions to marry. Appropriate letters of consent and clearness were delivered to the clerk, who read them to the Meeting and made the proper notations in the minutes. Following a report from the committee that no objection was found, the couple was granted liberty to proceed with the marriage. Friends were appointed to attend the marriage to ensure that orderly procedure was followed. They were also required to report the orderly completion of the marriage at the following Monthly Meeting and see that the certificate was properly recorded. The Overseer of the Meeting was ultimately responsible for all records and would then examine the entry to make certain all was correct.

If, for any reason, the marriage certificate was not recorded, certain assumptions can be made from the minutes. According to an entry at the beginning of the Woodbridge Monthly Meeting minutes, "it can be assumed that the marriage took place one week after the date permission was granted or three weeks before the date it was reported accomplished." A comparison of the minutes and properly recorded certificates shows this statement to be highly accurate, although exceptions can by found.

The procedure for an orderly marriage within the discipline usually took five weeks from the first announcement to the marriage day. This delay was deemed necessary to give the couple time to cool off and consider. With disturbing frequency, couples elected to bypass procedure and marry outside of Friends by ceremonies performed by a "hireling priest," a minister of another denomination, or by a justice or magistrate. This was always cause for disciplinary action. If the member wished to remain in unity with Friends, he or she was required to bring a letter condemning the act to a Monthly Meeting and read it before Friends. The individual was also required to bring a copy of the marriage certificate. If the person charged were truly contrite and no corrections were necessary in the condemnation letter, Friends could elect to accept the letter and continue in unity. If conditions did not appear to be in order, the Meeting usually continued the case until the following Monthly Meeting. Failure to accept and follow the order of discipline usually led to disownment. The most serious marriages out of unity were those involving close relatives, such as first cousins. This almost always led to disownment. Marriages between second cousins were occasionally permitted but always discouraged, and marriages between third cousins were both permitted and common. Unlike assumptions that can be made from entries in the minutes granting permission to marry or reporting its accomplishment, no assumptions can be made from entries reporting marriages out of unity, because the marriage may have occurred from days to years prior to the entry. In these cases, the reader is advised to seek a copy of the civil marriage license from New Jersey Archives in Trenton.

Friends believed that the use of the names of the days and months was a "vulgar practice" because the origin of many of these names could be traced back to pagan gods, such as the Viking god Thor for Thursday, or deified rulers, such as Julius Caesar, Caesar Augustus, and Octavian. Consequently, Friends numbered their days and months. Days of the week began with Sunday as "First Day" and were never a problem; however, two calendars, the Julian and Gregorian, were in use by Friends during the period of this book, each with a different number corresponding to the name of the month. Briefly the rule is this: For dates before November 1, 1751, the first month of the year was March, the second was April, and so on; from November 1, 1751, to the present, January was designated the first month.

MORAVIAN CHURCH

In an article by George B. Macaltioner in *Notes On Old Gloucester County New Jersey*, Vol. 1, pp. 77-86, published by The New Jersey Society of Pennsylvania (1917), he describes the conditions of Swedish churches in the area which led to the loss of ministers. He states that the Moravian Church in New Jersey found its beginning at this time, owing to the fact that the Swedish churches were without pastors and the German Lutheran Church, at Friesburg, was neglected.

On 13 January, 1742/3, Paul Daniel Bryzelius proposed to supply the need for ministers for very little salary. He had been ordained at Frankford, Pennsylvania, as a Presbyter according to the orders of Count Zinzendorf, founder of the Moravian Church. He was given charge of three Swedish churches and one German Lutheran, at Friesburg, or Chohansey. The Swedish churches were at Maurice River, Raccoon, and Penns Neck.

The church at Pilesgrove, Oldmans Creek, or Woolwich, was begun in 1747, by Laurence T. Nyberg, a Moravian minister who had been shut out of the German church at Lancaster, Pennsylvania. In 1749, the membership of this church included the following persons: George Avis, Nicholas Dahlberg and wife, Charles Dorsan, Andrew Holstein, Lawrence Holstein, Sr., and his son Lawrence, Jr., Larse Hopman, Michael Kett, Mons Kyn, Peter Lauterbach, Adam Lehberger, Saml. Lynch, Christopher Linmyer, Bateman Lloyd, Obediah Lloyd, Alexander Mueller, John Roalin Samson a slave, Garret Van Immen and wife, John Van Immen and wife, William Van Immen and wife, Andrew Van Immen and wife, Jechoniah Wood, and Jeremiah Wood. By 1793, the congregation began to dwindle. From 1798 to 1800, there was no pastor. The last pastors served from 1801 until 1803. In 1834, the Episcopalians were granted use of the building. This was the last Moravian church in New Jersey until the modern church was established.

SWEDES

For information on early Swedish settlers in Gloucester County, see Peter Stebbins Craig, *The 1693 Census Of The Swedes On The Delaware*. Winter Park, FL: SAG Publications (1993).

BIRTHS AND DEATHS IN HADDONFIELD MONTHLY MEETING 1658-1825

Children of Thomas Sharp and Sarah, his wife: Elizabeth Sharp, b. 2nd da, 9th mo, 1687; Thomas Sharp, b. 25th da, 7th mo, 1689; Samuel Sharp, b. 21st da, 5th mo, 1691; Mary Sharp, b. 10th da, 1st mo, 1692; Martha Sharp, b. 27th da, 11th mo, 1694; Sarah Sharp, b. 9th da, 10th mo, 1696; Joseph Sharp, b. 22nd da, 12th mo, 1698.

Children of Thomas Sharp and his second wife, Elizabeth Winn: John Sharp, b. 5th da, 4th mo, 1703.

Children of Timothy Hancock: Elizabeth Hancock, b. 16th da, 1st mo, 1686; Mary Hanock, b. 11th da, 1st mo, 1688; Sarah Hancock, b. 3rd da, 11th mo, 1689; Ann Hancock, b. 30th da, 7th mo, 1691; John Hancock, b. 30th da, 4th mo, 1693; Hannah Hancock, b. 14th da, 4th mo, 1695.

Children of Francis Estlake born in Bermudas: Hepezabeth Estlake, b. 21st da, 1st mo, 1658; Mary Estlake, b. 15th da, 1st mo, 1660; Ruth Estlake, b. 3rd da, 9th mo, 1663; Sarah Estlake, b. 17th da, 5th mo, 1665; George Estlake, b. 19th da, 6th mo, 1667; Meriam Estlake, b. 30th da, 4th mo, 1669; Jeremiah Estlake, b. 3rd da, 12th mo, 1671; Joseph Estlake, b. 16th da, 9th mo, 1674.

Children of Thomas A. Thackrea and Hepzabeth, his wife: Thomas Thackrea, b. 7th da, 8th mo, 1690; Francis Thackrea, b. 5th da, 7th mo, 1693; Hepzabeth Thackhrea, Jr., b. 23rd da, 11th mo, 1695.

Children of John Wood and Allis, his wife: Constantine Wood, b. 24th da, 7th mo, 1683; John Wood, b. 24th da, 1st mo, 1687. Constantine Wood was the first child of English parents born at Woodbury Creek.

Child of Henry Wood of Woodbury Creek: Mary Wood, b. 11th da, 6th mo, 1706.

Children of Samuel Sharp and Martha, his wife: Elizabeth Sharp, b. 5th da, 3rd mo, 1719; Thomas Sharp, b. 7th da, 12th mo, 1720.

Sarah Sharp, wife of Thomas Sharp, d. 2nd da, 9th mo, 1699, buried at Newton.

Elizabeth Sharp, the second wife of Thomas Sharp, d. 4th da, 8th mo, 1709, buried at Newton.

Katherine Sharp, third wife of John Sharp, d. 23rd da, 9th mo, 1720, buried at Newton.

Henery Wood, father of the said John Wood, d. 19th da, 8th mo, 1686 aged 83 years and was buried at Woodbury Creek.

Allice, wife of John Wood, d. 3rd mo, 8th mo, 1693 aged about 47

years. Jeremiah Wood, son of John d. 2nd da, 9th mo, 1694 about 22 years of age.
Rebeka, wife of Henery Wood, d. 1703.
John Wood, of Woodbury Creek, d. 30th da, 8th mo, 1706 aged about 36 years.
Anthony Sharp, d. 1st da, 11th mo, 1694.
Hannah Atkinson, wife of James Atkinson, d. 3rd da, 2nd mo, 1698.
Mary Lord, dau of Joshua and Sarah Lord, d. 22nd da, 9th mo, 1695.
John Lord, son of Joshua Lord, d. 10th da, 6th mo, 1693.
Sarah Lord, wife of Joshua Lord, d. 30th da, 3rd mo, 1702.
Sarah Lord, dau of Joshua Lord, d. 20th da, 7th mo, 1702.

Sarah Sharp, dau of William Sharp, b. 2nd da, 2nd mo, 1696.
Jeremiah Sharp, b. 5th da, 3rd mo, 1699.
Children of John Sharp and Elizabeth, his wife: William Sharp, b. 2nd da, 10th mo, 1689; Elizabeth Sharp, b. 4th da, 3rd mo, 1692; John Sharp, b. 8th da, 10th mo, 1693; Thomas Sharp, b. 23rd da, 6th mo, 1698; Hannah Sharp, b. 1st da, 10th mo, 1700; Samuel Sharp, b. 5th da, 7th mo, 1702; Sarah Sharp, b. 30th da, 4th mo, 1705.

Elizabeth Sharp, wife of John, d. 28th da, 9th mo, 1705, buried at burying ground near William Evens's house.
Simeon Ellis, d. 29th da, 1st mo, 1715, was buried at Newton burying grounds.

Children of Josiah Kay and Rebekah, his wife: John Kay, b. 24th da, 8th mo, 1715; Josiah Kay, b. 17th da, 12th mo, 1717; Francis Kay, b. 19th da, 7th mo, 1720; Rebekah Kay, b. 23rd da, 10th mo, 1722.
Children of Joshua Lord and Sarah, his wife: John Lord, b. 19th da, 2nd mo, 1692; James Lord, b. 6th da, 8th mo, 1693.
Children of John Kay and Elizabeth, his wife: Joshua Kay, b. 28th da, 2nd mo, 1685 at Springwell; John Kay, Jr., b. 22nd da, 8th mo, 1686; Elizabeth Kay, b. 23rd da, 1st mo, 1688; Josiah Kay, b. 7th da, 10th mo, 1690; Joseph Kay, b. 23rd da, 7th mo, 1692; Benjamin Kay, b. 4th da, 7th mo, 1694; Samuell Kay, b. 28th da, 6th mo, 1696; Sarah Kay, b. 22nd da, 7th mo, 1698; Isaac Kay, b. 4th da, 11th mo, 1704.
Children of James Adames and Hester, his wife: Judedya Adames, b. 4th da, 5th mo, 1696; John Adames, b. 1st da, 2nd mo, 1698, d. 7th da, same mo; Thomas Adames, b. 12th da, 12th mo, 1698.
Children of Stephen Newby and Elizabeth, his wife: Marke Newby, b. 1st da, 6th mo, 1704; Hannah Newby, b. 11th da, 10th mo, 1705.

Joshua Kay, son of John Kay, d. 27th da, 7th mo, 1711.
Joseph Kay, son of John Kay, d. when struck by a falling log on the 16th da, 4th mo, 1724, buried at Newton burying grounds, aged 28 years.
Samuel Kay, d. 20th da, 1st mo, 1706, was buried at Newton, 10 years of age.
Elizabeth Kay, wife of John Kay, d. 11th da, 8th mo, 1713.
Esther Spicer and Esther Saxby, her servant, and Richard Thackera, the son of Thomas Thackrea of Newton, he being about 11 years, were slain by thunder 24th da, 7th mo, 1703. All buried at Newton burying grounds.

Children of Thomas Hutton and Mary, his wife: William Hutton, b. 2nd da, 9th mo, 1698; John Hutton, b. 7th da, 6th mo, 1700; Thomas Hutton, b. 5th da, 2nd mo, 1702; Mary Hutton, b. 29th da, 11th mo, 1703; Ann Hutton, b. 29th da, 11th mo, 1703; Ann Hutton, b. 22nd da, 12th mo, 1705.
Children of Thomas Frentch and Mary, his wife: Joseph Frentch, b. 23rd da, 7th mo, 1698; Thomas Frentch, b. 27th da, 8th mo, 1702.

Richard Heritage of New Garden, d. 16th da, 6th mo, 1702.

Children of Matthew Allen: Matthew Allen, b. 23rd da, 8th mo, 1688; Mercy Allen, b. 13th da, 1st mo, 1692; Mary Allen, b. 23rd da, 8th mo, 1695; Thomas Allen, b. 7th da, 2nd mo, 1697.
Children of William Evens and Elizabeth, his wife: Thomas Evens, b. 12th da, 12th mo, 1694; William Evens, b. 25th da, 7th mo, 1697; Jane Evens, b. 21st da, 8th mo, 1699; William Evens, b. 18th da, 10th mo, 1704.

Jane Evens, mother of William Evens, the elder, d. 6th da, 4th mo, 1697.
William Evens, the son of William Evens and Elizabeth, d. 31st da, 8th mo, 1698.
Archibald Mickle, d. 28th da, 1st mo, 1706.

Child of Thomas Sharp and Elizabeth Winn, his wife: John Sharp, b. 9th da, 1st mo, 1703.
Children of Samuel Sharp: Elizabeth Sharp, b. 21st da, 3rd mo, 1719; Thomas Sharp, b. 7th da, 12th mo, 1720.
Children of Joshua Lord and Sarah, his wife of Woodbury: Elizabeth

Lord, b. 12th da, 8th mo, 1690; John Lord, b. 19th da, 2nd mo, 1692; James Lord, b. 6th da, 8th mo, 1693; Mary Lord, b. 14th da, 9th mo, 1696; Joshua Lord, Jr., b. 1st da, 11th mo, 1698; Sarah Lord, b. 30th da, 3rd mo, 1702.

Children of Joshua Lord and Isabel, his second wife: Edmond Lord, b. 12th da, 11th mo, 1710/11.

Children of James Lord and Elizabeth, his wife belonging to the meeting at Woodbury were married 24th da, 1st mo, 1714 at Chesterfield in Burlington County: Sarah Lord, b. 30th da, 8th mo, 1717; Benjamin Lord, b. 18th da, 12th mo, 1719; James Lord, Jr., b. 13th da, 3rd mo, 1722; Phinehas Lord, b. 21st da, 1st mo, 1724; Ann Lord, b. 18th da, 7th mo, 1726.

Children of John Cooper and Ann, his wife of Woodbury: Mary Cooper, b. 12th da, 1st mo, 1712; Ann Cooper, b. 23rd da, 4th mo, 1716; John Cooper, b. 15th da, 1st mo, 1718/9; James Cooper, b. 11th da, 1st mo, 1721; Sarah Cooper, b. 1st da, 4th mo, 1723; David Cooper, b. 7th da, 12th mo, 1724/5; Hannah Cooper, b. 13th da, 12th mo, 1726/7; John Cooper, 2nd son of that name, b. 5th da, 11th mo, 1729.

Children of Joshua Lord and Sarah, his wife of Woodbury were married at Burlington: Hope Lord, b. 16th da, 8th mo, 1722; Caleb Lord, b. 14th da, 5th mo, 1724; Sarah Lord, b. 12th da, 11th mo, 1726/7; Joshua Lord, b. 1st da, 10th mo, 1728; James Lord, b. 12th da, 9th mo, 1730; Eunice Lord, b. 12th da, 11th mo, 1732; Jonathan Lord, b. 3rd da, 4th mo, 1735; Elizabeth Lord, b. 15th da, 6th mo, 1739.

Joseph Cooper, son of William and Margret Cooper, b. in Old England, County of Buckingham 1666 and Lydia, his wife, b. in Ireland of English parents, 1664.

Children of Joseph Cooper, Jr. and Mary, his wife of Newton Twp were married 17th da, 7th mo, 1713 at Philadelphia: Mary Cooper, b. 3rd da, 9th mo, 1714; William Cooper, b. 9th da, 5th mo, 1716; Joseph Cooper, b. 11th da, 6th mo, 1718; Joshua Cooper, b. 2nd da, 1st mo, 1720; Elizabeth Cooper, b. 2nd da, 12th mo, 1723/4; Lydia Cooper, b. 18th da, 8th mo, 1728.

Children of Job Whiteall and Jane, his wife of Woodbury: James Whiteall, b. 4th da, 9th mo, 1717; Hannah Whiteall, b. 19th da, 9th mo, 1720.

Child of James Smith and Jane, his wife, widow of Job Whiteall of Woodbury: Ruth Smith, b. 8th da, 7th mo, 1726.

Children of Abraham Chattin and Grace, his wife, of Woodbury: John Chattin, b. 6th da, 10th mo, 1717; Nickson Chattin, b. 7th da, 1st mo,

1718/19; Mary Chattin, b. 3rd da, 9th mo, 1721; Abraham Chattin, b. 18th da, 12th mo, 1723/4; James Chattin, b. 26th da, 2nd mo, 1726; Abisha Chattin, b. 5th da, 12th mo, 1728/9; Malachi Chattin, b. 23rd da, 11th mo, 1730/1; Sarah Chattin, b. 25th da, 3rd mo, 1732; Frances Chattin, b. 15th da, 7th mo, 1735; Josiah Chattin, b. 15th da, 11th mo, 1737; Ann Chattin, b. 10th da, 2nd mo, 1741.

Children of Robert and Elizabeth Lord of Woodbury: John Lord, b. 4th da, 2nd mo, 1698; Samuell Lord, b. 3rd da, 1st mo, 1699; Isaac Lord, b. 11th da, 8th mo, 1702; Sarah Lord, b. 28th da, 12th mo, 1704/5; Abraham Lord, b. 24th da, 12th mo, 1706/7; Rachel Lord, b. 8th da, 10th mo, 1708; Elizabeth Lord, b. 22nd da, 3rd mo, 1711; Robert Lord, b. 13th da, 7th mo, 1714; Joshua Lord, b. 3rd da, 7th mo, 1716; Abigail Lord, b. 15th da, 6th mo, 1719.

Child of Jonathan Ladd and Ann, his wife of Woodbury: Elizabeth Ladd, b. 13th da, 9th mo, 1724.

Children of John Wood, b. 24th da, 5th mo, 1686/7 and Mary, his wife, b. 10th da, 7th mo, 1690: Hannah Wood, b. 16th da, 7th mo, 1711; Sarah Wood, b. 1st da, 9th mo, 1714; James Wood, b. 24th da, 8th mo, 1716; Henry Wood, b. 27th da, 10th mo, 1720; Jonathan Wood, b. 27th da, 7th mo, 1723.

Children of Joseph Gibson and Elizabeth, his wife, of Woodbury: Rebeckah Gibson, b. 3rd da, 7th mo, 1721; Sarah Gibson, b. 2nd da, 12th mo, 1722; Elizabeth Gibson, b. 27th da, 8th mo, 1724; Joseph Gibson, b. 26th da, 3rd mo, 1726.

Child of Richard Bickham and Mary, his wife of Woodbury: Sarah Bickham, b. 6th da, 9th mo, 1726.

Children of Ebenezer Hopkins and Sarah, his wife of Haddonfield married at Woodbury 29th da, 2nd mo, 1737: John Estaugh Hopkins, b. 6th da, 5th mo, 1738; Elizabeth Estaugh Hopkins, b. 14th da, 12th mo, 1739; Haddon Hopkins, b. 30th da, 4th mo, 1743; Ebenezer Hopkins, Jr., b. 26th da, 8th mo, 1745; Sarah Hopkins, b. 4th da, 12th mo, 1748; Mary Hopkins, b. 31st da, 10th mo, 1750; Ann Hopkins, b. 17th da, 8th mo, 1752.

Children of William Forster and Hannah, his wife: Sarah Forster, b. 25th da, 12th mo, 1729/30; Elizabeth Forster, b. 20th da, 7th mo, 1731; Hannah Forster, b. 27th da, 3rd mo, 1734; Rebeckah Forster, b. 25th da, 5th mo, 1736; Amie Forster, b. 14th da, 10th mo, 1738; Mary Forster, b. 12th da, 12th mo, 1740; Josiah Forster, b. 20th da, 3rd mo, 1743; Martha Forster, b. 28th da, 7th mo, 1745; Abigail Forster, b. 22nd da, 8th mo, 1747; Phebe Forster, b. 8th da, 8th mo, 1749; William Forster, b. 14th da, 7th mo, 1751; Lidya Forster, b. 8th da, 3rd mo, 1757.

Children of Edward and Mary Richardson, married 4th da, 8th mo, 1728 at Woodbury Creek: Ruth Richardson, b. 22nd da, 6th mo, 1729; Jonah Richardson, b. 19th da, 6th mo, 1731; Martha Richardson, b. 22nd da, 5th mo, 1733; Mary Richardson, b. 5th da, 12th mo, 1735; Tabitha Richardson, b. 4th da, 5th mo, 1738; Ann Richardson, b. 16th da, 11th mo, 1741; Jesse Richardson, b. 8th da, 4th mo, 1744.

Children of Josiah Forster, b. 4th mo, 1682 and Amie, his wife, b. 4th da, 1st mo, 1685, married 3rd mo, 1705: William Forster, b. 13th da, 12th mo, 1706/7; Rebecca Forster, b. 1st da, 10th mo, 1708; Hannah Forster, b. 21st da, 10th mo, 1715; Hannah Forster, b. 21st da, 10th mo, 1715.

Hannah Forster, wife of above William, b. 17th da, 10th mo, 1710.

Children of David Cooper, b. 9th da, 12th mo, 1724/5, son of John and Ann Cooper and Sybil, his wife: Martha Cooper, b. 31st da, 10th mo, 1747: Amos Cooper, b. 1st da, 10th mo, 1749; Elizabeth Cooper, b. 7th da, 10th mo, 1751; Paul Cooper, b. 11th da, 1st mo, 1754; Ann Cooper, b. 8th da, 7th mo, 1756; William Cooper, b. 21st da, 6th mo, 1758.

Children of James Cooper, b. 11th da, 1st mo, 1719/20, son of John and Ann Cooper and Deborah, his wife, b. 18th da, 12th mo, 1728/9: Benjamin Clark Cooper, b. 15th da, 11th mo, 1748/9; James Cooper, Jr., b. 3rd da, 12th mo, 1750; James Cooper, second son by that name, b. 7th da, 2nd mo, 1754; Rebecca Cooper, b. 11th da, 10th mo, 1756.

Children of James Cooper and Mary, his second wife, formerly Jessup, b. 21st da, 3rd mo, 1728: Deborah Cooper, b. 5th da, 3rd mo, 1766; Samuel Cooper, b. 1st da, 1st mo, 1767; Sarah Cooper, b. 3rd da, 7th mo, 1768; William Cooper, b. 24th da, 9th mo, 1770; John Cooper, b. 9th da, 12th mo, 1774; Esther Cooper, b. 28th da, 10th mo, 1777.

Children of Frances Estlack, b. 30th da, 1st mo, 1707 and Phebe, his wife, b. 6th mo, 1711: Restore Estlack, b. 13th da, 2nd mo, 1734; Elizabeth Estlack, b. 14th da, 5th mo, 1736; Joseph Estlack, b. 20th da, 5th mo, 1738; Samuel Estlack, b. 20th da, 2nd mo, 1740; Sarah Estlack, b. 27th da, 5th mo, 1742; Ann Estlack, b. 8th da, 3rd mo, 1744; Mary Estlack, b. 7th da, 3rd mo, 1746; Phebe Estlack, b. 15th da, 5th mo, 1748.

Children of Samuel Burrough, son of Samuel and Hannah Burrough, b. 28th da, 9th mo, 1701 and Ann, his wife, dau of Richard and Joanna Gray, b. 29th da, 2nd mo, 1701: Hanah Burrough, b. 5th da, 4th mo, 1724; Sarah Burrough, b. 16th da, 8th mo, 1725; Samuel Burrough,

Jr., b. 10th da, 10th mo, 1727; Mary Burrough, b. 16th da, 3rd mo, 1730; Ann Burrough, b. 15th da, 10th mo, 1733; Joseph Burrough, b. 13th da, 12th mo, 1735/6; Abigail Burrough, b. 22nd da, 5th mo, 1738; Bathsheba Burrough, b. 14th da, 12th mo, 1739/40; Samuel Burrough, Jr., b. 4th da, 5th mo, 1742; Rachel Burrough, b. 15th da, 1st mo, 1743/4.

Samuel Tomlinson, son-in-law to Samuel Burrough, b. 24th da, 8th mo, 1732.

Children of Josiah Alberson of Gloucester twp, b. 1706 and Ann, his wife, b. 3rd da, 2nd mo, 1703: Hanah Alberson, b. 21st da, 1st mo, 1728; Mary Alberson, b. 16th da, 9th mo, 1730; Casandrew Albertson, b. 2nd mo, 1732; Elizabeth Albertson, b. 1st mo, 1734; Patience Albertson, b. 6th mo, 1736; Josiah Albertson, b. 8th mo, 1738; Sarah Albertson, b. 12th da, 10th mo, 1740; Kitturah Alberson, b. 1st da, 1st mo, 1743; Ann Alberson, b. 21st da, 6th mo, 1745.

Children of John Burrough, b. 18th da, 5th mo, 1705 and Phebe, his wife, dau of John Haines of Evesham, b. 6th da, 9th mo, 1710: Enoch Burrough, b. 28th da, 10th mo, 1726; John Burrough, b. 31st da, 5th mo, 1728; Samuel Burrough, b. 30th da, 6th mo, 1730; Hannah Burrough, b. 19th da, 9th mo, 1732; Josiah Burrough, b. 6th da, 10th mo, 1734; Esther Burrough, b. 18th da, 5th mo, 1737; Martha Burrough, b. 22nd da, 7th mo, 1739; Gideon Burrough, b. 3rd da, 11th mo, 1741; Mary Burrough, b. 21st da, 2nd mo, 1744; Benjamin Burrough, b. 11th da, 5th mo, 1746.

Joseph Heritage, son of Richard and Mary Heritage, b. 24th da, 2nd mo, 1675 at a place called Suttenander Brales in Gloucester Shire in old England, and Hannah, his wife, b. 13th da, 2nd mo, 1681 at Shrewsbury in east Jersey. He came over to America with his parents about the ninth year of his age, who settled in west Jersey,

Joseph Heritage, grandson to the above and son of Richard and Sarah Heritage, b. 25th da, 9th mo, 1746.

Daniel Roberts, grandson of the above and son of Jacob Roberts and Hannah, his wife, b. 4th da, 7th mo, 1752.

Children of Anthony Sharp, b. 20th da, 3rd mo, 1702 and Mary, his wife, b. 17th da, 10th mo, 1713: Elizabeth Sharp, b. 8th da, 5th mo, 1732; John Sharp, b. 26th da, 9th mo, 1735; Mary Sharp, b. 22nd da, 9th mo, 1739; Anthony Sharp, b. 20th da, 12th mo, 1741; Hosea Sharp, b. 16th da, 7th mo, 1744.

Children of Joseph Morgan and Agnis, his wife: Griffith Morgan, b. 22nd da, 6th mo, 1742; Joseph Morgan, b. 18th da, 1st mo, 1746/7; Hannah Morgan, b. 8th da, 11th mo, 1750; Elizabeth Morgan, b. 17th da, 3rd mo, 1753.

Child of Joseph Morgan and Mary, his second wife: Sarah Morgan, b. 27th da, 8th mo, 1759.

Children of Joseph Gibson and Sarah, his wife: James Gibson, b. 6th da, 11th mo, 1747; Joseph Gibson, b. 9th da, 1st mo, 1749/50; Joshua Gibson, b. 31st da, 3rd mo, 1752; Ann Gibson, b. 25th da, 12th mo, 1754; Jonathan Gibson, b. 17th da, 4th mo, 1757; Gideon Gibson, b. 2nd da, 7th mo, 1759.

Children of John Brown and Sarah, his wife: Zephaniah Brown, b. 14th da, 1st mo, 1748; Jonathan Brown, b. 4th da, 7th mo, 1749; Hannah Brown, b. 23rd da, 9th mo, 1750; Sophia Brown, b. 1st da, 2nd mo, 1753; Kezia Brown, b. 3rd da, 11th mo, 1755; Beulah Brown, b. 1st da, 2nd mo, 1758.

Children of Nehemiah Andrews, b. 4th da, 7th mo, 1712, son of Edward Andrews and Elizabeth, his wife, b. 15th da, 4th mo, 1718: Rachel Andrews, b. 6th da, 5th mo, 1740; Sarah Andrews, b. 25th da, 2nd mo, 1742; Hannah Andrews, b. 17th da, 11th mo, 1743/4; Edward and Joseph Andrews, twins, b. 25th da, 11th mo, 1745/6; Isaac Andrews, b. 23rd da, 8th mo, 1747; Nehemiah Andrews, b. 15th da, 5th mo, 1750; Paul Andrews, b. 14th da, 8th mo, 1752; Luke Andrews, b. 7th da, 3rd mo, 1755.

Children of William Snowden and Margaret, his wife: Sarah Snowden, b. 14th da, 1st mo, 1755; Elizabeth Snowden, b. 26th da, 7th mo, 1756; Mary Snowden, b. 3rd da, 8th mo, 1758; Isaac Ballenger Snowden, b. 31st da, 3rd mo, 1761.

Children of Ephraim Tomlinson, b. 29th da, 6th mo, 1695 and Sarah, his wife: Joseph Tomlinson, b. 23rd da, 1st mo, 1729; John Tomlinson, b. 5th da, 5th mo, 1732; Elizabeth Tomlinson, b. 30th da, 9th mo, 1735; Mary Tomlinson, b. 4th da, 12th mo, 1739; Ephraim Tomlinson, b. 17th da, 6th mo, 1742.

Children of Joshua Stokes, b. 8th da, 4th mo, 1716 and Ammy, his wife, b. 15th da, 12th mo, 1719: Thomas Stokes, b. 23rd da, 7th mo, 1742; Samuel Stokes, b. 24th da, 12th mo, 1743; Hannah Stokes, b. 18th da, 10th mo, 1745; Jacob Stokes, b. 18th da, 1st mo, 1748; Joshua Stokes, b. 31st da, 3rd mo, 1750; Elizabeth Stokes, b. 18th da, 2nd mo, 1752; Rachel Stokes, b. 23rd da, 2nd mo, 1754; John Stokes, b. 3rd da, 7th mo, 1758; Joseph Stokes, b. 4th da, 11th mo, 1760.

Children of Thomas Brown and Frances, his wife: John Brown, b. 15th da, 9th mo, 1747; Mary Brown, b. 28th da, 6th mo, 1749; David Brown, b. 13th da, 7th mo, 1751; James Brown, b. 29th da, 10th mo,

1753.

Children of Samuel Hopper and Mary, his wife: Mary Hopper, b. 4th da, 11th mo, 1739; John Hopper, b. 18th da, 5th mo, 1742; Elizabeth Hopper, b. 14th da, 7th mo, 1747.

Children of John Glover, b. 8th da, 2nd mo, 1729 and Mary, his wife, b. 24th da, 3rd mo, 1729: Thomas Glover, b. 12th da, 2nd mo, 1752; John Glover, b. 30th da, 2nd mo, 1753; William Glover, b. 24th da, 11th mo, 1755; Sarah Glover, b. 1st da, 5th mo, 1758; Isaac Glover, b. 14th da, 3rd mo, 1760.

Children of Archibald Mickle and Mary, his wife, b. 16th da, 3rd mo, 1730: Joseph Mickle, b. 5th da, 10th mo, 1750 o.s.; Sarah Mickle, b. 31st da, 6th mo, 1752 o.s.; Elizabeth Mickle, b. 3rd da, 6th mo, 1754; Samuel Mickle, b. 23rd da, 2nd mo, 1756; Isaac Mickle, b. 25th da, 1st mo, 1758.

Children of Nathaniel Lippincott, b. 2nd da, 5th mo, 1715 and Mary, his wife, b. 14th da, 9th mo, 1716: John Lippincott, b. 31st da, 6th mo, 1737 o.s.; Cabel Lippincott, b. 8th da, 12th mo, 1739/40; Martha Lippincott, b. 8th da, 2nd mo, 1742; Barzilla Lippincott, b. 15th da, 8th mo, 1744; Grace Lippincott, b. 17th da, 6th mo, 1747; Seth Lippincott, b. 14th da, 12th mo, 1749/50; Mary Lippincott, b. 30th da, 7th mo, 1753.

Children of John Gill, b. 7th da, 12th mo, 1721/2 and Amy, his wife, b. 20th da, 1st mo, 1724: Mary Gill, b. 4th da, 6th mo, 1743; Marcy Gill, b. 16th da, 4th mo, 1745; Hannah Gill, b. 2nd da, 9th mo, 1747; Hannah Gill, b. 13th da, 2nd mo, 1751; Elizabeth Gill, b. 15th da, 12th mo, 1752; Amy Gill, b. 16th da, 2nd mo, 1756; John Gill, b. 16th da, 7th mo, 1758; David Gill, b. 20th da, 4th mo, 1761; Marcy Gill, b. 9th da, 9th mo, 1764.

Children of Isaac Andrews and Elizabeth, his wife: Sarah Andrews, b. 25th da, 6th mo, 1739; Mary Andrews, b. 25th da, 4th mo, 1741; Jeremiah Andrews, b. 22nd da, 11th mo, 174/3/4; Elizabeth Andrews, b. 23rd da, 5th mo, 1747; Isaac Andrews, b. 21st da, 9th mo, 1749; Edward Andrews, b. 8th da, 10th mo, 1751; Lettitia Andrews, b. 7th da, 4th mo, 1754; Hannah Andrews, b. 27th da, 4th mo, 1757; Ebenezer Andrews, b. 13th da, 5th mo, 1761; Esther Andrews, b. 26th da, 11th mo, 1763.

Children of Samuel Mifflin and Mary, his wife: Edward Mifflin, b. 19th da, 10th mo, 1760; Mary Mifflin, b. 21st da, 4th mo, 1763.

Children of William Griscom, b. 30th da, 1st mo, 1715 and Sarah, his wife, b. 26th da, 1st mo, 1720: David Griscom, b. 16th da, 9th mo, 1741; Joseph Griscom, b. 5th da, 3rd mo, 1743; Deborah Griscom, b.

22nd da, 3rd mo, 1745; Deborah Griscom, b. 30th da, 11th mo, 1747; Sarah Griscom, b. 19th da, 6th mo, 1749; David Griscom, b. 20th da, 10th mo, 1751; Hannah Griscom, b. 10th da, 6th mo, 1754; William Griscom, b. 10th da, 4th mo, 1756; William Griscom, b. 1st da, 4th mo, 1758.

Children of Solomon Lippincott, b. 23rd da, 7th mo, 1720, son of Freedom Lippincott and Sarah, his wife, b. 20th da, 5th mo, 1720: Elizabeth Lippincott, b. 8th da, 3rd mo, 1746; Freedom Lippincott, b. 14th da, 7th mo, 1748; Martha Lippincott, b. 16th da, 10th mo, 1751; Jacob Lippincott, b. 12th da, 6th mo, 1754; Joshua Lippincott, b. 3rd da, 2nd mo, 1757; Daniel Lippincott, b. 22nd da, 3rd mo, 1760; Solomon Lippincott, b. 3rd da, 3rd mo, 1763.

Children of Jacob Cozens and Elizabeth, his wife: Sarah, b. 20th da, 5th mo, 1721; John Cozens, b. 18th da, 6th mo, 1724; Samuel Cozens, b. 21st da, 3rd mo, 1727; Mary Cozens, b. 28th da, 8th mo, 1729; Jacob Cozens, b. 5th da, 2nd mo, 1732; Joshua Cozens, b. 12th da, 12th mo, 1735; Elizabeth Cozens, b. 18th da, 9th mo, 1737; Daniel Cozens, b. 1st da, 9th mo, 1741.

Children of Samuel Cozens, son of Jacob, b. 21st da, 3rd mo, 1727 and Hannah, his wife: Elizat Cozens, b. 28th da, 8th mo, 1753; Jacob Cozens, b. 31st da , 1st mo, 1756; Benjamin Cozens, b. 2nd da, 9th mo, 1759; Samuel Cozens, b. 13th da, 7th mo, 1762.

Children of James Whitall, Jr., b. 22nd da, 12th mo, 1741 and Rebecca, his wife, b. 13th da, 9th mo, 1746: Mary Whitall, b. 26th da, 9th da, 1764; Deborah Whitall, b. 25th da, 9th mo, 1766; Lathia Whitall, b. 6th da, 6th mo, 1768; James Whitall, b. 11th da, 5th mo, 1770; Richard Whitall, b. 3rd da, 5th mo, 1772; George Whitall, b. 18th da, 6th mo, 1774; George Whitall, b. 5th da, 6th mo, 1776; William Whitall, b. 25th da, 7th mo, 1778; Rebecca Whitall, b. 20th da, 5th mo, 1780; Abraham Whitall, b. 30th da, 3rd mo, 1782.

Children of John Tatum, b. 4th da, 6th mo, 1739 and Sarah, his wife, b. 12th da, 7th mo, 1733: George Tatum, b. 12th da, 10th mo, 1763; Isaac Tatum, b. 19th da, 2nd mo, 1766; John Tatum, b. 11th da, 9th mo, 1767; Sarah Tatum, b. 11th da, 5th mo, 1770.

Children of Richard Gibbs: Hannah Gibbs, b. 6th da, 8th mo, 1762; Elijah Gibbs, b. 6th da, 11th mo, 1764; Solomon Gibbs, b. 11th da, 9th mo, 1766; Enoch Gibbs, b. 30th da, 12th mo, 1769; Phebe Gibbs, b. 9th da, 1st mo, 1772; Burrough Gibbs, b. 13th da, 7th mo, 1774; Sarah Gibbs, b. 16th da, 10th mo, 1776.

Children of William Bates, son of William Bates, dec'd, b. 4th da, 3rd mo, 1742 and Phebe, his wife, b. 27th da, 5th mo, 1741: Martha

Bates, b. 29th da, 3rd mo, 1771; John Bates, b. 3rd da, 8th mo, 1772; Marcy Bates, b. 11th da, 7th mo, 1774; Rebecca Bates, b. 4th da, 3rd mo, 1776.

Children of Samuel Paul: Joel Paul, b. 3rd da, 8th mo, 1767; Samuel Paul, b. 8th da, 9th mo, 1774.

Children of David Brown: Paul Brown, b. 5th da, 1st mo, 1763; Jessy Brown, b. 1st da, 1st mo, 1765; David Brown, b. 2nd da, 2nd mo, 1767; Hepsibah Brown, b. 31st da, 11th mo, 1769; John Brown, b. 1st da, 1st mo, 1776.

Children of Thomas Redman of Haddonfield, son of Thomas Redman, late of the city of Philadelphia, b. 31st da, 3rd mo, 1714 and Hannah, his wife, dau of Thomas Gill, late of Haddonfield, b. 7th da, 7th mo, 1719: Mary Redman, b. 21st da, 4th mo, 1738; Sarah Redman, b. 21st da, 11th mo, 1740/1; Thomas Redman, b. 22nd da, 9th mo, 1742; John Redman, b. 22nd da, 8th mo, 1744.

Child of Thomas Redman and Marcy, his second wife, b. 6th da, 12th mo, 1721/2: Joseph Redman, b. 18th da, 11th mo, 1749/50.

Children of Thomas Redman of Haddonfield, son of Thomas and Hannah Redman, b. 22nd da, 9th mo, 1742 and Rebecca, his wife, dau of Josiah and Rebecca White of Mt. Holly, b. 15th da, 3rd mo, 1745: Hannah Redman, b. 15th da, 11th mo, 1767; Rebecca Redman, b. 4th da, 11th mo, 1771; Mary Redman, b. 22nd da, 1st mo, 1774; Sarah Redman, b. 23rd da, 8th mo, 1776; Hannah Redman, b. 21st da, 11th mo, 1779; Thomas Redman, b. 26th da, 2nd mo, 1783; John E. Redman, b. 21st da, 1st mo, 1786.

Samuel Coles, b. 1st da, 1st mo, 1703 and Mary, his wife, b. 3rd da, 10th mo, 1710.

Children of David Davis and Martha, his wife removed from Pilesgrove and settled at Waterford in the compass of Haddonfield Monthly Meeting 17th da, 5th mo, 1772 having four children whose births are recorded at Salem: Martha Davis, b. 9th da, 9th mo, 1772; David Davis, b. 24th da, 12th mo, 1774; Benjamin Davis, b. 28th da, 11th mo, 1776.

Children of Joshua Lord, b. 1st da, 10th mo, 1728 and Hannah, his wife, b. 14th da, 7th mo, 1726, md. 9th da, 1st mo, 1748/9: Phinehas Lord, b. 21st da, 11th mo, 1749; Joshua Lord, b. 18th da, 9th mo, 1752; Sarah Lord, b. 19th da, 2nd mo, 1753; James Lord, b. 23rd da, 3rd mo, 1755; Ann Lord, b. 9th da, 2nd mo, 1757; Hannah Lord, b. 22nd da, 2nd mo, 1759; Eunice Lord, b. 2nd da, 3rd mo, 1761; Joshua Lord, b. 21st da, 4th mo, 1766; Jehu Lord, b. 27th da, 2nd mo, 1770.

Children of John Jessup: James Jessup, b. 6th da, 11th mo, 1769;

Sarah Jessup, b. 29th da, 9th mo, 1771; John Jessup, b. 16th da, 11th mo, 1773.

Child of William Keais and Alice, his wife: Frances Keais, b. 2nd da, 4th mo, 1765; Alice Keais, b. 19th da, 5th mo, 1769.

Child of William Keais and Sarah, his wife: William Keais, b. 15th da, 10th mo, 1775; Samuel Keais, b. 1st da, 5th mo, 1778.

Alice Keais, first wife of William Keais, d. 22nd da, 10th mo, 1770.

Children of Amos Cooper, b. 1st da, 10th mo, 1749 and Sarah, his wife, b. 31st da, 6th mo, 1752: Sybil Cooper, b. 20th da, 3rd mo, 1774; Mary Cooper, b. 26th da, 8th mo, 1776; Sarah Cooper, b. 10th da, 2nd mo, 1778; Hannah Cooper, b. 13th da, 10th mo, 1779; Joseph Cooper, b. 8th da, 2nd mo, 1781.

Children of Jonathan Brown, son of John Brown, b. 4th da, 7th mo, 1748: Mary Brown, b. 15th da, 8th mo, 1777; John Brown, b. 19th da, 3rd mo, 1780.

Children of Samuel Ladd and Sarah, his wife: Jonathan Ladd, b. 23rd da, 9th mo, 1755; Ann Ladd, b. 11th da, 7th mo, 1757; Hannah Ladd, b. 7th da, 11th mo, 1759; Eldad Ladd, b. 2nd da, 6th mo, 1762; John Ladd, b. 2nd da, 11th mo, 1764; Deborah Ladd, b. 23rd da, 9th mo, 1766; Samuel Ladd, b. 10th da, 11th mo, 1771.

Children of Job Whitall, son of James and Ann Whitall, b. 27th da, 1st mo, 1743 and Sarah, his wife, dau of John and Amy Gill, b. 28th da, 5th mo, 1751: David Whitall, b. 23rd da, 8th mo, 1771; Job Whitall, b. 27th da, 7th mo, 1773; Hannah Whitall, b. 26th da, 9th mo, 1775; Sarah Whitall, b. 11th da, 1st mo, 1779; John Gill Whitall, b. 7th da, 7th mo, 1781.

Children of Ebenezer Hopkins, b. 26th da, 8th mo, 1745 and Ann, his wife, b. 21st da, 6th mo, 1745: Isaac Hopkins, b. 23rd da, 8th mo, 1765; Sarah Hopkins, b. 5th da, 4th mo, 1767; Ebenezer Hopkins, b. 7th da, 9th mo, 1768; Josiah Hopkins, b. 25th da, 4th mo, 1770; Benjamin Hopkins, b. 29th da, 11th mo, 1771; Ann Hopkins, b. 25th da, 10th mo, 1773; Elizabeth Hopkins, b. 5th da, 10th mo, 1775; Samuel Hopkins, b. 7th da, 12th mo, 1777; Mary Hopkins, b. 19th da, 12th mo, 1780.

Children of Ephraim Tomlinson, son of Ephraim and Sarah Tomlinson, b. 17th da, 6th mo, 1764 and Ann, his wife, b. 24th da, 1st mo, 1750: Sarah Tomlinson, b. 18th da, 8th mo, 1768; Lydia Tomlinson, b. 8th da, 8th mo, 1770; Elizabeth Tomlinson, b. 21st da, 5th mo, 1773; Catherine Tomlinson, b. 23rd da, 2nd mo, 1775; James Tomlinson, b.

HADDONFIELD MONTHLY MEETING

16th da, 4th mo, 1778; Joseph Tomlinson, b. 28th da, 12th mo, 1780; Benjamin Tomlinson, b. 19th da, 4th mo, 1782.

Children of Joseph Mickle, son of Archibald Mickle, b. 5th da, 10th mo, 1750 and Hannah, his wife: Archibald Mickle, b. 8th da, 9th mo, 1772; Mary Mickle, b. 4th da, 7th mo, 1774; Elizabeth Mickle, b. 12th da, 5th mo, 1776; Sarah Mickle, b. 11th da, 4th mo, 1778; Deborah Mickle, b. 7th da, 8th mo, 1780; Keziah Mickle, b. 9th da, 3rd mo, 1784; Prisilla Mickle, b. 9th da, 2nd mo, 1786; Joseph Mickle, b. 8th da, 5th mo, 1788; Hannah Mickle, b. 11th da, 3rd mo, 1790; Lydia Mickle, b. 29th da, 8th mo, 1792; Martha Mickle, b. 9th da, 12th mo, 1794.

Children of Thomas Thorne, b. 10th da, 1st mo, 1739 and Abigail, his wife, b. 2nd da, 5th mo, 1738: Samuel Thorne, b. 11th da, 4th mo, 1762; John Thorne, b. 12th da, 8th mo, 1764; Joseph Thorne, b. 14th da, 3rd mo, 1767; Ann Thorne, b. 6th da, 5th mo, 1769; Isaac Thorne, b. 21st da, 8th mo, 1771; Mary Thorne, b. 26th da, 11th mo, 1773; Thomas Thorne, b. 17th da, 2nd mo, 1776; William Thorne, b. 6th da, 10th mo, 1778; Abigail Thorne, b. 11th da, 9th mo, 1781; Benjamin Thorne, b. 21st da, 8th mo, 1785.

Children of Thomas Stokes, b. 23rd da, 7th mo, 1742 and Sarah, his wife, b. 4th da, 1st mo, 1747: Abraham Stokes, b. 22nd da, 9th mo, 1765; Hannah Stokes, b. 14th da, 4th mo, 1767; Josiah Stokes, b. 24th da, 8th mo, 1768; Benjamin Stokes, b. 26th da, 5th mo, 1770; Esther Stokes, b. 11th da, 2nd mo, 1772; Elizabeth Stokes, b. 24th da, 8th mo, 1774; Joseph Stokes, b. 3rd da, 10th mo, 1776; William Stokes, b. 4th da, 2nd mo, 1779; Thomas and Joshua Stokes, twins, b. 19th da, 8th mo, 1780; Kezia Stokes, b. 22nd da, 5th mo, 1783.

Children of Samuel Burrough, Jr., son of Samuel Burrough, b. 4th da, 5th mo, 1742 and Sarah, his wife, dau of Jacob Lamb, b. 27th da, 7th mo, 1751: son, (not named), Burrough, b. 1st da, 9th mo, 1767; Abel Burrough, b. 31st da, 3rd mo, 1769; Samuel Burrough, b. 10th da, 7th mo, 1772; Eber Burrough, b. 19th da, 4th mo, 1775; Thomas Burrough, b. 13th da, 5th mo, 1779; Lydia Burrough, b. 16th da, 12th mo, 1781; Sarah Burrough, b. 23rd da, 9th mo, 1784; Samuel Burrough, b. 4th da, 8th mo, 1787.

Children of Elisha Hooton and Esther, his wife: Samuel Hooton, b. 4th da, 10th mo, 1774; William Hooton, b. 14th da, 11th mo, 1777; Martha Hooton, b. 18th da, 11th mo, 1779; Aaron Hooton, b. 22nd da, 1st mo, 1783; Elizabeth Hooton, b. 12th da, 3rd mo, 1785.

Children of Amos Ashead, b. 18th da, 12th mo, 1742/3 and Lydia, his wife, b. 31st da, 6th mo, 1746: John Ashead, b. 12th da, 4th mo,

1768; Mary Ashead, b. 28th da, 5th mo, 1770; Abel Ashead, b. 14th da, 9th mo, 1772; Eleanor Ashead, b. 20th da, 5th mo, 1779.

Children of Thomas Githens, b. 14th da, 10th mo, 1746 and Mary, his wife, b. 21st da, 5th mo, 1744: John Githens, b. 14th da, 8th mo, 1767; Thomas Githens, b. 26th da, 1st mo, 1771; Rebeckah Githens, b. 8th da, 2nd mo, 1773; Sarah Githens, b. 5th da, 1st mo, 1776; Mary Githens, b. 24th da, 7th mo, 1778; Phebe Githens, b. 16th da, 10th mo, 1780.

Children of Constantine Wilkins and Ann, his wife: Thomas Wilkins, b. 27th da, 9th mo, 1767; John Wilkins, b. 28th da, 11th mo, 1768; James Wilkins, b. 4th da, 9th mo, 1772; Benjamin Wilkins, b. 25th da, 8th mo, 1775; Joanna Wilkins, b. 16th da, 3rd mo, 1777.

Jedidiah Allen, son of Jedidiah Allen and Ann, his wife, b. 21st da, 8th mo, 1780.

Children of Josiah Albertson, Jr., b. 8th mo, 1738 and Eleanor, his wife, dau of John Tomlinson: Hannah Albertson, b. 2nd da, 2nd, mo, 1768; Isaac Albertson, b. 20th da, 10th mo, 1769; John Albertson, b. 16th da, 12th mo, 1771; Josiah Albertson, b. 26th da, 1st mo, 1774; Mary Albertson, b. 27th da, 3rd mo, 1776.

Children of John Sharp and Sarah, his wife: Anthony Sharp, b. 23rd da, 3rd mo, 1763; Nehemiah Sharp, b. 25th da, 9th mo, 1765; Sarah Sharp, b. 12th da, 12th mo, 1767; Mary Sharp, b. 15th da, 12th mo, 1769; John Sharp, b. 7th da, 3rd mo, 1772; Elizabeth Sharp, b. 25th da, 3rd mo, 1777.

Children of Samuel Webster, son of Thomas Webster, b. 20th da, 8th mo, 1735 and Sarah, his wife, b. 12th da, 10th mo, 1740: Ann Webster, b. 13th da, 4th mo, 1761; Thomas Webster, b. 1st da, 2nd mo, 1763; Elizabeth Webster, b. 2nd da, 1st mo, 1765; Josiah Webster, b. 8th da, 1st mo, 1767; Patience Webster, b. 14th da, 9th mo, 1768; Samuel Webster, b. 4th da, 3rd mo, 1771; Josiah Webster, b. 8th da, 11th mo, 1773; Isaac Webster, b. 12th da, 2nd mo, 1776; Jacob Webster, b. 22nd da, 2nd mo, 1778; Sarah Webster, b. 22nd da, 11th mo, 1779; Hannah Webster, b. 13th da, 1st mo, 1783.

Children of Richard Snowden and Sarah, his wife: John Snowden, b. 11th da, 8th mo, 1780 in Evesham; Leonard Snowden, b. 11th da, 10th mo, 1783 in Haddonfield; Mary Snowden, b. 3rd da, 10th mo, 1781 in Evesham; Rebecca Snowden, b. 17th da, 12th mo, 1785 in Northampton; Elizabeth and Sarah Snowden, twins, b. 18th da, 2nd mo, 1789 in Gloucester.

Children of John Gill, son of John and Amie Gill, b. 16th da, 7th mo, 1758 and Ann, his wife, dau of William Lovett and Mary Smith, b.

12th da, 2nd mo, 1758: Mary Gill, b. 9th da, 12th mo, 1788; John Gill, b. 9th da, 7th mo, 1795.

Children of William Bates, the elder and Elizabeth, his second wife, dau of Samuel and Ann Hooten, b. 20th da, 12th mo, 1736/7: Samuel Bates, b. 29th da, 11th mo, 1756; Samuel Bates, b. 9th da, 4th mo, 1758; Hezekiah Bates, b. 14th da, 12th mo, 1759; Hope Bates, b. 2nd da, 4th mo, 1761; Mary Bates, b. 6th da, 5th mo, 1763; Elizabeth Bates, b. 11th da, 1st mo, 1765; Ann Bates, b. 7th da, 10th mo, ----; Rebecca Bates, b. 22nd da, 8th mo, 1768; Sarah Bates, b. 4th da, 6th mo, 1772.

John Nickles and Hannah, his wife, no birth dates.

Joseph Kaighn, Sr. and Prudence, his wife, no birth dates.

Children of Michael Stratton, b. 6th da, 1st mo, 1766 and Rhoda, his wife, b. 8th da, 4th mo, 176?: Josiah Stratton, b. 21st da, 2nd mo, 1787; Charles Stratton, b. 5th da, 6th mo, 1790; Joseph Stratton, b. 15th da, 4th mo, 1792; Joshua Stratton, b. 1st da, 6th mo, 1796; Daniel Stratton, b. 8th da, 12th mo, 1797; Elizabeth Stratton, b. 10th da, 1st mo, 1800; Aaron Stratton, b. 31st da, 10th mo, 1801; Mary Stratton, b. 23rd da, 9th mo, 1805; Abigail Stratton, b. 17th da, 2nd mo, 1807; Michael Stratton, b. 13th da, 8th mo, 1808; George Stratton, b. 27th da, 11th mo, 1809.

Children of Benjamin Cooper, son of Samuel and Prudence Cooper, b. 9th da, 1st mo, 1775 and Elizabeth, his wife, dau of Joab and Amy Wills, b. 20th da, 4th mo, 1776: Samuel Cooper, b. 7th da, 10th mo, 1799; Rebecca Cooper, b. 17th da, 12th mo, 1800; Prudence Cooper, b. 6th da, 8th mo, 1802; Benjamin Cooper, b. 13th da, 1st mo, 1805; Elizabeth Cooper, b. 26th da, 11th mo, 1808; William, b. Cooper, b. 11th da, 6th mo, 1814.

Children of Joseph Kaighn, son of Joseph and Prudence Kaighn, b. 18th da, 3rd mo, 1774 and Sarah, his wife, dau of Joseph and Hannah Mickle, b. 11th da, 4th mo, 1778: John Kaighn, b. 7th da, 5th mo, 1796; Joseph Kaighn, b. 7th mo, 1798; Hannah Mickle Kaighn, b. 30th da, 5th mo, 1801; Hannah Mickle Kaighn, b. 27th da, 4th mo, 1804; Charles Kaighn, b. 30th da, 6th mo, 1806; William Kaighn, b. 10th da, 6th mo, 1808; Elizabeth Kaighn, b. 4th da, 4th mo, 1811; Sarah Kaighn, b. 2nd da, 6th mo, 1813; Mary Kaighn, b. 8th da, 3rd mo, 1816.

Children of Daniel Bassett, son of Daniel and Mary Bassett and Mary, his wife: Mary Bassett, no birth date; David Smith Bassett, b. 17th da, 11th mo, 1783.

Children of Daniel Bassett and Ruth, his second wife: Josiah Bassett, b.

26th da, 2nd mo, 1791; Hannah Bassett, b. 23rd da, 10th mo, 1793; Elizabeth Bassett, b. 1st da, 12th mo, 1796; Ruth Ann Bassett, b. 16th da, 2nd mo, 1799; Ebenezer Milton Bassett, b. 28th da, 2nd mo, 1801; Mark Bassett, b. 20th da, 4th mo, 1803.

Children of James Sloan and Rachel, his wife: Samuel Sloan, b. 10th da, 3rd mo, 1771; James Sloan, b. 8th da, 1st mo, 1773; Joseph Sloan, b. 14th da, 6th mo, 1774; Ruth Sloan, b. 23rd da, 12th mo, 1776; Mary Sloan, b. 16th da, 9th mo, 1778; William Sloan, b. 15th da, 4th mo, 1783; Rachel Sloan, b. 16th da, 3rd mo, 1786; Samuel Sloan, b. 18th da, 10th mo, 1787; John Sloan, b. 24th da, 8th mo, 1789; Rachel Sloan, b. 25th da, 12th mo, 1792.

Children of Isaac Mickle, son of Archibald and Mary Mickle, b. 25th da, 1st mo, 1758 and Sarah, his wife: Mary Mickle, b. 8th da, 3rd mo, 1789; Isaac Mickle, b. 15th da, 1st mo, 1791; John W. Mickle, b. 1st da, 1st mo, 1793; Rachel W. Mickle, b. 2nd da, 3rd mo, 1794.

Children of Isaac Mickle and Mary, his second wife: Archibald Mickle, b. 19th da, 5th mo, 1799; Andrew Ehrmstrong Mickle, b. 7th da, 6th mo, 1801; Benjamin Whitall Mickle, b. 31st da, 7th mo, 1803; Joseph Mickle, b. 7th da, 10th mo, 1806; Andrew Ehrmstrong Mickle, b. 28th da, 5th mo, 1810.

Children of Joshua Cooper and Abigail, his wife: William Cooper, b. 1st da, 1st mo, 1783; Joseph Ellis Cooper, b. 29th da, 8th mo, 1786; Cadwalder Cooper, b. 2nd da, 7th mo, 1789; Jacob S. Cooper, b. 12th da, 8th mo, 1790; Franklin Cooper, b. 13th da, 4th mo, 1793; Daniel Cooper, b. 21st da, 11th mo, 1795; George Cooper, b. 8th da, 10th mo, 1798; Sarah Ann Cooper, b. 6th da, 6th mo, 1801; Abigail Stokes Cooper, b. 25th da, 4th mo, 1803.

Child of Isaiah Burr and his wife: Ann Burr, b. 26th da, 11th mo, 1801.

Children of Daniel Arney and Elizabeth, his wife: Beulah Arney, b. 21st da, 11th mo, 1795, d. 25th da, 3rd mo, 1798; Ann Arney, b. 20th da, 8th mo, 1797; Barclay Arney, b. 19th da, 7th mo, 1799; Beulah Arney, b. 4th da, 11th mo, 1801; Charlotte Arney, b. 30th da, 7th mo, 1803; Daniel Arney, b. 13th da, 4th mo, 1807.

Daniel Arney, d. 8th da, 12th mo, 1806 aged 34 years.

Children of John Ward, son of George and Rachel Ward, b. 28th da, 1st mo, 1765 and Hannah, his wife, dau of James and Rebecca Mason, b. 17th da, 11th mo, 1762: Mason Ward, b. 6th da, 9th mo, 1788; Rebecca Ward, b. 11th da, 1st mo, 1790; Sarah Ward, b. 24th da, 6th mo, 1791; John Ward, b. 25th da, 11th mo, 1793; Lettitia Ward, b.

2nd da, 4th mo, 1796; Aaron 25th da, 6th mo, 1798; Rachel Ward, b. 24th da, 11th mo, 1800; George M. Ward, b. 20th da, 4th mo, 1804; Isaac, b. Ward, b. 21st da, 3rd mo, 1806; Hannah Ward, b. 4th da, 2nd mo, 1809; Richard Jordan Ward, b. 17th da, 6th mo, 1811.

Children of Richard M. Cooper and Mary, his wife: Elizabeth Cooper, b. 22nd da, 3rd mo, 1799, d. 21st da, 10th mo, 1803; Sarah West Cooper, b. 20th da, 10th mo, 1801; William M. Cooper, b. 21st da, 11th mo, 1802, d. 26th da, 12th mo, 1811; Elizabeth Brown Cooper, b. 13th da, 2nd mo, 1804; Caroline Cooper, b. 4th da, 1st mo, 1806; Abigail Matlack Cooper, b. 17th da, 1st mo, 1808; Alexander Cooper, b. 22nd da, 1st mo, 1810; Mary Volans Cooper, b. 1st da, 5th mo, 1812; Anna Cooper, b. 12th da, 10th mo, 1814, d. 22nd da, 2nd mo, 1818; Richard Matlack and William Daniel Cooper, b. 30th da, 8th mo, 1816; Anna F. Cooper, b. 12th da, 5th mo, 1819, d. 28th da, 3rd mo, 1822.

Children of William Knight and Elizabeth, his wife: Samuel Knight, b. 3rd da, 2nd mo, 1785; Sarah Knight, b. 28th da, 12th mo, 1786; Jonathan Knight, b. 6th da, 6th mo, 1788; Beulah Knight, b. 15th da, 9th mo, 1790; William Knight, b. 6th da, 9th mo, 1792; William Knight, b. 2nd da, 10th mo, 1794; Elizabeth Knight, b. 28th da, 11th mo, 1796.

Children of John Barton and Rebecca, his wife: Mary Barton, b. 2nd da, 1st mo, 1783; Meriba Barton, b. 5th da, 6th mo, 1784; Ann Barton, b. 19th da, 11th mo, 1787; Samuel Barton, b. 15th da, 10th mo, 1789; Hannah Barton, b. 15th da, 12th mo, 1791; Elizabeth and Rebecca Barton, twins, b. 2nd da, 1st mo, 1794; Amy Barton, b. 21st da, 10th mo, 1796; Beulah Barton, b. 10th da, 7th mo, 1799; David Barton, b. 26th da, 3rd mo, 1804.

Children of Joseph Sloan, b. son of James Sloan and Rachel, his wife: Jeremiah Haines Sloan, b. 13th da, 8th mo, 1800; Mary Sloan, b. 21st da, 12th mo, 1801, d. 5th da, 11th mo, 1802; Rachel Clement Sloan, b. 13th da, 2nd mo, 1804; William Sloan, b. 16th da, 10th mo, 1805; James Sloan, b. 30th da, 9th mo, 1807, d. 6th da, 8th mo, 1808; Joseph Sloan, b. 5th da, 10th mo, 1809; Marmaduke Sloan, b. 13th da, 7th mo, 1810; Edwin Sloan, b. 27th da, 3rd mo, 1813; Elizabeth Haines Sloan, b. 7th da, 8th mo, 1815.

Children of Josiah Atkinson and Priscilla, his wife: Lydia Atkinson, b. 11th da, 10th mo, 1801; Priscilla Atkinson, b. 9th da, 5th mo, 1804; Samuel B. Atkinson, b. 27th da, 9th mo, 1806, d. 20th da, 7th mo, 1807; Esther Ann Atkinson, b. 18th da, 9th mo, 1808; Josiah Atkinson, b. 30th da, 5th mo, 1812; Thomas B. Atkinson, b. 8th da,

10th mo, 1814; Charles Atkinson, b. 20th da, 7th mo, 1816.
Children of Amos Warner and Mary, his wife: Francis Warner, b. 25th da, 12th mo, 1786; Samuel Warner, b. 20th da, 6th mo, 1789; Agnes Warner, b. 2nd da, 1st mo, 1793; Lydia Warner, b. 20th da, 9th mo, 1800.
Children of James Kaighn and Hannah, his wife: Isaac Kaighn, b. 5th da, 1st mo, 1775; Mary Kaighn, b. 5th da, 4th mo, 1776; John Kaighn, b. 10th da, 5th mo, 1778; Elizabeth Kaighn, b. 28th da, 2nd mo, 1780; James Kaighn, b. 19th da, 8th mo, 1782; Hannah Kaighn, b. 10th da, 5th mo, 1784; Sarah Kaighn, b. 23rd da, 10th mo, 1787; Mary Kaighn, b. 25th da, 1st mo, 1789; Ann Kaighn, b. 24th da, 1st mo, 1792; Charity and Isaac Kaighn, twins, b. 7th da, 5th mo, 1795.
Children of Josiah Webster and Priscilla, his wife: Joshua Evens Webster, b. 6th da, 2nd mo, 1802; Samuel Webster, b. 19th da, 11th mo, 1803; Josiah Webster, b. 11th da, 12th mo, 1805; Josiah Webster, b. 11th da, 12th mo, 1805.
Children of Josiah Webster and Beulah, his wife: Elizabeth Webster, b. 17th da, 2nd mo, 1810; James G. Webster, b. 1st da, 3rd mo, 1812; Marmaduke Webster, b. 14th da, 9th mo, 1815.
Children of Joshua Evens, Jr. and Rebecca, his wife: Ann Evens, b. 13th da, 3rd mo, 1797; Samuel Evens, b. 10th da, 4th mo, 1798, d. 20th da, 10th mo, 1822; James Evens, b. 10th da, 4th mo, 1800, d. 6th da, 7th mo, 1804.
Children of Joseph Rogers and Sarah, his wife: Sarah Ann Rogers, b. 19th da, 1st mo, 1800; Hannah Rogers, b. 18th da, 6th mo, 1801; Abraham J. Rogers, b. 23rd da, 8th mo, 1804.
Children of Abel Clements, son of Abel Clements and Keziah, his wife, dau of Joseph Mickle: Hannah Mickle Clements, b. 27th da, 8th mo, 1803, d. 12th da, 1st mo, 1806; Mickle Clement, b. 9th da, 12th mo, 1804; Elizabeth Clement, b. 2nd da, 5th mo, 1811; Mary Clement, b. 26th da, 3rd mo, 1816; Aaron Clement, b. 24th da, 6th mo, 1816; Sarah Clement, b. 15th da, 3rd mo, 1818.
Children of Robert Rowand, son of Joseph and Rachel Rowand, b. 16th da, 8th mo, 1775 and Elizabeth, his wife, dau of John and Amy Barton, b. 30th da, 6th mo, 1779: Rachel Rowand, b. 4th da, 12th mo, 1799; Amy Rowand, b. 25th da, 4th mo, 1801, d. 22nd da, 8th mo, 1803; Samuel Rowand, b. 27th da, 1st mo, 1804; Mary Rowand, b. 9th da, 5th mo, 1805; Barton Rowand, b. 25th da, 10th mo, 1806; Elizabeth Rowand, b. 3rd da, 9th mo, 1808, d. 3rd da, 2nd mo, 1810; Charles Rowand, b. 30th da, 3rd mo, 1810; William Donaldson Rowand, b. 10th da, 4th mo, 1812.

Children of Isaac Glover, son of John and Mary Glover, b. 14th da, 3rd mo, 1760 and Phebe, his wife: Elizabeth Glover, b. 7th da, 12th mo, 1789; Mary Glover, b. 14th da, 4th mo, 1792; John Duell Glove, b. 27th da, 8th mo, 1797.

Children of Abel Nicholson, son of Abel and Rebecca Nicholson, b. 11th da, 10th mo, 1761 and Mary, his wife, dau of Isaac and Mary Ellis, b. 1st da, 9th mo, 1763: Rebecca Nicholson, b. 18th da, 12th mo, 1787; Isaac Nicholson, b. 18th da, 2nd mo, 1790; Samuel Nicholson, b. 18th da, 4th mo, 1793; Abel Nicholson, b. 11th da, 10th mo, 1795.

Children of Stephen Munson Day, son of Samuel and Nancy Day, b. in Morris Town, Morris County, 5th da, 2nd mo, 1778, d. 5th da, 11th mo, 1812 and Sarah, his wife, dau of Thomas and Rebecca Redman, b. 23rd da, 8th mo, 1776: Rebecca Day, b. 31st da, 7th mo, 1808, d. 13th da, 8th mo, 1808; Samuel Munson Day, b. 31st da, 3rd mo, 1810; Stephen Munson Day, b. 6th da, 8th mo, 1812, d. 15th da, 8th mo, 1812.

Samuel Cooper, son of Benjamin and Elizabeth Cooper, b. 25th da, 6th mo, 1744, d. 21st da, 9th mo, 1812 and Prudence, his wife, b. 27th da, 5th mo, 1739, d. 14th da, 8th mo, 1822.

Children of Joseph Burrough, Jr., son of Joseph and Kezia Burrough, b. 4th da, 9th mo, 1769 and his wife, Martha, dau of David and Martha Davis, b. 9th da, 9th mo, 1772: Kezia Burrough, b. 20th da, 6th mo, 1794; Martha Burrough, b. 6th da, 8th mo, 1797, d. 2nd da, 10th mo, 1802; Lydia Burrough, b. 1st da, 2nd mo, 1800; Joseph Burrough, b. 17th da, 9th mo, 1802; Rachel Burrough, b. 1st da, 6th mo, 1805; Aaron Burrough, b. 10th da, 12th mo, 1816.

Children of John Albertson, son of Josiah and Eleanor Albertson and Eleanor, b. 16th da, 12th mo, 1771 and Ann, his wife, dau of John and Rachel Pine, b. 16th da, 10th mo, 1775: Josiah Albertson, b. 28th da, 8th mo, 1795; Isaac Albertson, b. 16th da, 12th mo, 1797; Rachel Albertson, b. 1st da, 3rd mo, 1800; Eleanor Albertson, b. 24th da, 10th mo, 1802; Ann Albertson, b. 6th da, 6th mo, 1805; Hannah Albertson, b. 24th da, 12th mo, 1807; Mary and John Albertson, twins, b. 27th da, 7th mo, 1810, John d. 28th da, 12th mo, 1816; Ketuah Albertson, b. 3rd da, 5th mo, 1813; Chalkley Albertson, b. 9th da, 1st mo, 1816.

Children of Samuel Stokes, son of Joshua and Amy Stokes, b. 24th da 12th mo, 1743, d. 2nd da, 4th mo, 1802 and Hope, his wife: Aquila Stokes, b. 28th da, 7th mo, 1779; Priscilla Stokes, b. 21st da, 4th mo, 1781; Atlantick Stokes, b. 30th da, 3rd mo, 1783; Isaac Stokes, b. 12th da, 9th mo, 1784; Rachel Stokes, b. 1st da, 9th mo, 1786; Esther

Stokes, b. 25th da, 12th mo, 1788; Hezekiah Stokes, b. 12th da, 1st mo, 1790; Elisha Stokes, b. 25th da, 3rd mo, 1793; Mary Ann Stokes, b. 10th da, 8th mo, 1795; Martha Stokes, b. 5th da, 12th mo, 1799.

Children of Nathaniel Barton, son of John and Elizabeth Barton, b. 10th da, 5th mo, 1753 and Rachel, his wife, dau of Joshua and Amy Stokes, b. 23rd da, 2nd mo, 1754: Joshua Barton, b. 27th da, 9th mo, 1777; Benjamin Barton, b. 10th da, 10th mo, 1779; Amy Barton, b. 28th da, 8th mo, 1781; Rachel Barton, b. 6th da, 12th mo, 1783; John Barton, b. 1st da, 5th mo, 1785; Sarah Barton, b. 18th da, 3rd mo, 1788; Hannah Barton, b. 4th da, 10th mo, 1790; David Barton, b. 26th da, 7th mo, 1792; Nathaniel Barton, b. 15th da, 4th mo, 1794; Joseph Barton, b. 30th da, 4th mo, 1796; Elizabeth Barton, b. 9th da, 6th mo, 1798.

Children of Wallace Lippincott: Stacy Lippincott, b. 16th da, 2nd mo, 1796; Mary Lippincott, b. 28th da, 4th mo, 1798; Wallace Lippincott, b. 7th da, 9th mo, 1801; Sarah Ann Lippincott, b. 17th da, 9th mo, 1804.

Children of Joseph Glover, son of John and Mary Glover and Sarah, his wife, dau of James Mickle, b. 1st da, 2nd mo, 1776: Anna Glover, b. 8th da, 7th mo, 1797; Beulah Glover, b. 2nd da, 7th mo, 1799; James Mickle b. 16th da, 1st mo, 1802; Joseph Glover, b. 19th da, 2nd mo, 1804, d. 13th da, 4th mo, 1806; Arthur Glover, b. 17th da, 5th mo, 1806, d. 29th da, 10th mo, 1806; Elizabeth Glover, b. 16th da, 8th mo, 1807; Sarah Glover, b. 26th da, 3rd mo, 1810, d. 3rd da, 5th mo, 1817; Mary T. Glover, b. 9th da, 1st mo, 1813.

Children of Nathan Lippincott, b. 24th da, 3rd mo, 1757, son of Joshua Lippincott and Sarah, his wife, b. 2nd da, 6th mo, 1755: Abraham Lippincott, b. 18th da, 6th mo, 1787; Mary Lippincott, b. 20th da, 10th mo, 1790; Joshua Lippincott, b. 1st da, 12th mo, 1792; Nathan Lippincott, b. 10th da, 2nd mo, 1797.

Children of Samuel Thorne, son of Thomas and Abigail Thorne, b. 11th da, 4th mo, 1762 and Sarah, his wife, dau of Job Collins, b. 15th da, 11th mo, 1774: Mary H. Thorne, b. 18th da, 12th mo, 1794; Elizabeth Thorne, b. 16th da, 8th mo, 1796, d. 15th da, 7th mo, 1820; Job 11th da, 6th mo, 1798, d. 15th da, 7th mo, 1800; William Thorne, b. 22nd da, 6th mo, 1800; Abigail Thorne, b. 16th da, 7th mo, 1802; Samuel Collins Thorne, b. 13th da, 5th mo, 1805; Sarah S. Thorne, b. 15th da, 5th mo, 1807; Thomas Thorne, b. 27th da, 5th mo, 1809; Charles Haines Thorne, b. 23rd da, 8th mo, 1811; Clayton Thorne, b. 22nd da, 9th mo, 1813; Chalkley Thorne, b. 9th da, 8th mo, 1817.

Children of Joseph W. Bennett and Mary, his wife: Joseph M. Bennett,

b. 9th da, 11th mo, 1798; Louise Bennett, b. 14th da, 3rd mo, 1801; Martha R. Bennett, b. 16th da, 1st mo, 1803; Mary Bennett, b. 11th da, 7th mo, 1805; Caroline Bennett, b. 13th da, 11th mo, 1807.
Child of John Gill, late of Haddonfield, now of Salem County and Susannah, his wife, dau of David Branson, d. 4th da, 5th mo, 1796 being 40 years of age: David Gill, b. 14th da, 2nd mo, 1795.
Children of William Sloan and Hannah, his wife: Rebecca Sloan, b. 21st da, 7th mo, 1807, d. 8th da, 8th mo, 1807; William West Sloan, b. 4th da, 12th mo, 1808; James Clement Sloan, b. 13th da, 10th mo, 1810; Ann Brick Sloan, b. 10th da, 2nd mo, 1814, d. 28th da, 4th mo, 1814; Ann Eliza Sloan, b. 24th da, 8th mo, 1815.
Children of Samuel Brown, son of Samuel and Rebecca Brown and Mary, his wife, dau of Benjamin and Mary Hartley, d. 2nd da, 5th mo, 1813: Edmund Brown, b. 21st da, 4th mo, 1804; Mary Hartley Brown, b. 15th da, 8th mo, 1806; Elisha Brown, b. 28th da, 12th mo, 1807; Benjamin Hartley Brown, b. 30th da, 4th mo, 1809; Thomas Chalkley Brown, b. 19th da, 11th mo, 1810; Ezra Brown, b. 8th da, 11th mo, 1812.
Children of Samuel Brown and Martha, his second wife, dau of Daniel Hillman, b. 21st da, 12th mo, 1787: Rebecca Brown, b. 10th da, 10th mo, 1815; Martha H. Brown, b. 9th da, 10th mo, 1817, d. 18th da, 10th mo, 1817; Samuel Emlen Brown, b. 2nd da, 1st mo, 1820; Hannah H. Brown, b. 8th da, 3rd mo, 1823.
Children of Paul Troth, son of William and Esther Troth, b. 3rd da, 1st mo, 1759 and Mary, his wife, dau of James and Mary Hillman: Esther Troth, b. 15th da, 2nd mo, 1783; William Troth, b. 9th da, 7th mo, 1784; James Troth, b. 4th da, 11th mo, 1785; Jacob and Joseph Troth, twins, b. 29th da, 8th mo, 1788; Elizabeth Troth, b. 24th da, 2nd mo, 1791; Paul Troth, b. (stillborn) 3rd da, 6th mo, 1793.
Paul Troth married 2nd time to Sabyllah.
Children of Samuel Cresson, son of Joshua and Mary Cresson, b. 5th da, 3rd mo, 1791 and Elizabeth M., his wife, dau of John and Ann Blackwood, b. 31st da, 5th mo, 1792: Samuel Emlen Cresson, b. 25th da, 1st mo, 1814, d. 19th da, 8th mo, 1819, buried at Haddonfield; John B. Cresson, b. 9th da, 9th mo, 1817; Sarah Emlin Cresson, b. 20th da 3rd mo, 1821; Mary Ann Cresson, b. before 1821, d. 8th da, 12th mo, 1821; Elizabeth M. Cresson, b. 5th da, 3rd mo, 1824, d. 6th da, of same mo; Joshua Cresson, b. 19th da, 12th mo, 1825.
John Arnett Cresson, son of Joshua and Mary, b. in Philadelphia 13th da, 5th mo, 1784.
Children of Abraham Lippincott, son of Nathan and Sarah Lippincott,

b. 18th da, 6th mo, 1787 and Rachel, his wife: Joseph Lippincott, b. 17th da, 3rd mo, 1814; Benjamin Lippincott, b. 5th mo, 1815; Sarah Lippincott, b. 17th da, 4th mo, 1817; Lydia Lippincott, b. 6th da, 2nd mo, 1819; Esther Lippincott, b. 12th da, 11th mo, 1821, d. 7th da, 11th mo, 1822; Nathan Lippincott, b. 14th da, 11th mo, 1826.

Children of Simeon Eastlack, son of Samuel Eastlack, b. 13th da, 5th mo, 1772 and Rachel, his wife, dau of Nathaniel Barton, b. 17th da, 6th mo, 1783: Amy Eastlack, b. 4th da, 2nd mo, 1807; Sarah Eastlack, b. 7th da, 2nd mo, 1808; Elwood Eastlack, b. 12th da, 1st mo, 1810; Joseph B. Eastlack, b. 4th da, 4th mo, 1812; Elizabeth Eastlack, b. 5th da, 9th mo, 1813; Lydia S. Eastlack, b. 25th da, 6th mo, 1815; Hannah Eastlack, b. 20th da, 10th mo, 1817; Rachel Eastlack, b. 7th da, 1st mo, 1820.

Children of Isaac Nicholson, son of Abel and Mary Nicholson, b. 18th da, 2nd mo, 1790 and Prisilla, his wife, b. 15th da, 4th mo, 1789: Zebedea Nicholson, b. 13th da, 3rd mo, 1815; Mary Nicholson, b. 25th da, 8th mo, 1816; Joseph Nicholson, b. 5th da, 11th mo, 1818; Priscilla Nicholson, b. 9th da, 12th mo, 1820; Isaac Nicholson, b. 19th da, 8th mo, 1823, d. 9th da, 10th mo, 1823; Isaac W. Nicholson, b. 26th da, 1st mo, 1829.

Children of Charles Haines and Mary, his wife: Eliza Haines, b. 23rd da, 10th mo, 1814; Albert Haines, b. 15th da, 9th mo, 1816.

Children of John Sloan, son of James and Rachel Sloan, b. 24th da, 8th mo, 1789 and Beulah, his wife, dau of William and Sarah Knight, b. 15th da, 9th mo, 1790: Sarah Knight Sloan, b. 23rd da, 8th mo, 1812; Charles Sloan, b. 27th da, 11th mo, 1813; Amos Haines Sloan, b. 2nd da, 3rd mo, 1818, d. 7th da, 7th mo, 1822; Richard Sloan, b. 5th da, 9th mo, 1824.

John Kaighn, son of James and Hannah Kaighn, b. 10th da, 5th mo, 1778 and Elizabeth, his wife: Hannah Kaighn, b. 27th da, 9th mo, 1814; Ann Kaighn, b. 14th da, 7th mo, 1816; Rebecca Kaighn, b. 20th da, 4th mo, 1818; Rachel Kaighn, b. 10th da, 12th mo, 1819; John B. Kaighn, b. 13th da, 4th mo, 1822; Mary Kaighn, b. 7th da, 1st mo, 1826.

Children of Mason Ward, son of John and Hannah Ward, b. 6th da, 9th mo, 1788 and Hannah, his wife, dau of John and Rebecca Barton, b. 15th da, 12th mo, 1791: Thomas H. Ward, b. 26th da, 4th mo, 1818; Alexander Ward, b. 22nd da, 5th mo, 1819; Lydia Ward, b. 26th da, 5th mo, 1821; Mary C. Ward. b. 22nd da, 5th mo, 1823, d. 30th da, same mo; John B. Ward, b. 16th da, 4th mo, 1825; Mann Ward, b. 18th da, 10th mo, 1827.

Children of Abel Hillman, son of Daniel and Martha Hillman, b. 2nd da, 10th mo, 1791 and Sarah, his wife, dau of Nathaniel and Rachel Barton, b. 18th da, 3rd mo, 1788: Nathaniel Barton Hillman, b. 5th da, 11th mo, 1807; Martha E. Hillman, b. 3rd da, 2nd mo, 1819; Rachel Hillman, b. 14th da, 10th mo, 1820; Sarah H. Hillman, b. 22nd da, 9th mo, 1821; Richard J. Hillman, b. 29th da, 9th mo, 1822; Rebecca Hillman, b. 21st da, 9th mo, 1824; Joshua B. Hillman, b. 6th da, 12th mo, 1828.

Children of Samuel Eastlack, son of Samuel and Hannah, his wife, b. 5th da, 8th mo, 1781 and Elizabeth, his wife, dau of Isaac and Phebe Glover, b. 7th da, 12th mo, 1789: Isaac Glover Eastlack, b. 7th da, 12th mo, 1814; Charles H. Eastlack, b. 22nd da, 4th mo, 1822.

Children of Thomas Redman, Jr., son of Thomas and Rebecca Redman, of Haddonfield, b. 26th da, 2nd mo, 1783 and Elizabeth, his wife, b. 14th da, 5th mo, 1785, dau of James and Rebecca Hopkins of Haddonfield, married 7th da, 5th mo, 1807: Rebecca Hopkins Redman, b. 14th da, 4th mo, 1811, d. 1st da, 11th mo, 1814; Thomas Redman, b. 3rd da, 7th mo, 1813; James H. Redman, b. 30th da, 4th mo, 1815; Joseph Swatt Redman, b. 25th da, 5th mo, 1817; Elizabeth Estaugh Redman, b. 9th da, 4th mo, 18--; Sarah Hopkins Redman, b. 20th da, 12th mo, 1826.

Children of Isaac Thorne, son of Thomas and Abigail Thorne, b. 21st da, 8th mo, 1771 and Rachel, his wife, dau of Isaac and Elizabeth Horner: Sarah Ann Thorne, b. 31st da, 12th mo, 1800, d. 17th da, 1st mo, 1807; Isaac H. Thorne, b. 16th da, 3rd mo, 1802; Abigail Thorne, b. 20th da, 1st mo, 1806; Elizabeth Thorne, b. 2nd da, 8th mo, 1808; Richard Thorne, b. 12th da, 10th mo, 1811.

Children of Abel Haines, son of Jacob and Bathsheba Haines, b. 18th da, 5th mo, 1786 and Nancy, his wife, dau of Joseph and Mary Moore, b. 18th da, 1st mo, 1786: Jacob Haines, b. 8th da, 12th mo, 1808; Rachel M. Haines, b. 8th da, 10th mo, 1812; Samuel Haines, b. 26th da, 11th mo, 1818; Eliza Haines, b. 28th da, 12th mo, 1821; Abel Haines, b. 27th da, 4th mo, 1824; Joseph Haines, b. 15th da, 8th mo, 1826.

Children of James Zanes, b. 25th da, 4th mo, 1775, son of William Zanes and Mary, his wife, dau of Simeon Ellis, b. 22nd da, 10th mo, 1780: Simeon Ellis Zanes, b. 8th da, 7th mo, 1801; Sarah Zanes, b. 6th da, 9th mo, 1805; William Zanes, b. 17th da, 9th mo, 1808; Mary Zanes, b. 3rd da, 4th mo, 1812; Elizabeth Hillman Zanes, b. 29th da, 8th mo, 1820.

Child of Samuel Butcher and Mary, his wife: Morris Butcher, b. 18th da, 9th mo, 1820.

Children of Stacy Matlack, son of Samuel and Sarah Matlack, b. 11th da, 5th mo, 1790 and Eleanor, his wife, dau of Samuel and Hannah Glover, b. 17th da, 4th mo, 1790, d. 17th da, 5th mo, 1823: Hannah Ann Matlack, b. 14th da, 3rd mo, 1814; Samuel Glover Matlack, b. 22nd da, 9th mo, 1816; Benjamin Matlack, b. 25th da, 4th mo, 1819; Sarah S. Matlack, b. 15th da, 2nd mo, 1822.

Child of William Thorne, son of Thomas Thorne, b. 6th da, 10th mo, 1778 and Hannah, his wife: Hannah D. Thorne, b. 13th da, 10th mo, 1821.

Children of John B. Cooper, son of Joseph Cooper, b. 1st da, 17th mo, 1794 and Hannah W., his wife, b. 3rd da, 12th mo, 1793: Charles Morris Cooper, b. 19th da, 9th mo, 1817; Sarah Buckley Cooper, b. 12th da, 24th mo, 1819, d. 7th da, 10th mo, 1821; Samuel Willis Cooper, b. 10th da, 10th mo, 1823, d. 30th da, same mo; Joseph Buckley Cooper, b. 22nd da, 5th mo, 1828.

Children of Samuel C. Cooper and Elizabeth, his wife: Alfred Cooper, b. 2nd da, 3rd mo, 1821; Charlottee Louisa Cooper, b. 17th da, 7th mo, 1823.

Child of Isaac Burrough and Mary, his wife: Isaac Burrough, b. before 1822, d. 13th da, 1st mo, 1822 aged 2 years.

Joseph Boggs d. 9th da, 7th mo, 1823.

Children of William Hooton, son of Elisha Hooton, b. 14th da, 11th mo, 1777 and Hannah, his wife, dau of Isaac Kay, b. 21st da, 8th mo, 1780: Ann Hooton. b. 16th da, 7th mo, 1799; Esther Hooton, b. 31st da, 11th mo, 1802; Alexander Hooton, b. 10th da, 9th mo, 1804; Isaac Hooton, b. 19th da, 12th mo, 1805; Elisha Hooton, b. 6th da, 2nd mo, 1808; Samuel Hooton, b. 15th da, 3rd mo, 1810; William Hooton, b. 25th da, 6th mo, 1811; Benjamin Hooton, b. 10th da, 6th mo, 1812; Benjamin Hooton, b. 10th da, 6th mo, 1813; Hannah Hooton, b. 12th da, 4th mo, 1815; Aaron Hooton, b. 7th da, 2nd mo, 1818; Martha Hooton, b. 18th da, 6th mo, 1821; Elizabeth Hooton, b. 1st da, 1st mo 1826.

Child of Jonathan Petit and Ann, his wife: Sarah Petit, b. 24th da, 11th mo, 1820.

Children of William E. Hopkins and Ann, his wife: Hannah W. Hopkins, b. 15th da, 1st mo, 1797; Griffith M. Hopkins, b. 6th da, 10th mo, 1799; Sarah Hopkins, b. 10th da, 5th mo, 1801; Rebecca M. Hopkins, b. 27th da, 7th mo, 1803; Mary Ann Hopkins, b. 26th da, 8th mo,

1806; Elizabeth Lord Hopkins, b. 11th da, 9th mo, 1808; John Estaugh Hopkins, b. 6th da, 5th mo, 1811.

Children of William Glover and Mary, his wife: George Mickle Glover, b. 21st da, 12th mo, 1800; Sarah Glover, b. 7th da, 8th mo, 1802; Ann Glover, b. 18th da, 9th mo, 1804; Thomas Glover, b. 15th da, 9th mo, 1806; Hannah Glover, b. 24th da, 11th mo, 1808; Eliza Glover, b. 17th da, 4th mo, 1812; Sophia Glover, b. 15th da, 2nd mo, 1814; Susannah Mickle Glover, b. 7th da, 11th mo 1816, d. 19th da, same mo; Addaline Glover, b. 21st da, 5th mo, 1817; Gulilimor Maria Glover, b. 30th da, 7th mo, 1819, d. 30th da, 1st mo, 1820.

Children of Daniel Hillman, son of Daniel Hillman, b. 6th da, 6th mo, 1786 and Esther, his wife, dau of Samuel Stokes, b. 25th da, 12th mo, 1788: Samuel Stokes Hillman, b. 18th da, 8th mo, 1816; Daniel Ellis Hillman, b. 21st da, 4th mo, 1819; Aquilla Shinn Hillman, b. 18th da, 11th mo, 1821; Mary Ann Hillman, b. 16th da, 10th mo, 1826.

Children of Benjamin Dugdale, son of Thomas Dugdale, b. 26th da, 7th mo, 1788 and Hannah Dugdale, dau of James Kaighn, b.10th da, 5th mo, 1784: Sarah Dugdale, b. 13th da, 4th mo, 1812; Sarah Dugdale, b. 25th da, 2nd mo, 1814; James Dugdale, b. 17th da, 10th mo, 1815; Benjamin Dugdale, Jr., b. 12th da, 9th mo, 1817, d. 28th da, 1st mo, 1819; Benjamin Dugdale, Jr. b. 9th da, 9th mo, 1819, d. 27th da, 5th mo, 1820; Samuel Dugdale, b. 2nd da, 6th mo, 1821.

Children of Isaac Webster, son of Samuel Webster, b. 2nd da, 12th mo, 1776 and Sarah, his wife: Marmaduke Webster, b. 20th da, 12th mo, 1801, d. 16th da, 7th mo, 1807; Hannah Willis Webster, b. 3rd da, 10th mo, 1803; Joseph Webster, b. 19th da, 7th mo, 1809; Sarah Ann Webster, b. 26th da, 8th mo, 1813; Elizabeth Webster, b. no date.

Children of Jacob Troth, son of Paul Troth, b. 29th da, 9th mo, 1788 and Rebecca, his wife, dau of Abel Nicholson, b. 18th da, 12th mo, 1787: Joseph Nicholson Troth, b. 17th da, 9th mo, 1811; Mary H. Troth, b. 16th da, 11th mo, 1816; Paul Hillman Troth, b. 11th da, 5th mo, 1818; Rebecca Troth, b. 27th da, 9th mo, 1820.

Children of David Borton and Elizabeth, his wife, dau of Paul Troth, b. 24th da, 2nd mo, 1791: Mary H. Borton, b. 4th da, 8th mo, 1814; Martha Barton, b. 5th da, 10th mo, 1815; Elizabeth T. Borton, b. 13th da, 7th mo, 1817; David Borton, b. 11th da, 5th mo, 1819, d. 12th da, 9th mo, 1819; Deborah A. Borton, b. 27th da, 5th mo, 1820.

Children of Joseph H. Lippincott and Keturah, his wife married at Cookwell, 16th da, 11th mo, 1815: John Haines Lippincott, b. 1st da, 10th mo, 1816; Jesse Lippincott, b. 26th da, 1st mo, 1819; Mary Lippincott, b. 1st da, 12th mo, 1826.

Children of Griffith M. Cooper, son of James Cooper and Elizabeth, his
wife: Thomas H. Cooper, b. 20th da, 3rd mo, 1815, d. 13th da, 10th
mo, 1822; James B. Cooper, b. 12th da, 7th mo, 1817; Caroline
Cooper, b. 12th da, 7th mo, 1819, d. 25th da, 10th mo, 1822; Mary H.
Cooper, b. 3rd da, 11th mo, 1821.

Children of John A. Glover, son of John T. Glover and Ann, his wife,
dau of John Inskip: John Inskip Glover, b. 19th da, 2nd mo, 1818;
Catharine Ridgway Glover, b. 2nd da, 9th mo, 1820; Mary Thorne
Glover, b. 7th da, 9th mo, 1823; Ephraim Inskip Glover, b. 2nd da,
8th mo, 1828.

Children of Samuel L. Wilkins, son of Jacob Wilkins, b. 17th da, 8th
mo, 1795 and Rebecca, his wife, dau of Samuel Clement, b. 19th da,
9th mo, 1795: Mary C. Wilkins, b. 20th da, 2nd mo, 1821; Sarah Ann
Wilkins, b. 27th da, 12th mo, 1822..

Children of Benjamin M. Haines, b. 22nd da, 9th mo, 1795 and Kezia,
his wife, dau of Joseph and Martha Burrough, b. 20th da, 6th mo,
1794: Martha B. Haines, b. 12th da, 22nd da, 1818; Elizabeth M.
Haines, b. 14th da, 6th mo, 1820..

Children of Samuel Brick and Elizabeth, his wife: Elizabeth Brick, b.
17th da, 12th mo, 1793; Benjamin H. and Charles F. Brick, twins, b.
6th da, 3rd mo, 1797; Mariah Brick, b. 29th da, 4th mo, 1799; William
Brick, b. 25th da, 5th mo, 1801; Harriet Brick, b. 1st da, 11th mo,
1804; Mercy H. Brick, b. 22nd da, 10th mo, 1805; John Hartley Brick,
b. 15th da, 8th mo, 1806; Elizabeth Brick, b. 15th da, 8th mo, 1807;
Charlotte Brick, b. 23rd da , 3rd mo, 1810; Anne Mariah Brick, b. 3rd
da, 7th mo, 1812; Rebecca Brick, b. 17th da, 10th mo, 1815.

Children of James Glover, son of John Thorne and Elizabeth Glover, b.
30th da, 10th mo, 1785 and Elizabeth, his wife, dau of Joseph and
Lydia Davis, b. 3rd da, 3rd mo, 1791: Joseph Davis Glover, b. 25th
da, 7th mo, 1819; John Thorne Glover, b. 6th da, 7th mo, 1821; Lydia
Glover, b. 22nd da, 1st mo, 1824; Maria Wood Glover, b. 26th da, 7th
mo, 1826.

Children of Joseph Jennings, son of Jacob Jennings and Sarah, his
wife: Hannah Jennings, b. 17th da, 9th mo, 1804; Ann Jennings, b.
18th da, 4th mo, 1806; Charles Jennings, b. 23rd da, 3rd mo, 1808;
Mary Jennings, b. 3rd da, 5th mo, 1810, d. 15th da, 3rd mo, 1812;
Jacob H. Jennings, b. 7th da, 4th mo, 1812; Sarah Jennings, 20th da,
5th mo, 1814; Joseph Jennings, b. 1st da, 8th mo, 1816; Barclay
Jennings, b. 10th da, 3rd mo, 1819; Kezia Jennings, b. 13th da, 3rd
mo, 1821; May Jennings, b. 13th da, 7th mo, 1823; Keturah Jennings,
b. 12th da, 10th mo, 1825; Margaret Jennings, b. 18th da, 4th mo,

1828, d. 2nd mo, 1829.
Children of Job Willets and Mary, his wife, b. 20th da, 10th mo, 1790: Jeremiah L. Willetts, b. 6th da, 12th mo, 1821, d. 11th mo, 7th da, 1822; Sarah A. Willets, b. 28th da, 12th mo, 1822; Mary Willets, b. 30th da, 11th mo, 1824, d. 18th da, 10th mo, 1825; Nathan L. Willets, b. 15th da, 5th mo, 1827, d. 3rd da, 7th mo, 1827.
Children of John M. Kaighn, son of Joseph and Sarah Kaighn, b. 7th da, 5th mo, 1796 and Rebecca W., his wife, dau of Benjamin and Elizabeth Cooper, b. 17th da, 12th mo, 1800: Sarah M. Kaighn, b. 8th da, 2nd mo, 1822; Elizabeth C. Kaighn, b. 29th da, 7th mo, 1825; Joseph Mickle Kaighn, b. 24th da, 2nd mo, 1827.
Children of Benjamin Burrough and Hannah, his wife, b. 20th da, 2nd mo, 1761: Ann Burrough, b. 23rd da, 2nd mo, 1784.

Hannah Gouldy, wife of William Gouldy, b. 6th da, 5th mo, 1775.
Beulah Clement, wife of Samuel and mother of Ruth Wood, wife of Richard Wood, d. 11th da, 9th mo, 1822.

Child of James Wood, son of Richard Wood, d. 20th da, 10th mo, 1807 and Ruth, his wife, dau of Samuel and Beulah Clement: Rebecca Wood, b. 11th da, 2nd mo, 1803, d. 7th mo, 1822; James Wood, b. no date.
Children of Hezebiah Estlack and Margaret, his wife: Isaiah Estlack, b. 14th da, 9th mo, 1808; George Estlack, b. 19th da, 1st mo, 1810; Margarett H. Estlack, b. 29th da, 7th mo, 1812.
Child of Thomas Clark, son of Thomas Clark and Deborah, his wife: Anna Clark, b. 10th da, 8th mo, 1823.
Child of John Gill and Anna, his wife: John Gill, b. 9th da, 7th mo, 1795.
Children of John Gill and Sarah, his wife, dau of William E. Hopkins, b. 10th da, 5th mo, 1801: John S. Gill, b. 18--, d. 19th da, 8th mo, 1820; Rebecca Maryan Gill, b. 27th da, 8th mo, 1821; Ann Smith Gill, b. 27th da, 8th mo, 1823; Charlotte Gill, b. 30th da, 8th mo, 1826.
Children of Josiah Albertson, son of John and Ann Albertson, b. 28th da, 8th mo, 1795 and Abigail, his wife, dau of Thomas Hodson: John P. Albertson, b. 30th da, 8th mo, 1823; Thomas H. Albertson, b. 8th da, 6th mo, 1825.
Children of Isaac Jones, son of Joseph and Sarah Jones, b. 14th da, 3rd mo, 1775 and Amy, his wife, dau of Nathaniel Borton, b. 28th da, 8th mo, 1781: Amy Jones, b. 16th da, 2nd mo, 1811; Eliza Jones, b. 7th da, 8th mo, 1813; Joseph Jones, b. 6th da, 2nd mo, 1815; Beulah

28 EARLY CHURCH RECORDS OF GLOUCESTER COUNTY

Jones, b. 16th da, 2nd mo, 1817; Mary H. Jones, b. 22nd da, 11th mo, 1818; Rebecca Jones, b. 7th da, 12th mo, 1820; Isaac Jones, b. 12th da, 2nd mo, 1823.
Child of Edward Bullock and Hannah, his wife: Rebecca Bullock, b. 13th da, 10th mo, 1819, d. 28th da, 12th mo, 1825.
Benjamin Blackwood, son of John Blackwood and Mary Ann, his wife, dau of William O. Hopkins, b. 20th da, 8th mo, 1806.

Judith Willets, wife of Nathan Willetts, son of Jeremiah Willetts, d. 22nd da, 9th mo, 1822.
Jeremiah Elforth, d. 11th da, 3rd mo, 1825.

Richard Jordon, b. 12th da, 9th mo, 1756, d. 16th da, 10th mo, 1826 and Pharaby, his wife, b. 8th da, 3rd mo, 1752, d. 2nd da, 3rd mo, 1825.
Catharine White, b. 14th da, 4th mo, 1778.
Children of Samuel Brazington, b. 16th da, 4th mo, 1787 and Lydia, his wife, b. 8th da, 10th mo, 1798.
Children of Stacy Lippincott, son of Wallace Lippincott, b. 16th da, 2nd mo, 1795 and Hannah, his wife, dau of Kendal and Sarah Coles: Sarah Ann Lippincott, b. 22nd da, 3rd mo, 1822; Nathaniel Lippincott, b. 12th da, 4th mo, 1825; Hope Lippincott, b. 1st da, 1st mo, 1828.
Children of Thomas Evans, b. 5th da, 3rd mo, 1753 and Abigail, his wife, b. 6th da, 10th mo, 1785: Charles Evans, b.10th mo, 1805; Josiah Evans, b. 7th mo, 6th da, 1811.
Benjamin Whitale Mickle, son of Isaac P. and Mary Mickle, b. 7th da, 31st da, 1801 and Ann, his wife, dau of John and Ann Blackwood, b. 1st da, 1st mo, 1802.

DEATHS OF HADDONFIELD MONTHLY MEETING

Martha Sharp, d. 10th da, 8th mo, 1716.
Sarah Sharp, wife of Thomas Sharp, d. 2nd da, 9th mo, 1699.
Elizabeth Sharp, wife of sd Thomas Sharp, d. 1st da 8th mo, 1709.
Katharine Sharp, wife of sd. Thomas Sharp, d. 28th da, 9th mo, 1720.
Sarah Lord, Jr., d. 20th da, 7th mo, 1702.
Sarah Lord, wife of Joshua Lord, d. 30th da, 3rd mo, 1702.
Isabel Lord, second wife of Joshua Lord, d. 16th da, 8th mo, 1712.
Joshua Lord, father of Sarah Lord, Jr., d. 6th da, 8th mo, 1713.

HADDONFIELD MONTHLY MEETING

James Lord, minister of the gospel, d. 24th da, 7th mo, 1727.
Elizabeth Lord, widow of James Lord, d. 11th da, 8th mo, 1728.
Benjamin Lord, d. 1st da, 2nd mo, 1727.
James Lord, d. 3rd da, 12th mo, ----.
Phineas Lord, d. 25th da, 2nd mo, ----.
Ann Lippincott, the dau of James Lord, d. 27th da, 11th mo, 1752.
John Cooper, son of William and Mary Cooper, d. 22nd da, 9th mo, 1730.
John Cooper, Jr., d. 7th da, 11th mo, 1728.
Sarah Lord, wife of Joshua Lord, d. 30th da, 1st mo, 1748.
Hope Lord, d. 3rd da, 6th mo, 1723.
Caleb Lord, d. 2nd da, 2nd mo, 1727.
Joshua Lord, d. 16th da, 4th mo, 1777.
James Lord, d. 1st da, 10th mo, 1749.
Jonathan Lord, d. 18th da, 2nd mo, 1737.
Joseph Cooper, d. 7th mo, 1731.
Lydia Cooper, d. 18th da, 8th mo, 1736.
Mary Cooper, wife of sd. Joseph Cooper, d. 16th da, 12th mo, 1728.
William Cooper, d. 29th da, 11th mo, 1727.
Joseph Cooper, d. 15th da, 12th mo, 1733/4.
Joshua Cooper, d. 18th da, 7th mo, 1727.
Elizabeth Cooper, d. 17--.
Lydia Cooper, d. 2nd da, 1st mo, 1751/2.
Job Whiteall, d. 6th da, 1st mo, 1722.
James Smith, d. 6th da, 1st mo, 1726/7.
Malichi Chattin, d. 14th da, 3rd mo, 1731.
Elizabeth Lord, parent, d. 26th da, 3rd mo, 1726.
Ebenezer Hopkins, d. 14th da, 4th mo, 1757.
Ebenezer Hopkins, d. 13th da, 6th mo, 1781.
Rebecca Foster, d. 5th da, 10th mo, 1751.
Ruth Richardson, d. 2nd da, 1735.
Jonath Richardson, d. 3rd da, 1737.
Sybil Cooper, d. 5th da, 5th mo, 1759.
Deborah Cooper, d. 12th da, 6th mo, 1759.
James Cooper, Jr., d. 17th da, 11th mo, 1753.
Sarah Cooper, d. 4th da, 9th mo, 1778.
Deborah Cooper, d. 6th da, 3rd mo, 1766.
Samuel Cooper, d. 15th da, 1st mo, 1767.
Phebe Eastlack, d. 16th da, 12th mo, 1779.
Hanah Burrough formerly Stiles, d. 20th da, 4th mo, 1756.
Samuel Burrough, Jr., d. 1st mo, 1729.

Mary Burrough formerly Mickle, d. 1743/4.
Rachel Davis formerly Burrough, d. 11th da, 8th mo, 1826.
Enoch Burrough, d. 22nd da, 1st mo, 1756.
Joseph Heritage, buried in Chesterfield burying grounds, d. 13th da, 11th mo, 1756.
Hannah Heritage, d. 19th da, 5th mo, 1745.
Elizabeth Sharp, d. 3rd da, 1737.
Mary Sharp, d. 6th mo, 1752.
Anthony Sharp, d. 6th da, 3rd mo, 1760.
Hosea Sharp, d. 10th da, 6th mo, 1752.
John Brown, d. 19th da, 2nd mo, 1775.
Sarah Brown, d. 3rd da, 3rd mo, 1774.
Hannah Brown, d. 14th da, 2nd mo, 1753.
Ephraim Tomlinson, d. 2nd da, 8th mo, 1780.
Joseph Tomlinson, d. 28th da, 6th mo, 1738.
John Tomlinson, d. 16th da, 3rd mo, 1760.
Joshua Stokes, d. 7th da, 5th mo, 1779.
Amy Stokes, d. 11th da, 3rd mo, 1781.
Joseph Stokes, d. 11th mo, 1766.
Archabald Mickle, d. 16th da, 9th mo, 1758.
Mary Mickle, d. 30th da, 8th mo, 1758.
Mary Lippincott, d. 1st da, 12th mo, 1787 aged 71 years.
Barzilla Lippincott, d. --- age about 5 years.
Amy Gill, wife of John Gill, d. 17th da, 10th mo, 1766.
Mary Gill formerly Roberts, d. 31st da, 1---.
Marcy Gill, d. 29th da, 3rd mo, 1760.
Hannah Gill, d. about 3 months old.
Hannah Gill, d. 23rd da, 3rd mo, 1760.
Sarah Andrews, d. 16th da, 12th mo, 1763.
Mary Andrews, d. 26th da, 5th mo, 1745.
Elizabeth Andrews, d. 31st da, 3rd da, 1760 age 13 years.
Edward Andrews, d. 11th da, 8th mo, 1752.
Lettitia Andrews, d. 8th da, 4th mo, 1760.
Hannah Andrews, d. 10th da, 7th mo, 1758.
Samuel Mifflin, d. 2nd da, 8th mo, 1762.
Edward Mifflin, d. 24th da, 1st mo, 1780.
David Griscom, d. 20th da, 6th mo, 1746.
Joseph Grisscom, d. 25th da, 6th mo, 1746.
Deborah Griscom, d. 9th da, 10th mo, 1746.
Sarah Griscom, d. 2nd da, 10th mo, 1758.
David Griscom, d. 30th da, 4th mo, 1760.

William Griscom, d. 13th da, 12th mo, 1757.
William Griscom, d. 4th da, 8th mo, 1759.
Freedom Lippincott, d. 8th da, 10th mo, 1752.
Martha Lippincott, d. 2 years old.
Solomon Lippincott, d. 2 ½ years old.
Jacob Cozens, d. 1st da, 2nd mo, 1760 age 60 years.
John Cozens, d. 4 years age.
Samuel Cozens, d. 21st da, 10th mo, 1762.
Mary Cozens, d. 2nd year of her age.
Elizabeth Cozens, d. 1761.
Samuel Cozens, d. 31st da, 10th mo, 1762.
Mary Miller, clerk of the monthly and quarterly meeting at
   Haddonfield, d. 5th da, 1st mo, 1770.
George Whitall, d. 8th da, 11th mo, 1775.
Abraham Whitall, d. 1st da, 4th mo, 1782.
Sarah Tatum, wife of John Tatum, d. 26th da, 8th mo, 1778.
George Tatum, d. 8th da, 9th mo, 1772.
Isaac Tatum, d. 13th da, 10th mo, 1766.
Elijah Gibbs, d. 7th da, 10th mo, 1767.
Martha Bates, d. 26th da, 4th mo, 1773.
Thomas Redman, d. 23rd da, 9th mo, 1766 aged 2 years 3 mo 10 days.
Hannah Redman, d. 4th da, 6th mo, 1746.
Mary Miller, wife of Mark Miller, d. 5th da, 1st mo, 1770.
Sarah Redman, d. 1st da, 5th mo, 1743.
Marcy Redman, widow of Thomas Redman, d. 15th da, 3rd mo, 1778.
Joseph Redman, d. 21st da, 11th mo, 1778.
Hannah Redman, d. 28th da, 10th mo, 1770.
Samuel Coles, d. 11th da, 10th mo, 1772.
Mary Coles, d. 14th da, 10th mo, 1775.
Martha Davis, wife of David Davis, d. 19th da, 7th mo, 1780 aged 43
   years.
Joshua Lord, an elder, d. 16th da, 4th mo, 1777.
James Lord, d. 11th da, 3rd mo, 1777.
Alice Kays, d. 22nd da, 10th mo, 1770.
Francis Keais, d. 1772.
Jonathan Ladd, d. 6th da, 6th mo, 1760.
Eldad Ladd, d. 11th da, 8th mo, 1776.
Deborah Ladd, d. 3rd da, 3rd mo, 1771.
Ebenezer Hopkins, d. 13th da, 6th mo, 1781.
Sarah Tomlinson, d. 6th da, 5th mo, 1777.
Lydia Tomlinson, d. 17th da, 12th mo, 1778.

James Tomlinson, d. 8th da, 3rd mo, 1779.
Archiblad Mickle, d. 9th mo, 1777 aged 5 years.
Mary Mickle, d. 7th mo, 1783.
Deborah Mickle, d. 14th da, 12th mo, 1791.
Lydia Mickle, d. 14th da, 6th mo, 1796.
Abraham Stokes, d. 9th da, 11th mo, 1766.
David Brown, d. 7th mo, 1796.
John Clement, d. 30th da, 9th mo, 1784.
Sarah Clement d. 8th da, 9th mo, 1778.
Elizabeth Lippincott, d. 6th da, 7th mo, 1774.
Hannah Lippincott, d. 5th da, 10th mo, 1776.
Abel Burrough, d. 8th da, 2nd mo, 1775.
Samuel Burrough, d. 5th da, 7th mo, 1778.
Eber Burrough, d. 18th da, 7th mo, 1778.
Esther Wooten, d. 12th da, 3rd mo, 1786.
Mary Ashead, d. 28th da, 5th mo, 1770.
Rebecca Githens, d. 10th da, 8th mo, 1774.
Constantine Wilkins, d. 4th da, 2nd mo, 1778.
Ann Allen, widow of Constantine Wilkins, d. 16th da, 12th mo, 1780.
Mary Albertson, d. 2nd da, 10th mo, 1777.
Elizabeth Albertson, d. 13th da, 6th mo, 1779.
Josiah Webster, d. 27th da, 4th mo, 1767.
Jacob Webster, d. 16th da, 7th mo, 1778.
John Snowden, d. 26th da, 2nd mo, 1780.
Elizabeth Snowden, d. 13th da, 2nd mo, 1791.
Samuel Bates, d. 1757.
Hope Bates, d. 27th da, 7th mo, 1778.
Elizabeth Bates, d. 27th da, 7th mo, 1778.
Rebecca Bates, d. 23rd da, 4th mo, 1788.
Sarah Bates, d. 1st da, 8th mo, 1778.
John Mickle, d. 9th mo, 1744.
Hannah Mickle, d. 1st mo, 1737.
Joseph Kaighn, Sr., d. 18th da, 5th mo, 1797.
Mary Bassett, dau of Daniel and Ruth Bassett, d. 7th da, 10th mo, 1798.
Josiah Bassett, d. 4th da, 12th mo, 1794.
Samuel Sloan, d. 31st da, 3rd mo, 1785.
Rachel Sloan, d. 2nd da, 4th mo, 1792.
Cadwalder Cooper, d. 16th da, 7th mo, 1789.
Franklin Cooper, d. 3rd mo, 1794.
Beulah Arney, d. 25th da, 3rd mo, 1798.

William Knight, d. 6th da, 2nd mo, 1793.
Elizabeth Knight, d. 19th da, 11th mo, 1799.
Elizabeth Kaighn, d. 21st da, 4th mo, 1777.
Mary Kaighn, d. 10th mo, 1778.
Atlantick Stokes, d. 6th da, 9th mo, 1788.
Rachel Stokes, d. 22nd da, 9th mo, 1789.
Hannah Borton, d. 7th da, 9th mo, 1793.
David Borton, d. 27th da, 8th mo, 1793.
John Barton, the elder, d. 29th da, 1st mo, 1798.
Susanah Gill, d. 4th da, 5th mo, 1796 aged 40 years.

MARRIAGES CERTIFICATES OF HADDONFIELD MONTHLY MEETING

James Atkinson of Philadelphia and Hannah Newby of Newton, Gloucester Co., m. at Newton 9th mo, 16th da, 1684.
John Ladd and Sarah Wood, dau of Jonathan Woods, Sr., both of province of New Jersey, m. at Newton 10th mo, 13th da, 1685.
Walter Forest [Fforest] of Bybury Mill, Bucks Co., PA. and Ann Alberson, dau of William Alberson, Sr. of Newton, m. 9th mo, 10th da, 1686.
Thomas Shakle of Compton house in the province of West Jersey and Allis Sealles of Newton, m. at the house of James Atkinson 12th mo, 25th da, 1686.
Samuel Tomes and Rachell Woods, dau of Jonathan Woods, Sr. both being of West Jersey, m. at Newton 2nd mo, 6th da, 1686.
Joshua Fearne, son of Robert and Elizabeth (Eggington) Fearne of Bonsall, Derbyshire, England and Abigail Bate, dau of William Bate, Sr., m. at Newton Twp 4th mo, 9th da, 1687.
William Clarke of West Jersey and Mary Heritage, dau of Richard Heritage of Sutton, New Garden, m. at Newton 9th mo, 13th da, 1687.
John Hugg, Jr. carpenter, son of John Hugg and Priscilla Collins, dau of Francis and Sarah (Mayham) Collins of Mountewell, Gloucester Co., m. at Mountewell 12th mo, 13th da, 1688.
Joseph Cooper, son of William and Margaret Cooper of Pinepoynt and Lydea Riggs of Pinepoynt, dau of George Riggs, having his parents consent, m. at Pinepoynt 8th mo, 11th da, 1688.
Joshua Lord, son of James Lord of Baroye in Lankeshire in Ould England and Sarah Woods, dau of John and Alice (Sales or Seilles)

Woods of Woodbury Brooke, Gloucester Co., m. at Newton 4th mo, 13th da, 1689.

Thomas Willard, late of Hopewell, West Jersey and Judeth Woods, dau of Henry and Hannah Woods of Hopewell, having consent of her father, m. 5th mo, 10th da, 1689. Thomas produced a certificate from Barbados dated 2nd mo, 3rd da, 1689.

Thomas Thachera, Sr. and Hepzibah Eastlak, dau of Francis Eastlak, both of Newton Twp, m. 7th mo, 21st da, 1689.

John Butcher of Springfield, Burlington Co., and Mary Walker, Gloucester Co., m. 4th mo, 7th da, 1691 or 1692.

William Hollingshead, son of John Hollingshead of Northampton River, Burlington Co., and Elizabeth Adams, Jr., dau of John and Elizabeth Adams, of same place, having consent of their parents, m. 1st mo, 23rd da, 1692.

Simeon Ellis of Spring well, Gloucester Co., son of Thomas Ellis of Woodale and Sarah Bate, dau of William Bate, Sr. of Newton, having her parents consent, m. at Newton 4th mo, 16th da, 1692.

Daniel Cooper, son of William and Margaret Cooper of Pinepoynte, Gloucester and Abygall Woods, dau of Henry and Hannah Woods of Hopewell in the said county, having the consent of their parents, m. 3rd mo, 4th da, 1693.

Daniel Cooper, son of William and Margaret Cooper, and Sarah Spicer, dau of Samuel and Esther (Tilton) Spicer, having consent of their parents, m. 12th mo, 26th da, 1695.

Joseph Nicholson, son of Samuel and Anne Nicholson of Alloways Creek, Salem Co. and Hannah Wood, dau of Henry and Hannah Wood, of Burlington, having consent of their parents, m. 1st mo, 3rd da, 1695.

William Sharpe and Jemima Eastlake, dau of Francis Eastlake, both of Newton Twp, having consent of their parents, m. at Newton 4th mo, 18th da, 1695.

Edward Buzby of Dublin, Philadelphia Co., and Susannah Adams, dau of John and Elizabeth Adams of Chester, Burlington Co., having consent of their parents, m. 3rd mo, 7th da, 1696.

Francis Austin of Evesham Twp, Burlington Co., and Mary Borton of Evesham, dau of John and Ann Borton, having consent of their parents, m. at Evesham 7th mo, 15th da, 1696.

John Whiteall and Hannah Thackrea, dau of Thomas Thackrea, both of Newton Twp, having consent of their parents, m. at Newton 9th mo, 13th da, 1696.

Joseph Heritage, son of Richard and Mary (Times) Heritage of Sutton,

New Garden, Gloucester Co. and Hannah Allin of the said providence, dau of Juda and Mary (Woolley), dec'd, Allin of Shrewsbury, having consent of his parents, m. at Sutton, New Garden 11th mo, 26th da, 1697.

Thomas Eves, son of Thomas Eves of Wellingborough and Mary Roberts, dau of John and Sarah (Marks) Roberts of Chester, having consent of her parents, m. 10th mo, 27th da, 1699.

Samuel Burrows, son of Samuel and Hannah Burrows and Hannah Roberts, dau of John, dec'd, and Sarah (Marks) Roberts, both of Chester, having consent of her mother, m. at Chester 10th mo, 27th da, 1699.

Thomas Thackrea, Jr. of Newton, son of Thomas and Esther Thackera and Ann Parker, late of Philadelphia, m. at Newton 3rd mo, 22nd da, 1699.

Juda Allin [Allen] of Burlington Co., son of Juda and Mary (Wooley) Allen of Shrewsbury, Monmouth Co., and Deborah Adams [Addams] of the county aforesaid, dau of John and Elizabeth Adams, m. at Chester, 10th mo, 15th da, 1701.

Joseph Bate and Mercy Clemence, dau of James Clemence of Flushing, Long Island, both of Gloucester Co., m. 10th mo, 16th da, 1701.

Hugh Sharp, son of William and Hannah Sharp of Pensbury, Bucks Co., PA. and Rachel Allen of Chester, Burlington Co., widow of Matthew Allen, dau of Thomas and Jane (Atkins) French, m. 12th mo, 9th da, 1702.

John Estaugh and Elizabeth Haddon both of Gloucester Co., dau of John Haddon of London, England, m. 4th mo, 1st da, 1702.

William Newbury of Evesham, Burlington Co., and Mercy Hasker, dau of William and Elizabeth Hasker of same place, having consent of their parents, m. at Evesham 10th mo, 20th da, 1705.

Henry Newbury and Sarah Boyes, of Burlington, both single, having consent of their parents, m. at Evesham 7th mo, 16th da, 1703.

Stephen Newbury of Newton, son of Edward and Hannah Newbury and Elizabeth Woods, both single, having consent of their parents, m. at Newton 8th mo, 6th da, 1703.

Henry Clifton of Philadelphia, weaver and Joane Engle, widow of Robert Engle of Evesham, having consent of their parents, m. 9th mo, 22nd da, 1703.

Emanuel Straten of Evesham, son of William Straten of Stratford on Avon, England and Hannah Hancock, dau of Timothy and Rachel (Simon) Hancock, m. at Evesham 9th mo, 25th da, 1703.

John Mickle, son of Archibald, Sr. and Isabel Mickle of Newton and

Hannah Cooper, dau of William, Jr. and Mary (Bradway) Cooper, both dec'd, having consent of their relations, m. at Cooper Point 9th mo, 8th da, 1704.

Josiah Southwick and Elizabeth Collins, dau of Frances and Sarah (Mayham) Collins, having consent of their parents, m. 9th mo, 28th da, 1705.

Enoch Core, son of Enoch and Mary (Humphreys) Core of Gloucester Co., and Sarah Roberts of Chester, dau of John and Sarah (Marks) Roberts, having consent of their parents, m. 2nd mo, 10th da, 1706.

John Heritage of Sutton, New Garden, Gloucester Co., yeoman, son of Richard and Mary (Times) Heritage and Sarah Slocum late of Shrewsbury, dau of Nathaniel and Hannah Slocum, having consent of their parents, m. 4th mo, 19th da, 1706.

John Ingle [Engle] of Burlington Co., yeoman and Mary Ogburn of the same place, having consent of their parents, m. at Evesham 10th mo, 4th da, 1707.

John Kay, son of John and Elizabeth (Fern) Kay of Spring well, yeoman and Sarah Langston of same county, having consent of their parents, m. at Newton 12th mo, 11th da, 1707.

Benjamin Wood of Hopewell, son of Henry, dec'd, and Hannah Wood and Elizabeth Kay of Spring well, dau of John and Elizabeth (Fern) Kay, both of Waterford Twp, having consent of their parents, m. 3rd mo, 1st da, 1707.

Samuel Mickle of Gloucester Co., yeoman, son of Archibald, Sr. and Isabel Mickle and Elizabeth Cooper, dau of Joseph and Lydia (Riggs) Cooper of Cooper's Point in Gloucester Co., having consent of their parents, m. 2nd mo, 20th da, 1708.

Simon Breach and Mary Dennis both of Newton, having consent of their parents, m. at Newton 2nd mo, 27th da, 1709.

Robert Bradock of Burlington Co., and Elizabeth Hancock of the same, dau of Timothy and Rachel (Firman) Hancock, having consent of their parents, m. at Evesham 9th mo, 17th da, 1709.

Joseph Stokes of Burlington Co., son of Thomas and Mary (Barnard) Stokes and Judith Lippincott of the same place, dau of Freedom and Mary (Curtis or Customs) Lippincott, having consent of their relations, m. at Evesham 9th mo, 9th da, 1710.

Thomas Lippincott of Evesham, son of Freedom and Mary (Curtis or Customs) Lippincott and Mary Haines of same place, dau of John and Esther (Borton) Haines, having consent of their parents, m. at Evesham 10th mo, 19th da, 1711.

Abraham Brown, Jr. of Wellingborough Twp, Burlington Co., son of

Abraham and Mary Browne and Hannah Adams of Burlington Co., dau of John and Elizabeth Adams, having consent of their parents, m. at Chester, Burlington Co. 1st mo, 20th da, 1711.

Daniel Mickle of Newton, son of Archibald and Sarah (Watts) Mickle and Hannah Dennis of Newton, dau of Jonathan and Rachel Dennis, having consent of their parents, m. at Newton 1st mo, 27th da, 1711.

Thomas Smith of Evesham, son of Thomas and Joyce Smith and Sarah Hancock, dau of Timothy and Rachel (Firman) Hancock, having consent of their parents, m. at Evesham 2nd mo, 4th da, 1711.

Mark Straten of Burlington Co., son of William Straten of Stratford on Avon, Warwickshire, England and Ann Hancock, dau of Timothy and Rachel (Firman) Hancock, m. at Evesham 8th mo, 8th da, 1712.

Emmanuel Straton of Evesham, Burlington Co., husbandman and Hannah Hancock, dau of Timothy Hancock of said county, having consent of their parents, m. 9th mo, 15th da, 1713.

Henry Allen of Shrewsbury, son of Jedediah and Elizabeth (Howland) Allen and Abigail Adams, dau of John and Elizabeth Adams, m. 2nd mo, 12th da, 1714.

John Hugg, Jr., carpenter, Gloucester Co., and Elizabeth Newby, widow, having consent of their relations, m. at Newton 7th mo, 23rd da, 1714.

Thomas Evens, son of William and Elizabeth (Hanks) Evens of Evesham and Esther Haines, dau of John and Esther (Borton) Haines, having consent of their parents, m. at Evesham 10th mo, 1st mo, 1715.

John Adamson, and Ann Shuw [probably Chew], m. 3rd mo, 14th da, 1716.

Thomas Robinson of Newton and Sarah Low of the same place, having consent of their parents, m. at Newton 4th mo, 21st da, 1716.

Job Whiteall of Deptford Twp, Gloucester Co., son of James and Hannah Whiteall and Jane Siddon, dau of Ezekiel Siddon of Newton, having consent of their parents, m. at Newton 8th mo, 4th da, 1716.

William Hudson, son of William and Mary (Richardson) Hudson of Philadelphia and Jane Evens, dau of William and Elizabeth (Hanke) Evens of Evesham, having consent of their parents, m. at Evesham 8th mo, 29th da, 1717.

John Gill of Haddonfield and Mary Heritage, dau of Joseph and Hannah (Allen) Heritage of Chester Twp, Burlington Co., m. at Chester 8th mo, 23rd da, 1718.

John Sharp, Evesham, Burlington Co., and Jane Fritz Randle of the same, widow, having consent of their relations, m. at Evesham 10th mo, 24th da, 1719.

Abraham Haines of Evesham, son of Richard and Mary (Carlisle) Haines and Grace Hollingshead of Chester Twp, dau of John, Jr. and Agnes (Hackney) Hollingshead, having consent of their parents, m. at Evesham 3rd mo, 14th da, 1719.

Henry Warrington of Chester Twp, Burlington Co., and Elizabeth Austin, dau of Francis and Mary (Borton) Austin, having consent of their parents, m. at Evesham 6th mo, 11th da, 1719.

Joseph Gibson of Deptford, Gloucester, son of Thomas and Ann Gibson and Elizabeth Tindall, dau of Joseph and Dorcas (Erwin) Tindall of Waterford, having consent of their parents, m. at Newton 2nd mo, 21st da, 1720.

Thomas Eayre of Northampton Twp, Burlington Co., son of Richard Eayre and Priscilla Hugg, dau of John and Priscilla (Collins) Hugg of Gloucester Co., having consent of their parents, m. at Newton 3rd mo, 5th da, 1720.

Timothy Matlack of Waterford Twp, Gloucester Co., son of William and Mary (Hancock) Matlack, and Mary Haines, dau of Richard and Mary (Carlisle) Haines of Evesham, having consent of their parents, m. at Evesham 4th mo, 3rd da, 1720.

Jedidiah Adams of Chester Twp, Burlington Co., son of James and Esther (Allen) Adams and Margaret Christian of same place, having consent of their parents, m. at Chester 5th mo, 29th da, 1720.

Luke Gibson of Deptford, Gloucester Co., and Sarah Clarke, dau of William and Mary (Heritage) Clarke of Gloucester Twp, m. at Newton 9th mo, 2nd da, 1721.

Amos Cooper, son of David and Sybil(Matlack) Cooper of Deptford and Sarah Mickle, dau of Archibald, dec'd, and Mary (Burroughs) Mickle of Newton, m. at Newton 11th mo, 24th da, 1722.

John Rathmell of Burlington Co., and Mary Ballinger, dau of Henry and Mary (Harding) Ballinger of Evesham, having consent of their parent, m. at Evesham 4th mo, 20th da, 1723.

Thomas Sharp, son of John and Elizabeth (Paine) Sharp of Evesham and Elizabeth Smith, dau of Thomas Smith, Jr., having consent of their parents, m. at Evesham 10th mo, 3rd da, 1724.

Isaac Albertson and Rachel Haines, dau of Richard and Mary (Carlise) Haines, m. 12th mo, 14th da, 1725/6.

Joseph Kraighn of Gloucester Co., son of John and Sarah (Dole-Griscom) Kaighn and Mary Estaugh, dau of James of Philadelphia, a wheelwright and Mary (Lawson)Estaugh, having consent of their parents, m. at Haddonfield 3rd mo, 18th da, 1727.

Ephraim Tomlinson of Gloucester Co., son of Joseph and Elizabeth Tomlinson and Sarah Carbret of the same place, having consent of their parents, m. at Haddonfield 4th mo, 22nd da, 1727.

Henry Warrington of Chester Twp, Burlington Co., and Elizabeth Bishop, dau of Thomas Bishop of Burlington Co., having consent of their parents, m. at Evesham 11th mo, 9th da, 1728.

Moses Ward, son of James Ward of Gloucester Co., and Mary Clark, Jr., dau of William and Mary (Heritage) Clark of the same place, having consent of their parents, m. at Haddonfield 4th mo, 20th da, 1728.

George Ward, Jr., a fuller, of Deptford, son of George and Hannah (Warrington) Ward and Margaret Bennett, dau of Alexander and Sarah Bennett of the same place, m. at Woodbury Creek 8th mo, 29th da, 1729.

Joseph Parker of Chester Co., PA., yeoman and Mary Ladd, dau of John and Mary (Woods) Ladd of Gloucester Co., m. at Woodbury Creek 3rd mo, 21st da, 1730.

Bartholomew Wayatt, Jr., son of Bartholomew and Sarah (Ashton) Wyatt of Mannington Twp, Salem Co., and Elizabeth Tomlinson of Evesham, Burlington Co., dau of Joseph and Elizabeth Tomlinson, having consent of their parents, m. at Evesham 6th mo, 20th da, 1730.

Anthony Sharp, son of William and Jemaima (Eastlack) Sharp of Gloucester and Mary Dimmick of the said county, having consent of their parents, m. at Haddonfield 6th mo, 19th da, 1731.

Thomas Clark of the city of Philadelphia, carpenter, son of William Clark of Gloucester Twp and Meribah Parker, having consent of their parents, m. at Evesham 8th mo, 7th da, 1731.

William Mickle, son of John and Hannah (Cooper) Mickle of Gloucester Co., and Sarah Wright, dau of John and Elizabeth (Champion) Wright of same place, having consent of their parents, m. at Haddonfield 8th mo, 19th da, 1732.

Thomas Edgerton of Newton Twp and Sarah Stephens, Newton, having consent of their relations, m. at Haddonfield 10th mo, 20th da, 1733.

Peter White of Gloucester Co., and Rebecca Burr, dau of Henry and Elizabeth (Hudson) Burr of Burlington Co., having consent of their parents, m. at Haddonfield 1st mo, 21st da, 1733.

Francis Eastlake of Greenwich Twp and Phebe Driver, dau of Samuel Driver of same place, m. at Woodbury Creek 5th mo, 20th da, 1733.

Josiah White of Northampton Twp, Burlington Co., and Rebecca Foster, dau of Josiah and Amie Foster of Evesham Twp, having consent of their parents, m. at Evesham 10th mo, 5th da, 1734.

John Cowperthwaite of Burlington Co., son of John and Sarah (Adams) Cowperthwaite and Rachel Stokes, dau of Thomas and Rachel (Wright) Stokes of Gloucester, having consent of their parents, m. at Haddonfield 9th mo, 7th da, 1734.

Timothy Matlack and Martha (Burr) Haines, widow of Josiah Haines, dau of Henry and Elizabeth (Hudson) Burr, m. 1st mo, 12th da, 1735.

David Stratton of Evesham Twp, Burlington Co., tailor, son of Mark and Ann (Hancock) Stratton and Mary Elkenton, dau of Joseph, dec'd, and Elizabeth (Antrim) Elkenton of Northampton Twp, having consent of their parents, m. at Chester Twp 1st mo, 7th da, 1736/7.

Thomas Redman, Jr., son of Thomas, dec'd, and Sarah (Harriott or Marriott) Redman of Philadelphia, bricklayer and Hannah Gill, dau of John and Mary (Heritage) Gill of Haddonfield, having consent of their parents, m. at Haddonfield 2nd mo, 28th da, 1737.

Ebenezer Hopkins, a vintner, son of Benjamin, dec'd, late of London, and Sarah (Haddon) Hopkins and Sarah Lord, dau of James and Elizabeth (Clarke) Lord, he being dec'd, having consent of the surviving parents, m. at Woodbury Creek 2nd da, 29th mo, 1737.

Thomas Thorne, son of John and Ann (Hinchman) Thorne of Gloucester Co., and Mary Harrison, dau of Samuel Harrison of the same place, having consent of their parents, m. at Haddonfield 7th mo, 29th da, 1737.

Robert Stephens of Newton Twp and Ann Dent of the same place, having consent of their relations, m. at Haddonfield 10th mo, 13th da, 1739.

Charles French, Burlington Co., bricklayer, son of Charles and Eleanor French and Ann Clement, dau of Jacob and Ann (Harrison) Clement, he being dec'd, late of Gloucester, having consent of the surviving parents, m. 10th mo, 6th da, 1739.

Joseph White, son of William and Sarah White, late of Falls Twp, Bucks Co., PA. and Martha Lippincott, dau of Samuel and Hope (Wells) Lippincott of Evesham, Burlington Co., m. at Evesham 1st mo, 20th da, 1739.

William Griscom of Haddonfield, son of Tobias and Deborah (Gabitas) Griscom and Sarah Davis of Pilesgrove in Salem Co., dau of David and Dorothy (Cousins or Cozens) Davis, having consent of their parents, m. at Pilesgrove 9th mo, 6th da, 1740.

Samuel Stokes, son of Joseph Stokes of Burlington Co., and Hannah Hinchman, dau of John and Sarah Hinchman, having consent of their parents, m. at Haddonfield 3rd mo, 7th da, 1741.

Joshua Stokes, son of Thomas Stokes, dec'd, of Gloucester, yeoman and Amy Hinchman, dau of Joseph Hinchman, dec'd, late of same place, having consent of their parents, m. 10th mo, 10th da, 1741.

John Gill, son of John and Mary (Heritage) Gill of Haddonfield and Amy Davis, dau of David and Dorothy (Cousins or Cozens) Davis of Pilesgrove, having consent of their parents, m at Pilesgrove 10th mo, 1st da, 1741.

Thomas Hooton of Evesham, Burlington Co., and Mary Bate of Waterford, Gloucester Co., m. 5th mo, 1st da, 1742.

Ebenezer Andrews, son of Thomas and Abigail Andrews and Patience Lippincott, dau of Thomas and Mary (Haines) Lippincott, m. 9th mo, 8th da, 1742. Thomas Andrews was son of Roger Andrews of Evesham.

Benjamin Heritage, son of Joseph and Hannah (Allen) Heritage of Burlington Co., and Kezia Matlack, dau of John and Mary (Lee) Matlack of Gloucester Co., having consent of their parents, m. at Haddonfield 2nd mo, 28th da, 1743.

William Allen, son of Matthew Allen, dec'd, and Judith Stokes, dau of Joseph and Judith (Lippincott) Stokes, m. 1st mo, 10th da, 1745/6.

John Brown of Deptford Twp, son of John, dec'd, and Phebe (Chatfield) Brown and Sarah Cooper, dau of John and Ann (Clarke) Cooper, he being dec'd, m. at Deptford 1st mo, 28th da, 1746.

Jonathan Brown of Deptford Twp, son of John, dec'd, and Sarah (Cooper) Brown of Deptford and Sarah Ballinger of the same place, dau of Amariah, dec'd, and Mary (Elwell-Ashbrook) Ballinger, having consent of relations, m. at Woodbury 4th mo, 19th da, 1746.

Samuel Atkinson, son of John and Hannah (Shinn) Atkinson, of Burlington, and Esther Evans [or Evens], dau of Thomas and Esther (Haines) Evans [or Evens] m. 2nd mo, 24th da, 1746.

James Cooper, son of John, late of Deptford, dec'd, and Ann (Clarke) Cooper and Deborah Matlack of Waterford, dau of Richard and Rebecca (Haines) Matlack, having consent of their relations, m. at Haddonfield 4th mo, 5th da, 1746.

Thomas Redman, Jr., son of Thomas, dec'd, and Sarah (Harriott or Marriott) Redman of Haddonfield and Mary Davis, dau of David and Dorothy (Cousin or Cozens) Davis of Pilesgrove, having consent of their parents, m. at Pilesgrove 7th mo, 29th da, 1747.

William Matlack, Jr., son of William and Ann Matlack and Mary Turner, dau of John and Jane Turner, m. at Haddonfield 10th mo, 1st da, 1748.

Joshua Evens, son of Thomas and Rebecca (Owens) Evens, a

bricklayer, and Priscilla Collins, dau of John and Elizabeth (Kemble) Collins of Waterford, having consent of their relations, m. at Haddonfield 3rd mo, 20th da, 1753.

Samuel Clement of Newton Twp, son of Samuel and Rebecca Clement and Beulah Evans of Newton, dau of Dr. John, late of Evesham, dec'd, and Ruth (Nicholson) Evans, having consent of the surviving parents, m. at Haddonfield 1st mo, 19th da, 1758.

John Miller, son of Ebenezer Miller of Greenwich, Cumberland Co., and Sarah Andrews, daughter of Isaac Andrews, of Newton, Gloucester Co., having consent of their parents, m. 11th mo, 23rd da, 1758.

John Brackney of Burlington Co., cordwainer, son of Mathias and Frances (Andrews) Brackney and Mary Cheasman, dau of Thomas Cheasman, Gloucester Co., having consent of their parents, m. at Haddonfield 2nd mo, 23rd da, 1758.

John Branson, son of David of Newton Twp and Mary (Bullock) Branson and Sarah Sloan, dau of James and Mary (Cooper) Sloan of the same place, having consent of their parents, m. at Haddonfield 10th mo, 25th da, 1759.

Aaron Wills, son of Daniel and Elizabeth (Woolston) Wills of Burlington Co., and Rachel Warrington, dau of Henry and Elizabeth (Bishop) Warrington, having consent of parents, m. at Chester, Burlington Co. 1st mo, 18th da, 1759.

Samuel Webster, son of Thomas, dec'd, and Sarah (Venicomb) Webster, late of Gloucester Twp and Sarah Albertson of the same place, dau of Josiah and Ann (Austin) Albertson, having consent of their relations, m. at Haddonfield 6th mo, 28th da, 1759.

Thomas Rodgers of Philadelphia, a shopkeeper, son of Nicholas Rodgers, dec'd, and Elizabeth Craige, dau of John, dec'd, and Elizabeth (Parrott) Craige, late of Newton, having consent of their relations, m. at Haddonfield 11th mo, 20th da, 1760.

Constantine Lord of Deptford, son of Edmond, dec'd, and Elizabeth (Wood) Lord and Sarah Albertson of Gloucester Twp, dau of Benjamin Albertson, having consent of their relations, m. at Haddonfield 12th mo, 4th da, 1760.

Samuel Mifflin of Deptford, son of Edward Mifflin, dec'd, of VA. and Mary Jessup, dau of John, dec'd, and Margaret (Whitaker) Jessup of Deptford, having consent of the surviving parents, m. at Woodbury Creek 1st mo, 25th da, 1760.

Richard Gibbs, son of John Gibbs, of Mansfield Twp, Burlington Co., and Mary Burrough, dau of John and Phebe (Haines) Burroughs, of

Waterford Twp, having consent of their relations, m. at Haddonfield 11th mo, 19th da, 1761.

Jacob Jennings of Gloucester Co., son of Isaac Jennings, dec'd, and Mary Smith, dau of Isaac and Elizabeth (Norris) Smith, he being dec'd, having consent of their relations, m. at Haddonfield 12th mo, 3rd da, 1761.

Isaac Borton of Waterford Twp, son of John Borton, late of the same place, dec'd, and Mary Hooton, dau of Samuel and Ann (Goodbody) Hooton, having consent of their relations, m. at Haddonfield 5th mo, 28th da, 1761.

Elnathan Zane of Haddonfield, son of Ebenezer Zane, dec'd, and Bathsheba Hartly of Haddonfield, dau of Roger and Rebecca (Parker) Hartley, having consent of their relations, m. at Haddonfield 8th mo, 20th da, 1761.

David Davis of Pilesgrove, Salem Co., son of David, late of the same place, dec'd, and Dorothy (Cousins or Cozens) Davis and Martha Coles, dau of Samuel and Mary (Lippincott) Coles of Waterford Twp, having consent of their parents, m. at Haddonfield 10th mo, 21st da, 1762.

John Mickle, son of William Mickle of Greenwich Twp and Sarah (Wright) Mickle and Elizabeth Estaugh Hopkins, dau of Ebenezer, late of Newton, dec'd, and Sarah (Lord) Hopkins, having consent of their parents, m. at Haddonfield 3rd mo, 18th da, 1762.

James Whital of Deptford Twp, son of James and Ann (Cooper) Whital of same place and Rebekah Matlack, dau of Richard and Mary (Wood-Coles) Matlack of Waterford Twp, having consent of their parents, m. at Haddonfield 4th mo, 19th da, 1762.

Stephen Thackery of Newton Twp, son of Joseph and Hannah (Newby) Thackery and Elizabeth Sloan, dau of James and Mary (Cooper) Sloan of Newton, having consent of their relations, m. at Haddonfield 5th mo, 20th da, 1762.

John Tatum, son of John Tatum, late of Deptford, dec'd, and Sarah (Lord) Tatum and Sarah Wood, dau of George, dec'd, and Margaret (Bennett) Wood of Deptford, having consent of their relations, m. at Woodberry Creek 9th mo, 17th da, 1762.

Thomas Stoakes [Stokes], son of Joshua and Amy (Hinchman) Stokes, of Waterford Twp and Sarah Inskip, dau of Abraham and Sarah (Ward) Inskip of Waterford, having consent of their parents, m. at Haddonfield 10th mo, 25th da, 1764.

Ebenezer Hopkins of Haddonfield, son of Ebenezer, dec'd, and Sarah (Lord) Hopkins and Ann Albertson, dau of Josiah and Ann (Austin)

Albertson of Gloucester, having consent of their parents, m. at Haddonfield 11th mo, 22nd da, 1764.

James Cooper of Deptford Twp, son of John and Ann (Clarke) Cooper and Mary Mifflin, widow of Samuel Mifflin, late of Gloucester Twp, dec'd, dau of John and Margaret (Whitaker) Jessup, dec'd, having consent of their relations, m. at Woodbury Creek 11th mo, 23rd da, 1764.

Caleb Lippincott, son of Nathaniel and Mary (Engle) Lippincott of Waterford and Anna Venicomb, dau of Frances and Rachel (Lippincott) Venicomb of Northampton Twp, Burlington Co., having consent of their parents, m. at Mt. Holly 12th mo, 16th da, 1764.

James Starr, son of Moses Starr of Maiden Creek, Berks Co., PA. and Elizabeth Lord, dau of Joshua, dec'd, and Sarah (Wills) Lord, late of Deptford, having consent of their relations, m. at Woodbury Creek 8th mo, 15th da, 1764.

William Cooper, son of Daniel and Mary (West) Cooper of Newton Twp, and Abigail Matlack, dau of Richard and Mary (Wood-Cole) Matlack of Waterford Twp, having consent of their parents, m. at Haddonfield 4th mo, 18th da, 1765.

William Wells of Philadelphia, son of Edward Wells, dec'd, and Annah Craig of Philadelphia, dau of John, dec'd, and Elizabeth (Parrott) Craig late of Haddonfield, having consent of their relations, m. at Haddonfield 5th mo, 23rd da, 1765.

John Jessup, son of John Jessup, late of Deptford, dec'd, and Margaret (Whittaker) Jessup and Elizabeth Ballinger, dau of Amariah, late of the same place, dec'd, and Elizabeth (Garwood) Ballinger, having consent of their relations, m. at Woodbury Creek 10th mo, 17th da, 1766.

Isaac Townsend, son of Isaac and Sarah (Willets) Townsend of Cape May Co., and Keturah Albertson, dau of Josiah and Ann (Austin) Albertson of Gloucester Twp, having consent of their parents, m. at Haddonfield 12th mo, 11th da, 1766.

Mark Miller of Deptford Twp, shopkeeper, son of Ebenezer and Sarah Miller of Greenwick Twp, Cumberland Co., and Mary Redman of Newton, dau of Thomas, dec'd, and Hannah (Gill) Redman, having consent of their relations, m. at Haddonfield 10th mo, 15th da, 1767.

John Gill of Haddonfield, Gloucester Co., son of John, dec'd, and Mary (Heritage) Gill and Abigail Hillman of same place, widow of Daniel Hillman and dau of Samuel and Sarah (Burrough) Nicholson, having consent of their relations, m. at Haddonfield 11th mo, 12th da, 1767.

John Redman of Newton Twp, son of Thomas, dec'd, and Hannah (Gill)

HADDONFIELD MONTHLY MEETING 45

Redman, and Rachel Branson, dau of David and Mary (Bullock) Branson of same place, having consent of their parents, m. at Haddonfield 4th mo, 13th da, 1767.

Josiah Albertson, Jr., son of Josiah and Ann (Austin) Albertson and Elenor Tomlinson, dau of John Tomlinson, dec'd, having consent of the surviving parents, m. 4th mo, 4th da, 1767.

Caleb Cresson of Philadelphia, a merchant, son of James, late of the same, dec'd, and Sarah (Emlen) Cresson and Sarah Hopkins, dau of Ebenezer, late of Haddonfield, dec'd, and Sarah (Lord) Hopkins, having consent of their parents, m. at Haddonfield 5th mo, 7th da, 1767.

Aquilla Jones of Philadelphia, son of Griffith, late of the same place, dec'd, and Elizabeth Cooper, dau of Isaac and Hannah (Coate) Cooper of Newton, having consent of their relations, m. at Haddonfield 6th mo, 4th da, 1767.

Samuel Browne, son of Ebenezer, late of Newton Twp, dec'd, and Elizabeth (Ives) Browne and Rebecca Branson, dau of David and Mary (Bullock) Branson of the same place, having consent of their parents, m. at Haddonfield 12th mo, 15th da, 1768.

Jacob Haines of Waterford, son of Samuel, dec'd, and Lydia (Stokes) Haines and Bathsheba Burrough, dau of Samuel and Ann (Gray) Burrough of same place, having consent of their parents, m. at Haddonfield 4th mo, 28th da, 1768.

Job Whitall of Deptford Twp, son of James and Ann (Cooper) Whital of same place and Sarah Gill, dau of John and Amy (Davis) Gill of Haddonfield, having consent of their parents, m. at Haddonfield 12th mo, 21st da, 1769.

Jonathan Iredell of Deptford, house carpenter, son of Abraham Iredell, dec'd, and Elizabeth Hillman, dau of Daniel, late of Gloucester and Abigail (Nicholson) Hillman, having consent of their parents and guardian, m. at Haddonfield 10th mo, 18th da, 1770.

James Sloan of Newton Twp, son of James, dec'd, and Mary (Cooper) Sloan, and Rachel Clement, dau of Samuel, dec'd, and Ruth (Nicholson-Evans) Clement of Newton, having consent of their parents, m. at Haddonfield 4th mo, 19th da, 1770.

Joshua Cresson of Philadelphia, a merchant, son of James, late of the same, dec'd, and Sarah (Emlen) Cresson and Mary Hopkins, dau of Ebenezer, late of Haddonfield, dec'd, and Sarah (Lord) Hopkins, having consent of their relations, m. at Haddonfield 4th mo, 26th da, 1770.

Isaac Buzby, son of Thomas and Margaret (Haines) Buzby of

Wellingborough, Burlington Co., and Martha Lippincott, dau of Nathaniel and Mary (Engle) Lippincott of Waterford Twp, having consent of their parents, m. at Haddonfield 11th mo, 14th da, 1771.

Joseph Gibson, son of Joseph, Jr. and Sarah (Lord) Gibson of Deptford Twp and Sarah Haines, dau of William, dec'd, and Sarah (Lippincott) Haines having consent of their parents, m. at Greenwich 11th mo, 21st da, 1771.

Phineas Lord of Deptford, son of Joshua and Hannah (Lippincott) Lord and Marcy Gibbs, dau of Benjamin and Phebe Gibbs, having consent of their relations, m. at Woodbury 11th mo, 22nd da, 1771.

Benjamin Clarke Cooper, son of James and Deborah (Matlack) Cooper of Deptford and Ann Black, dau of William, dec'd, of Waterford Twp and Mary (Gibbs) Black, having consent of their parents, m. at Haddonfield 11th mo, 19th da, 1772.

Thomas Wright, son of Amos and Ann (Black) Wright of New Hanover Twp, Burlington Co. and Mary Branson, dau of David and Mary (Bullock) Branson of Newton, having consent of their parents, m. at Haddonfield 11th mo, 5th da, 1772.

Joseph Mickle, son of Archibald, Jr., dec'd, and Mary (Burroughs) Mickle of Newton and Hannah Burrough, dau of Isaac and Deborah (Jennings) Burrough of same place, having consent of their relations, m. at Haddonfield 2nd mo, 13th da, 1772.

William Mickle, son of William and Sarah (Wright) Mickle of Greenwich Twp and Sarah Lord, dau of Joshua and Hannah (Lippincott) of Deptford, having consent of their relations, m. at Woodbury Creek 5th mo, 1st da, 1772.

Amos Cooper, son of David Cooper of Deptford, Gloucester Co., yeoman and Sarah Mickle, dau of Archibald Mickle, dec'd, having consent of the surviving parents, m. 24th da, 11th mo, 1772.

Samuel Allinson of city of Burlington, son of Joseph, dec'd, and Elizabeth (Scattergood) Allinson and Martha Cooper of Deptford, Gloucester Co., dau of David and Sybil (Matlack) Cooper, having consent of their relations, m. at Woodbury 1st mo, 29th da, 1773.

George Ward, son of George, dec'd, and Margaret (Bennet) Ward and Ann Branson, dau of David and Mary (Bullock) Branson of Newton Twp, having consent of their parents, m. at Haddonfield 5th mo, 20th da, 1773.

John Barton of Waterford Twp, son of John, dec'd, and Elizabeth (Champion) and Amy Shivers of same place, dau of John and Mary Shivers, having consent of their relations, m. at Haddonfield 7th mo, 27th da, 1773.

HADDONFIELD MONTHLY MEETING

James Stewart of Alloways Creek, Salem Co., son of John and Mary (Wade) Stewart and Mary Ballinger of Deptford Twp, dau of Amariah, dec'd, and Mary (Elwell-Ashbrook) Ballinger, having consent of their relations, m. at Woodbury Creek 11th mo, 24th da, 1774.

Enoch Allen of Evesham, Burlington Co., house carpenter, son of Matthew Allen, dec'd, and Martha (Stokes) Allen and Hannah Collins of Waterford Twp, Gloucester Co., dau of Samuel and Rosanna (Stokes) Collins, having consent of their relations, m. at Haddonfield 12th mo, 1st da, 1774.

William Keais of Deptford Twp, son of William Keais, late of Rhode Island, dec'd, and Sarah Pedrick of Deptford, dau of Philip Pedrick, dec'd, having consent of their relations, m. at Woodbury 12th mo, 23rd da, 1774.

Joseph Reeves of Deptford, son of Thomas and Sarah (Biddle) and Elizabeth Morgan, dau of Joseph and Sarah (Mickle) Morgan, having consent of their parents, m. at Haddonfield 3rd mo, 31st da, 1774.

Joshua Stretch of Alloways Creek, Salem Co., son of Joseph, dec'd, and Deborah (Smith) Stretch and Lydia Tomlinson of Gloucester Twp, dau of Joseph, dec'd, and Lydia (Wade) Tomlinson, having consent of their relations, m. at Haddonfield 3rd mo, 31st da, 1774.

William Zane, Jr. of Greenwich Twp, son of Robert, Jr., dec'd, and Mary (Chattin) Zane and Elizabeth Hillman of Haddonfield, dau of James, dec'd, and Mary (Smallwood) Hillman, having consent of their parents, m. at Haddonfield 9th mo, 13th da, 1774.

Benjamin Cathrall of Newton Twp, shopkeeper, son of Edward and Rachel Cathrall and Esther Brown, dau of Ebenezer, dec'd, and Elizabeth (Ives) Brown, having consent of their relations, m. at Haddonfield 9th mo, 15th da, 1774.

Samuel Mickle of Greenwich Twp, son of William and Sarah (Wright) Mickle and Ann Lord of Deptford, dau of Joshua and Hannah (Lippincott) Lord, having consent of their relations, m. at Woodbury 11th mo, 30th da, 1775.

John Haines, son of William late of Greenwich Twp, dec'd, and Sarah (Lippincott) Haines and Hipparchia Hinchman, dau of James and Sarah (Bickham) Hinchman of Woolwich Twp, having consent of their friends, m. at Upper Greenwich 12th mo, 21st mo, 1775.

Joab Wills of Evesham, Burlington Co., son of Micajah and Rebecca (Hewlings) Wills and Amy Gill, dau of John and Amy (Davis) Gills, having consent of their parents, m. at Haddonfield 3rd mo, 9th da, 1775.

48 EARLY CHURCH RECORDS OF GLOUCESTER COUNTY

William Edgerton of Haddonfield, joiner, son of Thomas Edgerton and Tabitha Henson of same place, dau of John Henson, having consent of their relations, m. at Haddonfield 6th mo, 22nd da, 1775.

Caleb Lippincott, son of Nathaniel and Mary (Engle) Lippincott of Waterford and Zilphah Shinn, dau of James Shinn of Hanover, Burlington Co., having consent of their parents, m. at Evesham 7th mo, 20th da, 1775.

Nathaniel Barton of Waterford Twp, son of John and Elizabeth (Champion) and Rachel Stokes of the same place, dau of Joshua and Amy (Hackman) Stokes, having consent of their parents, m. at Haddonfield 3rd mo, 28th da, 1776.

John Clement of Haddonfield, house carpenter, son of Jacob and Elizabeth (Tyler) Clement, and Hannah Griscom, dau of William Griscom and Sarah (Davis) Griscom, having consent of their parents, m. at Haddonfield 4th mo, 8th da, 1776.

Jedediah Allen, son of Judiah Allen of Salem Co., dec'd, and Ann Wilkins, widow of Constantine Wilkins, dau of John and Sarah (Kay) Hooton, having consent of their relations, m. at Upper Springfield 8th mo, 16th da, 1776.

David Branson of Newton Twp, weaver, son of David and Mary (Bullock), dec'd, Branson and Elizabeth Evens of the same place, dau of Joshua and Priscilla (Collins), dec'd, Evens, having consent of their relations, m. at Haddonfield 10th mo, 23rd da, 1777.

Samuel Tomlinson of Gloucester Twp, son of Joseph, dec'd, and Catherine (Fairlane) Tomlinson and Martha Mason of the same, dau of Solomon, dec'd, and Anna (Kemble) Mason, having consent of their relations, m. at Haddonfield 6th mo, 19th da, 1777.

Joshua Evens, a bricklayer, son of Thomas and Rebecca (Owens) Evens and Ann Kay of Haddonfield, widow of Joseph Kay, dec'd, having consent of their relations, m. at Haddonfield 8th mo, 12th da, 1777.

Job Cowperthwaite of Chester Twp, Burlington Co., son of Thomas and Mary (Borden) Cowperthwaite and Ann Vickers of Newton Twp, dau of Peter and Anna (Knight) Vickers, having consent of their parents, m. at Haddonfield 8th mo, 21st da, 1777.

William Wood, son of William, dec'd, and Rachel (Stockdell) Wood of Deptford Twp and Hannah Ladd, dau of Samuel and Sarah (Hambilton) Ladd of same place, having consent of their relations, m. at Woodbury 9th mo, 19th da, 1777.

William White of Greenwich Twp, son of William White, dec'd, and Ann Paul of the same place, dau of Samuel and Isabel (English) Paul, having consent of their relations, m. at Upper Greenwich 12th mo,

24th da, 1778.
Joseph Burrough of Waterford Twp, son of Samuel, dec'd, and Ann (Gray) Burrough and Lydia Stretch, widow of Joshua Stretch, dau of Joseph and Catherine Tomlinson, having consent of their relations, m. at Haddonfield 2nd mo, 19th da, 1778.
Marmaduke Cooper of Newton Twp, son of Isaac, dec'd, and Hannah (Coate) Cooper and Mary Jones of Newton, dau of Aquilla and Rebecca (Wills) Jones, having consent of their parents, m. at Haddonfield 3rd mo, 26th da, 1778.
Samuel Stokes of Waterford, son of Joshua and Amy (Hinchman) Stokes and Hope Hunt of same place, dau of Robert, dec'd, and Martha Hunt, having consent of their parents, m. at Haddonfield 1st mo, 21st da, 1779.
Benjamin Test of Pilesgrove, Salem Co., son of Francis, dec'd, and Elizabeth (Bacon) Test and Elizabeth Thackery of Newton Twp, widow of Stephen Thackery, dau of James, dec'd, and Mary (Cooper) Sloan, m. at Haddonfield 10th mo, 14th da, 1779.
Richard Snowden of Evesham, Burlington Co., tanner, son of Leonard and Jane Snowden and Sarah Brown of Newton Twp, dau of Ebenezer and Elizabeth (Ives), dec'd, Brown, having consent of the surviving parents, m. at Haddonfield 11th mo, 18th da, 1779.
James Hinchman of Deptford Twp, son of James and Sarah (Bickham) Hinchman and Sarah Morgan of Waterford Twp, dau of Joseph and Mary (Stokes) Morgan, having consent of their parents, m. at Haddonfield 3rd mo, 18th da, 1779.
Joshua Paul of Greenwich Twp, son of Nathan and Deborah (Vinneman) Paul and Mary Lippincott, dau of Restore and Deborah Lippincott, having consent of their parents, m. at Greenwich Twp 3rd mo, 4th da, 1779.
Richard Wood, son of Richard and Hannah (Ellis-Warrington) Wood of Greenwich, Cumberland Co., and Ann Cooper, dau of David and Sybil (Matlack) Cooper of Deptford, having consent of their parents, m. at Woodbury 11th mo, 24th da, 1780.
Samuel Tomlinson of Gloucester Twp, son of Joseph, dec'd, and Catherine (Fairlane) Tomlinson and Mary Bates of Waterford, dau of William, dec'd, and Elizabeth (Hooten) Bates, having consent of their relations, m. at Haddonfield 12th mo, 14th da, 1780.
Benjamin Hooten, son of John and Sarah (Key) Hooten of Greenwich and Sarah Snowden, dau of William and Margaret (Ballinger) Snowden of Deptford Twp, having consent of their parents, m. at Woodbury 3rd mo, 31st da, 1780.

William Lippincott of Woolwich Twp, son of Caleb and Hannah (Wills) Lippincott and Elizabeth Folwell of the same, dau of Thomas and Elizabeth (Atkinson) Folwell, having consent of their relations, m. at Upper Greenwich 4th mo, 13th da, 1780.

John Tatum of Deptford, son of John, dec'd, late of Deptford and Sarah (Lord) Tatum and Elizabeth Cooper, dau of David and Sybill (Matlack) Cooper of the same place, having consent of their relations, m. at Woodbury 6th mo, 23rd da, 1780.

Isaac Ballinger Snowden, son of William and Margaret (Ballinger) Snowden of Deptford and Mary Bassett of Greenwich Twp, dau of William Bassett, dec'd, having consent of their relations, m. at Upper Greenwich 10th mo, 11th da, 1781.

John Webb of Waterford, joiner, son of John Webb, dec'd, and Amey Wills of Newton Twp, widow of Joab Wills, dau of John and Amy (Davis) Gills, having consent of their parents, m. at Haddonfield 11th mo, 22nd da, 1781.

Edward Gibbs of Newton Twp, son of John Gibbs and Hepzibah Evens, dau of John, dec'd, and Ruth (Nicholson) Evens of same place, having consent of their parents, m. at Haddonfield 12th mo, 20th da, 1781.

Peter Thompson [Thomson] of Newton Twp, son of Edward Thompson [Thomson] and Mary Glover, widow of Thomas Glover, dau of Robert and Hannah (Burrough) Stiles of same place, having consent of relations, m. at Haddonfield 1st mo, 18th da, 1781.

John Gill of Haddonfield, son of John, dec'd, and Mary (Heritage) Gill and Sarah Prickett of Waterford, widow of Josiah Prickett, dau of John and Rachel (Stokes) Cowperthwaite, having consent of their relations, m. at Chester, Burlington Co. 3rd mo, 15th da, 1781.

Robert Zane, son of Robert, dec'd, and Mary (Chattin) Zane of Greenwich Twp and Elizabeth Butler of the same place, dau of John Butler, dec'd, having consent of their relations, m. at Upper Greenwich 3rd mo, 15th da, 1781.

Daniel Hillman, Jr. of Waterford, carpenter, son of Daniel, dec'd, and Abigail (Nicholson) Hillman and Martha Ellis of Waterford, dau of Isaac and Mary (Shivers) Ellis, having consent of their relations, m. at Haddonfield 5th mo, 24th da, 1781.

George Ward of Deptford, son of Josiah, dec'd, and Kesiah (Albertson) Ward and Hannah Wood of Deptford, widow of William Wood, dau of Samuel and Sarah (Hambleton) Ladd, both of Newton, having consent of their parents, m. at Woodbury 10th mo, 25th da, 1782.

Preston Lippincott of Newton Twp, a fuller, son of Samuel and Mary (Preston) Lippincott and Deborah Even of the same, dau of Julius,

HADDONFIELD MONTHLY MEETING 51

dec'd, and Sarah (Middleton) Even, having consent of their parents, m. at Haddonfield 11th mo, 14th da, 1782.

Joshua Harlan of Deptford Twp, son of Joel and Hannah Harlan and Sarah Hinchman, dau of James and Sarah (Bickham) Hinchman of same place, having consent of their parents, m. at Woodbury 12th mo, 20th da, 1782.

Joshua Cooper of Newton Twp, son of Daniel, dec'd, and Mary (West) Cooper and Abigail Stokes, dau of Jacob Stokes of the same place, having consent of their parents, m. at Haddonfield 2nd mo, 21st da, 1782.

John Barton of Waterford, son of John, dec'd, and Elizabeth (Champion) and Rebecca Engwine, dau of John Engwine, dec'd, of same place, having consent of the surviving relations, m. at Haddonfield 3rd mo, 7th da, 1782.

John Reeve of Cumberland Co., son of John and Elizabeth (Brick) Reeve and Beulah Brown of Gloucester Co., dau of John and Sarah (Cooper), having consent of their relations, m. at Woodbury 4th mo, 12th da, 1782.

David Ware of Lower Alloways Creek, Salem Co., son of John Ware, dec'd, and Sarah Shinn of Greenwich Twp, dau of Azariah, dec'd, and Sarah (Haines-Lippincott) Shinn, having consent of their relations, m. at Woodbury 9th mo, 30th da, 1782.

Asher Brown, son of Samuel, dec'd, and Ann (Buffin) Brown and Mary Ward, dau of George, dec'd, and Rachel (Wilkins) Ward, having consent of their relations, m. at Woodbury 12th mo, 19th da, 1783.

Zaccheus Test of Newton, son of Benjamin and Sarah (Dunn) Test and Rebecca Davis of Deptford, dau of Gabriel, dec'd, and Sarah (Battin) Davis, having consent of their parents, m. at Woodbury 1st mo, 19th da, 1783.

Isaac Stiles of Newton Twp, son of Robert, dec'd, and Hannah (Burrough) Stiles and Rachel Glover of Gloucester Twp, dau of John and Mary (Thorne) Glover, having consent of their parents, m. at Haddonfield 3rd mo, 13th da, 1783.

Jacob Jennings of Gloucester town, son of Isaac, dec'd, and Ann Hopkins of Newton, widow of Ebenezer Hopkins, dau of Josiah and Ann (Austin) Albertson, having consent of their parents, m. at Haddonfield 7th mo, 24th da, 1783.

Darling Haines of Waterford Twp, son of Amos and Mary (Connaro) Haines and Mary Lippincott of same, dau of Caleb and Anna (Venicomb) Lippincott, having consent of their parents, m. at Haddonfield 10th mo, 21st mo, 1784.

James Mickle, son of William late of Greenwich Twp, dec'd, and Sarah
(Wright) Mickle and Hannah Lord, dau of Joshua, dec'd, and Hannah
(Lippincott) Lord of Deptford Twp, having consent of their relations,
m. at Woodbury 11th mo, 12th da, 1784.
Jonathan Morgan, son of Jonathan and Mary Morgan of Deptford and
Elizabeth Fisher, dau of Jonathan Fisher of Greenwich Twp, having
consent of their relations, m. at Woodbury 11th mo, 26th da, 1784.
James Thackry, son of Stephen, dec'd, late of Newton Twp and
Elizabeth (Sloan) Thackry and Jane Gaunt of same place, dau of
John and Jane (Satterthwaite) Gaunt, having consent of their
parents, m. at Haddonfield 2nd mo, 19th da, 1784.
William Knight of Newton Twp, son of Jonathan and Isabella Knight
and Elizabeth Webster of same, dau of Samuel and Sarah (Albertson)
Webster, having consent of their parents, m. at Haddonfield 3rd mo,
18th da, 1784.
Charles Fogg of Alloways Creek, Salem Co., son of Charles, dec'd, and
Sarah Fogg and Ann Bates of Waterford Twp, dau of William, dec'd,
and Elizabeth (Hooten) Bates, having consent of their relations, m. at
Haddonfield 4th mo, 15th da, 1784.
James Hopkins of Newton Twp, son of John Estaugh and Sarah
(Mickle) Hopkins, and Rebecah Clement of same place, dau of
Samuel, Jr. and Beulah (Evans) Clement, having consent of their
parents, m. at Haddonfield 5th mo, 27th da, 1784.
John Evens of Newton Twp, son of Joshua and Priscilla (Collins) Evens
and Elizabeth Browning of Newton, dau of Joseph and Sarah
(Matlack-Rowland) Browning, having consent of their parents, m. at
Newton 10th mo, 19th da, 1785.
Daniel Roberts of Waterford Twp, son of Jacob, dec'd, and Hannah
(Heritage) Roberts and Hannah Stokes, dau of Thomas and Sarah
(Inskip) Stokes, having consent of their relations, m. at Haddonfield
3rd mo, 17th da, 1785.
Abraham Warrington, son of Thomas and Mary (Roberts) Warrington
of Chester Twp, and Rachel Evens, dau of Joshua and Priscilla
(Collins) Evens of Newton, having consent of their parents, m. at
Newton 3rd mo, 18th da, 1785.
Peter Thompson of Gloucester town, son of Edward Thompson and
Sarah Stevenson of Newton Twp, widow of Jennings Stevenson,
having consent of their relations, m. at Newton 6th mo, 15th da,
1785.
John Stewart of Alloways Creek, Salem Co., son of John and Mary
(Wade) Stewart and Deborah Griscom of Newton, dau of William and

Sarah (Davis) Griscom, having consent of their parents, m. at Haddonfield 6th mo, 16th da, 1785.

Isaac Jones of Haddonfield, a cordwainer, son of Henry and Naomi (Cheeseman), dec'd, Jones and Sarah Atkinson of Newton Twp, widow of Empson Atkinson, dau of Noah and Rebecca (Leeds) Ridgway, having consent of the surviving parents, m. at Newton 10th mo, 16th da, 1788.

Francis Boggs of Newton Twp, son of James and Sarah Boggs, she being dec'd, and Ann Haines of the same place, dau of Thomas and Mary Haines, having consent of guardian and relations, m. at Newton 11th mo, 13th da, 1788.

Caleb Atkinson of Newton Twp, bricklayer, son of Samuel and Esther (Evans) Atkinson and Sarah Champion of Haddonfield, dau of Thomas and Deborah (Clark) Champion, having consent of their parents, m. at Haddonfield 11th mo, 13th da, 1788.

William Rogers of Evesham, son of William and Grace (Allen-Eayre) Rogers and Mary Davis, dau of David and Martha (Coles) Davis of Waterford, having consent of surviving parents, m. at Haddonfield 2nd mo, 26th da, 1789.

Joseph Davis of Waterford Twp, son of David and Martha (Coles), dec'd, Davis and Mary Haines of same place, dau of Amos and Mary (Connaro) Haines, having consent of surviving parents, m. at Haddonfield 3rd mo, 26th da, 1789.

William Letchworth of Philadelphia, son of John, dec'd, and Diana Letchworth and Mary Pryor of Haddonfield, dau of Thomas, dec'd, and Hannah Pryor, having consent of relations, m. at Haddonfield 4th mo, 16th da, 1789.

John Thorne of Waterford Twp, son of Thomas and Abigail (Burroughs) Thorne and Mary Dubree of the same place, dau of William and Mary Dubree, she being dec'd, having consent of surviving parents, m. at Haddonfield 4th mo, 30th da, 1789.

Samuel Glover of Gloucester Twp, son of John and Mary (Thorne) Glover and Hannah Albertson of Waterford, dau of Josiah, Jr. and Eleanor (Tomlins) Albertson, having consent of relations, m. at Haddonfield 4th mo, 3rd da, 1789.

Thomas Middleton Potter of Haddonfield, house carpenter, son of James, dec'd, and Guili (Middleton) Potter and Mary Glover of Gloucester, dau of John and Mary (Thorne) Glover, having consent of surviving parents, m. at Haddonfield 10th mo, 14th da, 1790.

James Wood of Salem town, son of Richard and Hannah (Ellis-Warrington) Wood and Ruth Clement of Haddonfield, dau of Samuel, dec'd, and Beulah (Evans) Clement, having consent of surviving parents, m. at Haddonfield 10th mo, 21st da, 1790.

Josiah Kay of Haddonfield son of Joseph, dec'd, and Ann (Thompson) Kay and Elizabeth Horner of Gloucester Twp, dau of Isaac, dec'd, and Elizabeth (Kay) Horner, having consent of surviving parents, m. at Haddonfield 11th mo, 18th da, 1790.

Thomas Knight, son of Jonathan, dec'd, and Isabella Knight of Newton and Hannah Branson, dau of John, dec'd, and Sarah (Sloan) Branson, having consent of surviving parents, m. at Newton 9th mo, 16th da, 1790.

George Abbot of Warrington, Salem Co., son of William and Rebecca (Tyler) Abbot of Salem and Mary Redman of Haddonfield, dau of Thomas and Rebecca (White) Redman, having consent of parents, m. 10th mo, 20th da, 1791.

Samuel Abbott of Elsingborough, Salem Co., son of William and Rebecca (Tyler) Abbott and Marcia Gill of Haddonfield, dau of John and Amie (Davis) Gill, having consent of parents, m. at Haddonfield 11th mo, 24th da, 1791.

Jeremiah Wood of Deptford Twp, son of Jehu, dec'd, and Mary Wood and Mary Horner of Waterford Twp, dau of Isaac, dec'd, and Elizabeth (Kay) Horner, having consent of surviving parents, m. at Haddonfield 11th mo, 24th da, 1791.

John Gill, son of George and Elizabeth Gill, of Gloucester Twp and Susanna Branson of Newton Twp, dau of David and Mary (Bullock) Branson, having consent of parents, m. at Newton 11th mo, 15th da, 1792.

Joseph Burrough, Jr. of Waterford, Gloucester Co., son of Joseph and Kezia Burrough and Martha Davis, dau of David and Martha, dec'd, Davis of same place, having consent of surviving parents, m. 10th mo, 18th da, 1792.

Jesse Lippincott, son of Caleb and Anne (Venicomb), dec'd, Lippincott of Waterford and Mary Ann Kay of same, dau of Isaac, Jr., dec'd, and Hannah (Shinn) Kay, having consent of surviving parents, m. at Haddonfield 2nd mo, 1st da, 1793.

Joseph Cooper, son of Samuel and Providence (Brown) Cooper, of Newton and Sarah Powell Buckley of the same place, dau of William and Sarah Buckley, having consent of parents, m. at Newton 3rd mo, 14th da, 1793.

Jacob Glover, son of John and Mary (Thorne) Glover of Gloucester Twp and Mary Branson, dau of John, dec'd, and Sarah (Sloan) Branson of Newton Twp, having consent of surviving parents, m. at

Newton 10th mo, 17th da, 1793.

Marmaduke Burr of Northampton Twp, Burlington Co., son of Joseph and Rachel (Coate) Burr, and Ann Hopkins of Haddonfield, dau of Ebenezer, dec'd, and Sarah (Lord) Hopkins, having consent of surviving parents, m. at Haddonfield 10th mo, 24th da, 1793.

Abraham Silver of Pilesgrove, Salem Co., son of Abel and Hope Silver and Sarah Knight of the town of Gloucester, dau of Jonathan, dec'd, and Sarah Knight, having consent of surviving parents, m. at Haddonfield 11th mo, 14th da, 1793.

Joshua Roberts, son of John and Phebe (Andrews) Roberts of Evesham and Rachel Coles, dau of Job and Elizabeth (Tomlinson) Coles of Waterford, having consent of relations, m. at Haddonfield 12th mo, 19th da, 1793.

Obadiah Engle of Evesham, son of Joseph and Mary (Borton) Engle and Patience Coles of Waterford Twp, dau of Job and Elizabeth (Tomlinson) Coles, having consent of parents, m. at Haddonfield 3rd mo, 13th da, 1794.

George C. Ward of Deptford, a blacksmith, son of Isaac and Rebecca Ward and Deborah Saunders of Gloucester Twp, dau of John and Elizabeth (Lippincott) Saunders, having consent of relations, m. at Haddonfield 10th mo, 16th da, 1794.

Benjamin Hopkins of Haddonfield, house carpenter, son of Ebenezer and Ann (Albertson), dec'd, Hopkins, and Rebecca Ward of the same, dau of Dr. Isaac and Rebecca Ward, she being, dec'd, having consent of relations, m. at Haddonfield 10th mo, 23rd da, 1794.

John Albertson, son of Josiah Albertson, Jr., dec'd, and Eleanor (Tomlinson) Albertson and Ann Pine, dau of John Pine, dec'd, and Rachel (Burrough) Pine, having consent of surviving parents, m. at Haddonfield 11th mo, 20th da, 1794.

Isaac Ballinger of Waterford Twp, blacksmith, son of Thomas and Priscilla (Corson) Ballinger and Esther Stokes of same place, dau of Thomas and Sarah (Inskip) Stokes, having consent of parents, m. at Haddonfield 2nd mo, 19th da, 1795.

Joseph Kaighn, son of Joseph and Prudence (Butcher-Rogers) Kaighn of Newton Twp and Sarah Mickle, dau of Joseph and Hannah (Burrough) Mickle of same place, having consent of parents, m. at Newton 4th mo, 16th da, 1795.

Job Bishop of Evesham Twp, taylor, son of Isaac, dec'd, and Mary Bishop and Sarah Jones of Newton Twp, dau of Hugh and Esther Jones, she being dec'd, having consent of surviving parents, m. at Haddonfield 4th mo, 16th da, 1795.

Jesse Smith, son of Thomas, dec'd, and Rebecca Smith and Mary Paul, widow of Josiah Paul, both of Newton Twp, dau of Israel and Rebecca Cassell, having consent of relations, m. at Newton 8th mo, 20th da, 1795.

William Estaugh Hopkins, son of John Estaugh and Sarah (Mickle) Hopkins and Ann Morgan of same place, dau of Griffith, dec'd, and Rebecca (Clement) Morgan, having consent of surviving parents, m. at Haddonfield 10th mo, 22nd da, 1795.

Joseph Glover of Gloucester Twp, son of John and Mary (Thorne) Glover and Sarah Mickle of same place, dau of James and Letitia (Wood), dec'd, Mickle, having consent of surviving parents, m. at Haddonfield 5th mo, 12th da, 1796.

Aaron Pancoast of Greenwich Twp, son of William, Jr. and Mary (Copeland) Pancoast and Ann Cooper of Waterford, widow of William Cooper, having consent of surviving parents, m. at Haddonfield 11th mo, 24th da, 1796.

Joseph W. Bennett of Mt. Holly, Burlington Co., son of John and Ruth Bennett, she being dec'd, and Mary Morgan of Waterford Twp, dau of Joseph and Mary (Stokes), dec'd, Morgan, having consent of her father, m. at Haddonfield, 12th mo, 22nd da, 1796.

Reuben Braddock of Evesham, son of Reuben and Abigail (Borton), dec'd, Braddock and Elizabeth Stokes of Waterford Twp, dau of Thomas and Sarah (Inskip) Stokes, having consent of surviving parents, m. at Haddonfield, m. 12th mo, 29th da, 1796.

Peter Hannay [Hanna] of Newton Twp, clothier, son of Samuel Hannay [Hanna], now or late of North Britain in Europe, and Hannah Duell of Gloucester Twp, dau of John and Elizabeth (Cowperthwaite), dec'd, Duell, having consent of relations, m. at Haddonfield 3rd mo, 16th da, 1797.

Joseph Cooper Swett of Waterford Twp, son of Benjamin and Mary Swett and Ann Harrison Clement of Haddonfield, dau of Samuel, dec'd, and Beulah (Evans) Clement, having consent of surviving parents, m. at Haddonfield 4th mo, 20th da, 1797.

William Vinecomb of Northampton Twp, Burlington Co., son of Francis and Rachel (Lippincott) Vennicomb and Hannah Kay, widow of Isaac Kay, Jr., dau of Jacob and Hannah (Rakestraw-Lippincott) Shinn, having consent of relations, m. at Haddonfield 11th mo, 23rd da, 1797.

Jonathan Knight, son of Jonathan, dec'd and Isabella Knight of Newton Twp, Gloucester Co., and Elizabeth Kaighn, dau of James and Hannah Kaighn of same place, having consent of surviving parents,

m. 12th mo, 16th da, 1797.
Joseph Burr of Burlington, son of Joseph and Rachel (Coats), dec'd, Burr and Mary Sloan, dau of James and Rachel (Clement) Sloan of Gloucester Twp, having consent of surviving parents, m. at Newton 12th mo, 20th da, 1798.
Abel Ashead, Waterford Twp, son of Amos and Lydia Ashead and Ann Jenings, dau of Levi and Sarah (Robeson) Jennings, having consent of parents, m. at Haddonfield 12th mo, 27th da, 1798.
Richard Matlack Cooper of Newton Twp, son of William, dec'd, and Abigail (Matlack) Cooper and Mary Cooper, dau of Samuel and Prudence (Brown) Cooper of Waterford Twp, having consent of surviving parents, m. at Newton 5th mo, 24th da, 1798.
James A. Alexander of Philadelphia, son of Adam and Hannah Alexander and Hannah Redman, dau of Thomas and Rebecca (White) Redman, having consent of parents, m. 5th mo, 24th da, 1798. [marriage book calls him John Adamson Alexander].
Robert Rowand, son of Joseph and Rachel (Cole) Rowand of Waterford Twp and Elizabeth Barton, dau of John and Amy (Shivers) Barton of Waterford, having consent of relations, m. at Newton 1st mo, 17th da, 1799.
William Roberts of Chester Twp, Burlington Co., blacksmith, son of Joseph and Susanne (Coles) Roberts and Ann Brick of Waterford Twp, dau of John and Abigail (French) Brick, having consent of parents, m. at Haddonfield 5th mo, 16th da, 1799.
Isaac Thorne of Waterford Twp, son of Thomas and Abigail (Burroughs) Thorne and Rachel Horner of the town of Gloucester, dau of Isaac, dec'd, and Elizabeth (Kay) Horner, having consent of surviving parents, m. at Haddonfield 5th mo, 23rd da, 1799.
Samuel Hooten of Waterford, son of Elisha and Esther (Hunt), dec'd, Hooton and Sarah Ballinger of same place, dau of Thomas and Priscilla (Corson) Ballinger, having consent of surviving parents, m. at Haddonfield 11th mo, 14th da, 1799.
Joshua Reeve of Greenwich, Cumberland Co., son of Benjamin and Rachel (Tyler) and Milisent Carr of Haddonfield, dau of Job, dec'd, and Catharine Carr, having consent of surviving parents, m. at Haddonfield 4th mo, 17th da, 1800.
Enoch Allen and Mrs. Ann (Haines) Kirby, dau of William and Elizabeth (Ballinger) Haines, widow of Amos Kirby, m. 5th mo, 7th da, 1800.
Thomas Middleton Potter of the city of Trenton, druggist, son of James, dec'd, and Guila Potter and Rebecca Redman of Haddonfield,

dau of Thomas and Rebecca Redman, having consent of surviving parents, m. 5th mo, 22nd da, 1800.

Samuel Edgerton, son of William and Tabitha, dec'd, Edgerton of Newton, Gloucester Co., and Elizabeth Wilkins, dau of William, dec'd and Sarah Wilkins of same place, having consent of surviving parents, m. 10th mo, 16th da, 1800.

Josiah Webster of Newton, Gloucester Co., son of Samuel and Sarah Webster and Priscilla Evens, dau of Joshua and Priscilla, dec'd, Evens of same place, having consent of surviving parents, m. 11th mo, 13th da, 1800.

Josiah Atkinson of Newton, son of Samuel and Esther (Evans), dec'd, Atkinson and Priscilla Ballinger of Waterford Twp, dau of Thomas and Priscilla (Corson) Ballinger, having consent of surviving parents, m. at Haddonfield 11th mo, 20th da, 1800.

Joshua Haines of Philadelphia, son of John and Mary (Shreve) Haines and Mary Pine of Gloucester Twp, dau of John, dec'd, and Rachel (Burrough) Pine, having consent of surviving parents, m. at Haddonfield 12th mo, 18th da, 1800.

Samuel Lippincott of Newton Twp, Gloucester Co., son of Caleb and Hannah, dec'd, Lippincott and Patience Webster, dau of Samuel and Sarah Webster of Newton, having consent of surviving parents, m. 3rd mo, 12th da, 1801.

Amos Haines, Jr., of Newton, Gloucester Co., son of Amos and Mary Haines of Waterford and Elizabeth Knight, dau of Samuel and Sarah Webster of Newton, having consent of parents, m. 3rd mo, 26th da, 1801.

Daniel Gaunt of Mansfield, Burlington Co., son of John and Jane, dec'd, Gaunt and Mary Githens, dau of Thomas and Mary Githens of Haddonfield, having consent of surviving parents, m. 3rd mo, 18th da, 1802.

Abel Clements, Jr., of Deptford Twp, Gloucester Co., yeoman, son of Abel and Elizabeth Clement and Keziah Mickle, dau of Joseph and Hannah Mickle of Newton, having consent of the surviving parents, m. 9th mo, 11th da, 1802.

Samuel Langstaff of Cumberland Co., yeoman, son of Laban, dec'd, and Mary Langstaff and Hannah Pine, dau of Benjamin and Priscilla, dec'd, Pine of Waterford, having consent of parents, m. 6th mo, 23rd da, 1803.

Samuel Fisher of the city of Philadelphia, PA., merchant, son of William Fisher, late of same, a merchant, dec'd, and Sarah Fisher and Sarah Ward Cooper, dau of William, late of Gloucester, dec'd and

Abigail Cooper, having consent of surviving parents, m. 12th mo, 22nd da, 1803.

Samuel Brown, Jr., of Haddonfield, Gloucester Co., tanner, son of Samuel and Rebecca, dec'd, Brown and Mary Hartley, dau of Benjamin and Mary, dec'd, Hartley of same place, having consent of surviving parents, m. 12th mo, 22 da, 1803.

David Bassett of Gloucester Twp, merchant, son of Daniel and Mary, dec'd, Bassett and Sarah Tomlinson, dau of Ephraim and Ann, dec'd, Tomlinson, having consent of surviving parents, m. 3rd mo, 14 da, 1805.

Bethuel Borton of Evesham, Burlington Co., yeoman, son of Benjamin and Charity Borton and Rebecca Cliffton, dau of Nathan and Mary Cliffton of same place, having consent of parents, m. 4th mo, 18th da, 1805.

Stephen M. Day of Haddonfield, Gloucester Co., son of Samuel, dec'd and Nancy Day and Sarah Redman, dau of Thomas and Rebecca, dec'd, Redman of same place, having consent of surviving parents, m. 11th mo, 14th da, 1805.

Abraham Lippincott of Chester, Burlington Co., son of Samuel and Priscilla Lippincott and Abigail Thorne, dau of Thomas and Abigail Thorne of Waterford, Gloucester Co., having consent of parents, m. 3rd mo, 13th da, 1806.

Simeon Eastlack of Newton, Gloucester Co., yeoman, son of Samuel and Hannah Eastlack and Rachel Borton, dau of Nathaniel and Rachel Borton of Waterford, having consent of surviving parents, m. 6th mo, 19th da, 1806.

John Brown of Newton, Gloucester Co., son of Jonathan and Sarah Brown of Deptford and Ruth Sloan, dau of James and Rachel Sloan of Newton, having consent of parents, m. 3rd mo, 12th da, 1807.

Thomas Redman, Jr., of Haddonfield, Gloucester Co., merchant, son of Thomas and Rebecca, dec'd, Redman and Elizabeth S. Hopkins, dau of James and Rebecca, dec'd, Hopkins of same place, having consent of surviving parents, m. 5th mo, 7th da, 1807.

Nathan Evens of Waterford, Gloucester Co., son of Nathan, dec'd, and Syllania Evens and Rebecca Evens, widow of John Evens, having consent of surviving parents, m. at Haddonfield 11th mo, 12th da, 1807.

Josiah Webster of Newton, Gloucester Co., son of Samuel and Sarah Webster and Beulah Graseberry, widow, dau of Anthony and Elizabeth Warwick of Gloucester, having consent of parents, m. 4th mo, 13th da, 1808.

Enoch Roberts of Evesham, Burlington Co., son of John and Phebe Roberts and Ann Thorne, dau of Thomas and Abigail Thorne of Waterford, having consent of parents, m. 4th mo, 27th da, 1809.
Samuel Allen of Mannington, Salem Co., yeoman, son of David and Rebecca, dec'd, Allen and Mary Elfirth, dau of Jeremiah and Mary Elfirth of Newton, having consent of surviving parents, m. 11th mo, 23rd da, 1809.
Abraham Haines of Evesham, Burlington Co., yeoman, son of Benjamin and Elizabeth, dec'd, Haines and Deliverance Haines, dau of Amos, dec'd, and Mary Haines of Waterford, having consent of surviving parents, m. 4th mo, 25th da, 1810.
John Jacobs, son of Israel Jacobs, late of Montgomery Co., PA., dec'd, and Amelia Cox, dau of Israel Cox of Charlestown, Chester Co., dec'd, having consent of relations, m. 10th mo, 25th da, 1810.
Jacob Troth of Newton, Gloucester Co., son of Paul and Mary, dec'd, Troth and Rebecca Nicholson, dau of Abel and Mary Nicholson of Newton, having consent of surviving parents, m. 11th mo, 22nd da, 1811.
Allen Moore of Wateford, Gloucester Co., son of Bethuel and Martha, dec'd, Moore and Ann T. Kay of Waterford, dau of Josiah, dec'd, and Elizabeth Kay, having consent of surviving parents, m. 2nd mo, 14th da, 1811.
Isaac Comley, son of Isaac and Asanath Comley of Byberry, Philadelphia Co., PA. and Meribah Barton, dau of John and Rebecca Barton of Newton, Gloucester Co., having consent of parents, m. 6th mo, 20th da, 1811.
Charles Stratton of Goshen, Columbiana Co., OH., yeoman, son of Michael and Rhoda Stratton and Hannah Mickle of Gloucester Co., dau of James and Hepanah Mickle, having consent of parents, m. 11th mo, 14th da, 1811.
Benjamin Dugdale of Camden, Gloucester Co., son of Thomas and Sarah Dugdale of Bristol, Bucks Co., PA and Hannah Kaighn, dau of James and Hannah, dec'd, Kaighn of Newton, having consent of surviving parents, m. 5th mo, 16th da, 1811.
John Sloan of Newton, Gloucester Co., son of James and Rachel Sloane and Beulah Knight, dau of William, dec'd, and Elizabeth Knight having consent of surviving parents, m. at Haddonfield 11th mo, 21st da, 1811.
David Borton of Evesham, Burlington Co., son of John, dec'd, and Hannah Borton and Elizabeth Troth, of Newton, Gloucester, dau of Paul and Mary, dec'd, Troth of Newton, having consent of surviving

parents, m. at Haddonfield 10th mo, 15th da, 1812.

Samuel Cresson of Newton, Gloucester Co., son of Joshua and Mary, dec'd, Cresson of Philadelphia and Elizabeth Blackwood of Gloucester Co., dau of Ann Blackwood, having consent of surviving parents, m. at Haddonfield 10th mo, 22nd da, 1812.

Joseph Walmsley of Byberry, Philadelphia Co., PA, son of William and Abigail Walmsley and Ann Borton, dau of John and Rebecca Borton of Newton, having consent of parents, m. at Haddonfield 11th mo, 19th da, 1812.

Hugh F. Hollingshead of Newton, Gloucester Co., son of Hugh, dec'd, and Eleanor Hollingshead and Martha Mickle, dau of Joseph and Hannah, dec'd, Mickle, having consent of surviving parents, m. at Haddonfield 9th mo, 28th da, 1812.

Stacy Matlack of Evesham, Burlington Co., son of Daniel and Sarah Matlack and Eleanor Glover, dau of Samuel, dec'd, and Hannah Glover, having consent of surviving parents, m. Haddonfield 2nd mo, 18th da, 1813.

Josiah Siddons of Philadelphia, PA., son of Job and Rachel Siddons of Newton, Gloucester Co., and Mary Albertson, widow of Aaron Albertson, having consent of parents, m. at Haddonfield 6th mo, 24th da, 1813.

Samuel Eastlack of Newton, Gloucester Co., son of Samuel and Hannah Eastlack and Elizabeth Glover, dau of Isaac and Phebe Glover of Newton, having consent of parents, m. at Haddonfield 3rd mo, 4th da, 1814.

Henry Hull of Stanford Duchess Co., NY and Sarah Cooper of Newton, dau of Samuel, dec'd, and Prudia Cooper, having consent of surviving parents, m. at Haddonfield 9th mo, 2nd da, 1814.

Samuel Brown of Newton, Gloucester Co., son of Samuel and Rebecca, dec'd, Brown and Martha Hillman of Waterford, dau of Daniel and Martha, dec'd, Hillman, having consent of surviving parents, m. at Haddonfield 11th mo, 17th da, 1814.

Seth Matlack of Evesham, Burlington Co., son of Samuel and Sarah Matlack and Sarah B. Glover, of Newton, dau of Jacob and Mary Glover, having consent of parents, m. at Haddonfield 2nd mo, 16th da, 1815.

Daniel Hillman of Waterford, Gloucester Co., son of Daniel and Martha, dec'd, Hillman and Esther Stokes, dau of Samuel, dec'd, and Hope Stokes of Waterford, having consent of surviving parents, m. at Haddonfield 10th mo, 11th da, 1815.

Paul Troth of Newton, Gloucester Co., yeoman and Hannah Glover of same place, widow of Samuel Glover, having consent of relations, m. at Haddonfield 1st mo, 11th da, 1816.

Benjamin M. Haines of Waterford, Gloucester Co., son of John and Elizabeth Haines and Kezia Burrough, dau of Joseph and Martha Burrough of the same place, having consent of parents, m. at Haddonfield 11th mo, 20th da, 1816.

Thomas Buzby of Evesham, Burlington Co., son of Jabes, dec'd, and Sarah Buzby and Esther Borton, dau of Joseph, dec'd, and Elizabeth Borton of Evesham, Burlington Co., having consent of surviving parents, m. at Haddonfield 11th mo, 14th da, 1816.

Abel Hillman of Waterford, Gloucester Co., son of Daniel and Martha, dec'd, Hillman and Sarah Barton, dau of Nathaniel and Rachel Barton of Waterford, having consent of parents, m. 11th mo, 21st da, 1816.

Zachariah Reeves of Northampton, Burlington Co., son of Henry and Rachel, dec'd, Reeves and Sarah T. Coles, dau of Job and Elizabeth Coles, having consent of surviving parents, m. at Haddonfield 1st mo, 17th da, 1817.

Mason Ward of Newton, Gloucester Co., son of John and Hanna Ward and Hannah Barton of same place, dau of John and Rebecca Barton, having consent of parents, m. at Haddonfield 2nd mo, 13th da, 1817.

Samuel Noble of the Northern liberties of the city of Philadelphia, PA., son of Samuel and Lydia, dec'd, Noble and Sarah Webster, dau of Samuel, late of Newton and Sarah Webster, dec'd, having consent of surviving parents, m. Haddonfield 10th mo, 16th da, 1817.

Isaac Tyson, Jr., of the city of Baltimore, MD., son of Jesse and Margaret, dec'd, Tyson of said city and state and Hannah Ann Wood, dau of James, dec'd, and Ruth Wood, having consent of surviving parents, m. at Haddonfield 6th mo, 14th da, 1818.

James Wood of the city of Philadelphia, PA., son of William, dec'd, and Catharine Wood and Deborah Eldridge, dau of Job and Tacy, dec'd, Eldridge, having consent of surviving parents, m. at Haddonfield 3rd mo, 19th da, 1818.

John Gill, Jr., of Gloucester Twp, son of John and Anna Gill and Sarah Hopkins, dau of William E. and Ann Hopkins, having consent of parents, m. 4th mo, 21st da, 1818.

Thomas Richardson of Middletown, Bucks Co., PA., son of William and Elizabeth Richardson, both dec'd, and Abigail Blackwood, dau of John and Ann Blackwood, both dec'd, of Newton, having consents of relations, m. at Haddonfield 10th mo, 22nd da, 1818.

Joshua Pine, son of William and Judith Pine of Greenwich, Gloucester

Co., and Mary H. Thorne, dau of Samuel and Sarah Thorne of Waterford, having consent of parents, m. 3rd mo, 18th da, 1819.

Samuel T. Wilkins of Deptford, Gloucester Co., son of Jacob and Theoscia Wilkins and Rebecca Clement, dau of Samuel and Mary Clement of Haddonfield, having consent of parents, m. at Haddonfield 4th mo, 13th da, 1820.

Reuben Haines of Waterford, Gloucester Co., son of John and Elizabeth Haines and Ann Hooton, dau of William and Hannah Hooton of Waterford, having consent of parents, m. at Haddonfield 11th mo, 16th da, 1820.

Enos Sharpless of Delaware Co., PA., son of Daniel and Hannah, dec'd, Sharpless and Hannah Webster of Newton, dau of Samuel and Sarah Webster, having consent of surviving parents, m. at Haddonfield 23rd da, 11th mo, 1820.

Job Willets of Little Eggharbor, Burlington Co., son of Jeremiah and Mary Willets, and Mary Lippincott, dau of Nathan and Sarah Lippincott of Newton, having consent of parents, m. at Haddonfield 3rd mo, 22nd da, 1821.

John M. Kaighn of Newton, son of Joseph and Sarah Kaighn and Rebecca M. Cooper, dau of Benjamin and Elizabeth Cooper of Waterford, having consent of parents, m. at Haddonfield 4th mo, 26th da, 1821.

Josiah Albertson of Gloucester Twp, son of John and Ann Albertson and Abigail C. Hodson, dau of Thomas and Mary, dec'd, Hodson of Gloucester Twp, having consent of surviving parents, m. at Haddonfield 3rd mo, 21st da, 1822.

David Shinn of Woolwich, Gloucester Co., son of Peter, dec'd, and Grace Shinn and Susan Reeves, dau of Clement, late of the city of Philadelphia, dec'd, and Sarah Reeves, having consent of surviving parents, m. at Haddonfield 6th mo, 20th da, 1823.

Abel Nicholson of Newton and Sarah Day, widow of Stephen Munson Day, having consent of relations, m. at Haddonfield 1st mo, 15th da, 1824.

Benjamin W. Blackwood of Gloucester town, son of John and Ann, dec'd, Blackwood and Mary Ann Hopkins, dau of William E. Hopkins, late of Newton, dec'd, and Ann Hopkins, having consent of surviving parents, m. 11th mo, 18th da, 1824.

Josiah Thorne of Waterford, Gloucester Co., son of Joseph and Esther Thorne and Hannah B. Engle, dau of Job and Sarah Engle, having consent of parents, m. at Haddonfield 12th mo, 23rd da, 1824.

William Evans of the city of Philadelphia, PA., druggist, son of

Jonathan and Hapizah Evans and Elizabeth Borton, dau of John, dec'd, and Rebecca Borton of Newton, m. having consent of surviving parents, m. 12th mo, 23rd da, 1824.

Benjamin Mickle of Newton, son of Isaac and Mary Mickle and Ann Blackwood, dau of John Blackwood and Ann, his wife, both, dec'd, of Gloucester Co., having consent of surviving parents, m. 1st mo, 13th da, 1825.

Moses Rulon of Woolwich, son of Moses and Susanna Rulon and Ealanor Albertson, dau of John and Ann Albertson of Gloucester Twp, having consent of parents, m. at Haddonfield 3rd mo, 24th da, 1825.

George Horner of Woolwich, Gloucester Co., son of Malachi and Elizabeth, dec'd, Horner and Mary Burrough late Evans of Newton, dau of Jacob and Abigail, dec'd, Evans, having consent of parents, m. at Haddonfield 9th mo, 17th da, 1825.

SECOND TIME MARRIAGE DECLARATIONS OF INTENTIONS

Under this heading, we indicate the appearance of couples who declare their intentions to marry. The marriage generally took place about two months afterward.

5th mo, 11th da, 1706. Joseph Brown of Philadelphia and Martha Spicer, dau of Samuel and Esther (Tilton) Spicer.

10th mo, 19th da, 1706. Edward Newby, son of Mark and Hannah Newby and Hannah Chew.

7th mo, 11th da, 1707. Benjamin Thacara, son of Thomas, Jr., and Hepzibeth (Eastlack) Thacara and Mary Cooper, dau of William, Jr., and Mary (Bradway) Cooper.

8th mo, 9th da, 1707. John Townsend of Cape May, son of Richard and Elizabeth (Wickers) Townsend of Oyster Bay, Long Island, NY. and Mercy Willits, widow. John Holloway of Darby, PA., son of John Holloway and Elizabeth Sharp, dau of Thomas and Sarah (Fearne) Sharp.

7th mo, 13th da, 1708. Ezekiel Siddon, son of John Siddon and Sarah Mickle, dau of Archibald and Sarah (Watts) Mickle.

1st mo, 13th da, 1709/10. Thomas Bull and Susanna Nelson. Joshua Lord, son of James and Elizabeth Lord and Isabella Watts.

7th mo, 12th da, 1709. John Harvey, son of Peter and Sarah (Curtis) Harvey and Sarah Hasker, dau of William and Elizabeth Hasker.

HADDONFIELD MONTHLY MEETING 65

2nd mo, 10th da, 1710. William Harrison, son of Samuel and Sarah (Hunt) Harrison and Ann Hugg, dau of John, Jr., and Priscilla (Collins) Hugg. James Dilke and Ann Barker.

5th mo, 10th da, 1710. John Wood, son of John and Alice (Sale) Wood and Mary Whitall, dau of James and Hannah Whitall.

8th mo, 9th da, 1710. Thomas Sharp and Katherine Hollingham, widow of Isaac Hollingham of Newton.

3rd mo, 14th da, 1711. Samuel Dennis and Ruth Tindall, dau of Thomas and Isabel Tindall.

6th mo, 11th da, 1713. William Matlack, Jr., son of William and Mary (Hancock) Matlack and Ann Antrim, dau of John and Frances (Butcher) Antrim.

7th mo, 10th da, 1713. Thomas Nixon and Maudland Belges.

8th mo, 12th da, 1713. Samuel Ladd, son of John and Sarah (Woods) Ladd and Mary Medcalfe, dau of Matthew and Dorothy Medcalf. Dorothy Medcalf gave her consent.

2nd mo, 12th da, 1714. Joseph Dole, son of John and Mary Dole and Hannah Somers, dau of John, Sr., and Hannah (Hodgkins) Somers.

7th mo, 13 da, 1714. Thomas Hackney of Burlington, son of William and Sarah Hackney and Rebecca Wilkins, dau of Thomas and Susanna Wilkins. John Cook (or Cock) and Lydia Cooper, Jr., dau of Joseph and Lydia (Riggs) Cooper.

9th mo, 8th da, 1714. John Antrim, son of John and Francis (Butcher) Antrim and Amy Andrews, dau of Roger and Lydia Andrews.

10th mo, 12th da, 1715. Henry Wood, son of John and Alice (Selles) Wood and Hannah Whitall, widow.

1st mo, 1st da, 1715. Thomas Stokes and Rachel Wright of Westbury, Long Island.

1st mo, 14th da, 1716/7. Abraham Chattin and Grace Mills [or Miller], dau of John and Mary Mills [or Miller].

4th mo, 11th da, 1716. Francis Richardson and Sarah Cooper, widow of Daniel Cooper, formerly Sarah Dennis.

5th mo, 9th da, 1716. William Sharp, son of John and Elizabeth (Paine) Sharp and Mary Austin, dau of Francis and Mary (Borton) Austin.

6th mo, 10th da, 1716. Job Whitall and Jane Siddon.

1st mo, 10th da, 1717. John Borton and Ann Darling. Benjamin Cooper, son of Joseph and Lydia (Riggs) Cooper and Rachel Mickle, dau of Archibald, Sr. and Sarah (Watts) Mickle.

2nd mo, 8th da, 1717/8. William Wickward and Sarah Mason, dau of John Mason.

3rd mo, 1st da, 1717. George Nicholson and Alice Lord.

8th mo, 14th da, 1717. Alexander Morgan, son of Griffith and Elizabeth (Ibbs-Coles) Morgan and Hannah Cooper, dau of Joseph and Lydia (Riggs) Cooper.

2nd mo, 14th da, 1718. James Whitall, son of John and Hannah (Thackara) Whitall and Sarah Rakestraw, dau of William and Elizabeth Rakestraw.

6th mo, 11th da, 1718. Samuel Sharp, son of Thomas and Sarah (Fearne) Sharp and Martha Hall. Thomas Rakestraw of Philadelphia, son of William, Sr. and Grace (Wyron) Rakestraw and Mary Wilkins, dau of Thomas and Susanna Wilkins.

8th mo, 13th da, 1718. John Hill and Sarah Whitall.

1st mo, 1st da, 1719/20. George Ward, Sr. and Hannah Newby, widow of Edward Newbury, formerly Hannah Chew.

4th mo, 8th da, 1719. John Hancock, son of Timothy and Susannah (Ives) Hancock and Mary Gurnell, late of Europe.

7th mo, 12th da, 1720. Joshua Reaper of Burlington, son of Thomas and Abigail (Perkins) Raper and Sarah Cooper, dau of Joseph and Lydia (Riggs) Cooper.

9th mo, 1st da, 1720. Thomas Adams and Hannah Sharp.

3rd mo, 8th da, 1721. John Lord and Mary Tindall, dau of Joseph and Dorcas (Erwin) Tindall.

5th mo, 10th da, 1721. Richard Haines, Jr., son of Richard and Mary (Carlisle) Haines and Agnes Hollingshead, dau of John, Jr., and Agnes (Hackney) Hollingshead.

6th mo, 1st da, 1721. Richard Matlock and Rebecca Hains.

8th mo, 9th da, 1721. Jacob Coffin, Jr., and Hannah Wilkins, dau of Thomas and Hannah Wilkins.

10th mo, 11th da, 1721. Carlisle Haines, son of Richard and Mary (Carlisle) Haines and Sarah Matlack, dau of William and Mary (Hancock) Matlack of Chester. Samuel Burrough, son of Samuel and Hannah (Taylor) Burrough and Ann Gray, from England, dau of Richard and Joanna (Kelson) Gray.

1st mo, 12th da, 1722/3. Zachary Prickett, son of Zachariah and Ellington Prickett and Mary Troth, dau of William and Elizabeth (Field) Troth.

2nd mo, 9th da, 1722. Samuel Nicholson, son of Joseph and Hannah (Wood) Nicholson and Sarah Burrough, dau of Samuel and Hannah (Taylor) Burrough.

3rd mo, 14th da, 1722. John Haines, son of Richard and Margaret Haines, and Hannah Wood, widow of Henry Wood.

5th mo, 9th da, 1722. James Coffee of Duck Creek and Margaret Zane, dau of Nathaniel and Grace (Rakestraw) Zane.

6th mo, 9th da, 1722. Joseph Matlack, son of William and Mary (Hancock) Matlack of Chester Twp and Rebecca Haines, dau of John and Esther (Borton) Haines of Evesham.

8th mo, 8th da, 1722. Thomas Ellis, son of Simeon and Sarah (Bate) Ellis and Catharine Collins, dau of Joseph and Katherine (Huddleston) Collins.

1st mo, 9th da, 1723/4. William Garwood, son of Thomas and Jane (White) Garwood and Jane Troth, dau of William and Elizabeth (Field) Troth of Evesham.

3rd mo, 13th da, 1723. Joseph Mickle, son of Archibald, Sr. and Sarah (Watts) Mickle and Elizabeth Eastlake, dau of John and Sarah (Thackara) Eastlack.

9th mo, 1st da, 1723. John Pimm of Abington, son of John and Elizabeth Pimm of Nottinghamshire and Lydia Briggs, dau of John and Sarah (Briggs).

10th mo, 7th da, 1723. Jonathan Ladd, son of John and Sarah (Woods) Ladd and Ann Wills, dau of John and Hope (Delafosse) Wills.

10th mo, 14th da, 1724. Henry Willard, son of Thomas and Judith (Wood) Willard and Elizabeth Ballinger, dau of Henry and Mary (Harding) Ballinger of Evesham.

2nd mo, 8th da, 1724. John Darnelly of Salem, and Hannah Borton, dau of John, Jr., and Elizabeth Borton.

3rd mo, 11th da, 1724. Benjamin Clark of Philadelphia, son of William and Mary (Heritage) Clark and Mary Hooton, dau of Thomas and Mary (Lippincott) Hooton.

6th mo, 10th da, 1724. John French of Burlington, son of Thomas and Jane (Atkins) French and Sarah Wickware, widow, dau of John Mason. William Wilkins, son of Thomas and Susannah Wilkins and Mary Buckken.

8th mo, 12th da, 1724. John Lendell and Hannah Ward.

1st mo, 14th da, 1725/6. John Burrough, son of Samuel and Hannah (Taylor) Burrough and Phebe Haines, dau of John and Esther (Borton) Haines of Evesham.

2nd mo, 12th da, 1725. Richard Bickman, Jr., and Mary Wood.

8th mo, 11th da, 1725. Amariah Ballinger, son of Henry and Mary (Harding) Ballinger and Elizabeth Garwood, dau of Thomas and Jane (White) Garwood.

9th mo, 8th da, 1725. Thomas Bickman and Elizabeth Hopper, dau of John Hopper.

10th mo, 13th da, 1725. James Smith of Tredhave Creek, MD., son of

John Smith and Jane Whiteall, widow, dau of Ezekiel Siddon.

2nd mo, 12th da, 1726. John Hudson, son of William and Mary (Richardson) Hudson of Philadelphia and Hannah Wright. Robert Jones from New England and Sarah Siddon. James Wills, son of John and Hope (Delafosse) Wills and Sarah Clement, dau of Jacob and Ann (Harrison) Clement.

9th mo, 4th mo, 1726. Nathan Crosby of Burlington, son of John and Mary (Shinn) Crosby and Elizabeth Garwood, dau of John Garwood.

11th mo, 9th da, 1726. John Wills of Burlington, son of Daniel and Elizabeth Wills and Elizabeth Kaighn, dau of Eliakim and Lydia (Perkins) Wardell.

5th mo, 12th da, 1727. Jonas Cattle of Burlington and Mary Engle, widow, dau of Samuel and Jane (Curtis) Ogborne.

7th mo, 11th da, 1727. William Clark, Jr., son of William and Mary (Heritage) Clark and Phyllis Ward.

8th mo, 9th da, 1727. Derrick Tyson, son of Roger and Ann Hooten, dau of Thomas Hooten. Josiah Alberson of Gloucester Twp, son of William and Hannah (Druett-Stockel) and Ann Austin, dau of Francis and Mary (Borton) Austin.

12th mo, 12th da, 1727/8. Thomas Wilkins, Jr., son of Thomas and Susannah Wilkins and Mary Core, dau of Enoch and Sarah (Roberts) Core. John Haines, Jr., of Goshen, PA., son of John and Esther (Borton) Haines and Jane Smith, widow of James Smith, dau of Ezekiel Siddon.

3rd mo, 1st da, 1728. Robert Ingle, son of John and Mary (Ogborne) Engle and Rachel Venicomb, dau of William and Mary (Stockton-Jones) Venicomb. 1st time.

4th mo, 10th da, 1728. Moses Ward and Mary Clark.

6th mo, 1st da, 1728. Edward Richardson and Mary Richard, or Richardson.

7th mo, 9th da, 1728. Richard Clark, son of William and Mary (Heritage) Clark and Elizabeth Flamington.

10th mo, 9th da, 1728. Henry Warrington, son of John Warrington and Elizabeth Bishop, dau of Thomas Bishop.

11th mo, 13th da, 1728/29. Isaac Knight, son of Isaac and Mary (Carver) Knight and Elizabeth Wright, dau of Joshua, Jr., and Rebecca (Stacy) Wright.

3rd mo, 12th da, 1729. William Forster of Rhode Island, son of Josiah and Amie (Borden) Forster and Hannah Core, dau of Enoch , Jr., and Sarah (Roberts) Core.

5th mo, 14th da, 1729. Thomas Wright of Salem and Mary Thackara, widow of Benjamin Thackara, dau of William, Jr., and Mary (Bradway) Cooper. Thomas Pedric and Rebecca Bickham.

8th mo, 13th da, 1729. John Turner and Jane Engle, dau of John and Mary Ogborne Engle. John Swain and Mary Buzby, dau of Nicholas and Mary (French) Buzby.

9th mo, 10th da, 1729. Richard Heritage, son of Joseph and Hannah (Allen) Heritage and Sarah Tindle, dau of Joseph and Dorcas (Irwin) Tindle.

12th mo, 1st da, 1729. Timothy Matlack and Martha Hains.

2nd mo, 13th da, 1730 John Barton, Jr., son of John and Elizabeth Barton and Elizabeth Lord, dau of Robert and Elizabeth Lord. Joseph Parker, of Chester County, Pa., and Mary Ladd.

4th mo, 8th da, 1730 John Kay, son of Garvis and Sarah Kay and Sarah Ellis, widow of Simeon Ellis, dau of William Bate, Sr.

6th mo, 10th da, 1730 Hasker Newberry, son of William and Mercy (Hasker) Newberry and Mary Heritage, dau of John and Sarah (Slocum) Heritage. David Price of Herford, Merion, and Grace Zane.

8th mo, 12th da, 1730 Thomas Potts, Jr., and Sarah Beakes, dau of William, Jr., and Ruth (Stacy) Beakes.

9th mo, 6th da, 1730 Isaac Cowgill of Chesterfield, and Rachel Brigg.

11th mo, 11th da, 1730/1. William Hooton, son of Thomas and Mary (Lippincott) Hooton and Ann Sharp, widow of John Sharp, dau of Thomas and Elizabeth (Austin) Haines.

12th mo, 1st da, 1730 John Saunders and Elizabeth Wilkins.

1st mo, 1st da, 1731. --- Mills and Elizabeth Erwin.

2nd mo, 12th da, 1731. John Buzby of Burlington, son of Nicholas and Mary (French) Buzby and Hannah Adams, dau of James and Esther (Allen) Adams. William Borton, Jr., son of John Borton, Jr., and Deborah Hedger, dau of John and Meribah Hedger. Thomas Wilkins and Joanna Wood, dau of Constantine and Alice Wood. Samuel Sharp, son of John, dec'd, and Elizabeth (Paine) Sharp and Mary Tomlinson, dau of Joseph and Elizabeth Tomlinson.

6th mo, 1st da, 1731. Thomas Clark, of Philadelphia and Meribah Parker of Burlington. Daniel Morgan from England, now of Byberry and Mary Haines, widow of Jonathan Haines, dau of William and Mary (Hancock) Matlack.

7th mo, 13th da, 1731. Thomas Jennings of Burlington and Ann Borton, dau of John, Jr., and Elizabeth Borton.

9th mo, 8th da, 1731. John Cripps of Burlington, son of Nathaniel and Grace (Whitten) Cripps and Mary Eves, dau of Thomas , Jr., and Mary (Roberts) Evesham. Samuel Coles, Jr., son of Samuel and Mary

(Kendall) Coles and Mary Lippincott, dau of Samuel and Hope (Wills) Lippincott.

10th mo, 13th da, 1731. Amos Haines of Burlington, son of Thomas and Elizabeth (Austin) and Rebecca Troth, dau of William and Elizabeth (Field) Troth.

7th mo, 11th da, 1732. Philip Pedrick of Salem and Hannah Bickham. William Mickle and Sarah Right, or Wright, 7th mo, 1732.

8th mo, 9th da, 1732. Thomas French, son of Thomas and Mary French and Mary Cattle, widow, dau of Samuel and Jane (Curtis) Ogborne.

9th mo, 13th da, 1732. John Ladd, Jr., son of John and Sarah (Woods) Ladd and Hannah Mickle, dau of John and Hannah (Cooper) Mickle. John Wills, Jr., son of John and Hope (Delafosse) Wills and Abigail Lippincott, dau of John and Mary (Haines) Lippincott.

12th mo, 1st da, 1733. Peter White, late of Egg Harbor, Philadelphia, and Burlington, and Rebecca Barr or Burr of Burlington.

2nd mo, 9th da, 1733. Joseph Hopewell and Sarah Briggs.

3rd mo, 14th da, 1733. Thomas Garwood, Jr., son of Thomas and Margaret (Hancock) Garwood and Mary Ballinger, widow, dau of Richard and Abigail (Stockton) Ridgway.

7th mo, 10th da, 1733. Richard Chew and Abigail Wood, dau of Constantine and Alice Wood. John Wilkins, son of John and Sarah Wood, dau of John and Mary (Whitall) Wood. David Price of Harford, PA. and Grace Zane.

8th mo, 8th da, 1733. Samuel Abbott, Salem Co., son of George and Mary Abbott of Salem Co., and Hannah Foster, dau of Josiah and Anny (Borden) Foster. David Davis and Mary Musgrove. Francis Dudley, from Europe and Rachel Wilkins, dau of Thomas and Susannah Wilkins.

9th mo, 12th da, 1733. Obadiah Gibbs and Mary Lord, widow, dau of Joseph and Dorcas (Erwins) Tindall. Thomas Egerton, with a certificate from Colledine, Ireland, and Sarah Stephens.

11th mo, 14th da, 1733. Thomas Sunderland and Ann Hooper.

12th mo, 11th da, 1733/4.Richard Bidgood, from PA. and Hannah Burrough, dau of John and Hannah Taylor, widow of Samuel Burrough.

2nd mo, 8th da, 1734.Barzillai Newbold of Chesterfield and Sarah Core, dau of Enoch and Sarah (Roberts) Core. William Ward and Hannah Wood.

3rd mo, 13th da, 1734. John Howell of Chester, PA. and Katherine Ladd, dau of John and Sarah (Wood) Ladd. Hugh Hollingshead, son of John, Jr., and Agnes (Hackney) Hollingshead and Anna Eves, dau of Thomas, Jr., and Mary (Roberts) Eves.

7th mo, 1st da, 1734. John Cowperthwaite and Rachel Stokes.

8th mo, 14th da, 1734. Samuel Haines of Burlington, son of William and Sarah (Paine) Haines and Lydia Stokes, dau of Thomas, Jr., and Deliverance (Horner) Stokes. Josiah White and Rebecca Forster.

9th mo, 11th da, 1734. Samuel Hopper, son of John Hopper, Sr. and Mary Johnson.

1st mo, 8th da, 1735/6. Edward Barton of Burlington, son of Thomas and Ann (Butcher) Barton and Margaret Tomlinson, dau of Joseph and Elizabeth Tomlinson.

2nd mo, 12th da, 1735. Nathan Haines of Burlington, son of William and Sarah (Paine) Haines and Sarah Austin, dau of Francis and Mary (Borton) Austin. Joseph Cooper and Hannah Dent.

8th mo, 13th da, 1735. Nathan Beaks, son of William and Ruth (Stacy) Beakes and Elizabeth Hooton, dau of Thomas and Mary (Lippincott) Hooton.

3rd mo, 10th da, 1736. Thomas Bishop of Burlington, son of Thomas and Rachel Matlack, dau of William, Jr., and Ann (Antrim) Matlack.

4th mo, 4th da, 1736. Nathaniel Lippincott, son of Thomas and Mary (Haines) Lippincott and Mary Engle, dau of John and Mary (Ogborne) Engle.

10th mo, 30th da, 1736. Walter Fawcett and Margaret Rylins [or Rillings].

1st mo, 14th da, 1737/8. Daniel Garwood, son of Thomas and Margaret (Hancock) Garwood and Susanna Collins, dau of John and Ruth Collins. Ebenezer Hopkins and Sarah Lord.

1th mo, 13th da, 1737/8. John Tanner and Susanna Alcott.

2nd mo, 11th da, 1737. Jacob Taylor and Ann Andrews, dau of Thomas and Abigail Andrews. William Sharp and Elizabeth Robson [or Robinson]. John Jessop and Margaret Whitaker.

3rd mo, 9th da, 1737. Jonathan Ellis, son of Simeon and Sarah (Bate) Ellis and Mary Hollingshead, dau of John, Jr., and Agnes (Hackney) Hollingshead.

5th mo, 11th da, 1737. Andrew Griscom, son of Tobias and Deborah (Gabitas) Griscom and Susannah Hancock, dau of John and Mary (Gurnell) Hancock.

6th mo, 1st da, 1737. Benjamin More and Marcy Newberry.

7th mo, 12th da, 1737. Jacob Howell, Jr., of Chester, son of John and Mary Howell and Mary Cooper, dau of Joseph and Mary (Hudson) Cooper.

8th mo, 10th da, 1737. John Maxfield and Hannah Matlack, dau of

John and Mary (Lee) Matlack. Matthew Allen, son of Matthew and Martha Stokes, dau of Joseph and Judith (Lippincott) Stokes. Ebenezer Brown of Nottingham Twp, and Elizabeth Ives. Edmund Hollingshead, son of John, Jr., and Agnes (Hackney) Hollingshead and Mary Morgan, dau of Alexander and Hannah (Cooper) Morgan. James Wood, son of John and Mary (Whitall) Wood and Sarah Kimsey.

9th mo, 14th da, 1737. Isaac Decow of Chesterfield, son of Jacob and Elizabeth (Powell-Newbold) Decow and Mary Cripps, widow of John Cripps, dau of Thomas, Jr., and Mary (Roberts) Eves.

10th mo, 12th da, 1737. Robert French, son of Thomas and Mary French, of Chester Twp and Hannah Cattell, dau of Jonas and Mary Cattell of Chester.

12th mo, 1st da, 1737. John Tanner and Susanna Allcut.

1st mo, 12th da, 1738/9. Thomas Budd, Jr., of Burlington, son of Thomas and Deborah (Langston) Budd, and Rebecca Atkinson, dau of Samuel and Ruth (Stacy-Beakes) Atkinson. William Earl, Jr., of Burlington, son of William Earl and Mary Sharp of Philadelphia, widow of Samuel Sharp, dau of Joseph and Elizabeth Tomlinson.

3rd mo, 8th da, 1738. Thomas Eagerton and Esther Bate, widow.

8th mo, 9th da, 1738. John Higby and Mary Barton.

11th mo, 14th da, 1739/40. Thomas Rakestraw, son of Thomas and Mary (Wilkins) Rakestraw and Mary Mason, dau of James and Lydia (Buzby) Mason of Evesham. Isaac Lippincott, son of Thomas and Mary (Haines) Lippincott and Hannah Engle, dau of John and Mary (Ogborne) Engle. William Wood, son of Constantine and Alice Wood and Rachel Stockdell, dau of Jarvis and Mary (Allen) Stockdell.

12th mo, 2nd da, 1739. Joseph White, of Falls, Buck Co., PA, and Martha Lippincott.

1st mo, 10th da, 1739/40. Joseph Lippincott of Burlington, son of Jacob and Mary (Burr) Lippincott and Elizabeth Evans, Jr., dau of Thomas and Esther (Haines) Evans. John Saunders and Elizabeth Wilkins, dau of Thomas and Susannah Wilkins.

4th mo, 11th da, 1739. Isaac Warren of Philadelphia and Priscilla Matlack, dau of Timothy and Mary (Haines) Matlack.

9th mo, 12th da, 1739. Freedom Lippincott, son of Samuel and Hope (Wills) Lippincott and Hannah Rakestraw, dau of Thomas, dec'd, and Mary (Wilkins) Rakestraw of Philadelphia. James Whitall, son of Job and Jane (Siddon) Whitall and Ann Cooper, dau of John and Ann (Clarke) Cooper.

1st mo, 9th da, 1740/1. Habbakuk Ward and Hannah Lord, dau of

Joshua Lord, decd.

2nd mo, 14th da, 1740. Jonathan Haines, Jr., son of Jonathan and Mary (Matlack) Haines and Hannah Sharp, dau of William and Mary (Austin) Sharp. John Lippincott of Burlington, son of James and Anna (Eves) Lippincott and Elizabeth Elkinton, dau of Joseph and Elizabeth Elkinton.

3rd mo, 12th da, 1740. Jacob Hinchman and Abigail Harrison. Thomas Middleton and Esther Borton. Thomas Kimsey, Jr., and Hannah Ward, widow of William Ward, dau of John, Jr., and Mary (Whitall) Wood.

8th mo, 13th da, 1740. David Elwell and Mary Haines.

9th mo, 10th da, 1740. Abraham Iredell of Abington, PA. and Sarah Coffin, 1st time. Samuel Butcher, Jr., son of Samuel and Silence (Bunting) Butcher and Mercy Newberry, dau of William and Mercy (Hasker) Newbury.

10th mo, 8th da, 1740. Daniel Packer, son of Philip and Rebecca Packer and Ruth Warrington, dau of Henry and Elizabeth (Austin) Warrington.

11th mo, 12th da, 1740/1. Michael Miller, son of John and Mary Miller and Sarah Moore, dau of Benjamin and Sarah (Stokes) Moore.

1st mo, 1st da, 1741. Samuel Stokes, son of Joseph Stokes and Hannah Hinchman, daughter of John Hinchman.

2nd mo, 13th da, 1741. William Borton, son of John, Jr., and Abigail Lord, dau of Robert, decd, and Elizabeth Lord. Joshua Ballinger, son of Thomas, decd, and Elizabeth (Elkington) Ballinger and Martha Stratton, dau of Emanuel and Hannah (Hancock) Stratton.

4th mo, 8th da, 1741. William Austin, son of Francis and Mary (Borton) Austin and Mary Roberson.

8th mo, 10th da, 1741. Joshua Roberts, son of John Roberts and Rebecca Stokes, daughter of Joseph Stokes. William Albertson, 3rd son of William Albertson, Jr. and Esther (Willis) Albertson, and Jane Turner, widow of John Turner, dau of John and Mary (Ogborne) Engle. Thomas Stokes, son of Thomas, Jr., and Rachel (Wright) Stokes and Abigail Matlack, dau of John and Mary (Lee) Matlack.

9th mo, 9th da, 1741. Samuel Wickward, son of William and Sarah (Mason) Wickard and Sarah Buzby, dau of Nicholas and Mary (French) Buzby.

3rd mo, 10th da, 1742. John Ashead, son of Amos Ashead and Mary Middleton, dau of Thomas and Mary (Hudson) Middleton.

1st mo, 9th da, 1742. Samuel Mickle, son of John and Hannah (Cooper) Mickle and Laetitia Matlack, dau of Timothy and Mary (Haines)

Matlack.

2nd mo, 12th da, 1742. John Roberts, Sr., son of John and Mary (Elkington) Roberts and Esther Lippincott, dau of Thomas and Mary (Haines) Lippincott. Silvester Sharp, son of William Sharp and Mary Mills, dau of Francis, dec'd, and Elizabeth Mills.

3rd mo, 10th da, 1742. Isaac Burrough, son of Samuel and Hannah (Taylor) Burrough and Deborah Jennings, dau of Isaac and Judith Jennings. Thomas Hooten and Mary Bates

6th mo, 9th da, 1742. Jonathan Davis of New Garden, Chester Co., PA., son of David and Jane (Jones) Davis and Esther Haines, dau of Jonathan and Mary (Matlack) Haines, both dec'd, of Evesham.

12th mo, 14th da, 1742/3. Robert Down, Sr. and Catharine Ladd, dau of Samuel, dec'd, and Mary (Metcalf) Ladd.

1st mo, 12th da, 1743/4. Samuel Lippincott, son of Freedom, Jr., and Elizabeth (Wills) Lippincott and Abigail Bates, dau of Joseph and Mercy (Clement) Bates. Abraham Haines, Jr., and Sarah Ellis, dau of Thomas Ellis. Jonathan French, son of Richard and Mary French and Esther Matlack, dau of John and Mary Matlack. Benjamin Heritage and Kezia Matlack.

3rd mo, 9th da, 1743. John Mitchner of Abington, PA. and Sarah Wilkins, dau of Thomas and Mary (Core) Wilkins.

4th mo, 13th da, 1743. Robert Zane, son of Robert, Jr., and Jane Zane and Mary Chattin, dau of Abraham, Sr. and Grace (Mills) Chattin.

8th mo, 10th da, 1743. George Matlack, Jr., son of George and Mary Matlack and Rebecca Hackney, dau of Thomas and Rebecca (Wilkins) Hackney. Freedom Lippincott, Jr., son of Freedom and Mary (Curtis or Custom) Lippincott and Elizabeth Ballinger, widow, dau of George and Mary (Humphreys) Elkinton. Henry Wood, son of John and Mary (Whitall) Wood and Ruth Dennis, dau of Samuel and Ruth (Tindall) Dennis.

9th mo, 14th da, 1743. Daniel Fortner and Rebecca Smith. Joseph Wilkins and Sarah Hartman. Eber Decow and Sarah Eves.

10th mo, 12th da, 1743. Gabriel Davis, Jr., of Salem, son of Gabriel and Jane Davis and Sarah Ballinger, dau of Amariah and Elizabeth (Garwood) Ballinger. William Pinyard and Mary Young.

12th mo, 13th da, 1743/4. Robert Stiles, son of Robert and Sarah (Rudderow) Stiles and Hannah Burrough, dau of Samuel and Ann (Gray) Burrough. Daniel Hillman, Jr., son of Daniel and Elizabeth (Ashbrook) Hillman and Abigail Nicholson, dau of Samuel and Sarah (Burrough) Nicholson.

1st mo, 11th da, 1744/5. John Green of Chesterfield and Katherine

Huestis, dau of Jonathan and Mary (Brandreth) Huestis.

2nd mo, 9th da, 1744. Samuel Nicholson, son of Joseph and Hannah (Wood) Nicholson and Deborah Saint. James Debzel [Delzel] and Elizabeth Hancock, dau of John and Mary (Gurnell) Hancock. John Warrington, son of Henry and Elizabeth (Austin) Warrington and Hannah Ellis.

6th mo, 11th da, 1744. John Rowen, [or Rowell], and Sarah Matlack, daughter of Joseph Matlack.

8th mo, 1st mo, 1744. Solomon Lippincott, son of Freedom, and Sarah Cousins [or Cozens], dau of Jacob Cousins [or Cozens]. Edward Barton, son of John and Ann (Butcher) Barton and Elizabeth Middleton, dau of William and Sarah (Branson) Middleton.

9th mo, 12th da, 1744. Job Siddons and Achsah Matlack, dau of Timothy and Mary (Haines) Matlack.

11th mo, 1st da, 1744. Amariah Ballenger, Jr., son of Thomas Ballenger, dec'd, and Ruth Collins.

1st mo, 10th da, 1745/6. Aaron Lippincott, son of Samuel and Hope (Wills) Lippincott and Elizabeth Jennings, dau of Isaac and Judith Jennings.

9th mo, 11th da, 1745. Isaac Evans [Evens] son of Thomas and Esther (Haines) Evans and Bathsheba Stokes, dau of Joseph and Judith (Lippinocott) Stokes.

10th mo, 4th da, 1745. Joseph Morgan, son of Alexander and Hannah (Cooper) Morgan and Sarah Mickle, dau of Joseph and Elizabeth (Eastlack) Mickle by license. Thomas Lippincott, Jr., son of Thomas and Mary (Haines) Lippincott and Rebecca Eldridge. Richard Matlack, son of William and Mary (Hancock) Matlack and Mary Cole, widow of Joseph Cole, dau of Benjamin and Elizabeth (Kay) Wood.

11th mo, 13th da, 1745/6. Abraham Chattin, Jr., son of Abraham and Grace (Mills) Chattin and Mary Wood, dau of John, decd, and Mary (Whitall) Wood.

12th mo, 10th da, 1745/46. Hudson Middleton, son of Thomas and Mary (Hudson) Middleton and Christian Hopewell, dau of Nathaniel, decd, and Elizabeth (Briggs) Hopewell. Jacob Shinn, son of John, Jr., and Mary Shinn of Burlington and Hannah Lippincott, widow of Freedom Lippincott, dau of Thomas and Mary (Wilkins) Rakestraw. John Brown, son of John Brown, dec'd, and Sarah Cooper, daughter of John Cooper. William Allen, son of Matthew Allen, dec'd, and Judith Stokes, daughter of Joseph Stokes.

1st mo, 1st da, 1746. Samuel Atkinson, son of John Atkinson of Burlington Co., and Esther Evens, daughter of Thomas Evens.

Samuel Hammack, son of George Hammack, decd, and Esther Sharp, dau of William and Mary (Austin) Sharp.

2nd mo, 14th da, 1746. John Garwood, son of Thomas and Margaret (Hancock) Garwood and Charity Wright, dau of Josiah and Prudence Wright. Enoch Stratton, son of Mark and Ann (Hancock) Stratton and Amy Elkinton, dau of Joseph and Elizabeth (Antrim) Elkinton. James Cooper, son of John Cooper, and Deborah Matlack, daughter of Richard Matlack.

4th mo, 9th da, 1746. John Hillman, son of Daniel and Elizabeth (Ashbrook) Hillman and Hannah Nicholson, dau of Samuel and Sarah (Burrough) Nicholson.

6th mo, 1st da, 1746. Henry Wood, and daughter of Isaac Williams of Philadelphia. Jacob Spicer, son of Thomas and daughter of Jacob Lippincott, of Salem.

8th mo, 13th da, 1746. Timothy Middleton, son of William and Sarah (Brandreth) Middleton and Elizabeth Barton.

9th mo, 10th da, 1746. Francis Collins, son of John and Elizabeth (Kemble) Collins and Ann Haines, widow of Nehemiah Haines, dau of Launcelot and Joan (Whitlack) Brown. Samuel Noble, son of Joseph Noble of Philadelphia and Lydia Cooper, dau of Isaac and Hannah (Coate) Cooper. Joseph Stokes, son of Thomas and Mary (Barnard) Stokes and Ann Haines, widow of John Haines, dau of Amos Ashead.

10th mo, 8th da, 1746. George Ward, Jr., son of George Ward and Martha Bates, dau of Joseph and Elizabeth Bates.

11th mo, 12th da, 1746/7. Joseph Gibson, Jr., son of Joseph Gibson of Salem and Sarah Lord, dau of Joshua and Sarah (Wills) Lord.

12th mo, 9th da, 1746/7. Richard Wood of Salem and Hannah Warrington, widow.

1st mo, 14th da, 1747/8. Michael Lents and Rachel Richardson.

10th mo, 14th da, 1747. Jacob Clement, son of Samuel and Rebecca (Collins) Clement and Hannah Albertson, dau of Josiah and Ann (Austin) Albertson.

3rd mo, 11th da, 1747. Joseph Butcher, son of Samuel and Silence (Bunting) Butcher and Prudence Rogers, dau of William and Ann (Stockdell) Rogers. Thomas Warrington, son of Henry and Elizabeth Warrington and Mary Roberts, dau of John and Mary (Elkinton) Roberts.

4th mo, 8th da, 1747. Jacob Wills, son of James of Morris Co. and Sarah (Clement) Wills and Deborah Ladd, dau of Samuel, decd, and Mary (Medcalf) Ladd.

8th mo, 12th da, 1747. John Fisher of Philadelphia and Grace Mason, widow. Jonathan Austin, son of Francis and Mary (Borton) Austin and Rebecca Mason, dau of James and Lydia (Buzby) Mason.

11th mo, 11th da, 1747/8. William Miller of Chesterfield and Elizabeth Woodward, widow of Joseph Woodward, dau of Alexander and Hannah (Cooper) Morgan.

2nd mo, 11th da, 1748. William Haines, son of Nathan and Sarah (Austin) Haines and Elizabeth Ballinger, dau of Thomas and Elizabeth (Elkinton) Ballinger. Samuel Collins, Jr., son of Samuel, and Rosanna Stokes, daughter of Thomas.

3rd mo, 8th da, 1748. John Jeffreys and Mercy Butcher, widow of Samuel, dau of William and Mercy (Hasker) Newberry.

4th mo, 13th da, 1748. Joseph Lewdon of Newark, PA. and Rebecca Howell.

8th mo, 1st da, 1748. William Matlack, son of William Matlack, dec'd, and Mary Turner, daughter of John Turner, dec'd.

9th mo, 14th da, 1748. Samuel Clement, son of Jacob and Ann (Harrison) Clement and Ruth Evans, widow, dau of Abel and Mary (Tyler) Nicholson. Benjamin Champion, son of Nathaniel and Mary (Combe) Champion and Amy Hughet. Daniel Wills, Jr., of Burlington, son of Daniel and Elizabeth (Woolston) Wills and Sarah Foster, dau of William and Hannah (Core) Foster.

10th mo, 8th da, 1748. Ebenezer Andrews, son of Thomas and Abigail Andrews and Mary Warrington, dau of Henry and Elizabeth (Austin) Warrington.

11th mo, 19th da, 1748/9. Joseph Huestis, son of Jonathan and Mary (Brandreth) Huestis and Sarah Lord, dau of Samuel and Mary Lord. Joseph Cowgill and Ann Arnold.

1st mo, 12th da, 1749/50. William Middleton, Jr., son of William and Sarah (Brandreth) Middleton and Ann Borton [or Barton]. Jacob Stokes, son of Thomas Stokes, dec'd, and Priscilla Ellis, daughter of Joseph Ellis.

2nd mo, 10th da, 1749. James West of Philadelphia, son of Charles West and Mary Cooper, dau of Isaac and Hannah (Coate) Cooper. Samuel Nicholson, son of Joseph and Hannah (Wood) Nicholson and Jane Albertson, widow, dau of John and Mary (Ogborne) Engle. Jacob Evans, son of Thomas and Esther (Haines) Evans and Rachel Eldridge. John Jeffreys and Mary Butcher, widow of Samuel Butcher.

4th mo, 12th da, 1749. Job Haines, son of Jonathan, dec'd, and Mary (Matlack) Haines and Esther Hammack, widow of Samuel Hammack, dau of William and Mary (Austin) Sharp. Robert Hunt, son of Robert and Elizabeth (Woolman-Paine) Hunt and Martha Ward, widow of

George Ward, Jr., dau of Joseph and Elizabeth Bates.
5th mo, 10th da, 1749. William Austin, son of Francis and Mary (Borton) Austin and Hannah Thomas, dau of Philip Thomas.
8th mo, 9th da, 1749. Aaron Silver, son of Archibald and Mary (Cowgill) Silver of Salem and Hannah Hall. Obadiah Borton, son of John , Jr., and Mary Driver, dau of Samuel Driver. John Pinyard, son of John Pinyard and Martha Wilkins, dau of William Wilkins.
9th mo, 13th da, 1749. Archibald Mickle, son of Joseph and Elizabeth (Eastlack) Mickle and Mary Burrough, dau of Samuel and Ann (Gray) Burrough. Ezekiel Lindsey and Rachel Shores.
1st mo, 11th da, 1750/1. Enoch Burrough, son of John and Phebe (Haines) Burrough and Deborah Middleton, dau of Thomas and Mary (Hudson) Middleton. Thomas Hinchman and Leticia Mickle, widow. She was the mother of Samuel Mickle, the merchant and Diarist of Woodbury.
2nd mo, 1st da, 1750. Benjamin Matlack and Susanna Hewit. Jacob Ellis, son of Simeon and Sarah (Collins) Ellis and Cassandra Albertson, dau of Josiah and Ann (Austin) Albertson. Nathaniel Brown of Philadelphia and Mary Bircham [or Burdsall]. Thomas Eyres of Burlington, son of Richard and Mary Eyres and Sarah Milles, widow, dau of Benjamin and Sarah (Stokes) Moore.
3rd mo, 8th da, 1750. John Lippincott, son of Nathan and Mary (Engle) Lippincott and Anna Matlack, dau of John, Jr., and Hannah (Shrive) Matlack.
7th mo, 10th da, 1750. Thomas West of Philadelphia, son of Charles West and Deborah Wills, widow, dau of Samuel and Mary (Medcalf) Ladd of Haddonfield. John Thorn, son of Joseph and Mary (Bowne) Thorn and Mary Gill, widow of John Gill, dau of Joseph and Hannah (Allen) Heritage.
8th mo, 8th da, 1750. Daniel Basset, Jr., of Salem, son of Daniel and Mary (Lawrence) Bassett and Mary Lippincott, dau of Freedom and Elizabeth (Wills) Lippincott. John Risdon, son of George and Ann Risdon of Philadelphia and Sarah Turner, dau of John, dec'd, and Jane (Engle) Turner.
10th mo, 10th da, 1750. William Cozens, son of George Cozens and Phebe Young, dau of Joseph Young, dec'd. John Barton, son of John and Ann (Butcher) Barton and Elizabeth Champion, dau of Nathaniel, dec'd, and Mary (Combe) Champion. Isaac Mason, son of James and Lydia (Buzby) Mason and Sarah Price, dau of William Price. Jonathan Fisher, Jr., son of John and Mary Fisher and Hannah Hutchinson, dau of John and Elizabeth Hutchinson. Joseph

Browning, son of Joseph, dec'd, and Kezia Stokes, dau of Thomas and Rachel (Wright) Stokes.

1st mo, 11th da, 1751. Jacob Burrough, son of Samuel dec'd, and Hannah (Taylor) Burrough and Sarah Thorn, dau of Thomas and Letitia (Horner) Thorne.

2nd mo, 11th da, 1751. Robert Braddock, son of Robert and Elizabeth (Hancock) Braddock, and Frances Norcross, dau of John and Mary (Antrim) Norcross. Thomas Evens, son of Thomas, dec'd, and Hannah Roberts, daughter of John Roberts, dec'd. Amariah Ballinger, Jr., son of Thomas and Elizabeth (Elkington) Ballinger and Mary Ashbrook, widow of Greenwich. John Glover, son of Richard Glover of Bucks Co., PA. and Rachel (Clark) Gibbs and Mary Thorne, dau of John and Ann (Hinchman) Thorne.

3rd mo, 13th da, 1751. Joseph Bispham, son of Benjamin and Sarah (Backhouse) Bispham and Elizabeth Hinchman, dau of John and Ann (Harrison-Clement) Hinchman. Isaac Wilkins, son of Thomas and Mary (Core) Wilkins and Elizabeth Bliss, dau of George and Elizabeth (Wills) Bliss.

7th mo, 9th da, 1751. Ebenezer Cook, and Elizabeth Zane, dau of Robert Zane.

9th mo, 11th da, 1751. James Lippincott, Jr., of Burlington, son of James and Anna (Eves) Lippincott and Elizabeth Lippincott, widow of Aaron Lippincott, dau of Isaac and Judith Jennings.

12th mo, 11th da, 1751. Simon Breach and Mary Shores, widow. Enoch Burrough, son of John and Deborah Middleton, daughter of Thomas Middleton.

1st mo, 13th da, 1752. Thomas Eyres, Jr., son of Thomas and Priscilla (Hugg) Eyres of Burlington and Keturah Moore, dau of Benjamin Moore, Jr.

2nd mo, 10th da, 1752. Samuel Hugg and Elizabeth Collins, dau of John Collins.

3rd mo, 1st da, 1752. Restore Lippincott, of Burlington, son of Jacob and Ann Lord, daughter of James Lord. Thomas Bates, son of Joseph and Mercy (Clement) Bates and Sarah Pancoast, dau of John Hugg, widow of Benjamin Pancoast, of Mansfield twp.

5th mo, 11th da, 1752. James Hinchman, son of Joseph, dec'd, and Sarah Hinchman and Sarah Bickham, dau of Richard, dec'd, and Mary (Wood) Bickman. Benjamin Haines, son of Abraham and Grace (Hollingshead) Haines and Elizabeth Roberts, dau of John, Jr., decd, and Mary (Elkington) Roberts. Charles West, Jr., of Philadelphia, son of Charles West and Hanna Cooper, dau of Isaac and Hannah (Coate)

Cooper.

6th mo, 28th da, 1752. Joseph Low, son of Joseph Low, decd, and Rachel Waite, dau of Benjamin, decd. and Jane Waite. Abner Woolman of Burlington, son of Samuel, decd, and Elizabeth (Burr) Woolman and Mary Aaronson, dau of Aaron and Rebecca (Powell-Satterthwaite) Aaronson.

7th mo, 13th da, 1752. John Eves, son of Samuel and Mary (Shinn) Eves and Jane Evans, dau of John, dec'd, and Ruth (Nicholson) Evans. Joseph Wilcox and Sarah Iredale.

9th mo, 1st da, 1752. Richard Satterthwaite, of Chesterfield and Elizabeth Wright, dau of Joshua Wright, dec'd. Thomas Andrews, of Burlington, son of Peter Andrews, and Katherine Webster, daughter of Thomas Webster.

10th mo, 9th da, 1752. Caleb Lippincott, son of Freedom and Elizabeth (Wills) Lippincott and Hannah Wilkins, dau of Thomas Wilkins of Evesham. Thomas Robson and Sarah Chattin, dau of Abraham and Grace (Mills) Chattin.

11th mo, 13th da, 1752. William Sharp, Jr., son of William, dec'd, and Mary (Austin) Sharp and Mary Haines, dau of Abraham and Grace (Hollingshead) Haines. Francis Wood, son of Constantine and Alice Wood and Rachel Zane, dau of Robert Zane.

12th mo, 11th da, 1752. John Lawton of Phil and Elizabeth Stephens, dau of Robert Stephens. Julius Ervan [or Ersan] of Burlington and Sarah Middleton, dau of William and Sarah (Brandick) Middleton.

1st mo, 8th da, 1753. James Wood, son of John, Jr., and Mary (Whitall) and Sarah Bickham, widow of Martin Bickham, dau of Robert and Margaret Gerrard.

4th mo, 9th da, 1753. John Ballinger, son of Thomas and Elizabeth (Elkington) Ballinger and Mary Andrews, dau of Henry and Elizabeth (Austin) Warrington, widow of Ebenezer Andrews.

5th mo, 14th da, 1753. Henry Burr, son of Joseph and Jane (Abbott) Burr and Elizabeth Foster, dau of William and Hannah (Core) Foster.

6th mo, 8th da, 1753. Aaron Lippincott of Burlington, son of James and Anna (Eves) Lippincott and Elizabeth Tomlinson, dau of Ephraim and Sarah (Corbut) Tomlinson.

7th mo, 9th da, 1753. Nathan Lord, son of John, decd, and Mary (Tindall) Lord and Ruth Snowden, dau of John and Sarah (Whitall) Snowden.

9th mo, 10th da, 1753. Joseph Johnson, Jr., son of Joseph Johnson of Great Egg Harbor and Mary Ellis. Thomas Middleton and Jane Nicholson, widow of Samuel Nicholson, dau of John and Mary

(Ogborne) Engle. Nathan Beakes of Chesterfield, son of William and Ruth (Stacy) Beakes and Lydia Morgan, dau of Alexander, dec'd, and Hannah (Cooper) Morgan. Thomas Cummings and Mary Craig, dau of John, dec'd, and Elizabeth (Parrott) Craig.

11th mo, 12th da, 1753. Robert Stephens and Mary Kaighn, widow of Joseph Kaighn, dau of James and Mary (Lawson) Estaugh of Philadelphia. Jacob Burroughs, son of Samuel and Hannah (Taylor) Burroughs and Cassandra Ellis, widow, dau of Josiah and Ann (Austin) Albertson.

1st mo, 1st da, 1754. William Rogers and Sarah Warrington, dau of Henry Warrington.

3rd mo, 12th da, 1754. Brizallah Prickett, son of Jacob and Hannah (Bishop) Prickett and Sarah Sharp, dau of William and Hannah (Austin) Sharp.

4th mo, 8th da, 1754. William Snowden, son of John and Sarah (Whitall) Snowden and Margaret Ballinger, dau of Amariah, dec'd, and Elizabeth (Garwood) Ballinger.

5th mo, 13th da, 1754. Edward Darnell, son of John and Hannah (Borton) Darnell and Jane Driver, dau of Samuel and Sarah Driver from Old England.

7th mo, 8th da, 1754. Samuel Burrough, son of John and Phebe (Haines) Burrough and Hannah Spencer.

8th mo, 1754. John Sleeper and Hannah Haines, daughter of Nehemiah Haines.

10th mo, 14th da, 1754. Joseph Buzby, son of Thomas and Margaret (Haines) Buzby and Hannah Warrington, dau of Henry and Elizabeth (Bishop) Warrington.

11th mo, 11th da, 1754. Samuel Andrews, son of Peter and Esther (Butcher) Andrews of Burlington, and Phebe Cowperthwaite, dau of Thomas and Mary (Borton) Cowperthwaite. William Wilkins, son of Thomas and Mary (Core) Wilkins of Evesham and Elizabeth Swaine, dau of John and Mary (Buzby) Swain.

12th mo, 9th da, 1754. Amos Haines, son of Nathan, dec'd, and Sarah (Austin) Haines and Mary Connaro, dau of Darling and Deliverance (Stokes) Connaro.

3rd mo, 10th da, 1755. John Hatkinson, and Elizabeth Bispham, widow of Joseph Bispham, dau of John and Ann (Harrison-Clement) Hinchman. William Cathcart of Philadelphia and Mary Orin.

4th mo, 14th da, 1755. John Hillman, son of John and Elizabeth (Bate) Hillman and Mary Horner, dau of Jacob and Mary (Corbett) Horner. Isaac Ballinger, son of Amariah, dec'd, and Elizabeth (Garwood)

Ballinger and Patience Albertson, dau of Josiah and Ann (Austin) Albertson.

8th mo, 11th da, 1755. Joseph Hackney, son of Thomas and Rebecca (Wilkins) Hackney and Agnes Haines, dau of Abraham and Grace (Hollingshead) Haines.

2nd mo, 2nd da, 1756. John Lippincott, son of Nathaniel Lippincott, and Anna Matlack, dau of John Matlack, Jr. William Bate and Elizabeth Hooten, dau of Samuel and Ann (Goodbody) Hooton.

3rd mo, 2nd da, 1756. Ezekial Lippincott, son of Jacob Lippincott, dec'd, and Bathsheba Matlack, daughter of John Matlack, Sr. Isaac Horner, son of Jacob, dec'd, and Mary (Corbett) Horner and Elizabeth Kay, dau of Isaac and Mary Ann (Gregory) Kay.

4th mo, 1st da, 1756. Joshua Lippincott, son of Freedom Lippincott, and Rachel Dudley, dau of Frances Dudley. Edward Andrews, son of Peter and Esther (Butcher) Andrews and Tabitha Richardson, dau of Edward Richardson, dec'd, and Mary (Richardson) Richardson.

5th mo, 10th da, 1756. John Newbold of Chesterfield, son of Michael Newbold and Mary Coles, dau of Samuel and Mary (Lippincott) Coles. Jacob Evans, son of Thomas and Esther (Haines) Evans and Mary Cherrington, dau of Clement Cherrington.

6th mo, 14th da, 1756. Caleb Evans, son of Thomas and Rebecca (Owen) Evans and Abigail Hunt, dau of Robert and Abigail (Bates-Ward) Hunt.

9th mo, 13th da, 1756. Benjamin Gaskill of Burlington and Sarah Heustis, widow of Joseph Huetis, dau of Samuel and Mary Lord.

10th mo, 13th da, 1756. Constantine Jeffries, son of John, dec'd, and Letitia (Wood) Jefferies and Patience Butler, dau of Samuel, Jr., dec'd, and Mercy (Newberry) Butcher.

12th mo, 12th da, 1756. Caleb Hughes [Hewes] of Philadelphia, son of William, dec'd, and Mary (Witters) Hewes and Abigail Ellis, dau of Joseph Ellis. William Montgomery of Philadelphia and Mary Ellis.

3rd mo, 14th da, 1757. Joshua Gibbs, son of Isaac Gibbs and Hannah Burrough, dau of John and Phebe (Haines) Burrough. Josiah Burrough, son of John and Phebe (Haines) Burrough and Sarah Morgan, dau of Alexander and Hannah (Cooper) Morgan.

4th mo, 11th da, 1757. William Troth, son of Paul, dec'd, and Deborah Troth of Evesham and Hester Borton, dau of William and Deborah (Hedgers) Borton. David Satterthwait, son of William , Jr., and Mary (Osborne) Satterthwaite of Chesterfield, and Mary Wright, dau Joshua Wright, decd.

HADDONFIELD MONTHLY MEETING

5th mo, 9th da, 1757. Joseph Stoakes, son of Joseph and Judith (Lippincott) Stokes and Atlantic Bispham, dau of Joshua and Mary (Lawrence) Bispham. Hudson Middleton, son of Thomas and Mary (Hudson) Middleton and Sarah Haines, dau of Nathan and Sarah (Austin) Haines. Robert Stiles, son of Robert and Sarah (Rudderow) Stiles and Mary Ellis, widow of Jonathan Ellis, dau of John, Jr., and Agnes (Hackney) Hollingshead.

11th mo, 14th da, 1757. Abraham Eldridge of Evesham, son of James and Esther (Rogers) Eldridge and Mary Lippincott, dau of Isaac and Hannah (Engle) Lippincott.

12th mo, 12th da, 1757. Jacob Wilkins, son of Thomas Wilkins and Ann French, dau of Charles, Jr., and Ann (Clement) French. Samuel Clement, Jr., son of Samuel Clement, and Beulah Evins, daughter of John Evins.

1st mo, 1st da, 1758. John Brackney, son of Mathias Brackney, dec'd, and Mary Cheesman, dau of Thomas Cheesman.

2nd mo, 13th da, 1758. John Peacock, son of John and Elizabeth (Prickett) Peacock and Susanna Ballinger, dau of Thomas, dec'd, and Elizabeth (Elkinton) Ballinger. James Wood and Rebecca (or Sarah) Wilkins, daughter of William Wilkins.

3rd mo, 13th da, 1758. Jacob Prickett, son of Jacob and Hannah (Bishop) Prickett and Elizabeth Phillips, dau of Peter Phillips. Daniel Tomlinson, son of William and Rebecca (Wills) Tomlinson and Mary Bate, dau of William Bate.

5th mo, 8th da, 1758. Isaac Haines, son of Abraham, dec'd, and Grace (Hollingshead) Haines and Deborah Roberts, dau of John and Mary (Elkington) Roberts. Abel Lippincott, son of Freedom, dec'd, and Hannah (Rakestraw) Lippincott and Jemima Evans, dau of Thomas and Rebecca (Owens) Evans. John Buzby of Burlington, son of John, dec'd, and Hannah (Cripps) Buzby and Sarah Ellis, dau of Joseph Ellis, dec'd. Caleb Austin, son of Amos and Esther (Haines) Austin and Lydia Mason, dau of James and Lydia (Buzby) Mason.

6th mo, 12th da, 1758. William Sharp of Woodbury, and Elizabeth Lippincott, widow of John Lippincott, son of Joseph and Elizabeth (Antrim) Elkinton.

8th mo, 14th da, 1758. John Haines, son of Nathan, dec'd, and Sarah (Austin) Haines and Mary Shreve, dau of Amos Shreve.

9th mo, 11th da, 1758. Samuel Tomlinson, son of William and Rebecca (Wills) Tomlinson and Ann Burrough, dau of Samuel, Sr. and Ann (Gray) Burrough. Joseph Morgan, son of Alexander Morgan, and Mary Stoaks, daughter of Joseph Stokes.

10th mo, 9th da, 1758. Joseph Morgan, son of Alexander and Hannah (Cooper) Morgan and Mary Stokes, dau of Joseph and Judith (Lippincott) Stokes.

11th mo, 13th da, 1758. Isaac Holloway, son of George Holloway and Mary Haines, dau of Nathan, dec'd, and Sarah (Austin) Haines.

12th mo, 11th da, 1758. Ephraim Haines of Salem, son of Richard Haines of Pilesgrove and Sarah Cheesman, dau of Thomas Cheesman.

2nd mo, 1st da, 1759. Brizallah Prickett, son of Jacob and Hannah (Bishop) Prickett and Sarah Sharp, dau of William Sharp.

3rd mo, 12th da, 1759. Samuel Sharp, son of William and Mary (Austin) Sharp and Rosanna Prickett, dau of Jacob and Hannah (Bishop) Prickett.

4th mo, 9th da, 1759. John Moore, son of Benjamin Moore and Hannah Eyres, dau of Thomas Eyres. George Turner, son of John and Jane (Engle) Turner and Hannah Thorne, dau of Thomas and Laetitia (Hinchman) Thorne. Lewis Darnell, son of John and Hannah (Borton) Darnell and Grace Thomas, dau of Philip Thomas. John Mason, son of James and Lydia (Buzby) Mason and Mary More, dau of Joseph and Patience (Woolman) More.

5th mo, 14th da, 1759. Thomas Thorn, son of Thomas, dec'd, and Letitia (Hinchman) Thorn and Abigail Burrough, dau of Samuel and Ann (Gray) Burrough.

9th mo, 1st da, 1759. Clayton Newbold, son of Michael Newbold and Mary Forster, daughter of William Forster.

10th mo, 8th da, 1759. John Painter, son of John Painter and Susannah Stratton, dau of David and Mary (Elkinton) Stratton. Clayton Newbold, son of Michael Newbold and Mary Forster, dau of William and Hannah (Core) Forster.

12th mo, 20th da, 1759. James Wilkins, son of John Wilkins and Mary Ward, dau of George Ward. Mary Ward died before the next meeting held on 1st mo, 14th da, 1760.

1st mo, 14th da, 1760. John Starr of Exeter Co., son of Moses Starr and Eunice Lord, dau of Joshua and Sarah (Wills) Lord.

4th mo, 1st da, 1760. Joseph Engle, son of Robert and Rachel (Venicomb) Engle, and Mary Borton, dau of Obadiah Borton.

5th mo, 12th da, 1760. Obadiah Engle, son of Robert and Rachel (Venicomb) Engle and Patience Coles, dau of Job and Elizabeth (Tomlinson) Coles.

9th mo, 8th da, 1760. John Brick of Salem, son of John Jr., dec'd, and Ann (Nicholson) Brick and Abigail French, dau of Charles, Jr., and Ann (Clement) French.

10th mo, 13th da, 1760. Thomas Champion, son of Nathaniel and Mary (Combe) Champion and Deborah Clark, dau of William and Phillis (Ward) Clark.
11th mo, 10th da, 1760. Chatfield Brown, son of John, dec'd, and Phebe (Chatfield) Brown and Hannah Andrews, dau of Peter and Esther (Butcher) Andrews.
3rd mo, 1st da, 1761. John Sharp, son of Anthony and Mary (Dimock) Sharp and Sarah Andrews, daughter of Nehemiah and Elizabeth (Lippincott) Andrews.
5th mo, 11th da, 1761. Simeon Zane, son of Robert and Mary (Chattin) Zane and Sarah Hooton, dau of John and Sarah (Kay) Hooton.
10th mo, 1st da, 1761. Jacob Jennings, son of Isaac Jennings, and Mary Smith, dau of Isaac Smith, dec'd.
1st mo, 11th da, 1762. Jacob Cozens, son of Jacob and Elizabeth Cozens and Esther Zane, dau of Robert, Jr., and Jane Zane.
5th mo, 10th da, 1762. John Estaugh Hopkins, son of Ebenezer and Sarah (Lord) Hopkins and Sarah Mickle, dau of William and Sarah (Wright) Mickle.
10th mo, 10th da, 1763. James Gardiner, son of Joseph and Catharine (Ridgway) Gardiner and Mary Tomlinson, dau of Ephraim and Sarah (Corbet) Tomlinson.
1st mo, 9th da, 1764. Job Kimsey, son of Thomas Kimsey, dec'd, and Elizabeth Eastlack, dau of Francis and Phebe (Drive) Eastlack.
12th mo, 11th da, 1765. Joseph Burrough, son of Samuel and Ann (Gray) Burrough and Mary Pine, dau of Benjamin and Hannah Pine.
3rd mo, 11th da, 1765. Jonathan Knight, son of Thomas and Sarah Knight and Elizabeth Delap, dau of Nathan Delap.
5th mo, 10th da, 1765. James Brown, son of John and Phebe (Chatfield) Brown and Catherine Andrews, widow of Thomas Andrews, dau of Thomas and Sarah (Venicomb) Webster.
2nd mo, 10th da, 1766. Griffith Morgan, son of Joseph and Agnes (Evans) Morgan and Rebecca Clement, dau of Samuel, dec'd, and Rebecca Collins Clement.
9th mo, 1st da, 1766. Constantine Jefferies, son of John, dec'd, and Patience Butcher, daughter of Samuel Butcher, dec'd.
2nd mo, 9th da, 1767. Constantine Wilkins, son of Thomas and Joanna (Wood) Wilkins and Ann Hooton, dau of John and Sarah (Kay) Hooton.
3rd mo, 1st da, 1767. Jacob Hains, son of Samuel Hains, dec'd, and Bathsheba Burroughs, dau of Samuel Burrough.
6th mo, 8th da, 1767. Joshua Lippincott, son of Jacob, dec'd, and Mary

86 EARLY CHURCH RECORDS OF GLOUCESTER COUNTY

(Burr) Lippincott and Rebecca Wood, widow. Isaac Townsend, Jr., of Cape May, and Caturah Albertson, daughter of Josiah Ablertson.

12th mo, 8th da, 1766. Joseph Gibson, Jr., and Mary Ballinger.

2nd mo, 9th da, 1767. John Wilkins, Jr., son of John and Sarah (Wood) Wilkins and Rachel Wood, dau of William, dec'd, and Rachel (Stockdell) Wood.

7th mo, 13th da, 1767. Robert Cooper, son of Thomas and Mary Hopper, dau of Samuel, dec'd, and Mary (Johnson) Hopper.

9th mo, 1st da, 1767. Mark Miller, son of Ebenezer Miller, and Mary Redman, daughter of Thomas Redman.

10th mo, 1st da, 1767. John Gill and Abigail Hillman, widow.

10th mo, 1st da, 1768. Jeremiah Andrews, son of Isaac Andrews, and Ann Wood, daughter of James Wood.

11th mo, 14th da, 1768. Thomas Saunders, son of John, dec'd, and Elizabeth (Wilkins) Saunders and Rachel Stephens, dau of Isaac Stephens, dec'd.

11th mo, 1st da, 1769. John Saunders, son of John, dec'd and Elizabeth (Wilkins) Saunders and Elizabeth Lippincott, dau of Solomon and Sarah (Cozens) Lippincott.

11th mo, 1st da, 1769. Jesse Thomas of Haverford, son of John Thomas, dec'd, and Sarah Becket, dau of Peter Becket.

2nd mo, 1st da, 1770. William Bates, son of William and Rebecca (Wills-Tomlinson) Bates and Phebe Butcher, dau of Samuel, Jr., and Mercy (Newbury) Butcher.

10th mo, 12th da, 1770. Thomas Adams, son of James and Esther (Allen) Adams and Hannah Sharp, dau of John and Elizabeth (Paine) Sharp.

6th mo, 1st da, 1771. Joseph Matlack, son of Richard and Mary (Wood-Cole) Matlack and Hannah Whitall, dau of James Whitall.

7th mo, 1771. Isaac Andrews, son of Nehemiah and Elizabeth (Lippincott) Andrews and Heziah Chew, dau of Jeremiah and Hannah (Ashbrook) Chew, 1st time.

9th mo, 1st mo, 1771. Joshua Borton, son of William, dec'd, and Abigail (Lord) Borton, and Mary Lippincott, dau of Nathaniel and Mary (Engle) Lippincott.

4th mo, 13th da, 1772. James Mickle, son of William and Sarah (Wright) Mickle and Latitia Wood, dau of William, dec'd, and Rachel (Stockdell) Wood. Joseph Platt, son of William Platt and Martha Pinyard, dau of William Wilkins, widow of John Pinyard. 1st time.

8th mo, 9th da, 1772. William White, son of William White and Hannah Fisher, dau of Jonathan and Hannah (Hutcheson) Fisher.

10th mo, 1st da, 1772. Jacob French, son of Charles French, and Elizabeth Stoaks, dau of Joshua Stoaks.

11th mo, 1st da, 1772. Samuel Roberts, son of Enoch Roberts, and Hannah Stiles, daughter of Robert Stiles.

12th mo, 1st da, 1772. Samuel Allison, son of Joseph Allison, dec'd, and Martha Cooper, dau of David Cooper.

2nd mo, 11th da, 1773. Samuel Thompson, son of James Thompson, dec'd, and Sarah Wood, dau of William, dec'd, and Rachel (Stockdell) Wood.

4th mo, 1st da, 1773. George Ward, son of George Ward, dec'd, and Ann Branson, dau of David Branson.

5th mo, 1st da, 1773. John Barton, son of John Barton, dec'd, and Amy Shivers, daughter of John Shivers.

7th mo, 10th da, 1773. Isaac Tomlinson, son of John, dec'd, and Mary (Fairlamb) Tomlinson and Elizabeth Ballinger, dau of Amariah Ballinger, dec'd.

10th mo, 1st da, 1773. John Wood, son of Henry, dec'd, and Ruth (Dennis) Wood and Mary Branson, dau of Jonathan Branson.

11th mo, 10th da, 1773. William Lippincott, son of Restore and Deliverance (Cooper) Lippincott and Elizabeth Beckett, dau of Peter Becket.

2nd mo, 1st da, 1774. Joshua Stretch, of Salem, son of Joseph, dec'd, and Lydia Tomlinson, dau of Joseph Tomlinson, dec'd. Joseph Reeves, son of Thomas Reeves, and Elizabeth Morgan, dau of Joseph Morgan. James Thackara, son of Stephen, dec'd, and Elizabeth (Sloan) Thackara and Jane Gaunt, dau of John and Jane (Satterthwaite) Gaunt at Haddonfield.

8th mo, 10th da, 1774. Israel Morris of Philadelphia, son of Anthony Morris and Mary Harrison, dau of Joseph Harrison.

9th mo, 12th da, 1774. Solomon Lippincott, son of Freedom, Jr., and Elizabeth (Wills) Lippincott and Sarah Cozens, dau of Jacob, Jr., and Elizabeth Cozens.

11th mo, 1st da, 1774. Solomon Lippincott, son of Freedom, Jr., and Elizabeth (Wills) Lippincott and Mary Zane, widow of Robert Zane, dau of Abraham and Grace (Mills) Chattin, 1st time.

12th mo, 10th da, 1774. Mark Nicholson, son of Joseph and Rachel (Lindsay) Nicholson and Mary Haines, dau of William dec'd, and Sarah (Lippincott) Haines.

1st mo, 10th da, 1775. Thomas Glover, son of John and Mary (Thorne) Glover and Mary Stiles, dau of Robert, dec'd, and Mary (Hollingshead-Ellis) Glover.

8th mo, 1st da, 1775. John Middleton, son of Thomas Middleton, dec'd, and Sarah Matlack, dau of John, Jr., dec'd, and Hannah (Shrivers) Matlack.

HADDONFIELD MONTHLY MEETING
"GOING OUT IN MARRIAGE"

The following are members who married outside the Society. The dates given are the dates on which it marriage was noted at the monthly meeting.

4th mo, 1712. John Dennis
5th mo, 1712 Mary, daughter of Simeon Ellis.
9th mo, 1715. John Matlack.
11th mo, 1715. Robert Champion, son of John and Sarah (Williams) Champion m. Mary Carson, daughter of Peter Carson, widow of Joseph Mapes.
11th mo, 1717. Wm Cooper; Joseph Hugg; Joseph Kay; Gervias Kay; Hannah Mickel, widow of Daniel Mickel; Sarah Kay, licensed to marry James Morris; Sarah Cooper.
11th mo, 1719. George Ward.
4th mo, 1720. John Kay and Jane Smith.
1st mo, 1725. William and Sarah Albertson.
2nd mo, 1725. William Dennis; Simeon Ellis.
3rd mo, 1725. Thomas Whiteall and Margaret Till, dau of John and Margaret Till, m. at First Presbyterian Church at Philadelphia, 2nd mo, 18th da, 1723.
7th mo, 1725. William and Cartharine Ellis.
4th mo, 1726. Robert and Sarah Jones.
1st mo, 1731. George Matlack and Mary Burnell, widow of John Hancock.
8th mo, 1731. Joseph Thackery to Hannah (Newbie) Alberson, widow of John Wilkins by license 6th mo, 1st da, 1731; Elizabeth Mills; Ann Shrivers; dau of Joshia Shrivers to Azra Bates by license.
3rd mo, 1735. William Sharp to Hannah Austin, his former wife's sister by license 5th da, May 1735; William Sharp and Mary Austin m. 5th mo, 2 da, 1716.
6th mo, 1735. Robert Hunt by license 19th da, Dec 1733 to Abigail Wood.
10th mo, 1736. Thomas Hooten to Rachel Barnes.

4th mo, 1737. Edmond Lord to Susanna Atwood by license 5th da, Dec 1736.
12th mo, 1737. Joseph Kaighn.
4th mo, 1738. Letitia (Wood) Jeffries to John Jeffries m. 24th da, Feb 1736.
11th mo, 1741. John Hornere and Wife; Mary Siddons m. Elijah Sharp Mar 1738.
12th mo, 1741. Jacob and Azubah Horner m. 28th da, Feb 1740.
2nd mo, 1742. Daniel Stratton and Mary Sharp m. 1st da, May 1739; Rebecca Bates, widow formerly Tomlinson to William Bates 6th mo (Aug) 1741.
4th mo, 1742. John and Elizabeth Hutchinson.
5th mo, 1742. James Cattle to Ann Rogers, widow of William Rogers m. 18th da, May 1738. William Rogers d. 1736 at Evesham.
8th mo, 1743. Edward Hollingshead.
1st mo, 1744. John Engle and Hannah Middleton by license 1st da, Nov, 1737; Benjamin Cooper.
1st mo, 1745. Thomas Bates; John Matlack, Jr.; John Heritage to Ann Hugg by license 22nd da, Aug 1741; Nehemiah Cowgill by license 1st da, Aug, 738 Esther Davis.
12th mo, 1745. John and Ann Stratton.
2nd mo, 1746. Amos Austin and Esther Haines, dau of Caleb Haines of Burlington Co., 27th da, Sep 1736 by license.
3rd mo, 1746. Elizabeth Mills.
5th mo, 1746. Joseph Morgan and Sarah Mickle m. 10th mo, 1745.
12th mo, 1746. John Heritage, Jr to Ruth Haines by license 14th da, Oct 1746.
1st mo, 1747. Abraham Chattin to Jane Caldwell by license 27th da, Feb 1746.
6th mo, 1747. Andrew and Mary Sloan.
1st mo, 1748. Samuel Moore to Mary Lord 6th da, Dec 1746 by license.
2nd mo, 1748. Francis Kay to Jemimiah French 7th da, Jul 1743.
5th mo, 1748. Hope Lippincott.
6th mo, 1748. Martha Low, dau Joseph Low; Rachel Morris.
12th mo, 1748. James Child; Rebecca Hartley, widow with unborn child.
4th mo, 1749. Rebecca Osgden.
5th mo, 1749. Benjamin Moore, Jr.
6th mo, 1749. Wm. Middleton to Mary Kimble m. 9th da, Oct 1746.
9th mo, 1749. John Pimm; Sarah Phillips.

11th mo, 1749. Miron Chattin to Hannah Cox 23rd da, May, 1749 by license; John Hopewell.

1st mo, 1750. Joseph and Sarah Huestes.

6th mo, 1750. Robert Braddock to Elizabeth Bates 24th da, Nov 1737 by license.

10th mo, 1750. Hugh and Ann Sharp (Stratton) 1st da, Nov 1748; Abraham Chattin; Prudence Thomas

12th mo, 1750. John Sharp son of John and Ann (Haines) Sharp to Dinah Peacock, dau John Peacock; Robert Down to Ann Sharp at Philadelphia by license 4th da, Feb 1746.

8th mo, 1751. Frances Austin to Deborah Allen, widow of Benjamin Allen.

9 month 1751. Enoch Roberts; Thomas French to Jamimah Ellenton by license 8th da, May 1746; Thomas French m. 1st mo, 13th da, 1751 (Thomas French made acknowledgement 1st mo, 13th da, 1752; Jeremiah Matlack; Benjamin Bates.

10th mo, 1751. John Hugestes [Heustis] to Martha Austin, dau of Thomas, Sr. and Mary (Boston) Austin.

3rd mo, 1752. John Stokes to Ann Champion by license 8th da, Jul 1751.

3rd mo, 1752. Enoch Burrough; James Kay son of Josiah Kay; Hugh Middleton.

4th mo, 1752. Deborah Burrough, wife of Enoch Burrough.

5th mo, 1752. Abraham Chattin to Dorcas Hughes 28th da, April 1752.

6th mo, 1752. Alice Wilkens, dau of Thomas Wilkens to Andrew Helms.

7th mo, 1752. Josiah Ward to Kezia Albertson m. 1st da, Mar 1750.

8th mo, 1752. Joseph Browning; Ann, wife of John Stokes; Kezia Brown.

9 month 1752. John Pritchett to Jane Garwood; Wm and Jane Troth.

10th mo, 1752. Dorcas Chattin.

3rd mo, 1753. Thomas Hackney, Jr.; Cassandra Albertson to Jacob Ellis m. 1750.

4th mo, 1753. Amos Sharp to Deborah Haines, dau of John and Ann Haines by license 2nd da, May 1751; Thomas Ellis, Jr.

8th mo, 1753. Samuel Atkinson Jr.; Joseph Thackery.

3rd mo, 1754. Joseph Haines, son of Richard Haines; Margaret Jessup, widow, Henry Stevens 8th da, Nov 1753.

5th mo, 1754. Isaac Matlack.

8th mo, 1754. David Fortines to Bathsheba French by license 28th da, Jul 1748.

9th mo, 1754. Ann Hinchman.

10th mo, 1754. Joseph Lord to Eleanor Chester 13th da, Mar 1750.
11th mo, 1754. Isaac Kay, the elder.
2nd mo, 1755. Joseph Nicholson to Rachel Lindsey by license 10th da, May 1748.
11th mo, 1755. Mary Higbee.
12th mo, 1755. Hannah Story.
6th mo, 1756. Mary Redman, wife of Andrew Redman; Esther Clement, wife of Judah.
7th mo, 1756. Samuel Cozens, son of Jacob Cozens by license 23rd da, Apr 1753 to Hannah.
11th mo, 1756. Samuel Ladd and Sarah Hamilton by license 2nd da, Oct 1754; Elizabeth Roberts.
12th mo, 1756. Amos Wilkins to Sarah Haines 17th da, Jan 1756; Reston Eastlock.
1st mo, 1757. Isaac and Ann Stratton; Thomas Cowperthwaite.
2nd mo, 1757. Jonathan Knight to Sarah Heppard 4th da, May 1756.
5th mo, 1757. Simeon Ellis, son of Thomas Ellis.
8th mo, 1757. George Cozen.
3rd mo, 1758. Samuel Cozen, son of George Cozen.
5th mo, 1758. Reston Eastlack.
6th mo, 1758. John Buzby and Sarah Ellis by license 9th da, May 1758; John Ware to soon after death of his wife.
10th mo, 1758. Benjamin Matlack.
3rd mo, 1759. Susannah Shute.
5th mo, 1759. Daniel Smith and Hannah Thackerell by license 3rd da, Dec 1757; Benjamin Ellis to Sarah Bates
6th mo, 1759. Thomas and Elizabeth Thackery.
10th mo, 1759. Benjamin Cheeseman to Mary Ashbrook by license 13th da, Jun 1758; Mary Price to Thomas Kinsey by license 25th da, Mar 1758.
11th mo, 1759. Thomas Ellis, Jr to Hannah Alberston by license 25th da, Sep 1759.
1st mo, 1760. Deborah Armstrong; Samuel Gashell to Sybella Collins 19th da, Dec 1759.
3rd mo, 1760. John Sanders and wife, Sarah.
9th mo, 1760. Daniel Lippincott produced an acknowledgment at Concord Monthly Meeting.
4th mo, 1760. Abel Nicholson and Rebecca Scattergood dau of Aaron and Rebecca Scattergood.
5th mo, 1760. Elizabeth Hollingshead late Conarro.
5th mo, 1760. John Ballinger to Sarah Cheeseman by license 8th da,

92 EARLY CHURCH RECORDS OF GLOUCESTER COUNTY

Nov 1760.
8th mo, 1760. Susannah Hulton late Stevens.
11th mo, 1760. Thomas Edgerton to Elizabeth Saint by license 27th da, Apr 1759.
8th mo, 1760. Daniel Tomlinson to Mary Borton.
9 month 1760. Daniel Lippincott and Hannah Coles by license 12th da, Nov, 1759.
9 month 1760. John Down.
1st mo, 1761. Joshua Cozens by Pennsylvania license 19th da, Apr 1760 to Martha Cheeseman; Frances Chattin to Elizabeth Clarke of Salem Co., by license 22th da, Jul 1760.
2nd mo, 1761. George Ward.
3rd mo, 1761. Humphrey Owen by license 8th da, Dec 1756 to Ruth Flewelling; Thomas Weaver by license 24th da, Dec 1756 to Abigail Cheeves [Shrives], dau of Joseph and Ann (Bates) Shrives.
4th mo, 1761. Joseph Browning; Abraham Chatten, Jr. by Pennsylvania license 22nd da, Jul 1760 to Ruth Wood.
5th mo, 1761. George and Rachel Ward; Josiah Chatten; Sarah Shinn, dau of Azariah Shinn; Isaac Albertson Jr. by license 29th da, Jan to Deborah Thorne.
6th mo, 1761. Jack Mickle of Gloucester.
11th mo, 1761. Isaac Burrough by Pennsylvania license 8th da, Apr 1761 to Abigail Hullings.
5th mo, 1764. William Clark to Susanna Attwood by license 3rd mo, 28th da, 1763.
4th mo, 1763. Elizabeth Mayfield now Graseberry.
4th mo, 1773. Hannah Matlack.
4th mo, 1778. Elizabeth Matlack.
4th mo, 1779. Caleb Matlack.
3rd mo, 1780. Tacy Lewis, late Matlack.
10th mo, 1790. Lydia Matlack.
3rd mo, 1809. Nathaniel Allen.
5th mo, 1809. Nathaniel Allen.
8th mo, 1809. Hope Ware.

4th mo, 1795 Sarah Allen and dau, Gartrew received into membership.
4th mo, 1762 Jane Matlack received into membership.
4 mo, 1773 Hannah Matlack wife of John received into membership.

CERTIFICATES

Mark Newby and Will Bates from county of Wicklow in Ireland 21st da, 6th mo, 1681.
Thomas Dennis from county of West Meath near Ashborne (Athlone?), in Ireland 21st da, 6th mo, 1681.
Jonathan Wood, a weaver and his family from the County of Ardmagh in the north of Ireland 8th da, 8th mo, 1683.
Thomas Thackra, his wife, Esther and family from Dublin 16th da, 6th mo, 1681.
William Cooper of Coleskill, County of Hertford, a blacksmith, his wife and family 5th da, 12th mo, 1678.
Richard Heritage of Brayles, county of Warwicks, a carpenter, his wife and family 3rd da, 6th mo, 1684.
Samuell Spicer and Esther, his wife from Grandsand on Long Island 29th da, 3rd mo, 1686.
John Kay, son of Gerias Kay of Mealehill, 7th da, 4th mo, 1683.
Henry Wood of Cliftshire in the county of Lanksshire and John Wood, his son, both now of Newport on Rhode Island 12th da, 5th mo, 1687.

Thomas Willard was granted a certificate to Barbados 3rd da, 2nd mo, 1689.
Simon Ellis, son of Thomas Ellis of Wooldae at Monk Britton 7th da, 4th mo, 1683.
John Adams, his wife and children from Long Island 29th da, 6th mo, 1691.
John Estaugh of Dunmow at Cogshall quarterly meeting in Essex 26th da, 7th mo, 1700.
Richard Gave and John Estaugh from Bermuda and Barbados dated 11th da, 1st mo, 1705.
Thomas Willard presented a certificate from a meeting held at Thomas Pilgrim's house, Barbados Island, signed by Thomas Robinson, 3rd da, 2nd mo, 1689.
Simeon Ellis, son of Thomas, of Wooddale, presented certificate dated 1st, 4th mo 1683.

8/12/1710. Tobias Griscom desires a certificate concerning his clearness from marriage engagements in order to take a wife in Burlington.
John Haines in behalf of his son John requests a certificate to PA.
12/12/1710. William MacClock requests to join.
4/3/1711. Thomas Smith the elder to remove with his family to live in

Burlington; requests certificate.

14/3/1711. Matthew Allin intends to marry a young woman in PA and desires a certificate.

8/8/1711. Thomas Adams intends to marry a young woman of Chesterfield Monthly Meeting and requests a certificate.

14/11/1711. John Roberts intends to take a young woman to wife who belongs to Burlington Monthly Meeting.

14/2/1712. John Estaugh produced a certificate from London for himself and his wife Elizabeth. William MacClock condemned his being overtaken with passion and striking or abusing Jacob Houlings. Joseph Tindall complained that John Erwin neglected to pay the legacies to his two daus. Mary Tindall and Elizabeth Tindall, which was willed to them by their grandmother Margret Erwin.

12/3/1712. Philip Paul disowned for cutting and carrying away timber from some land which is supposed to be the property of another. Elizabeth Kay produced a certificate from London.

11/6/1712. Henry Wood intends to marry a Friend in Chester Monthly Meeting, PA.

8/10/1712. Thomas Ballinger requests certificate signifying his clearness from marriage engagements.

12/11/1712. John Cooper intends to marry a friend in Chesterfield; requests certificate. Concern about John Coppertwhaite and his wife Sarah toward each other.

13/2/1713. Joseph Low requests certificate concerning his clearness from marriage engagements.

8/4/1713. John Hay produced certificate from Monthly Meeting at Lurgan in Ireland.

13/5/1713. Joseph Cooper Jr., desires certificate regarding his clearness from marriage engagements.

10/6/1713. William Macblock Jr. signifies his intention of taking Ann Antrum to wife and desires certificate.

14/7/1713. Thomas Nixon intends to take Maudland Bolges of Philadelphia to wife and desires certificate.

11/11/1713. John Hanes signifies that his son Isaac intends to remove to PA for a season and desires certificate.

8/12/1713. William Hunt produced a certificate from Gisbrough Monthly Meeting in Yorkshire in Old England for himself and wife.

8/1/1713/14. John Chambers produced certificate from Yorkshire in Old England; certificate recorded in Philadelphia.

10/11/1714. James Lord requests certificate in order to take to wife a young woman of Crosswick Monthly Meeting.

HADDONFIELD MONTHLY MEETING

14/1/1714. John Chambers signified that he intended to remove with his family to PA and requests certificate.

11/5/1715. Thomas Stouks [Stokes] signified that he intended to join himself in marriage with Rachell Right of Westbury Monthly Meeting in Long Island and desires cert.

12/7/1715. Nathaniel Champion desires certificate signifying his clearness from marriage engagements. Henry Wood desires certificate signifying his clearness from marriage engagements.

12/9/1716. Certificate requested for Anthony Fryer now gone for Great Britain - signifying his clearness from marriage engagements.

5/2/1717. John Bourton requests certificate to Monthly Meeting of Salem to marry Anne Daroling.

9/7/1717. John Eves produced certificate from Monthly Meeting of Burlington for himself and family. John Sharpe signified that his son John intends to marry a friend of Burlington Monthly Meeting and desires certificate.

10/12/1717. Henry Ballinger the younger signified his intention of removing to Salem Co. and desires certificate signifying his clearness from marriage engagements. James Mason intends to marry young woman of Burlington Monthly Meeting.

14/4/1718. Thomas Thornbrough produced certificate from Cootehill meeting.

13/8/1718. John Gibson desires certificate signifying his clearness from marriage engagements, to Burlington Monthly Meeting.

9/1/1718. John Haines in behalf of his son Kaleb (Caleb) desires certificate to take a wife of another meeting.

12/8/1719. Judah Williams being removed into the eastern division of the province desires certificate.

11/11/1719. Thomas Denis, Jr. intends to take Sarah Wyeth to wife, of Concord Monthly Meeting, PA.

14/1/1719. Samuel Atkinson brought a certificate from Monthly Meeting of Chesterfield for himself and wife.

9/3/1720. Judediah Addams intends to marry Margaret Christian. [rejected by monthly meeting]. Benjamin Wright who formerly lived in Philadelphia, now belonging to Woodbury Creek Meeting, brought certificate from the Monthly Meeting of Philadelphia.

14/9/1720. Hugh Clifton who formerly lived in Philadelphia but now belonging to Woodberry Creek Meeting brought a certificate from Monthly Meeting of Philadelphia.

10/2/1721. Certificate requested for Josiah Ballanger signifying his clearness from marriage engagements. [He removed to within the compass of Salem Monthly Meeting.]

9/8/1721. Joshua Lord requests certificate in order to marry young woman within verge of Burlington Monthly Meeting.

12/9/1721. Joseph Cooper, Jr., desires certificate to marry young woman of Philadelphia Monthly Meeting.

12/1/1721. Certificate prepared for Jacob Medcalf, signifying his clearness from marriage engagements.

11/4/1722. Hugh Clifton requests certificate signifying his clearness from marriage engagements.

13/6/1722. John Hollowell produced certificate from Monthly Meeting at Derby.

8/8/1722. William Hunt signified he and his wife intended to remove within the compass of Salem Monthly Meeting and requests certificate

12/9/1722. Certificate for Joseph Francks, signifying his clearness from marriage engagements.

14/11/1722. Certificate requests for Samuel Shiver, to marry young woman of Burlington Monthly Meeting. John Hains requests certificate for his son Josiah to marry young woman of Burlington Monthly Meeting.

11/12/1722. Certificate for Joshua Wright and his wife from Chesterfield Monthly Meeting.

8/5/1723. Benjamin Kidd produced two certificates, one from Monthly Meeting in Settle in Yorkshire and another from the meeting of Ministering Friends held in York in Old England. Certificate from Monthly Meeting of Horsly Down in London and ... morning meeting concerning John Estaugh and his wife.

11/9/1723. Thomas Greslye produced certificate from Ridgly Monthly Meeting in Great Britain. Wm. Clark in behalf of his brother Joseph Clark desires certificate to Salem Monthly Meeting.

9/1/1723/4. Thomas Sharp signifies his intention of marriage to woman of Monthly Meeting of Abington and desires certificate.

10/6/1724. Thomas Sharp made application by the request of his son in law John Holowell (who removed from Derby Monthly Meeting and lives hereabout two years and returned thither again for a certificate. Certificate for Mary Rothmall to Burlington Monthly Meeting. Certificate requested for Mary Clark who has lately married and removed within the verge of Philadelphia Monthly Meeting. William Wilkins requests certificate in order to marry Mary Buckken.

14/7/1724. Certificate requested for Elizabeth Holloway, lately removed within the compass of Darby Monthly Meeting. Certificate for Jno.

Hollowell to Derby Monthly Meeting. Thomas Greasly and his father being removed to PA, request certificate.

9/9/1724. Joseph Copper, Jr. produced certificate in behalf of John Hollowell and his wife Elizabeth which was signed.

11/11/1724. Certificate prepared for Thomas Grasly, wife and father.

8/12/1724. Henry Ballanger has been seen in actions unseemly with a woman of ill fame - disowned.

8/1/1724/5. Certificate requested for Hannah Lewden.

14/4/1725. Certificate requested for Hannah Whiteall who has removed to Philadelphia.

11/8/1725. Thomas Davis desires a certificate to Kennet Monthly Meeting. Samuel Sharp, son of John Sharp requests certificate to Monthly Meeting at Burlington Monthly Meeting to marry.

-/12/1725/6. Jos. Cooper requests, in behalf of his son Isaac, a certificate in order to marry young woman of Burlington Monthly Meeting.

14/1/1725/6. Certificate for John Adamson. Certificate for Eliza. Evens who plans to travel to Long Island.

9/3/1726. Certificate requested for Francis Jones, Jr.

10/2/1727. Certificate requested for Eliza. Wills who is late removed within verge of Burlington Monthly Meeting. Certificate requested for Jacob Horner to marry young woman in Phila Monthly Meeting.

12/4/1727. Certificate requested for Eliza. Crosby who was married within the verge of this meeting but now lives within the verge of Burlington Monthly Meeting.

14/6/1727. Robt. Stephens produced certificate for himself and family from Monthly Meeting at Colletine of County Wexford, Ireland.

9/8/1727. Certificate requested for Gersham Benbow to North Wales.

8/11/1727. Certificate requested for Ann Tyson.

13/3/1728. Jos: Knight desires certificate to Monthly Meeting at Abington, PA. Robert Ingle, son of John Ingle, decd. signified that he intended to take Rachel Vinson to wife, being a young woman of Burlington Monthly Meeting. Certificate requested for Thomas Dennis. Certificate requested for Jane Haines, now the wife of John Haines, Jr., formerly Jane Smith.

8/5/1728. Samuel Garwood by John Hollinghead requests certificate to Burlington Monthly Meeting to marry. Certificate requested for Hannah Siddons, dau. of Mary Siddens, to monthly meeting of Goshen, PA.

14/8/1728. Certificate requested by Timothy Matlack for his brother Jos: Matlack to Nottingham Monthly Meeting.

1/10/1728. Isaac Stephens from Ireland produced certificate from Monthly Meeting at Collydine. Certificate produced for Jane Haines to Monthly Meeting at Goshen.

10/1/1729. Jno. Burroughs requests certificate to Monthly Meeting of Goshen.

12/3/1729. Jos. Cooper, Jr., produced certificate for Grace Zane.

9/4/1729. Certificate requested for Sarah Hains to Burlington Monthly Meeting.

14/5/1729. Saml. Lippancott produced certificate in behalf of Sarah Haines, wife of Nathan Haines.

8/7/1729. Constantine Wood requests certificate in behalf of Thos. Predrick and his wife.

13/8/1729. Robt. Lord requests certificate to marry Friend of Abington Monthly Meeting. Rachel Seaman and Pheby Willits produced certificates from their Monthly Meeting at Westbury on Long Island.

8/10/1729. Joseph Dickinson produced certificate in his behalf from Mount Meleck Monthly Meeting in Ireland. John Wood and Abraham Chalton produced certificate in behalf of Robt. Lord to Burlington Monthly Meeting. Certificate requested for Edward Wever to marry young woman of Burlington Monthly Meeting. Jno. Jessop produced certificate from Dublin for himself and wife Jane.

9/1/1729. Certificate for Judith Sharp to Abbington Monthly Meeting.

13/2/1730. Thomas Evens requests certificate signifying his clearness from marriage engagements, to Monthly Meeting at Burlington. Thomas Wilkins at last monthly meeting presented his intentions of marriage with Joanna Wood.

11/3/1730. Certificate for Joshua Lord signed.

8/4/1730. Certificate requested for Mary Parker. Jno. Hollingshead requests certificate on behalf of Joshua Wright and family for a removal to Chesterfield Monthly Meeting.

10/6/1730. Jno. Hank produced certificate from Breash in County Derby, Great Britain. Ephraim Tomlinson requests certificate for Jno. Hugg to marry friend of Burlington Monthly Meeting.

14/7/1730. Certificate requested for Jno. Evans to marry young woman within verge of Salem Monthly Meeting. Certificate requested for Eliza. Wyat.

14/7/1730. Certificate for Martha Wall requested. Certificate requested for Eliza. Wight. Certificate requested for Stacy Beakes to Falls Monthly Meeting.

14/10/1730. Certificate requested for Rachel Cowgill to Chesterfield Monthly Meeting.

HADDONFIELD MONTHLY MEETING

8/12/1730. Henry Francklen from Great Britain produced two certificates, one from Monthly Meeting in York where he belonged and other from meeting of Ministers in said city.

21/2/1731. Certificate requested for Sarah Pots to Monthly Meeting at Chesterfield.

9/6/1731. Wm. Tomlinson requests certificate to Monthly Meeting at Burlington to marry.

13/7/1731. Certificate for Eliza. Wilcox to Burlington Monthly Meeting. Certificate for Grace Price to Friends where she dwells. Certificate requested for Jno. Borton to Wrightstown Monthly Meeting in PA in order to marry. Certificate requested for Jno. Hank to Derby in PA. Thos. Hooton requests certificate for son Thomas to Friends in Barbados. Certificate requested for Thomas Thornbury and wife to New Garden, PA.

11/8/1731. Roger Bragg signified he was about to remove to Goshen in Chester Co. and requests certificate.

13/10/1731. Certificate requested for Jno. Adams to marry Friend of Burlington. Paul Johnston produced certificate from Monthly Meeting in Dublin.

10/11/1731. Certificate requested for Mary Crips to Burlington Monthly Meeting.

14/12/1731. Thomas Lippencott requests certificate to marry in Burlington Monthly Meeting.

13/1/1731/2. Certificate requested for Meribah Clark to Philadelphia Monthly Meeting.

10/2/1732. Thomas Hooton requests certificate for his son to Friends in Barbados. Wm. Cooper requests certificate in order to marry dau. of Francis Rawle, dec., of Philadelphia Monthly Meeting.

12/4/1732. Robt. Pond produced certificate from Burlington Monthly Meeting for himself and wife Sarah. Certificate requested for Jos. Dickinson to Friends in PA. Certificate requested for Mercy Adams to Shrewsbury Monthly Meeting "for the time she lived amongst us."

14/6/1732. Mongo Bewly produced certificate from Monthly Meeting at Edenderry in Ireland. Saml. Stephens produced certificate form Monthly Meeting at Lambstown. Hannah Dent produced certificate from Monthly Meeting at Richmond in Yorkshire and another from meeting of minsters held at York. Isaac Stephens requested certificate by Timothy Mattlack in order to recommend him to Friends at Ireland.

13/9/1732. Obadiah Borton requests certificate to marry young woman within verge of Burlington Monthly Meeting.

100 EARLY CHURCH RECORDS OF GLOUCESTER COUNTY

12/12/1732. Isaac Stephens requests certificate to Friends in Ireland and elsewhere.

12/1/173/3. Rowlon Owen produced certificate from Burlington Monthly Meeting.

9/2/1733. Certificate for Hannah Patrick to Salem Monthly Meeting.

14/3/1733. Jno. Borton requests certificate for himself and wife to Burlington Monthly Meeting.

11/4/1733. Robt. Hunt produced certificate from Burlington Monthly Meeting signifying his orderly conversation and clearness from marriage engagements. Certificate requested for Sarah Hopewell to Phila.

10/10/1733. Robert Stephens produced certificate from Monthly Meeting at Colledine, County Wexford, Ireland. Certificate requested for Hannah Abbott to Salem Monthly Meeting.

14/11/1733. Certificate requested Jos. Hopewell to Philadelphia.

11/12/1733/4. Jos. Tomlinson requests certificate to marry within the verge of Salem Monthly Meeting.

13/3/1734. Thomas Hooton requests certificate for his son Thomas to Friends in Ireland or elsewhere.

-/5/1734. Certificate requested for Sarah Newbould to Chesterfield Monthly Meeting.

12/6/1734. Francis Smith produced certificate for himself and wife. James Darbe produced certificate from Monthly Meeting at Goshen. Saml. Bown and Richd. Hallet produced certificate from Monthly Meeting at Flushing.

9/7/1734. Richd. Bidgood produced certificate form Monthly Meeting at Falls. Certificate requested for Hugh Coperthwait to Monthly Meeting at Burlington.

11/9/1734. Thomas Hooton, Jr. produced certificate from Monthly Meeting Dublin, signifying his clearness from marriage engagements. Ralph Cowgill produced certificate from Monthly Meeting at Chesterfield. Certificate requested for Jane Seaton to Friends in Chester Co.

13/11/1734. Certificate requested for Ann Moss to Salem Monthly Meeting and Lydia Hains to Burlington Monthly Meeting.

10/1/1735. Certificate for Lydia Hains to Burlington Monthly Meeting.

4/2/1735. Joseph Cooper intends to take Hannah Dent to wife and requests certificate to Philadelphia Monthly Meeting. Certificate prepared for Thomas Evens.

12/3/1735. Report that Wm. Sharp has taken his former wife's sister in marriage.

HADDONFIELD MONTHLY MEETING

8/7/1735. Certificate from Philadelphia Friends was produced for Hannah Cooper, wife of Jos: Cooper.

13/8/1735. Thomas Evens produced certificate from Newport Friends.

10/9/1735. Certificate requested for Nathan Beaks and his wife to Monthly Meeting at Chesterfield.

12/11/1735. Isaac Stephens produced certificate from Monthly Meeting at Lambertown in Ireland, signifying his clearness from marriage engagements. Isaac Stephens requests certificate to marry young woman in verge of Monthly Meeting at London Grove or New Garden.

9/12/1735. Jane Seaton produced certificate from Monthly Meeting at Concord, signifying her clearness from marriage engagements.

12/2/1736. Certificate requested for Margret Barton to Burlington Monthly Meeting. Certificate requested for Joseph Gibson and his wife to Monthly Meeting at Salem.

14/4/1736. Thomas Hooton in behalf of his son Thomas requests certificate to Chesterfield Monthly Meeting in order to settle there.

12/5/1736. Certificate requested for Nathan Lippincott and wife to Monthly Meeting at Goshen.

13/7/1736. Thomas Redman produced certificate from Monthly Meeting at Philadelphia.

11/8/1736. John Tomlinson requests certificate in order to marry Friend in Chester Co.

13/10/1736. Jno. Maxell produced certificate from monthly meeting in Chester Co., signifying his clearness from marriage engagements.

14/4/1737. Certificate requested for Jane Seaton to Burlington Monthly Meeting.

11/5/1737. Wm. Ives produced certificate from Friends at East Nottingham, clear from marriage engagements. Certificate requested for Mary Sharp to Philadelphia Monthly Meeting.

12/7/1737. Certificate requested for Joshua Humphrey to marry Burlington Monthly Meeting. Saml. Lippincott requests certificate for his brother Freedom Lippincott in order for marriage within the compass of Chesterfield Monthly Meeting.

13/12/1737. Certificate requested for Mary Howell to Chester Monthly Meeting.

13/1/1737/8. Certificate requested for Joseph More to marry at monthly meeting of Burlington.

10/2/1738. Saml. Butcher produced certificate from Burlington Monthly Meeting for himself and wife. Joseph Tomlinson requests certificate to marry within compass of Providence Monthly Meeting. Certificate requested for Ruth Adams to Philadelphia Monthly Meeting. Certificate requested for Saml. Lippencott to marry a member of Chesterfield Monthly Meeting.

12/4/1738. Certificate requested for Hannah Engle to Goshen Monthly Meeting.

14/6/1738. Wm. Griscom produced certificate from Philadelphia Monthly Meeting, clear from marriage engagements. Certificate requested for Ruth Dennis to Newark Monthly Meeting in New Castle Co.

11/7/1738. Saml. Butcher, Jr. and his sister Pheby produced certificate from Burlington Monthly Meeting. Certificate requested for Amos Wilkins to marry at Chesterfield.

9/38/1738. Rowland Owen produced certificate from monthly meeting in Burlington for himself and wife. Robert Powel produced certificate for himself from Burlington Monthly Meeting, clear from marriage engagements. Certificate for Joshua Lord prepared.

13/9/1738. Daniel Elwell produced certificate for himself from Philadelphia Monthly Meeting, clear from marriage engagements. James Whiteall produced certificate for himself from Goshen Monthly Meeting, clear from marriage engagements. Certificate requested for James Staugh and family to Philadelphia Monthly Meeting.

12/1/1728/9. Francis Smith about to remove beck again to Burlington and requests certificate for himself and wife. Certificate requested for Mary Decow to Chesterfield Monthly Meeting. Certificate requested for Mary Stogdale to Burlington Monthly Meeting. Sarah Heritage is a widow in need of some support.

9/2/1739. Saml. Adkins requests certificate to Burlington Monthly Meeting. Certificates requested for Mary Earl, Rebekah Budd, Rachel Cowgill. Ebenezer Brown requests certificate for himself and wife to monthly meeting at Nottingham. Josiah Fowler requests certificate in his journey to Rhode Island.

11/3/1739. Certificate for Joseph Heritage.

11/4/1739. Certificate requested for Jno. Dennis [son of Saml. Dennis] to monthly meeting of Newark Monthly Meeting. John Howel requests certificate for himself and wife to monthly meeting in Philadelphia.

9/5/1739. Thomas Parvin produced certificate from monthly meeting of Gwynedd, PA, for himself and wife. Isaac Andrews produced certificate from monthly meeting of Burlington.

13/6/1739. Saml. Butcher appointed overseer in room of Thomas Ballenger, late of Evesham, dec.

HADDONFIELD MONTHLY MEETING 103

12/9/1739. Certificate requested for Benja. Tindal to Salem Monthly Meeting. [His father, Jos: Tindal, desires that a settlement be made between them before he has a certificate.]

11/10/1739. Joseph Dobbins produced certificate from monthly meeting at Providence in Chester Co.

10/11/1739. John Heritage produced certificate from monthly meeting of Burlington, clear from marriage engagements. Certificate requested for Ketherine Parvin to monthly meeting of North Wales (Gwynedd). Certificate prepared for Hannah Cooper for her intended visit.

10/1/1739/40. Certificate produced for Thos. Norbury and wife from monthly meeting of Goshen.

12/3/1740. Francis Smith produced certificate from Burlington Monthly Meeting for himself, wife and dau. Certificate requested for Jos: Hollingshead to Burlington Monthly Meeting. Certificate requested for Eliza. Lippincott, dau. of Thos. Evans.

9/4/1740. Certificate prepared for Martha White.

11/6/1740. James Stephens by his brother Robt. Stephens requests certificate for marriage and settlement within verge of Philadelphia Monthly Meeting. William Griscom by his uncle Jos: Kaighin requests certificate for marriage to Salem Monthly Meeting. Andrew Griscom requests certificate for himself and wife to monthly meeting at Eggharbour.

8/7/1740. Certificate requested for Esther Bidgood to monthly meeting at Falls in Buck Co.

13/8/1740. Joseph Edgerton by Jos: Cooper produced certificate from Lamberton, County of Wexford in Ireland, clear from marriage engagements. Certificate requested for Sarah Barnes to Salem Monthly Meeting.

8/10/1740. Certificate requested for Sarah Jerdall to monthly meeting of Abington.

9/12/1740. Certificate requested for Jos: Morgan, son of Alexr. Morgan to marry at Abington Monthly Meeting.

13/2/1741. Certificate requested for Thomas Sharp and family to Friends of Shinodando [Shenandoah?].

11/3/1741. Ebenezer Brown produced certificate from monthly meeting of East Nottingham for himself and wife. Nathanael Lippincott produced certificate from monthly meeting of Goshen for himself and wife. John Mickle requests certificate in order to marry a member of Burlington Monthly Meeting. Certificate requested for Josiah Kay, Jr., to monthly meeting in Salem.

13/5/1741. John Haines produced certificate from Goshen Monthly Meeting for himself and wife and son Wm.

10/6/1741. Robt. Down requests to come under the care of Friends. Edward Hollingshead by his father requests certificate for marriage at Cape May.

12/8/1741. Certificate requested for Thos. Moore to Burlington Monthly Meeting to marry.

9/9/1741. Certificate prepared for John Gill. Certificate requested for Ralph Cowgill and another for Isaac Cowgill and his wife, to Burlington Monthly Meeting. Certificate requested for John Gill, Jr. to Salem Monthly Meeting, in order to marry.

11/10/1741. Certificate from Burlington Monthly Meeting for Saml. Wickward.

8/12/1741. Certificate for Benjamin Tindal approved. [The affair of Benja. and his father apparently resolved.]

8/1/1741/2. John Barton produced certificate from Burlington Monthly Meeting, for himself and wife. Nehemiah Andrew sent certificate from Little Eggharbor for himself and wife. Certificate for Isaac Cowgill and wife.

12/2/1742. Samuel Clement requests to come under the care of Friends. Certificate requested for John Stratton to Friends of Shannods [Shenandoah?]. Certificate requested for Mary Stone to Friends of North Wales.

10/3/1742. Certificate for Hannah Fowler to Friends in Long Island. Certificate requested for Saml. Butcher for himself, wife, son and dau. to Burlington Monthly Meeting.

12/5/1742. Jos: Saul produced certificate from Philadelphia Monthly Meeting.

9/6/1742. Certificate requested for Mary Bickham to Chester Monthly Meeting. Certificate requested for Esther Davis to Goshen Monthly Meeting.

8/9/1742. Informed that Danl. Stratton and wife have returned from Shanadore [Shenandoah?] in order to dwell in these parts again; therefore not certificate is required. Jos: Edgerton requests certificate to marry in verge of Laycock and Sadsbury monthly meeting in Lancaster Co., PA.

10/11/1742. William Hulings requests certificate to marry at Burlington Monthly Meeting.

14/1/1742/3. Certificate for Solomon Lippincott to marry within verge of Chesterfield Monthly Meeting. Certificate requested for Rebekah Ballenger to monthly meeting of Philadelphia.

HADDONFIELD MONTHLY MEETING

9/3/1743. Certificate for Nehemiah Andrews and wife to Friends of Little Eggharbour.

13/4/1743. Saml. Butcher produced certificate from monthly meeting of Burlington for himself, wife and son Josh. and dau. Phebe.

13/5/1743. John Straton returned certificate to recommend him at Shanadnore in VA he not making any long stay there.

8/6/1743. Certificate for Abigail Cooper, dau. of Wm. Cooper to Friends of Philadelphia. Certificate requested for Sarah Michner [wife of John Michner] to Abington Monthly Meeting.

10/8/1743. Certificate requested for Thomas Cowgill, son of Nehemiah Cowgill to Falls Monthly Meeting. Certificate requested for Saml. Sharp to Derby Monthly Meeting.

14/9/1743. Certificate requested for Rebeckah Conoro to Burlington Monthly Meeting. Certificate requested for Ann Sharp, dau. of Saml. Sharp to Philadelphia Monthly Meeting.

13/12/1743/4. Certificate requested for John Allen to marry in Burlington Monthly Meeting. Certificate requested for Sarah Holloway, dau. of Tobias Holloway, dec., to Philadelphia Monthly Meeting.

12/1/1743/4. Joseph Tomlinson requests certificate for his brother Othnial Tomlinson to Salem Monthly Meeting.

9/2/1744. Certificate for Sarah Decow to Chesterfield Monthly Meeting. Abraham Chattin produced certificate from monthly meeting of Salem for Robt. Lodge and his wife.

9/5/1744. David Elwell requests certificate for himself and family to Philadelphia Monthly Meeting. Certificate requested for Rebeckah White to monthly meeting of Philadelphia.

8/8/1744. Richd. Matlack by his brother Timothy requests certificate to marry at Salem Monthly Meeting.

12/9/1744. Certificate requested for Joseph Saul to marry at Philadelphia Monthly Meeting.

14/11/1744. Caleb Haines requests certificate for himself, wife and two daus.: Eliza., and Patience, to Burlington Monthly Meeting.

11/12/1744/5. John Thorn requests to be taken under the care of Friends. Thos. Webster produced certificate for himself and wife from Burlington Monthly Meeting.

11/1/1744/5. John Borton produced certificate from Buckingham Friends in Bucks Co., PA. Certificate requested for Eliza. Delzel to Philadelphia Friends.

8/2/1745. Jno. Allen requests certificate to Burlington Monthly Meeting.

13/3/1745. Certificate requested for Jos: Saul to Philadelphia Monthly Meeting.
10/4/1745. Restore Lippincott produced certificate from monthly meeting of Burlington.
12/6/1745. Certificate requested for Abraham Haines, Jr. and wife to Opeckon, Fredericksburg, VA.
9/7/1745. Certificate requested for Nixon Chattin to monthly meeting of Philadelphia.
14/8/1745. Joseph Heritage requests certificate for his son John Heritage to monthly meeting of Philadelphia. Michael Linch requests to be taken under the care of Friends.
13/11/1745/6. Joshua Wright, Jr. and his wife produced certificate from Chesterfield Monthly Meeting. Certificate requested for Rachel Maddock to monthly meeting [at Kennet or Center].
10/12/1745/6. Certificate requested for George Cousins and wife to Philadelphia Monthly Meeting. Restore Lippincott, son of Jacob Lippincott requests certificate to Philadelphia Monthly Meeting.
10/1/1745/6. Joshua Haines, son of Abraham Haines, requests certificate to where he has gone to settle [Opeckon, VA].
14/2/1746. Timothy Matlack requests certificate for himself, wife and dau., Sabilla, in order to settle in Philadelphia, she, clear from marriage engagements.
12/3/1746. Certificate requested for Esther Adkinson to Burlington Monthly Meeting.
14/5/1746. Certificate requested for Thos. Southerlin and wife to Friends of Opeckon in Frederick Co., VA.
11/6/1746. Certificate requested for Jacob Taylor and Ann his wife to monthly meeting in Opekon in Frederick Co., VA. Henry Wood of Waterford requests certificate to join in marriage with a dau. of Isaac Williams of Philadelphia. Jacob Spicer, son of Thos. Spicer, requests certificate to join in marriage with dau. of Jacob Lippincott within verge of Salem Monthly Meeting. Ezekial Haines, son of Corlile Haines requests certificate to marry within verge of Burlington Monthly Meeting.
13/8/1746. Hugh Haines, son of Richd. Haines lately came from Opeckon in Frederick Co., VA, and expected that his father had made application for a certificate for him but being neglected; he is clear from marriage engagements.
10/9/1746. Thos. Redman in behalf of his apprentice Jon: Knight, age 17, produced certificate on his behalf from monthly meeting of Buckingham, Bucks Co.

HADDONFIELD MONTHLY MEETING

8/10/1746. Benja. Crispon produced certificate from monthly meeting of Burlington for himself, wife and two daus., Rebeckah and Martha.

12/11/1746/7. Certificate requested for David Cooper to monthly meeting of Philadelphia to marry.

9/1/1746/7. Jos. Cowgill produced certificate from monthly meeting at the Falls, Bucks Co., clear from marriage engagements. Grace Mason produced certificate from monthly meeting of Salem, clear from marriage engagements. Certificate requested for Lydia Noble to Philadelphia Monthly Meeting. Certificate requested for Rebeckah Hugg to Philadelphia Monthly Meeting.

13/2/1747. Certificate of Restore Lippincott returned, he not being likely to remove to Philadelphia. Certificate for John Millern and his wife Eliza., from monthly meeting of Chesterfield, having lived among them nearly 20 years and hath been gone to the new country about 2-3 years.

11/3/1747. James Sloan produced certificate in behalf of himself and wife from monthly meeting of Richland. Certificate requested for John Milban (Milborn) and Eliza., his wife to Frederick Co., VA. Certificate requested for Eliza. Woodward to monthly meeting of Philadelphia.

8/4/1747. Abraham Kelly produced certificate for himself, and wife from monthly meeting of Burlington. Certificate for Saml. Lippincott and wife Mary from monthly meeting of Philadelphia. Jacob Spicer requests certificate to Salem Monthly Meeting.

11/6/1747. Thomas Redman requests certificate to marry at Salem Monthly Meeting.

14/7/1747. Richd. Willet produced certificate from Little Eggharbour Monthly Meeting for himself and wife. Silas Crispin, Jr., produced certificate for himself and wife from monthly meeting at Burlington.

9/9/1747. Certificate requested for Grace Fisher to monthly meeting of Philadelphia.

8/12/1747/8. Certificate requested for Jona. Husted, Jr., to marry at monthly meeting of Great Eggharbour. John Burough, Jr., requests certificate to monthly meeting of Philadelphia, in order for marriage.

14/1/1747/8. Abraham Kelly requests certificate in order to remove himself and wife Rachel to Burlington Monthly Meeting.

9/3/1748. Restore Lippincott requests certificate to monthly meeting of Burlington.

11/5/1748. Certificate of Nixon Chattin from Philadelphia Monthly Meeting. Certificate requested for Rebeckah Lewden to monthly meeting at Newark.

12/7/1748. John Hughes requests to be taken under the care of Friends.

14/9/1748. Certificate requested for John Wills and his wife Abigail to monthly meeting of Woodbridge.

12/10/1748. Isaac Ellis, son of Simeon Ellis requests certificate in order to marry at monthly meeting of Salem.

9/11/1748. Josa. Lord requests certificate for son Josa., to marry at Salem Monthly Meeting.

13/12/1748. Certificate requested for Sarah Wills to Burlington Monthly Meeting. Certificate requested for Wm. Haines, son of John Haines, to Salem monthly meeting to marry.

13/1/1748/9. Certificate requested for Ruben Haines to Philadelphia Monthly Meeting.

10/2/1749. Josa. Humphreys and Increase his wife, request certificate to monthly meeting of Burlington to reside there. Saml. Lippincott and Abigail his wife request certificate to Salem Monthly Meeting.

12/4/1749. Josiah Fowler informed the meeting that he has removed to Mount Holly.

14/6/1749. John Pinyard requests to come under the care of Friends.

11/7/1749. Certificate requested for Joshua Ballenger to marry at Salem Monthly Meeting. Saml. Parker produced certificate from monthly meeting of Little Eggharbour; he also produced acknowledgment for his outgoing in marriage.

13/9/1749. Josiah Forster requests certificate for himself and wife to Burlington Monthly Meeting. Jos: Hancock produced certificate from monthly meeting at Burlington, a young man, clear from marriage engagements. Certificate requested for Anna Silver to Salem Monthly Meeting.

12/1/1749/50. Certificate requested for Jane Siddon to monthly meeting of Philadelphia.

9/2/1750. Certificate requested for Eliza. Evans to monthly meeting of Gwynedd and Mary West to monthly meeting of Philadelphia.

4/3/1750. Edward Tyler produced certificate from Salem Monthly Meeting for himself and wife.

11/4/1750. Nathan Haines requests a certificate for son William and his wife [Elizabeth] to Salem Monthly Meeting.

9/5/1750. Certificate requested for Jacob Heulings, Jr. to marry young woman in Bucks Co.

13/6/1750. Ephraim Tomlinson requests certificate to marry in Chesterfield.

10/7/1750. William Miller requests certificate for himself and wife

Elizabeth to Chesterfield.

12/9/1750. Job Haines and Enoch Stratton request certificates for themselves and wives to Burlington Monthly Meeting. Certificate requested for Mary Bassett to Salem Monthly Meeting.

11/12/1750. Marriage of Simon Breach and Mary Shores. Her previous husband had gone to Carolina and was killed by a falling tree.

MARRIAGES OF GLOUCESTER COUNTY
from court records of New Jersey

August 3, "1728." (evidently error for 172 7. - "14th year of King George"), Wm. Smith of Gloucester Co., and Dorothy Birch of same, spinster.

March 30, 17-- (1st George 11; I. e. 1728) Benjamin Wood of Gloucester Co., yeoman, and Mary Ashton of Philadelphia, spinster.

Jan 17, 1727. George Cozens of Gloucester Co., yeoman, and Ellena Chester of same, spinster.

Jan 29, 1727. Isaac Hoel of Gloucester Co., sawyer, and Mary Sharp of same, spinster.

Jan 5, 1727. Thomas Briand of Gloucester Co., yeoman, and Sarah Dunn of same, spinster.

July 25, 1727. William Ward of Gloucester Co., yeoman, and Mary Anne Warder of same, spinster.

July 29, 1727. Thomas Thorn, Providence of New York, cordwainer, and Littia Hinchman of Gloucester in Providence of New Jersey, spinster.

June 19, 1727. John Spence of Gloucester Co., Gentleman, and Rachel Richardson of same, spinster.

June 19, 1727. James Dubury of Gloucester Co., yeoman, and Jane Hodges of same, spinster.

May 11, 1727. Thomas Cheeseman of Gloucester Co., yeoman, and Sarah Colemons of same, spinster.

Nov 23, 1727. Edward Irwin of Gloucester Co., yeoman, and Sarah Woodath of same, spinster.

Sept 18, 1727. Joseph Ireland of Great Egg Harbor, Gloucester Co., yeoman, and Ruth Coderry, of same, spinster, daughter of William Coderry and Anne, his wife.

April 10, 1728. Gabriel Hugg of Gloucester Co., bricklayer, and Patience Erwin of same, spinster.

April 19, 1728. Jonathan Belton of Gloucester Co., cordwainer, and Mary Champion of same, widow.

July 29, 1728. John Jones of Gloucester Co., yeoman, and Sarah Gagard of same, spinster.

Nov 28, 1732. John Kaighn of Gloucester Co., yeoman, and Abigail Hinchman, spinster.

April 6, 1728. Henry Jones of Gloucester Co., yeoman, and Naomi Cheeseman of same spinster.

Dec 16, 1732. Elias Steelman of Great Eggharbour, Gloucester Co.,

yeoman, and Comfort Creesey of same, spinster.
Dec 30, 1732. James Mickell of Gloucester Co., yeoman, and Sarah Eastlacke.
Jan 2, 1732. Job Sommers of Great Egg Harbour, Gloucester Co., yeoman, and Eunice Creesey of Cape May Co., spinster.
March 18, 1732. Tobias Holloway of Newton, Gloucester Co., yeoman and Mary Ladd of same, widow.
March 6, 1732. Thomas Bate of Gloucester Co., farmer, and Mary Shivers of same, spinster.
Nov 29, 1732. Remberance (Rememberance) Lippincott of Gloucester Co., blacksmith, and Hannah Bates of same, spinster.
Dec 29, 1733. Michael Chew of Gloucester Co., yeoman, and Amey Brinn of same, widow.
Jan 16, 1733. John Dilks of Deptford, Gloucester Co., yeoman, and Hannah Chew.
July 24, 1733. John Preston of Waterford, Gloucester Co., yeoman, and Margaret Mackintosh, widow.
July 25, 1733. Andrew Blakeman of Great Eggharbour, Gloucester Co., yeoman, and Mary Allen of same, widow.
July 4, 1733. Richard Buckley of Gloucester Co., yeoman, and Mary Curtis of same, spinster.
June 22, 1733. Isaiah Ross of Waterford, Gloucester Co., yeoman, and Ruth Tindall of same, spinster.
May 2, 1733. Levi Pearce of Gloucester Co., yeoman, and Rosanna Ward of same.
May 28, 1733. Isaac Matlack of Waterford, Gloucester Co., carpenter, and Rebecca Bate of same, spinster.
Nov 1, 1733. Wm. Kent of Gloucester Co., yeoman, and Sarah Powell of Newton Township.
Oct 29, 1733. Samuel Eastlack of Newton, Gloucester Co., yeoman, and Ann Breach of same.
Dec 5, 1736. Edmond Lord of Racoon Creek of Gloucester Co., yeoman, and Susanna Attwood of same Co., spinster.
Jan 12, 1736. John Hampton of Gloucester Co., husbandman, and Ann Devall of Pilesgrove, Salem Co., spinster.
Jan 13, 1736. John Matlack, Jr. of Waterford, Gloucester Co., husbandman, and Hannah Shivers of same, spinster.
Dec 5, 1736. Edmond Lord of Racoon Creek, Gloucester Co., yeoman, and Susanna Attwood of same Co., spinster.
Dec 9, 1736. Blackston Ingledew of Philadelphia, butcher, and Mary Mickle of Gloucester Co., widow.

Dec 9, 1736. George Flaningham of Gloucester Co., farmer, and Sarah Jennings of same spinster.

Feb 22, 1736. Jacob Richman of Salem Co., yeoman, and Catharine Malson (Matson) of Gloucester County.

Jan 12, 1736. John Hampton of Gloucester Co., husbandman, and Ann Devall of Pilesgrove, Salem Co., spinster.

Jan 13, 1736. John Matlack Jr. of Waterford, Gloucester Co., husbandman, and Hannah Shivers of same, spinster.

July 9, 1736. John Shivers of Gloucester Co., yeoman, and Mary Clement of Newton, same Co., spinster.

March 14, 1736. (sic) James Robertson of Gloucester Co., Gentleman, and Esther Adman of Great Egg Harbor, spinster.

Nov 29, 1736. Henry Willard of Waterford of Gloucester Co., yeoman, and Ann Wetherill of same Co., widow.

Sept 1, 1736. Samuel Morton of Gloucester Co., yeoman, and Lydia Cock of same, yeoman (sic).

April 16, 1737. Joseph Alberson of Gloucester, Gloucester Co., yeoman, and Rose Hampton, spinster, daughter of Wm. Hampton.

April 7, 1737. Archibald Jolly of Waterford, Gloucester Co., cordwainer, and Deborah Cheesman, spinster, daughter of Richard Cheesman of same, yeoman.

Aug 12, 1737. Michael Fish of Gloucester Co., husbandman, and Diana Fish of same, spinster.

Aug 6, 1737. Abraham Alberson, Jr. of Gloucester Co., yeoman, and Hannah Medcalf of same, widow.

Dec 5, 1737. John Hopper of Deptford, Gloucester Co., yeoman, and Ann Garwood, spinster, daughter of Thomas. Garwood of Burlington Co., yeoman.

Feb 16, 1737. Wm. Kaighn of Gloucester Co., husbandman, and Abigail Cooper, spinster, dau of Benjn. Moore of Burlington Co., yeoman.

July 9, 1737. John Green of Gloucester Co., schoolmaster, and Elizabeth Browning of same, spinster.

June 24, 1737. John Eastlack of Newton, Gloucester Co., yeoman, and Mary Belton of same, widow.

May 30, 1737. Thomas Clement of Gloucester, Gloucester Co., cordwainer, and Mary Tyly, spinster, daughter of Hannah Allison.

May 30, 1737. Wm. Hugg of Gloucester, Gloucester Co., yeoman, and Sarah Harrison, spinster, daughter of Samuel Harrison of same, yeoman.

Sept 14, 1737. Philip Scull of Great Eggharbour, Gloucester Co., yeoman, and Abigail Townsend, spinster, dau of Ruddock Townsend of same, yeoman.

Aug 9, 1737. Samuel Church of Great Eggharbour, Gloucester Co., and Dorothy Edwards of same.

June 17, 1737. Elias Gandy of Cape May, and Mary English of Eggharbour Gloucester County.

April 2, 1738. Isaac Kay of Gloucester, Gloucester Co., yeoman, and Mary Ann Gregory, spinster, daughter of Joseph Gregory of Gloucester, yeoman.

Aug 2, 1738. James Hayes of Waterford, Gloucester Co., yeoman, and Margaret Magloughin of same, spinster.

March 3, 1738. Henry Siddons of Gloucester, Gloucester Co., yeoman, and Elizabeth Sharp, spinster, daughter of Samuel Sharp of Newton, same Co., yeoman.

Nov 15, 1738. Jonathan Thomas of Gloucester Co., husbandman, and Sarah Ellis of same, widow.

Sept 6, 1738. David Row of Gloucester Co., farmer, and Elizabeth Taber of same, widow.

Dec 14, 1738. John Willshire (Wiltshire) of Gloucester Co., husbandman, and Elizabeth Williams of same, spinster.

Dec 8, 1738. Daniel Barber of Gloucester Co., yeoman, and Margaret Hampton, spinster, daughter of Wm. Hampton of Gloucester, yeoman.

Jan 15, 1738. Jeremiah Adams of Great Eggharbour, Gloucester Co., yeoman, and Mary Homan, spinster, dau. of Andrew Homan of same, yeoman.

Jan 8, 1738. Robert Turner of Gloucester, Gloucester Co., husbandman, and Abigail Burne, spinster, dau of Mary Burne of Gloucester, widow.

Jan 5, 1738. Peter Cock of Gloucester Co., shoemaker, and Beata Lock of Salem County.

April 3, 1739. John Chew of Gloucester, Gloucester Co., weaver, and Ann Jennings, spinster, daughter of Isaac Jennings of same place, yeoman.

Aug 12, 1739. Isaac Smith of Haddonfield, Gloucester Co., blacksmith, and Elizabeth Norris of same place, spinster.

Aug 8, 1739. John Bryant of Great Eggharbour, Gloucester Co., taylor and Mary Dennis of same, widow.

Feb 8, 1739. John Gray of Newton, Gloucester Co., husbandman, and Esther Gilcott of same, spinster.

July 23, 1739. Samuel Tew of Waterford, Gloucester Co., yeoman, and Susanna Collins, spinster, dau of Edward Collins of Chatnel

Township, Philadelphia Co., mason.

June 1, 1739. Nehemiah Nicholson of Great Eggharbour, Gloucester Co., Gent., and Sarah Badcock of same, spinster.

March 11, 1739. Henry Moran of Gloucester, Gloucester Co., weaver, and Mary Lucas of same, spinster.

March 17, 1739. William Wallis of Newton, Gloucester Co., woolcomber, and Dorothy Connolly of same, widow.

March 307, 1740. James Ward of Haddonfield, Gloucester Co., husbandman, and Mary Mackenny of same, spinster.

May 15, 1740. John Chattin of Deptford, Gloucester Co., yeoman, and Priscilla Hugg of same, spinster.

Jan 11, 1741. Joseph Bellas [or Belles] of Waterford, Gloucester Co., cordwainder, and Susannah Fish of same, spinster, daughter of Elias Fish.

Jan 7, 1741. Robert Bramen of Greenwood, Gloucester Co., yeoman, and Martha Bright of same, widow.

Oct 17, 1741. Jacob Clement of Haddonfield, Gloucester Co., yeoman, and Elizabeth Tyley, spinster, daughter of Anna Ellison, late Anna Tyley.

Oct 26, 1741. Daniel Scull of Eggharbor, Gloucester Co., Gent., and Rachel Mannery of Great Eggharbor, spinster.

Aug 20, 1742. Owen Carty of Gloucester Co., husbandman, yeoman, and Esther Watson, spinster, daughter of Samuel Watson of Burlington Co., yeoman.

Feb 1, 1748. Hugh Neale of Great Egg Harbor, Gloucester Co., and Deborah Leeds of same, spinster. (But the bond shows this to be an error, and that Neale, or Neill, executed it to obtain a license for John Pullen of Eggharbour to marry Deborah Leeds, 1747-48. :84)

March 7, 1748. Joel Hillman of Gloucester Co., labourer, and Litesha Cheesman, spinster.

April 10, 1749. Thomas Nightingale of Philadelphia, cordwainer, and Sarah Champion of same, spinster. (But the bond states her residence as Waterford, Gloucester County. A -W :299.)

April 14, 1749. David Ward of Gloucester Co., yeoman, and Susannah Ward of same, spinster.

April 16, 1749. Abell Scull of Great Eggharbour, Gloucester Co., yeoman, and Martha Hew of City of Burlington, widow.

May 11, 1749. Uriah Cheesman of Gloucester Co., and Hannah Rowland of same, spinster.

June 5, 1749. Ezekiel Hutchinson, and Susannah Eldridge " of the same place," spinster. (Bond states his residence as Greenwich, Gloucester

County. A -W :185.)

May 24, 1749. John McColloch of Gloucester Co., yeoman, and Sarah Inskeep of same, spinster.

Sept 30, 1749. John English Jr. of Great Eggharbour, Gloucester Co., and Anne Inskeep of Burlington Co., spinster.

March 1, 1750. Josiah Ward of Gloucester township, yeoman, and Keziah Albertson of same, spinster.

March 13, 1750. Joseph Lord of Gloucester Co., yeoman, and Eleanor Chester of same, spinster.

Oct 23, 1750. John Gosling, Jr., and Hannah Cole. (Bond shows residence of both as Gloucester Co., and calls Hannah "widow."G :38.

MORAVIAN REGISTER, WEST JERSEY 1742-1794
(Births, Baptisms, Marriages and Deaths)

Transcribed from the original records in the archives at Bethlehem, Pennsylvania.

Catherine Izard, dau of Gabriel and Martha Izard of Morris River, b. 23 May 1742, bapt. by Rev. Paul Daniel Boyocelius.

John Wiseman, son of John Wiseman of Cohansey, b. Dec, bapt. 3 Apr 1743 by Leonhard Schnell.

Christina Petersen, dau of Luke and Christina Petersen of Morris River, b. 6 Jun 1743.

Isaac Guest, son of William and Christina Guest of Racoon, b. 6 Dec 1743, bapt. by Rev. Paul Daniel Boyocelius.

Catherine Hoffman, dau of Peter and Mary Hoffman of Morris River, b. 10 Feb 1744, bapt. 20 the same month by Rev. Paul D. Boyocelius.

Samuel Cobb, son of Samuel and Catherine Cobb of Morris River, b. 6 Jun 1744, bapt. by Rev. Paul D. Boyocelius.

Peter Lock, son of John and Rebecca Lock of Racoon, b. 22 Sep 1744, bapt. 25 of same month by Rev. Paul D. Boyocelius.

Magdalene Gill, dau of Matthew and Magdalene Gill, b. 6 Nov 1744, bapt. by Rev. Paul D. Boyocelius.

Eric Keen, son of Eric and Catherine Keen of Morris River, b. 25 Dec 1744, bapt. Apr 1745 by Rev. Abraham Reinke.

Seth Samuel Ward, son of Samuel and Sarah Ward of Racoon, b. ---, bapt. 23 Apr 1745 by Rev. Abraham Reinke.

Deborah Hoffman, dau of Laurence and Mary Hoffman of Raccoon, b. ---, bapt. 23 Apr 1745 by Rev. Abraham Reinke.

Priscilla Lock, dau of John and Rebecca Lock of Racoon, b. ---, bapt. 9 Jun 1745 by Rev. Abraham Reinke.

Elizabeth Philpot, dau of Nicholas Philpot of Penn's Neck, b. ---, bapt. 9 Jun 1745 by Rev. Abraham Reinke.

Mary Keen, dau of John and Rachel Keen of Raccoon, b. ---, bapt. 10 Jun 1745 by Rev. Abraham Reinke.

Margaret Rawlins, dau of John and Margaret Rawlins of Piles Grove, b. ---, bapt. 11 Jun 1745 by Rev. Abraham Reinke.

Jeremiah Petersen, son of Laurence and Susannah Petersen, b. ---, bapt. --- by Rev. Abraham Reinke.

Sarah Lynmeyer, dau of Christopher and Ann Lynmeyer of Penn's Neck, b. 19 Jun 1745, bapt. 7 Jul 1746 by Rev. John C. Poyrlaeus.

Jonah Jones, son of Joseph and Margaret Jones of Morris River, b. 1

Aug 1745, bapt. 6 Jul 1746 by Rev. J. C. Poyrlaeus.
Catherine Gill, dau of Matthew and Magdalene Gill, b. 2 Jan 1746, bapt. 2 Jan 1747 by Rev. Matthew Gottshalk.
Samuel Hoffman, son of John and Elizabeth Hoffman, b. 18 Jan 1746, bapt. 6 Jul 1746 by Rev. J. C. Poyraleus.
Mary Hoffman, dau of Peter and Mary Hoffman of Morris River, b. 1 Jun 1746, bapt. 6 Jul 1746 by Rev. J. C. Poyraleus.
Matthew Hoffman, son of Frederick and Catherine Hoffman of Morris River, b. 27 Jun 1746, bapt. 6 Jul 1746 by Rev. J. C. Poyraleus.
Zachariah Petersen, son of Zachariah and Magdalene Petersen of Raccoon, b. 30 Jun 1746, bapt. 7 Jul by Rev. J. C. Poyraleus.
Christopher Lynmeyer, son of Christopher and Ann Lynmeyer, b. 5 Jul 1746, bapt. 7 Jul 1746 by Rev. J. C. Poyraleus.
Nathaniel Guest, son of William and Christina Guest, b. 3 Oct 1746, bapt. 13 Oct 1746 by Rev. J. C. Poyraleus.
Rebecca Jones, dau of Abraham and Guila Jones of Morris River, b. 5 Dec 1746, bapt. 7 Dec 1746 by Rev. J. C. Poyraleus.
Elizabeth Lowlander, dau of Abraham and Elizabeth Lowlander of Morris River, b. ---, bapt. 7 Dec 1746 by Rev. Abraham Reinke.
William Cobb, son of Samuel and Catherine Cobb of Morris River, b. ---, bapt. 7 Dec 1746 by Rev. Abraham Reinke.
John and Abraham Keen, twin sons of Eric and Catherine Keen of Morris River, b. 10 May 1747, bapt. by Rev. M. Gottshalk.
John Mulicka, son of Eric and Catherine Mulicka of Morris River, b. 17 Dec 1747, bapt. by Rev. Laurence Nyberg.
Isaac Vanneman, son of John and Mary Vanneman of Piles Grove, b. 19 Dec 1747, bapt. by Rev. Laurence Nyberg.
Joseph Guest, son of William and Christina Guest of Raccoon, b. 25 Dec 1747, bapt. by John Wade.
Deborah Gill, dau of Matthew and Magdalene Gill of Raccoon, b. 1 Jan 1748, bapt. by Rev. John Wade.
Christina Lynmeyer, dau of Christopher and Ann Lynmeyer of Penn's Neck, b. 26 Mar, bapt. 23 Oct 1748 by Rev. A. Reinke.
Frederick Hoffman, son of Frederick and Catherine Hoffman of Morris River, b. 1 Aug, bapt. 30 Nov 1748 by Rev. Abraham Reinke.
Mary Holstine, dau of Lawrence Holstine of Piles Grove, b. 11 Nov, bapt. 27 Nov 1748 by Rev. A. Reinke.
Andrew Kemp, son of Paul and Jane Kemp of Morris River, b. 31 Mar, bapt. by Rev. John Wade.
Ann Gracebury, dau of William and Mary Gracebury of Penn's Neck, b. 28 Jun, bapt. 3 Jul 1749 by Rev. John Wade.

William Avise, son of George and Jane Avise of Oldman's Creek, b. 17 Aug 1749, bapt. by Rev. Lawrence Nyberg.

Thomas Keen, son of Eric and Catherine Keen of Morris River, b. 3 Dec 1749, bapt. 7 Dec 1749 by Rev. John Wade.

Nicholas Lynmeyer, son of Christopher and Ann Lynmeyer of Penn's Neck, b. 24 Feb 1750, bapt. by Rev. Lawrence Nyberg.

Mary Gill, dau of Matthew and Magdalene Gill, b. 15 Mar 1750, bapt. 21 Apr 1750 by Rev. Abraham Reinke.

Sarah Jones, dau of Joseph and Margaret Jones of Morris River, b. 30 Oct, bapt. 25 Jan 1751 by Rev. Abraham Reinke.

Catherine Guest, dau of William and Christina Guest of Racoon, b. 18 Nov 1750, bapt. 22 Jan 1751 by Rev. Abraham Reinke.

Abraham Hoffman, son of Frederick and Catherine Hoffman of Morris River, b. 10 Dec 1750, bapt. 19 Jan 1751.

James Avise, son of George and Jane Avise of Oldman's Creek, b. 2 Dec 1750, bapt. 16 Aug 1751 by Rev. Abraham Reinke.

Charles Lloyd, dau of Obadiah and Rebecca Lloyd of Piles Grove, b. 12 Mar, bapt. 12 Apr 1752 by Rev. Abraham Reinke.

Christiana Gill, dau of Matthew and Magdalene Gill, b. 16 Mar 1752, bapt. by Rev. Matthew Reitz.

Mary Guest, dau of William and Christiana Guest, b. 8 Oct 1752, bapt. by Rev. Matthew Reitz.

John Holstine, son of Lawrence and Margaret Holstine of Piles Grove, b. 10 Nov, bapt. 16 Nov 1752 by Rev. Matthew Reitz.

Catherine Hoffman, dau of John and Catherine Hoffman of Morris River, b. 21 Jan, bapt. 28 Jan 1753 by Rev. Matthew Reitz.

Peter Lauterbach, son of Conrad and Elizabeth Lauterbach of Piles Grove, b. 3 Feb, bapt. 5 Feb 1753 by Rev. Matthew Reitz.

Peter Vaneman, son of Catherine and Peter Vaneman of Penn's Neck, b. 9 Dec, bapt. 16 Dec 1753 by Rev. Matthew Reitz.

Susanna Holstein, dau of Lawrence and Margaret Holstein of Piles Grove, b. 19 Dec 1753, bapt. 6 Jan 1754 by Rev. Matthew Reitz.

Ann Lynmeyer, dau of Christopher and Ann Lynmeyer of Penn's Neck, b. 6 Jan 1754, bapt. by Rev. Matthew Reitz.

Michael Katz, son of Michael and Mary Katz of Penn's Neck, bapt. 8 Jan 1754 by Rev. Matthew Reitz.

Zaccheus Avise, son of George and Jane Avise of Oldman's Creek, b. 28 Jan 1754, bapt. by Rev. Matthew Reitz.

Sarah Lloyd, dau of Obadiah and Rebecca Lloyd of Piles Grove, b. 30 Mar, bapt. 7 Apr 1754 by Rev. Matthew Reitz.

Rebecca Lloyd, dau of Beekman and Lydia Lloyd of Piles Grove, b. 6

Nov 1754, bapt. 21 Mar 1755 by Rev. Ernest Gambold.
Adam and Mathias Lauterbach, twin sons of Conrad and Elizabeth Lauterbach, b. 28 Nov 1754, bapt. 30 Mar 1755 by Rev. Ernest Gambold.
Elizabeth Hoffman, dau of John and Elizabeth Hoffman of Morris River, b. 3 Jan, bapt. 6 Apr 1755 by Rev. Ernest Gambold.
Matthew Gill, son of Matthew and Magdalena Gill of Racoon Creek, b. 7 Feb, bapt. 720 Mar 1755 by Rev. Ernest Gambold.
Michael Kats, son of Jacob and Barbara Kats of Penn's Neck, b. 14 Mar, bapt. 9 Apr 1755 by Rev. Ernest Gambold.
George Shute, son of William and Ann Shute of Oldman's Creek, b. 18 Apr, bapt. 18 May 1755 by Rev. John Brandmiller.
Rebecca Lloyd, wife of Obadiah Lloyd, b. 4 Jul 1731, bapt. 20 Mar 1755 by Rev. A. Reinke.
Benjamin Guest, son of William and Christiana Guest of Racoon Creek, b. 20 Jul, bapt. 7 Aug 1755 by Rev. Ernest Gambold.
Mary Adams, dau of Abraham and Bridget Adams of Racoon Creek, bapt. 13 Jan 1756 by Rev. Ernest Gambold.
Ann Gambold, dau of Ernest and Eleanor Gambold of Oldman's Creek, b. 9 Feb, bapt. 19 Feb 1756 by Rev. Thomas Yarrell.
Rosine Kats, dau of Michael and Mary Kats of Penn's Neck, b. 1 Apr, bapt. 5 May 1756 by Rev. Ernest Gambold.
Joseph Avise, son of George and Jane Avise, b. 31 Mar, bapt. 27 May 1756 by Rev. Ernest Gambold.
William Holstine, son of Lawrence and Margaret Holstine of Piles Grove, b. 19 Mar, bapt. 15 May 1756 by Rev. Ernest Gambold.
Daniel Vanneman, son of Peter and Catherine Vanneman of Penn's Neck, b. 29 May, bapt. 2 Jun 1756 by Rev. Ernest Gambold.
Bateman Lloyd, son of Bateman and Lydia Lloyd of Piles Grove, b. 28 Aug, bapt. 24 Oct 1756 by Rev. Ernest Gambold.
Samuel Lloyd, son of Obadiah and Rebecca Lloyd of Piles Grove, b. 25 Oct, bapt. 18 Nov 1756 by Rev. Ernest Gambold.
William Shute, son of William and Annie Shute of Oldman's Grove, b. 6 Apr, bapt. 15 May 1757 by Rev. Ernest Gambold.
Martin Kats, son of Jacob and Barbara Kats of Penn's Neck, b. 15 May, bapt. 8 Jun 1757 by Rev. Ernest Gambold.
Conrad Lauterbach, son of Conrad and Elizabeth Lauterbach, b. 16 May, bapt. 22 Jun 1757 by Rev. Ernest Gambold.
Samuel Vanneman, son of Samuel and Sarah Vanneman of Morris River, b. 20 Mar 1756, bapt. 7 Jul 1757 by Rev. Ernest Gambold.
Mary Hoffman, dau of Frederick and Catherine Hoffman of Morris

River, b. 11 Jan 1755, bapt. 5 Dec 1757 by Rev. Ernest Gambold.

Margaret Vanneman, dau of David and Mehetabel Vanneman of Morris River, b. 6 Oct 1756, bapt. 3 Dec 1757 by Rev. Ernest Gambold.

Samuel Jones, son of Joseph and Margaret Jones of Morris River, b. 19 Apr 1756, bapt. 3 Dec 1757 by Rev. Ernest Gambold.

Rebecca Steelman, dau of Charles and Anne Steelman of Morris River, b. 7 Jan 1756, bapt. 3 Dec 1757 by Rev. Ernest Gambold.

Margaret Hoffman, dau of John and Elizabeth Hoffman of Morris River, b. 20 May 1756, bapt. 3 Dec 1757 by Rev. Ernest Gambold.

Jane Jones, dau of Abraham and Jane Jones of Morris River, b. 7 Jul 1756, bapt. 3 Dec 1757 by Rev. Ernest Gambold.

Andrew Holstein, son of Lawrence Holstein of Piles Grove, b. 6 Oct 1756, bapt. 1 Jan 1757 by Rev. Ernest Gambold.

Priscilla Adams, dau of Abraham and Bridget Adams of Racoon Creek, b. 10 Sep 1756, bapt. 18 Mar 1757 by Rev. Ernest Gambold.

Hannah Avise, dau of George and Jane Avise of Oldman's Creek, b. 26 Apr, bapt. 2 Jul 1758 by Rev. Jasper Payne.

Joseph Shute, son of William, Jr., and Ann Shute of Oldman's Creek, b. 21 Sep 1758, bapt. by Rev. C. Otto Kemjstoop. Sponsors: Magdalena Gill, Obadiah Lloyd, William Guest and Christiana Guest.

Sarah Guest, dau of William and Christiana Guest of Racoon Creek, b. 9 Oct 1758, bapt. by Rev. C. O. Kemjstoop. Sponsors: Obadiah Lloyd, Magdalena Gill, William Shute and Ann Shute.

Daniel Lloyd, son of Obadiah and Rebecca Lloyd of Piles Grove, b. 31 Oct 1758, bapt. by Rev. C. O. Kemjstoop.

Josiah Gill, son of Matthew and Magdalena Gill of Racoon Creek, b. 21 Aug 1759, bapt. 6 Aug 1760 by Rev. Paul Daniel Boyocelius.

Rebecca Hoffman, dau of Lawrence and Sarah Hoffman of Piles Grove, b. 14 Feb, bapt. 5 Aug 1760 by Rev. Paul Daniel Boyocelius.

Sarah Holstein, dau of Lawrence and Margaret Holstein of Piles Grove, b. 17 Jun 1760, bapt. by Rev. Paul Daniel Boyocelius.

Marianna Kats, dau of Martin and Anne Kats, b. 30 Jan 1759, bapt. by Rev. Joseph Payne.

Jacob Kats, son of Jacob and Margaret Kats of Penn's Neck, b. ---, bapt. by Rev. Paul Daniel Boyocelius.

Elizabeth Jones, dau of Jacob and Ann Jones of Racoon Creek, b. ---, bapt. by Rev. Paul Daniel Boyocelius.

Mary Jones, dau of Andrew and Mary Jones of Racoon Creek, b. 18 May 1760, bapt. by Rev. Paul Daniel Boyocelius.

Martin Kats, son of Martin and Anna Kats of Penn's Neck, b. 17 Aug, bapt. 17 Sep 1750 by Rev. Paul Daniel Boyocelius.

Jaconias Lloyd, son of Obadiah and Rebecca Lloyd of Piles Grove, b. 25 Feb, bapt. 8 May 1761 by Rev. C.O. Kemjstoop. Sponsors: William and Christiana Guest, Ann Lynmeyer and Jaconias Wood.

Diana Shute, dau of William and Ann Shute of Oldman's Creek, b. 6 Nov 1760, bapt. 4 Mar 1761 by Rev. Christian O. Kemjstoop.

Rachel Avise, dau of George and Ann Avise of Oldman's Creek, b. 13 Jan, bapt. 4 Mar 1761 by Rev. C. O. Kemjstoop. Witnesses: William and Christian Guest, William and Ann Shute.

Jacob Lloyd, son of Bateman and Lydia Lloyd of Piles Grove, b. 10 Dec 1761, bapt. 28 Oct 1762 by Rev. George Neisser.

Benjamin Hoffman, son of Lawrence and Sarah Hoffman of Piles Grove, b. 25 Nov 1761, bapt. 29 Oct 1762 by Rev. George Neisser. Sponsors: Jackoniah Wood and Theodore Neisser.

Margaret Holstein, dau of Lawrence and Margaret Holstein of Piles Grove, b. 8 Oct, bapt. 1 Nov 1762 by Rev. George Neisser. Sponsors: William and Christiana Guest, Obadiah and Rebecca Lloyd.

Dorothea Kats, dau of Martin and Anne Kats of Penn's Neck, b. 29 Jan 1762, bapt. at Philadelphia, 6 Jul 1752 by Rev. George Neisser. Sponsors: Grandparents and Anna Parsons.

Isaac Lloyd, son of Obadiah and Rebecca Lloyd of Piles Grove, b. 22 May, bapt. 28 May 1763 by Rev. Chas. Godfrey Rundt. Sponsors: William and Catherine Guest.

William and Ann, twins of William, Jr., (dec'd) and Anne Shute, b. 4 Jun 1763, bapt. next day by Rev. Chas. Godfrey Rundt. Sponsors: William and Christiana Guest, Magdalena Gill, wife of Matthew.

Rebecca Avise, dau of George and Ann Avise of Oldman's Creek, b. 5 Feb, bapt. 5 Jun 1763 by Rev. Chas. Godfrey Rundt. Sponsors: William and Christiana Guest.

James Hoffman, son of Lawrence and Sarah Hoffman of Piles Grove, b. 26 Jan, bapt. 1 Apr 1764 by Rev. Chas. Godfrey Rundt.

James Gill, son of Matthew and Magdalene Gill of Racoon Creek, b. 3 Oct 1753, bapt. 1 Apr 1764 by Rev. Chas. Godfrey Rundt.

Lawrence and Hannah Holstein, twins of Lawrence and Margaret Holstein of Piles Grove, b. 27 Nov, bapt. 9 Dec 1764 by Rev. Geo. Neisser. Sponsors: William Guest and Obadiah Lloyd.

Elizabeth Murphy, dau of Henry and Isabel Murphy of Oldman's Creek, b. 2 May, bapt. 17 Aug 1765 by Rev. Nic. Henry Eberhardt. Sponsors: William and Christiana Guest and Mary Gill.

Alexander Linmeyer, son of Andrew and Elizabeth Linmeyer of Penn's Neck, b. 6 Oct, bapt. 28 Nov 1764 by Rev. Nicholas Henry Eberhardt. Sponsors: William Guest, Obadiah and Rebecca Lloyd.

Obadiah Lloyd, son of Obadiah and Rebecca Lloyd of Piles Grove, b. 15 Nov, bapt. 28 Nov 1765 by Rev. N. H. Eberhardt. Sponsors: John Lloyd, Laurence and Sarah Hoffman.

Uri Hoffman, son of Lawrence and Sarah Hoffman, b. 24 Feb, bapt. 23 Mar 1766 by Rev. N. H. Eberhardt. Sponsors: William Guest, Sr., Obadiah Lloyd and Mary Sparks.

Wood Lloyd, son of John and Polly Lloyd of Woodstown, b. 6 Feb, bapt. 17 Apr 1766 by Rev. N. H. Eberhardt. Sponsors: Obadiah Lloyd, Lawrence and Sarah Hoffman.

Catherine Kats, dau of Martin and Anne Kats of Penn's Neck, b. 12 Jan, bapt. 29 Jun 1766 by Rev. N. H. Eberhardt. Sponsors: Obadiah Lloyd, Andrew and Mary Vanneman.

Hannah Gill, dau of Matthew and Magdalene Gill of Racoon Creek, b. 17 Dec 1766, bapt. 8 Jan 1767 by Rev. N. H. Eberhardt. Sponsors: Sarah Eberhardt, Mary Sparks, Lawrence and Sarah Hoffman.

Hannah Guest, dau of William, Jr., and Hannah Guest, dec'd, of Greenwich Twp, b. 9 Sep 1766, bapt. 15 Jan 1767 by Rev. N. H. Eberhardt. Sponsors: William, Sr. and Christina Guest, Obadiah and Rebecca Lloyd.

Catherine Holstein, dau of Lawrence and Ann Holstein, b. 10 Sep 1766, bapt. 8 Feb 1767 by Rev. N. H. Eberhardt. Sponsors: William Guest, Jr., and Obadiah Lloyd.

William Shute, son of Henry and Lydia Shute, b. 25 Sep, buried 4 Oct 1767. (was not baptized)

Sarah Murphy, dau Henry and Isabel Murphy of Penn's Neck, b. 31 Oct, bapt. 25 Dec 1767 by Rev. Frederick Smith. Sponsors: George Avise, John and Agnes Avise.

Ann Avise, dau of John and Agnes Avise, b. 10 Jan, bapt. 7 Feb 1768 by Rev. Frederick Smith. Sponsors: George Avise, Matthew and Magdalene Gill.

Benjamin Lloyd, son of Obadiah and Rebecca Lloyd of Piles Grove, b. 14 Feb, bapt. 10 Mar 1768 by Rev. Frederick Smith. Sponsors: Lawrence and Sarah Hoffman, Mary Sparks.

Thomas Shute, son of Isaac and Susanna Shute of Oldman's Creek, b. 22 Apr, bapt. 4 May 1768 by Rev. Frederick Smith. Sponsors: the parents and Mary Dalbow.

Sarah Hoffman, dau of Lawrence and Sarah Hoffman of Piles Grove, b. 21 Apr, bapt. 29 May 1768 by Rev. Frederick Smith. Sponsors: Obadiah Lloyd, Mary Sparks and Magdalene Gill.

Lawrence Holstein, son of Lawrence and Ann Holstein, b. 6 Jun, bapt. 24 Jul 1768 by Rev. Frederick Smith. Sponsors: Obadiah Lloyd,

William Guest, Sr. and wife.
Joseph Eastlack, son of William and Mary Dorcas Eastlack bapt. by Rev. Frederick Smith.
John Kohl, son of John and Ann Kohl, b. 22 Aug, bapt. 9 Oct 1768 by Rev. Frederick Smith. Sponsors: John and George Avise, William Guest, Sr.
John Kats, son of Martin and Ann Kats, b. 5 Aug, bapt. 6 Nov 1768 by Rev. Frederick Smith. Sponsors: Andrew and Mary Vanneman, Obadiah Lloyd.
Sarah Agness Avis, wife of John Avis, b. 12 Nov 1747, bapt. 23 Nov 1768 by Rev. Frederick Smith. Sponsors: Bishop Nathaniel and Ann Johanna Seidel, George and Jane Avis and Sarah Smith.
Lawrence Linmeyer, son of Andrew and Elizabeth, b. 28 Oct, bapt. 4 Dec 1768 by Rev. Frederick Smith. Sponsors: Andrew and Mary Vannerman, William Guest, Sr.
Deborah Shute, dau of Henry and Lydia Shute, b. 13 Nov, bapt. 25 Dec 1768 by Rev. Frederick Smith. Sponsors: Joseph and Sarah Shute, Isaac and Susanna Shute.
Henry Shute (called William), b. 26 Feb 1746, bapt. 24 Mar 1769 and his wife, Lydia (called Hannah before), b. 22 Jan 1746, bapt. 24 Mar 1769 by Rev. Frederick Smith. Sponsors: William Guest and Joseph Shute.
Diana Estlack (named Mary), wife of William Estlack, bapt. 23 Nov 1769 by Rev. Frederick Smith. Sponsors: William Guest, Joseph Shute and Mary Sparks.
Ann Briarly, dau of John and Mary Briarly of Piles Grove, b. 2 Sep 1769; bapt. 4 Feb 1770 by Rev. Frederick Smith. Sponsors: Mary Sparks, John and Agnes Avis.
Catherine Weisner, dau of Jacob and Mary Weisner of Penn's Neck, b. 3 Oct 1769, bapt. 31 Dec 1769 by Rev. Frederick Smith. Sponsors: William Guest, Obadiah Lloyd and Sarah Smith.
Rebecca Lloyd, dau of Obadiah and Rebecca Lloyd of Piles Grove, b. 5 Feb, bapt. 18 Mar 1770 by Rev. Frederick Smith. Sponsors: Joseph and Sarah Shute and Mary Sparks.
Levi Shute, son of Isaac and Susanna Shute, b. 2 Apr, bapt. 10 Apr 1770 by Rev. Frederick Smith. Sponsors: the parents and Sarah Gill.
John Avis, son of John and Agnes Avis, b. 22 Mar, bapt. 15 Apr 1770 by Rev. Frederick Smith. Sponsors: Geo. and Jane Avis and Sarah Smith.
Thomas Estlack, son of William and Diana Estlack, b. 24 Nov 1768, bapt. 22 Jul 1770 by Rev. Frederick Smith. Sponsors: Joseph and

Sarah Shute and William Guest.

Ruth Shirbe, dau of Joseph and Sarah Shirbe, b. 24 Nov, bapt. 17 Dec 1770 by Rev. Frederick Smith. Sponsors: the parents, Sarah Smith and Sarah Agnes Avis.

Rebecca Murphy, dau of Henry and Isabel Murphy, b. 11 Nov 1770, bapt. 2 Jan 1771 by Rev. Frederick Smith. Sponsors: Sarah Agnes Avis, George, Sr. and Jane Avis.

Richard Holton, son of James and Christine Holton, b. 6 Dec 1770, bapt. 23 Mar 1771 by Rev. Frederick Smith. Sponsors: Obadiah Lloyd and Andrew Vannerman.

Sarah Kats, dau of Martin and Ann Kats of Penn's Neck, b. 23 Feb, bapt. 5 May 1771 by Rev. Frederick Smith. Sponsors: Joseph and Mary Shute, Mary Vanneman.

Idy Shute, dau of Henry and Lydia Shute, b. 5 May, bapt. 23 Jun 1771 by Rev. Frederick Smith. Sponsors: Isaac and Susanna Shute, William Guest, Sr.

Ann Hoffman, dau of Lawrence and Sarah Hoffman, b. 18 Jul, bapt. 11 Aug 1771 by Rev. Frederick Smith. Sponsors: Mary Sparks, John and Agnes Avis, Sarah Smith.

Flora, named Rhoda, a mulatto belonging to Joseph and Mary Aply, b. in East Jersey in Mar 1737, bapt. 29 Sep 1771 by Rev. Frederick Smith. Sponsors: Obadiah and Rebecca Lloyd, William and Christina Guest, Deborah Gill.

Sarah Estlack, dau of William and Diane Estlack, b. 21 Dec 1771, bapt. 3 Feb 1772 by Rev. Frederick Smith. Sponsors: Joseph and Sarah Shute, John and Agnes Avis.

Kesiah Kohl, dau of John and Ann Kohl, b. 2 Jun, bapt. 15 Jun 1772 by Rev. Frederick Smith. Sponsors: William and Christina Guest, Catherine Guest.

Sarah Briarly, dau of John and Mary Briarly, b. 6 Dec 1771, bapt. 21 Jun 1772 by Rev. Frederick Smith. Sponsors: John and Agnes Avis, Obadiah and Rebecca Lloyd.

Sarah Avis, dau of John and Agnes Avis, b. 23 Jul, bapt. 23 Aug 1772 by Rev. Frederick Smith. Sponsors: Geo. and Jane Avis, Joseph and Sarah Shute.

Joseph Uriel Shute, son of Isaac and Susanne Shute, b. 27 Oct, bapt. 13 Nov 1772 by Rev. Frederick Smith. Sponsors: the parents.

Elizabeth Dorsey, dau of Daniel and Elizabeth Dorsey, b. 8 May, bapt. 8 Dec 1772 by Rev. Frederick Smith. Sponsors: Andrew and Mary Vanneman, Henry Murphy.

James Holton, son of James and Christine Holton, b. 2 Dec, bapt. 25

Dec 1772 by Rev. Frederick Smith. Sponsors: John and Agnes Avis, William Guest and Mary Vanerman.

William Estlack, son of William and Diane Estlack, b. 26 Feb 1767, bapt. 5 Jun 1773 by Rev. Frederick Smith. Sponsors: the parents and Isaac Shute.

John Lloyd, son of Obadiah and Rebecca Lloyd, b. 25 Nov 1772, bapt. 10 Jan 1773 by Rev. Frederick Smith. Sponsors: John and Agnes Avis, Joseph and Sarah Shute.

Sarah Franklin, dau of William, dec'd, and Sarah Franklin, b. 26 May 1772, bapt. 10 Jan 1773 by Rev. Frederick Smith. Sponsors: William and Catherine Guest.

Rachel Hoffman, dau of John and Sarah Hoffman, b. 9 Dec 1770, bapt. 8 Feb 1773 by Rev. Frederick Smith. Sponsors: the parents and Lawrence Hoffman.

William Shute, son of Thomas and Sarah Shute, b. ---, bapt. 16 Feb 1773 by Rev. Frederick Smith. Sponsors: the parents.

Mary Wood, dau of Jachomiah and Christine Wood, b. 16 Mar, bapt. 4 Apr 1773 by Rev. Frederick Smith. Sponsors: the parents.

William Guest, son of Henry and Jane Guest b. 24 Jun, bapt. 8 Aug 1773 by Rev. Frederick Smith. Sponsors: William and Christine Guest, John and Agnes Avis.

Isaac Shute, son of Henry and Lydia Shute, b. 23 Jul, bapt. 15 Aug 1773 by Rev. Frederick Smith. Sponsors: Joseph and Sarah Shute, Isaac Shute and Wm. Guest, Sr.

Sarah Barber, dau of Aquila Barber, b. 4 Jun 1744, bapt. 4 Sep 773 by Rev. Frederick Smith.

John Murphy, son of Henry and Isabel Murphy, b. 31 Jul, bapt. 5 Sep 1773 by Rev. Frederick Smith. Sponsors: George and Jane Avis, Andrew and Mary Vaneman.

Joseph Holstein, dau of Lawrence and Ann Holstein, b. 14 Jan, bapt. 5 Sep 1773 by Rev. Frederick Smith. Sponsors: Andrew Lynmier, Andrew and Mary Vanerman.

Catherine Wood, dau of Jachomia and Christine Wood, b. 31 Jan, bapt. 10 Feb 1774 by Rev. Frederick Smith. Sponsors: John and Agnes Avis, Lawrence and Sarah Hoffman, Ann Lynmier.

Lydia Briarly, dau of John and Mary Briarly, b. 20 Jan, bapt. 3 Apr 1774 by Rev. Frederick Smith. Sponsors: Lawrence and Sarah Hoffman, John Avis and Mary Sparks.

Hannah Shute, dau of Isaac and Susanne Shute, b. 15 Mar, bapt. 10 Apr 1774 by Rev. Frederick Smith. Sponsors: Joseph and Sarah Shute, John and Agnes Avis.

Christine Avis, dau of James and Mary Avis, b. 15 Apr, bapt. 15 May 1774 by Rev. Frederick Smith. Sponsors: William and Christine Guest.

Samuel Estlack, son of William and Diane Estlack, b. 30 Apr, bapt. 29 May 1774 by Rev. Frederick Smith. Sponsors: Joseph and Sarah Shute, John and Agnes Avis.

Elizabeth Avis, dau of John and Agnes Avis, b. 3 Oct 1766, bapt. on her sickbed 14 Aug 1774 by Rev. Frederick Smith. Sponsors: the parents and George and Jane Avis.

Jesse Hoffman, son of Lawrence and Sarah Hoffman, b. 17 Sep, bapt. 9 Oct 1774 by Rev. Frederick Smith. Sponsors: Joseph and Sarah Shute, George and Jane Avis.

Mary Guest, dau of Joseph and Sarah Guest b. 24 Oct, bapt. 27 Nov 1774 by Rev. Frederick Smith. Sponsors: William and Christine Guest, George and Jane Avis, Gerrit Vanerman.

Nicholas Linmeyer Holton, son of James and Christine Holton, b. 20 Nov, bapt. 25 Dec 1774 by Rev. Frederick Smith. Sponsors: John and Agnes Avis, Joseph and Sarah Shute.

Jonathan Guest, son of Henry and Jane Guest, b. ---, bapt. 19 Feb 1775 by Rev. Frederick Smith. Sponsors: William and Christine Guest, George and Jane Avis.

Mary Avis, dau of John and Agnes Avis, b. 25 Feb, bapt. 25 Mar 1775 by Rev. Frederick Smith. Sponsors: George. and Jane Avis, Joseph and Sarah Shute, Sarah Gill.

Elizabeth Griffith, dau of John and Hannah Griffith of Penn's Neck, bapt. 6 Mary 1775 by Rev. Frederick Smith. Sponsors: Gerrit, Andrew and Mary Vaneman.

Hannah Avis, wife of George Avis, Jr., bapt. 18 Jun 1775 by Rev. Frederick Smith. Sponsors: her husband, Joseph and Sarah Shute.

Phoebe Armstrong, dau of William and Sarah Armstrong Penn's Neck, b. 21 Jun, bapt. 16 Jul 1775 by Rev. Frederick Smith. Sponsors: William and Christine Guest, John and Agnes Avis.

Samuel Shute, son of Henry and Lydia Shute, b. 30 Jun, bapt. 30 Jul 1775 by Rev. Frederick Smith. Sponsors: George and Jane Avis, Isaac and Susan Shute.

Benjamin Wood, son of Jachomia and Christiana Wood, b. 20 Sep, bapt. 12 Oct 1775 by Rev. Frederick Smith. Sponsors: the parents and William and Mary Gill.

Rebecca Estlack, dau of William and Diana Estlack, b. 20 Jan, bapt. 3 Mar 1776 by Rev. Frederick Smith. Sponsors: John and Agnes Avis, Isaac Shute, Sally Gill.

James Avis, son of James and Mary Avis, b. 25 Feb, bapt. 24 Mar 1776 by Rev. Frederick Smith. Sponsors: William Guest, John and Agnes Avis, Jane Avis.

Susana Linmein, with the name of Sarah, dau of Daniel and Sarah Cassell, (Quakers), b. 12 Dec 1734 at Brandywine, PA., bapt. 7 Apr 1776 by Rev. Frederick Smith. Sponsors: George and Jane Avis, John and Agnes Avis, Mary Vaneman.

James Holstein, son of Lawrence and Ann Holstein, bapt. 2 Jun 1776 by Rev. Frederick Smith. Sponsors: William and Christiana Guest, Garrit and Mary Vaneman.

Evie Hoffman, dau of John and Sarah Hoffman, b. 24 Apr, bapt. 16 Jun 1776 by Rev. Frederick Smith. Sponsors: Isaac and Susan Shute, William Guest, Sarah Hoffman.

Sarah Vaneman, dau of Gerrit and Catherine Vaneman, b. 6 Jun, bapt. 7 Jul 1776 by Rev. Frederick Smith. Sponsors: John and Agnes Avis, Mary Vaneman, Sarah and Deborah Gill.

Joseph Salsbury, son of John and Hannah Salsbury, b. 6 Jun, bapt. 14 Jul 1776 by Rev. Frederick Smith. Sponsors: Lawrence and Sarah Hoffman, William and Christiana Guest.

Peter Kats, son of Martin and Anna Kats, b. 10 Jun, bapt. 21 Jul 1776 by Rev. Frederick Smith. Sponsors: James and Mary Avis, Gerrit and Andrew Vaneman.

Sarah Pierson, dau of Zebulon and Mary Pierson, b. 29 Nov 1776, bapt. 12 Jan 1777 by Rev. Frederick Smith. Sponsors: William and Christine Guest, John and Agnes Avis.

Mary Holton, dau of James and Christine Holton, b. 1 Dec 176, bapt. 19 Jan 1777 by Rev. Frederick Smith. Sponsors: Andrew and Susan Linmier, Andrew and Catherine Vaneman.

James and Mary Guest, twins of Henry and Jane Guest, b. 20 Dec 1776, bapt. 9 Mar 1777 by Rev. Frederick Smith. Sponsors: William and Christine Guest, James and Mary Avis.

Susanna Shute, dau of Isaac and Susanna Shute, bapt. 22 Mar 1777 by Rev. Frederick Smith. Sponsors: George and Jane Avis, Joseph and Sarah Shute.

William Guest, son of Joseph and Sarah Guest, b. 2 Apr, bapt. 4 May 1777 by Rev. Frederick Smith. Sponsors: William and Christine Guest, James and Mary Avis.

Elizabeth Vaneman, dau of Peter and Rebecca Vaneman, b. 7 Feb, bapt. 4 May 1777 by Rev. Frederick Smith. Sponsors: Gerrit and Catherine Vaneman, John and Agnes Avis.

William Armstrong, son of William and Sarah Armstrong, b. 3 Mar, bapt. 11 May 1777 by Rev. Frederick Smith. Sponsors: George and Jane Avis, Andrew and Catherine Vaneman.

Ann Stratton, dau of Immanuel and Sarah Stratton, b. 4 Apr, bapt. 8 Jun 1777 by Rev. Frederick Smith. Sponsors: John and Anne Kohl, John and Agnes Avis.

Hannah Avis, dau of John and Agnes Avis, b. 23 Jun, bapt. 20 Jul 1777 by Rev. Frederick Smith. Sponsors: George and Jane Avis, James and Mary Avis.

Hannah Shute, dau of Joseph and Sarah Shute, b. 30 Jul, bapt. 24 Aug 1777 by Rev. Frederick Smith. Sponsors: Lawrence and Sarah Hoffman, William and Christine Guest.

Nathan Shute, son of Henry and Lydia Shute, b. 21 Oct, bapt. 4 Dec 1777 by Rev. Frederick Smith. Sponsors: Joseph and Sarah Shute, George and Jane Avis.

John Wood, son of Jochamia and Christine Wood, b. 17 Nov, bapt. 25 Dec 1777 by Rev. Frederick Smith. Sponsors: William Guest, Mary Gill, John and Agnes Avis.

William Avis, son of James and Mary Avis, b. 28 Feb, bapt. 8 Mar 1778 by Rev. Frederick Smith. Sponsors: Geo. and Jane Avis, Lawrence and Sarah Hoffman.

Mary Vaneman, dau of Gerrit and Catherine Vaneman, b. 25 Sep, bapt. 27 Oct 1778 by Rev. Frederick Smith. Sponsors: William Guest, Mary Gill, Sarah Gill and Andrew Vaneman.

Elizabeth Salsbury, dau of John and Hannah Salsbury, b. ---, bapt. 22 Nov 1778 by Rev. Frederick Smith. Sponsors: Joseph and Sarah Shute, John and Agnes Avis.

Christine Guest, dau of Henry and Jane Guest, b. ---, bapt. 29 Nov 1778 by Rev. Frederick Smith. Sponsors: William and Christine Guest, James and Mary Avis.

Christine Guest, dau of Joseph and Sarah Guest, b. 8 Dec, bapt. 10 Dec 1778 by Rev. Frederick Smith. Witnesses: the parents.

James Armstrong, son of William and Sarah Armstrong, b. 28 Nov 1778, bapt. 7 Jan 1779 by Rev. Frederick Smith. Sponsors: Andrew and Susana Linmeir, Gerrit and Mary Vaneman.

Samuel Burden, son of Samuel and Hannah Burden, b. 11 Mar, bapt. 2 Apr 1779 by Rev. Frederick Smith. Sponsors: George and Jane Avis, John and Agnes Avis.

Elizabeth Kats, dau of Mananna Kats, b. 23 Feb, bapt. 2 May 1779 by Rev. Frederick Smith. Sponsors: Martin Kats, John and Agnes Avis.

Mary Walker, dau of John and Dane Walker, b. 24 Aug 1778, bapt. 9 May 1779 by Rev. Frederick Smith. Sponsors: James and Mary Avis,

MORAVIAN REGISTER 129

William Guest.
Christine Holton, dau of James and Christine Holton, b. 29 Jul, bapt. 29 Aug 1779 by Rev. Frederick Smith.
Emmie Lauterbach, dau Mathias and Ann Lauterbach, b. 17 Jan, bapt. 30 May 1779 by Rev. Frederick Smith. Sponsors: William and Christine Guest, Elizabeth.
Lawrence Hoffman, son of John and Sarah Hoffman, b. 13 Jul, bapt. 5 Sep 1779 by Rev. Frederick Smith. Sponsors: Lawrence and Sarah Hoffman, James and Mary Avis.
George Straiten, son of Immanuel and Sarah Shute Straiten, bapt. 17 Sep 1779 by Rev. Frederick Smith. Sponsors: John and Ann Kohl, William Shute.
Jacob Helderman, son of George and Ann Helderman, bapt. 31 Oct 1779 by Rev. Frederick Smith. Sponsors: John and Agnes Avis, James and Mary Avis.
Mary Gill Wood, dau of Jochamia and Christine Wood, b. 22 Nov 1779, bapt. 8 Jan 1780 by Rev. Frederick Smith. Sponsors: the parents and Mary Gill.
John Estlack, son of William and Dinah Estlack, b. 13 Dec 1779, bapt. 16 Jan 1780 by Rev. Frederick Smith. Sponsors: George and Jane Avis, William Guest.
Elizabeth Avis, dau of Zekias and Susanna Avis, b. 9 Feb, bapt. 12 Mar 1780 by Rev. Frederick Smith. Sponsors: James and Mary Avis, George and Jane Avis.
Rebecca Shute, dau of Henry and Lydia Shute, b. ---, bapt. 24 Mar 1780 by Rev. Frederick Smith. Sponsors: Joseph and Sarah Shute, John and Agnes Avis.
Ebenezer Vaneman, son of Peter and Rebecca Vaneman, b. 31 Jan, bapt. 26 Mar 1780 by Rev. Frederick Smith. Sponsors: Gerrit and Catherine Vaneman, Andrew and Catherine Vaneman.
Charlotte Helderman, dau of Jacob and --- Helderman, b. 24 Mar, bapt. 7 May 1780 by Rev. Frederick Smith. Sponsors: the parents.
Hannah Salsbury, wife of John Salsbury, bapt. 14 May 1780 by Rev. Frederick Smith. Sponsors: George and Jane Avis, Lawrence and Jacob Hoffman.
Jane Guest, wife of Henry Guest, bapt. 14 May 1780 by Rev. Frederick Smith. Sponsors: William and Christine Guest, James and Mary Avis.
Joseph Shute, son of Joseph and Sarah Shute, bapt. 4 Jun 1780 by Rev. Frederick Smith. Sponsors: John and Agnes Avis, William and Daniel Easby.
Rebecca Avis, dau of John and Agnes Avis, b. 19 Jun, bapt. 15 Jul 1780

by Rev. Frederick Smith. Sponsors: George and Jane Avis, James and Mary Avis.

John Guest, son of Joseph and Sarah Guest, b. ---, bapt. 14 Oct 1780 by Rev. Frederick Smith. Sponsors: William and Christine Guest, Andrew and Catherine Vaneman.

Sarah Armstrong, dau of William and Sarah Armstrong, b. 15 Sep, bapt. 29 Oct 1780 by Rev. Frederick Smith. Sponsors: Gerrit and Catherine Vaneman, Andrew and Susanna Linmier.

Elizabeth Linmier, dau of Christopher and Rebecca Linmier, b. 13 Oct, bapt. 13 Dec 1780 by Rev. Frederick Smith. Sponsors: Andrew and Susanna Linmier, Andrew and Catherine Guest.

Catherine Avis, dau of James and Mary Avis, b. 8 Jan, bapt. 11 Jan 1781 by Rev. Frederick Smith. Sponsors: William and Christine Guest, George and Jane Avis.

Christine Vaneman, dau of Gerrit and Catherine Vanerman, b. 15 May, bapt. 10 Jun 1781 by Rev. Frederick Smith. Sponsors: Andrew and Catherine Vaneman, Mary Vaneman.

Jane Johnston, dau of Benjamin and Rachel Johnston, b. 19 Jul, bapt. 20 Jul 1781 by Rev. Frederick Smith. Sponsors: the parents and Jane Avis.

Martha Lauterbach, dau of Mathias and Ann Lauterbach, b. Jul 2, bapt. 12 Aug 1781 by Rev. Frederick Smith. Sponsors: John and Agnes Avis, Elizabeth Lauterbach.

Sarah Wood, dau of Jachomia and Christine Wood, b. 10 Sep, bapt. 20 Sep 1781 by Rev. Frederick Smith. Sponsors: the parents, Sarah and Polly Gill.

Samuel Salsbury, son of John and Hannah Salsbury, b. 13 Nov, bapt. 2 Dec 1781 by Rev. Frederick Smith. Sponsors: William and Christine Guest, James and Mary Avis.

Samuel Guest, son of Henry and Jane Guest, b. 8 Nov, bapt. 7 Dec 1781 by Rev. Frederick Smith. Sponsors: the parents.

Immanuel Straiten, son of Immanuel and Sarah Straiten, b. 31 Jul 1781, bapt. 6 Jan 1782 by Rev. Frederick Smith. Sponsors: William and Christine Guest and Ann Kohl.

Catherine Vaneman, dau of Peter and Rebecca Vaneman, b. 12 Dec 1781, bapt. 21 Jan 1782 by Rev. Frederick Smith. Sponsors: the parents.

Anna Holton, dau of James and Christine Holton, b. 29 Dec 1781, bapt. 17 Feb 1782 by Rev. Frederick Smith. Sponsors: Andrew and Susanna Linmeir, Andrew and Catherine Vaneman.

Mary Avis, dau of William and Ann Avis, b. 15 Jan, bapt. 10 Mar 1782

by Rev. Frederick Smith. Sponsors: George and Jane Avis, James and Mary Avis.
Susanna Avis, dau of Joseph and Sarah Avis, b. 10 Mar, bapt. 14 Apr 1782 by Rev. Frederick Smith. Sponsors: George and Jane Avis, John and Agnes Avis.
Deborah Hoffman, dau of John and Sarah Hoffman, b. 9 Mar, bapt. 29 Apr 1782 by Rev. Frederick Smith. Sponsors: James and Mary Avis, Sarah Hoffman.
William Armstrong, son of William and Sarah Armstrong, b. 7 May, bapt. 2 Jun 1782 by Rev. Frederick Smith. Sponsors: Andrew and Susanna Linmier, Andrew and Catherine Vaneman.
Isaac Shute, son of Joseph and Sarah Shute, b. 16 Aug, bapt. 15 Sep 1782 by Rev. Frederick Smith. Sponsors: William and Diana Easby, John and Agnes Avis.
Martha Avis, dau of John and Agnes Avis, b. 5 Sep, bapt. 30 Sep 1782 by Rev. Frederick Smith. Sponsors: George and Jane Avis, James and Mary Avis.
Jane Avis, dau of Zekias and Susanna Avis, b. 13 Oct, bapt. 14 Dec 1782 by Rev. Frederick Smith. Sponsors: George and Jane Avis, James and Mary Avis.
Harriet Lydia Lloyd, dau of Bateman and Abigail Lloyd, b. 14 Nov, bapt. 22 Dec 1782 by Rev. Frederick Smith. Sponsors: Mary Gill, Jochamia and Christine Wood.
Rebecca Avis, dau of James and Mary Avis, b. 1 Feb, bapt. 9 Mar 1783 by Rev. Frederick Smith. Sponsors: George and Jane Avis, John and Agnes Avis.
Elizabeth Guest, dau of John and Sarah Guest, b. 1 Apr, bapt. 27 Apr 1783 by Rev. Frederick Smith. Sponsors: William and Christine Guest, James and Mary Avis.
Henry Shute, son of Henry and Lydia Shute, b. 19 May, bapt. 29 Jun 1783 by Rev. Frederick Smith. Sponsors: John and Sarah Shute, William and Diane Easby.
Rebecca Linmeir, dau of Christopher and Rebecca Linmeir, b. 31 May, bapt. 29 Jun 1783 by Rev. Frederick Smith. Sponsors: Andrew and Susanna Linmeir, Andrew and Catherine Guest.
William Helderman, son of George and Anna Helderman, b. 28 Jul, bapt. 24 Aug 1783 by Rev. Frederick Smith. Sponsors: John and Agnes Avis, George and Jane Avis.
Jesse Johnson, son of Benjamin and Rachel Johnson, b. 22 Aug, bapt. 28 Aug 1783 by Rev. Frederick Smith. Sponsors: the parents.
Lylla Avis, dau of William and Anna Avis, b. 10 Aug, bapt. 5 Oct 1783

by Rev. Frederick Smith. Sponsors: George and Jane Avis, James and Mary Avis.

Harriet Smith Wood, dau of Jachomia and Christina Wood, b. 17 Sep, bapt. 19 Oct 1783 by Rev. Frederick Smith. Sponsors: the parents and Polly Gill.

Robert Guest, son of Henry and Jane Guest, b. 6 Oct, bapt. 30 Nov 1783 by Rev. Frederick Smith. Sponsors: James and Mary Avis, Andrew and Catherine Guest.

Lafford Lloyd, son of Bateman, Jr., and Abigail Lloyd, b. 29 Dec 1783, bapt. 27 Jan 1784 by Rev. Frederick Smith.

Jacob Fowler, son of John and Elizabeth Fowler, b. 3 Jan, bapt. 22 Feb, 1784 by Rev. Frederick Smith.

Daniel Vaneman, son of Peter, dec'd, and Rebecca Vaneman, b. 21 Dec 1783, bapt. 27 May 1784 by Rev. Frederick Smith.

Elisha Shute, son of Thomas and Sarah Shute, b. 27 Mar, bapt. 6 Jun 1784 by Rev. Frederick Smith.

Charles Avis, son of Joseph and Sarah Avis, b. 13 Jun, bapt. 11 Jul 1784 by Rev. Frederick Smith.

Benjamin Johnson, son of Benjamin and Rachel Johnson, b. 8 Sep, bapt. 3 Oct 1784 by Rev. Frederick Smith. Sponsors: John and Agnes Avis, James and Mary Avis.

John Lawrence Hoffman, married man, son of late Lawrence Hoffman, b. 8 Jan 1747, bapt. on his sick bed 5 Oct 1784 by Francis Bochler.

Ann Lauterbach, dau of Matthias and Ann Lauterbach, b. 16 Aug, bapt. 12 Sep 1784 by Rev. Frederick Smith.

Christopher Holton, son of James and Christine Holton, b. 29 Jul, bapt. 5 Sep 1784 by Rev. Frederick Smith.

Gerrit Guest, son of Joseph and Sarah Guest, b. 12 Sep, bapt. 7 Oct 1784 by Francis Bochler. Sponsors: Henry Guest and the grandmother, Christina Guest.

John Armstrong, son of William and Sarah Armstrong, b. 17 Sep, bapt. 17 Oct 1784 by Francis Bochler. Sponsors: Joseph Shute, Henry Shute, Jane Guest and Mary Sparks.

Mary Salsbury, dau of John and Hannah Salsbury, b. 1 Nov, bapt. 28 Nov 1784 by Francis Bochler. Sponsors: John and Agnes Avis.

Thomas Shute, b. 7 May 1748 and Sarah Shute, his wife, b. 22 Dec 1759, bapt. 5 Dec 1784 by Francis Bochler. Sponsors: Joseph Shute, John Avis, Martin Kats, Christine Guest, Magdalena Gill, Sarah Hoffmann (the elder).

Joseph Estlack, son of William and Mary Diana Estlack, b. 25 Jun 1770, bapt. about 4 weeks after by Rev. Frederick Smith. [This record appears with the records of 1784.]

Ann Fox, dau of Jacob and Lydia Fox, b. 18 Aug 1784, bapt. 20 Feb 1785 by Francis Bochler.

Samuel Lloyd, son of Daniel and Sarah Lloyd, b. 18 Jan, bapt. 20 Feb 1785 by Francis Bochler.

Sarah Christina Hoffman, wife of John Lawrence Hoffman, aged 35 years, bapt. on her sick bed 22 Feb 1785 by Francis Bochler. Sponsors: Christina Guest, Sarah Hoffman (the elder).

Elijah Hoffman, son of John Lawrence and Sarah Christina Hoffman, b. 26 Jan, bapt. 22 Feb 1785 by Francis Bochler. Sponsors: James Hoffman, Sarah Hoffman, Christina Guest.

Jesse Avis, son of John and Agnes Avis, b. 29 Jan, bapt. 27 Feb 1785 by Francis Bochler. Sponsors: James Avis, Henry Guest and Mary Avis.

Mary Avis, dau of James and Mary Avis, b. 8 Mar, bapt. 3 Apr 1785 by Francis Bochler. Sponsors: John Avis, Agnes Avis, Christina Guest.

Isaac Smallwood, married son of Mary Sparks by her first husband, b. 6 Sep 1755, bapt. 12 Jun 1785 by Francis Bochler. Sponsors: John Avis, James Avis.

Dorcas Taylor, a poor orphan bound to James and Mary Avis, b. 15 Feb, bapt. 8 Sep 1785 by Francis Bochler. Sponsors: James and Mary Avis.

Rebecca James, dau of Isarel and Rebecca James, b. 2 Apr, bapt. 11 Sep 1785 by Francis Bochler. Sponsors: John Avis, George Helderman, Agnes Avis, Susanna Shute.

George Helderman, son of George and Ann Helderman, b. 26 Aug, bapt. 2 Oct 1785 by Francis Bochler. Sponsors: John and Agnes Avis.

Benjamin Stratton, son of Immanuel and Sarah Shute Stratton, b. 22 Sep, bapt. 21 Nov 1785 by Francis Bochler.

Lydia Lloyd, dau of Bateman, Jr. and Abigail Lloyd, b. 20 Nov, bapt. 8 Nov 1785 by Francis Bochler at Woodstock.

John Holton, son of James and Christina Holton, b. 10 Nov, bapt. 18 Dec 1785 by Francis Bochler. Sponsors: John and Agnes Avis.

Peter Calhoon, son of Hugh and Judith Calhoon, b. 25 Nov, bapt. 26 Dec 1785 by Francis Bochler.

John Burden, son of Samuel and Hannah Burden, b. 31 Oct in Upper Penn's Neck, bapt. 27 Dec 1785 by Francis Bochler.

Jaconias Wood, son of Jachomia and Christina Wood, b. 10 Jan in Woodstock, bapt. 25 Jan 1786 by Francis Bochler.

Anny Avis, dau of William and Ann Avis, b. 23 Dec 1785, bapt. 29 Jan, 1786 by Francis Bochler. Sponsors: Anna Bohler, Mary Avis, James

Avis.

Sarah Kats, dau of Martin and Jane Kats, b. 28 Dec 1785, bapt. 29 Jan 1786 by Francis Bochler. Witnesses: Jane Avis, Agnes Avis, John Avis.

Mary Avis, dau of Zachreus and Susanna Avis, b. 20 Jan 1786, bapt. 19 Feb 1786 by Francis Bochler. Sponsors: Jane Avis, Mary Avis, James Avis.

Rachel Guest, dau of Henry and Jane Guest, b. 23 Jan 1786, bapt. 1 Mar 1786 by Francis Bochler. Sponsors: Ann Bohler, Mary Avis, James Avis.

Ann Lauterbach, formerly Cavey, wife of Mathias Lauterbach, b. 26 Nov 1758, bapt. 19 Mar 1786 by Francis Bochler. Sponsors: Anna Bohler, Christine Guest, Catherine Vanneman, Agnes Avis.

Sarah Gambel, dau of Luther and Mary Gambel, b. 3 Mar 1786 in Woodstock, bapt. 21 Mar 1786 at house of parents by Francis Bochler.

Lydia Shute, dau of William Henry and Hannah Lydia Shute, b. 13 Mar 1786 in Woodwich near Racoon Creek, bapt. at house of parents 26 Mar 1786 by Francis Bochler.

George Linmeyer, son of Christopher and Rebecca Linmeyer, b. 17 Jan 1786 in Upper Penn's Neck, bapt. 9 Apr 1786 by Francis Bochler. Sponsors: Thomas Shute, Joseph and Sarah Guest.

Josiah Gill, son of Matthew and Elizabeth Gill, b. 28 Jun 1786, bapt. 30 Jul 1786 by Francis Bochler. Sponsors: James Avis, I. Wood, Christina Guest, Sarah Gill, Mary Avis.

Isaac Lloyd, son of Daniel and Sarah Lloyd, b. 10 Jul 1786, bapt. 10 Sep 1786 by Francis Bochler. Sponsors: James Avis, Jachomiah Wood, Rebecca Lloyd.

William, son of Quamini and Susannah, Negroes, b. 8 Aug 1786, bapt. 24 Sep 1786 by Francis Bochler. Sponsors: James and Mary Avis.

William Chambles, son of Isaac, dec'd, and Regina Chambles, b. 28 Oct 1783, bapt. 30 Sep 1786 by Francis Bochler. (The child was sick, and bound to Bro. Andrew Vaneman and Catherine, his wife.)

Patience Lauterbach formerly Higgins, wife of Henry Lauterbach, b. 1 Jan 1752, bapt. 26 Nov 1786 by Francis Bochler. Sponsors: Ann Bochler, Magdalena Gill, Catherine Vaneman, Agnes Avis.

Sarah Guest, dau of Joseph and Sarah Guest, b. 13 Dec 1785, bapt. 25 Dec 1786 by Francis Bochler. Sponsors: Ann Bochler, the grandmother, Christina Guest and Henry Guest.

Ann Avis, dau of Joseph and Sarah Avis, b. 9 Aug 1786, bapt. 28 Dec 1786 by Francis Bochler. Sponsors: James Avis and Ann Bochler.

Anna Avis, dau of James and Mary Avis, b. 9 Jan 1787, bapt. 14 Jan 1787 by Francis Bochler. Sponsors: Anna Bochler and Christina Guest.

Elizabeth Johnson, dau of Benjamin and Rachel Johnson, b. 24 Dec 1786, bapt. 28 Jan 1787 by Francis Bochler. Sponsors: Jane Avis, Agnes Avis and James Avis.

Elizabeth Lauterbach, dau of Mathias and Ann Lauterbach, b. 6 Jan 1787, bapt. 18 Feb 1787 by Francis Bochler. Sponsors: Elizabeth Lauterbach (grandmother), Christina Guest and Henry Guest.

William Jordan, son of John and Mary Jordan, b. 29 Jan 1787 in Upper Penn's Neck, bapt. 9 Apr 1787 by Francis Bochler.

Sarah Fox, dau of Jacob and Lydia Fox, b. 10 Mar 1787 in Upper Penn's Neck, bapt. 9 Apr 1787 by Francis Bochler.

Ursula Step, dau of Martin and Susanna Step, b. 30 Sep 1786, bapt. 27 May 1787 by Francis Bochler.

Martha Murphy formerly Homes, wife of Henry Murphy, b. 1737, bapt. 8 Jul 1787 by Francis Bochler. Sponsors: Anna Bochler, Christina Holton and Agnes Avis.

Jane Ann Avis, dau of William and Ann Avis, b. 27 Oct 1787, bapt. 18 Nov 1787 by Francis Bochler. Sponsors: Jane Avis, Mary Avis and James Avis.

Andrew Quamine, negro, bapt. 2 Dec 1787 by Francis Bochler. Sponsors: James Avis, Martin Kats Sr., Joseph Shute and Mary Avis.

Agnes Avis, dau of John and Agnes Avis, b. 24 Nov 1787, bapt. 25 Dec 1787 by Francis Bochler. Sponsors: Anna Bochler, Ann Kohl, Jane Avis, George Helderman and James Avis.

Elizabeth Calhoons, dau of Hugh and Judith Calhoons, b. Feb 1787, bapt. 1 Jan 1788 by Francis Bochler.

John Williams, son of Justice and Agnes Williams, b. 24 Oct 1787, bapt. 13 Jan 1788 by Francis Bochler. Sponsors: grandparents of child's mother, Henry and Martha Murphy.

Lefferts Ware Lloyd, son of Bateman and Abigail Lloyd, b. 4 Feb 1788 at Woodstown, bapt. 2 Mar 1788 by Francis Bochler.

William Gambel, son of Luther and Mary Gambel of Woodstown, b. 5 Mar 1788, bapt. 30 Mar 1788 by Francis Bochler.

Benjamin Gill, son of Matthew and Elizabeth Gill of Racoon Creek, b. 14 Mar 1788, bapt. 13 Apr 1788 by Francis Bochler.

Catherine Elizabeth Shute, dau of Henry and Lydia Shute, b. 12 Apr 1788, bapt. 4 May 1788 by Francis Bochler. Sponsors: Catherine, Elizabeth Rutter and Sarah Shute.

Joseph James, son of Israel and Elizabeth James, b. 25 May 1788 in

Pilesgrove Twp, Salem County, bapt. 3 Jun 1788 by Francis Bochler. Sponsors: George Helderman, and the grandmother, Agnes Avis.

Christiana, dau of Andrew and Susanna (Negroes), b. 15 May 1788 in Woolwich Twp, bapt. sixth Sunday after Trinity by Francis Bochler. Sponsors: Rothe Flora, s.s. Negroes.

Samuel Wood, son of Jochamia and Christina Wood, b. 12 Jun 1787 at Woodstown, bapt. sixth Sunday after Trinity by Francis Bochler.

Abraham Smith, son of Joseph and Catherine Smith, b. 2 Jun 1788 in Piles Grove, bapt. 29 Jul 1788 by Francis Bochler.

Samuel Avis, son of Zacchaeus and Susanna Avis, b. 15 May 1788, bapt. 27 Jul 1788 by Francis Bochler.

Sarah Stratton dau of Immanuel and Sarah Stratton, b. 8 Jul 1788, bapt. 3 Sep 1788 by Francis Bochler.

RECEPTIONS INTO THE CONGREGATION 1765

William Guest, Sr.; Christina Guest; Obadiah Lloyd; Rebecca Lloyd; Obadiah Shute, Sr. ; Rebecca Shute; John Lloyd; Mary Lloyd; Bateman Lloyd; Lydia Lloyd; Jachomia Wood; Widow Wood; Laurence Hoffman; Sarah Hoffman; George Avis, Sr. ; Henry Guest, s.; Mary Gill, md.; Magdalena Gill, s.; Mary Sparks, md.; Widow Lauterbach;

January 24, 1768. John Avis; Agnes Avis; Henry Shute; Lydia Shute; Joseph Shute; Sarah Shute; Isaac Shute; Hannah Avis; George Avis, Jr.

Sep 11, 1768. Margaret Holstine

Nov 27, 1768. Martin Kats, md. Thomas Shute, md.; Anna Bauer, w.; Flora, negro.

Dec 11, 1768. Gerrit Vanerman, s.

Dec 16, 1770. Elizabeth Lippincott

Feb 8, 1771. Andrew Linmeyer and wife

May 19, 1771. Sarah Vanerman, s.

Dec 25 1772. James and Christina Holton

Sep 7, 1773. James Avis; Mary Avis; Nicholas Linmeyer, s.; Hannah Avis, s.; Andrew Vaneman, s.; Rebecca Hoffman, s.

Oct 31, 1773. --- Kohl, s.

Mar 13, 1773. Jane Guest, md.

Oct 9, 1773. John and Sarah Hoffman

May 14, 1775. Susanna Linmeyer

Feb 4, 1776. Anna Holstein, md.
June 2, 1776. ---- Holstein, md.; Susanna Holstein, s.
Jun 9, 1776. Mary Vaneman, s.
May 11, 1777. William Armstrong; Sarah Armstrong.

Wednesday, 23 Nov 1785, according to the directions of Bishop J. Wattinile, the congregation was reorganized and the following persons added: Matthew and Elizabeth Gill; William and Ann Avis; Martin and Jaen Kats; Joseph and Sarah Avis; Israel and Elizabeth James; Joseph Guest, md.; James Hoffman, s.; Alexander Linmeyer, s.; Thomas Estlack, s.; John Avis, s.; Joseph Estlack, s.; Richard Holton, s.; Ann Lauterbach, md.; Sarah Hoffman, s.; Ann Avis, s.; Deborah Shute, s.; Rebecca Barber, s.; Ruth Shute, s.; Rachel Hoffman, s.; Sarah Kats, s.; Ivy Shute, ; Ann Hoffman, s.; Hannah Bryant, s.; Sarah Avis, s.; Sarah Estlack, s.

Jan 1, 1786. Luther and Mary Gambel, md.; Patience Lauterbach, md.; Mar 25, 1787; Christina Avis, s.; Mary Guest, s.
June 10, 1787. Henry and Martha Murphy.
Aug 10, 1788. Jane Taylor, wd.

Record of Receptions into the Congregation by the Visitation of Rev. An. Nathaniel Seidel, Episcopus 23 Nov 1768.

Married men: William Guest; George Avis; Obadiah Lloyd; Lawrence Hoffman; Joseph Shute; Andrew Vaneman; John Avis; Isaac Shute.
Married Women: Christina Guest; Sarah Agnes Avis; Rebecca Lloyd; Susanna Shute; Sarah Hoffman; Sarah Noah; Jane Avis; Magdalena Gill; Mary Vaneman; Elizabeth Lauterbach, widow
Single Sisters: Catherine Guest; Elizabeth Guest; Sarah Gill; Catherine Gill; Deborah Gill; Mary Gill
William Henry and Hannah Lydia Shute by baptism 24 Mar 1769.
Mary Diana Estlack, md., by baptism 23 Nov 1769.
Rhoda Flora, mulatto, single, by baptism 29 Sep 1771.
Anna Kohl, md. by baptism 31 Oct 1773.
James and Mary Avis by baptism 18 Jun 1775.
Hannah Avis, wife of George Avis, Jr., by baptism 18 Jun 1775.
Gerret Vanmemens by baptism 5 Apr 1776.
William Estlack, md., by baptism 5 Apr 1776.
Susanna Linmeyer by baptism 7 Apr 1776.
Christina Wood by baptism 29 Nov 1778.

Sarah Guest by baptism 29 Nov 1778.
Christine Holton, md., by baptism 29 Nov 1778.
Hannah Salsbury by baptism 14 May 1780.
Jane Guest by baptism 14 May 1780.
John Lawrence Hoffman (on his sick bed) by baptism 5 Oct 1784.
Thomas and Sarah Shutes by baptism 5 Dec 1784.
Sarah Christina Hoffman, md., by baptism 22 Feb 1785.
Isaac Smallwood, md., by baptism 12 Jun 1785.
George Helderman by baptism 19 Jun 1785.
Jachomiah Wood by baptism 19 Jun 1785.
Andrew Van Nemen by baptism 12 Oct 1785.
Ann Lautebach, md., by baptism 19 Mar 1786.
William and Sarah Armstrong by baptism 2 Jul 1786.
Patience Lauterbach, md., by baptism 26 Nov 1786.
Martha Murphy, md., by baptism 8 Jul 1787.
Andrew and Quamim, negroes by baptism 2 Dec 1787.
Henry Murphy, md., by baptism 25 Dec 1787.
Jane Taylor, md., by baptism 18 Jan 1788.
Martin Kats, Jr., and his wife, Jane by baptism 12 Apr 1789.
Ann Helderman by baptism 31 Oct 1790.
Cathrine Smith by baptism 16 Jun 1793.

Records of Admissions to the Lord's Supper 1767.
November 23. On the consecration day at the First Lord's supper were present the following members:
Men: Obadiah Lloyd; William Guest; Lawrence Hoffman; Joseph Shute
Women: Rebecca Lloyd; Christina Guest; Sarah Hoffman; Sarah Shute; Mary Sparks; Mary Vanneman; Magd. Gill; Sarah Noah; Elizabeth Lauterbach, w.; Catharine Guest, s.; Catharine Gill, s.; Deborah Gill. s.

4 Nov 1769. Sarah Agnes Avis, md.
12 Apr 1770. John Avis, md.
16 May 1770. Isaac and Susanna Shutes.
3 Oct 1772. Jane Avis, md; Sarah Gill, s.
5 Aug 1775. Ann Kohl, md.
24 May 1777. Sarah Shute, md.
5 Nov 1778. James and Mary Avis.
22 May 1779. Gerret Vannemens, md.
24 Feb 1781. William and Mary Diana Estlack.
12 Apr 1781. Susanna Linmeyer, md.; Christiana Holton, md.

7 Sep 1782. Henry and Jane Guest.
13 Aug 1783. Martin Kats, md.
13 Apr 1786. Rhoda Flora, mulatto, s.
13 Aug 1786. Thomas and Sarah Shutes.
19 Jun 1787. George Helderman.
25 Nov 1787. Ann Lauterbach, md.
11 May 1788. Andrew Vanmeman, md.
2 Aug 1788. Jane Taylor, widow.
29 Aug 1790. William and Sarah Armstrong.

RECORD OF MARRIAGES

Jachomiah Wood, single to Christina Gill, single 6 Jul 1772 by Frederick Smith.
James Avis, single to Mary Guest, single 18 May 1772 by Frederick Smith.
Joseph Guest, single to Sarah Vanmemen, single 25 Dec 1772 by Frederick Smith.
Andrew Linmeyer to Susanna Clifton, widow, 17 May 1774 by Frederick Smith.
Gerrit VanMemen, single to Catharine Gill, single 18 Jul 1775 by Frederick Smith.
John Salsbury to Hannah Lippincoat 5 Dec 1775 by Frederick Smith.
Joseph Shute, widower, to Sarah Barber, single 30 Jan 1776 by Frederick Smith.
Andrew Vannemens, single to Cathrine Guest, single 29 Jan 1777 by Frederick Smith.
Zacheus Avis, single to Susanna Cabner, single 5 May 1777 by Frederick Smith.
William Tindel to Mary Ambler 27 May 1777 by Frederick Smith.
Christopher Linmyer to Catharine Corneliusin 23 Jun 1777 by Frederick Smith.
John Walker to Doni Allen 4 Nov 1777 by Frederick Smith.
Samuel Barden to Hannah Avis 7 Apr 1778 by Frederick Smith.
George Helderman to Anna Hayns 21 Oct 1778 by Frederick Smith.
Martin Kats, widower to Mary Weizel, widow 9 Nov 1778 by Frederick Smith.
David Goldin to Mary Bannister, widow 20 Mar 1781 by Frederick Smith.
Joshua Broder to Marianna Kats 11 Mar 1781 by Frederick Smith.

William Holstein to Elizabeth Banniston 4 Apr 1781 by Frederick Smith.
Joseph Avis, single to Sarah Riley, single 11 Dec 1781 by Frederick Smith.
Conrad Lauterbach, single to Mary Smith, single 9 Sep 1782 by Frederick Smith.
Quamini, Wm. Guest's negro man to Susanna (negress) 13 Nov 1782 by Frederick Smith.
William Shute, single to Sarah Adams, single 24 Feb 1783 by Frederick Smith.
Jacob Fox, single to Lydia Akirt, single 30 Sep 1783 by Frederick Smith.
William Avis, single to Ann Rumpert, single 23 May 1783 by Frederick Smith.
Abraham Farron, single to Mary Clark, single 15 Jul 1784 by Frederick Smith.
Nathan Avis, single to Rachel Roberts, single 16 Dec 1784 by Francis Bochler.
Luther Gambel, single to Mary Waters, single 4 Jan 1785 by Francis Bochler.
Martin Kats, single to Jane Avis, single 4 Apr 1785 by Francis Bochler.
James Christy, single to Sarah Barker, single 4 Aug 1785 by Francis Bochler.
Daniel Harker, single to Mary Shute, single 3 Jan 1786 by Francis Bochler.
Andrew Barns, single to Sarah Hoffman, widow 5 Feb 1786 by Francis Bochler.
Jacob Seers, widower to Susanna Shute, widow 20 Dec 1786 by Francis Bochler.
Andrew Crawford, single to Ann Hoffman, single 26 Mar 1787 by Francis Bochler.
John Raynold, single to Ann Avis, single 15 May 1787 by Francis Bochler.
William Cabner, single to Ann Avis, widow 21 Apr 1789 by Francis Bochler.
Alexander Forrister, M.D., single to Catharine Wood, single 20 Aug 1789 by Francis Bochler.
Thomas Estlack, single to Rebecca Howell, single 8 Apr 1790 by Francis Bochler.
Joseph Estlack, single to Hannah Salsbury, widow formerly Lippencoat, 20 Sep 1790 by Francis Bochler.

John Harker, son of Samuel Harker, dec'd, and Sarah formerly Garrison, single, farmer of Woolwick Twp, Gloucester, b. 25 Aug 1767 to Christiana Avis, b. 14 Apr 1774, dau of James Avis, cordwainer and tanner and Mary (Guest) Avis, m. 26 Aug 1791 by Francis Bochler, Deacon.

Conrad Weitzel, single, son of Jacob Weitzel, dec'd, and Anna Maria formerly Wenzel, (present wife of our brother Martin Kats, Sr.), farmer of Upper Penn's Neck, Salem County, b. May 1767, single and Margaret Holstein, single, b. 8 Oct 1762, dau of Lawrence Holstein and Margaret, both dec'd, m. 19 Jan 1792 by Francis Bochler, Deacon.

William Allen, single, farmer of Upper Penn's Neck, Salem County, son of Jeremiah and Bridget (Poulson) Allen, dec'd, and Sarah Murphy, single of same place, dau of Henry Murphy and Isabella formerly Avis, m. 8 Feb 1792 by Francis Bochler, Deacon.

Felix Kitts, single, farmer of Upper Penn's Neck, Salem County, b. 19 Oct 1773, son of Robert Kitts, tavern keeper and Jane, formerly Dickey, dec'd, and Mary Lauterbach, single of Piles Grove, Salem County, b. 7 Oct 1776, dau of Mathias Lauterbach, a farmer and Ann formerly Curry, m. 21 Mar 1793 by Francis Bochler, Deacon.

Thomas Snagg, single, farmer in Woolwich Twp, Gloucester County, son of Thomas and Margareth (Murphy) Snag, both dec'd, b. 15 Apr 1772 and Hannah Brant, single of same place, dau of Robert and Sarah (Spiarow) Brant, dec'd, b. 24 Aug 1771, m. 22 Aug 1793 by Francis Bochler, Deacon.

Job Scott, single, millwright of Trenton, Hunterton County, and Rachel Hoffman of Pilesgrove Twp, Salem County dau of John Hoffman and Sarah formerly Wright, both dec'd, b. 9 Dec 1770, m. 12 Sep 1793 by Francis Bochler, Deacon.

DEATHS

Before 1756.
Mary Holstein, wife of Lawrence Holstein.
John Holstein, son of Lawrence Holstein of Piles Grove.
Stephen Tussy, of Piles Grove.
Cathrine, wife of Stephen Tussy.
A strange servant man of Joseph Applins.
Mary Wiltse of Penn's Neck.
Peter Lauterbach, a child of Conrad Lauterbach.
Twins, still born of Christopher Linmyer.

Anne Linmyer, a child of Christopher Linmyer.
Magadalena Ritez, wife of Matthew Ritez.
Ann Shute, a child of William Shute of Oldman's Creek.
A child of Jacob Kats of Penn's Neck.
A child of Samuel Hewets of Oldman's Creek.
A child of Christopher Linmyer of Penn's Neck.
1756
Peter Vanneman d. 7 Oct 1756.
Christopher Linmyre d. 7 Nov 1756.
George, son of Christopher Linmyre d. 17 Dec 1757.
Jeremiah [Jochomiah] Wood of Pilesgrove d. 10 Aug 1757.
Catharine Hoffman, wife of Nicholas Hoffman of Pilesgrove d. Sep 1757.
William, a child of William Shute of Oldman's Creek d. Sep 1757.
Elizabeth Tussy, dau of Stephen Tussy of Pilesgrove d. 5 Mar 1758.
Benjamin Guest, son of William Guest of Bacon Creek d. 7 Nov 1758.
Nathaniel Guest, son of William Guest of Bacon Creek d. Jan, 1759.
Dorothea Kats, dau of Martin and Anne Kats d. 28 Sep 1762.
Isaac Noah, son of Michael and Sarah Noah of Penn's Neck d. 5 Jan 1763.
A child of James Thomas, (stillborn) of Penn's Neck d. Jan 1763.
William Shute, Sr. of Oldman's Creek d. 16 Mar 1763.
A child of William Sanders of Greenwich Twp, Gloucester County d. 1764.
Margaretha Hollstein, wife of Lawrence Hollstein of Pilesgrove d. 1765.
Lawrence Hollstein, son of Lawrence Hollstein and Margaretha d. 1765.
Anna Bauer, wife of --- Bauer of Oldman's Creek d. 20 Jan 1766.
John Gill's dau 9 days old d. 25 Feb 1766.
Urie Hoffman, a child of Lawrence and Sarah Hoffman d. 29 Aug 1766.
William Shute, Sr. d. 1 Oct 1766.
Hannah Guest, wife of William Guest, Sr. d. 17 Oct 1766.
Ann Shute, widow of William Shute, Sr. d. 6 Dec 1766.
Nicholas Hoffman d. 30 Sep 1767.
Catharine Wood, widow of Jeremiah [Jochamia] Wood d. 24 Dec 1766.
John Lloyd d. 28 Dec 1766.
Thomas Shute, son of Isaac and Susanna Shute d. 23 Apr 1766.
Jacob Kohl, son of John and Ann Kohl d. 9 Mar 1766.
Elizabeth Avis, 6 years old d. 21 Apr 1772.
Elizabeth Lippencoat, wife of Samuel Lippencoat d. 10 Aug 1766.
Joseph Uriel Shute d. 18 Nov 1766.

Elizabeth Guest d. 3 Jan 1773.
Sarah Guest d. 22 Jan 1773.
Michael Noah, husband of Sarah Noah d. 28 Jun 1774.
Sarah Franklin, dau of widow Franklin, age 3 years d. 13 Nov 1774.
Hannah Gill, dau of Matthew and Mary Gill d. 15 Nov 1774.
Jonathan Smith, son of widow Sarah Franklin age 17 years d. 28 Nov 1774.
Andrew Vannemens of Penn's Neck, husband of Mary Vannemens age 52 years d. 16 Dec 1774.
Mary Meoraig, wife of John Meoraig of Penn's Neck d. 4 Jul 1775.
Sarah Shute, wife of Joseph Shute d. 13 Aug 1775.
Errick Keen d. 30 Dec 1776.
Gebulon Pierson d. 10 Jan 1777.
Hannah Griffin d. 10 Jan 1777.
Daniel Dorsey d. 15 Jan 1777.
John Gill, son of Matthew Gill d. 2 Apr 1777.
George Shute d. 3 Apr 1777.
Lawrence Hollstein d. 8 Apr 1777.
A little dau of Mary Keen d. 15 Jun 1777.
Mary Apply d. 22 Jul 1777.
Lydia Lloyd d. 18 Dec 1777.
Diana Shute, a single woman, d. 4 Apr 1778.
Sarah Shute, age 2 years 1 ½ mos, d. 25 Aug 1778.
Catharine Linmyer d. 30 Nov 1778.
Rebecca Linmyer, a child of Christopher Linmyer d. 1778 (soon after the mother).
--- Guest, a child of Henry and Jane Guest 5 weeks of age d. 8 Dec 1778.
Anna Kats, wife of Martin Kats of Penn's Neck d. 6 Jan 1779.
John Bryerly, widower d. 7 Jan 1779.
Mary Gill Wood, child of Zacheus (Jachomia) and Christine Wood d. 11 Dec 1780.
Elizabeth Vannemens, dau of Peter and Rebecca Vannemens, 4 years old d. 26 Jan 1781.
Martin Kats, Sr. widower age 78 years d. 6 Dec 1781.
Ann Smith, mother of Christina Holten d. 13 Dec 1781.
Henry Shute, 3 weeks old d. 27 Feb 1782.
A child of George and Ann Helderman 2 weeks old d. 10 Mar 1782.
Gerrit Vannemens, husband of Catherine Vannemens d. 7 Apr 1782.
Magdalene Gill, dau of John Gill age 12 years d. 12 Apr 1783.
John Sharp, a married man in his 52nd year d. 23 Feb 1783.

Lawrence Hoffman d. 9 Mar 1783.
A child of Immanuel and Sarah Stratten d. 21 Mar 1783.
William Shute, son of Thomas and Sarah Shute age 12 years d. 20 Jun 1783.
A child of Mathias and Anna Lauterbach, 14 days old d. 25 Aug 1783.
Jesse Johnson, son of Benjamin and Rachel Johnson 7 days old d. 30 Aug 1783.
William Guest, a married man age 71 years d. 12 Oct 1783.
William Estlack, a married man d. 20 Dec 1783.
Peter Vannemens, a married man d. Jan 1784.
Isabel Sharp, a widow d. 14 Jan 1784.
John Vannemens, a child of Peter, dec'd, and Rebecca Vannemen d. 21 May 1784.
Catharine Vannemens, a child of Peter, dec'd, and Rebecca Vannemen 3 years old d. 1 Jun 1784.
Christopher Holton, son of James and Christina Holton 11 weeks 3 days old d. 19 Oct 1784.
9 Nov 1784 Anna Catharine Bochler, her maiden name Jack, wife of Brother Francis Bochler d. 8 Nov at 8 o'clock, buried the 9th. She was b. 3 Jun 1724 in Europe, Wetteravia, in the county of Issenberg, Marienborn, village Bergheim, came to the United Brethren's Congregation in those parts in the year 1743, was married to the present widower the 11 of Mar 1746. She came to America in 1752.
Susanna Holstein, dau of Lawrence and Margareth Holstein, dec'd, d. 12 Dec 1784 age 31 years.
A still born child of William and Sarah Shute d. 31 Dec 1784.
Ann Holstein, widow, third wife of Lawrence Holstein, dec'd, d. 27 Jan 1785.
Rosanna McCormick, wife of Patrick McCormick d. 1 Feb 1785.
A child of John and Mary Lloyd d. 18 Feb 1785.
Samuel Lloyd, son of Daniel and Sarah Lloyd aged 5 weeks d. 27 Feb 1785.
Sarah Christina Hoffman, wife of John Hoffman d. 10 Mar 1785. She was born in Bucks County, PA, 11 Mar 1750, was educated in the principles of the Quakers. After the delivery of a little son she was taken with dropsey. On the 22 of Feb from her sick bed she was added to the Congregation by baptism.
Elias Hoffman, child of John and Sarah Christina Hoffman, dec'd, d. 28 Mar 1785.
John Lloyd, a married man d. 17 Apr 1785.
Rebecca Lloyd, child of John, dec'd, and Mary Lloyd, widow aged 5

years d. 13 Aug 1785.
Rebecca Avis, child of John and Agnes Avis aged 5 years 2 mo 16 days d. 5 Sep 1785.
Dorcas Taylor, aged 7 mos 2 weeks d. 3 Oct 1785.
George Avis, Sr. d. 19 Oct 1785, age 96 years, b. in Old England in the year 1690, and as a child of about 8 years came to America with his parents.
Rebecca, dau of Israel and Elizabeth James aged 6 mos d. 29 Oct 1785.
Rebecca Estlack, a widow d. 1 Dec 1785.
Sarah Lloyd, b. 30 Mar 1754, dau of Obadiah Llyod and his surviving widow, Rebecca Lloyd d. 3 Mar 1786.
Hannah Holstein, youngest dau of Lawrence Holstein and his second wife d. 29 Mar 1786.
Samuel Levis aged 27 years d. 4 Jun 1786.
Jacob Anderson d. 30 Sep 1786.
Sarah Thomson aged 6 years d. 4 Oct 1786.
Isaac Lloyd, son of Samuel and Sarah Lloyd aged 4 mo d. 9 Nov 1786.
John Avis, Sr., b. 31 Oct 1742 at Oldman's Creek, d. 5 Mar 1787.
Israel Taylor, a married man d. 30 Mar 1787.
Ann Whilly aged 45 years d. 10 May 1787.
Mary Guest aged 10 years 5 mo d. 10 May 1787.
William Quamini, a negro child d. 30 May 1787.
Elizabeth Lauterbach, a child d. 31 May 1787.
Ann Elliot, wife of Thomas Elliot d. 22 Jul 1787.
William Avise, a married man d. 20 Sep 1787.
Thomas Christy, a child of James and Sarah Christy d. 8 Nov 1787.
Patrick McCormick, a widower d. 8 Jan 1788.
Rebecca Avise, dau of James and Mary Avise, 5 years 8 weeks old d. 13 Apr 1788.
Mary Salsbury aged 3 years 10 mos, 3 days d. 26 Sep 1788.
A child of James and Sarah Christy d. 4 Jan 1789.
Agnes Williams, wife of Justice Williams aged 19 years 6 mos d. 19 Feb 1789.
Sarah Noah, widow d. 22 Feb 1789, aged 102 11 mo 2 days. She was b. in Philadelphia 12 Mar 1685. She was married 3 times, had 13 children, 17 grandchildren and 2 great-grandchildren.
John McCraig, widower of Penn's Neck d. 24 Feb 1789.
Sarah Guest, a child of Joseph and Sarah Guest aged 2 years 4 mo d. 18 Jun 1789.
Elizabeth Lauterbach, widow aged 67 years d. 26 Oct 17899. Her husband Conrad Lauterbach departed 30 years prior. She had 5

children, 3 of whom are still living and 12 grand children.
Christiana Guest, widow, formerly Halten aged 76 years and 11 mos d. 29 Nov 1789. She was twice married, had 13 children, 31 grand children and 2 great-grand children.
John Kohl, husband of Ann Kohl d. 2 Dec 1789.
Levi Shute, son of the late Isaac and Susanna Shute aged 20 years d. 15 Mar 1790.
John Raynolds, husband of Ann Raynolds aged 30 years d. 14 Apr 1790.
Mary Huber, late widow of John Lloyd married to --- Huber of Pilesgrove d. 24 May 1790.
Bateman Lloyd, Sr., Esq. aged 66 years d. 3 Jun 1790.
Sarah Guest, age 35 years and 9 mos, formerly Vannemen, wife of Joseph Guest d. 4 Jul 1790.
Maria Forrester, a child of Alexander and Catharine Forrester d. 12 Nov 1790.
Henry Mitchel, a child of William and Ida Mitchel d. 17 Nov 1790.
Sarah Gill, a child of Matthew and Elizabeth Gill d. 22 Nov 1790.
Mary Shute, a child of William and Sarah Shute, d. 3 Mar 1790.
Susanna Avis, wife of Zacheus Avis d. 12 Mar 1790.
A child of Jacob and --- Lloyd d. 24 Mar 1790.
Ann Crawford, formerly Hoffman, wife of Andrew Crawford, shopkeeper in Woolwich Twp, b. 18 Jul 1771 in Pilesgrove Twp, Salem Co., d. 21 May 1790. She married to the present widower 25 Mar 1787, had 3 sons two which are alive. Barnes Crawford, b. 31 Mar 1789 and James Crawford, b. May 1791. Her age 19 years 10 mo and 3 days.
Henry Murphy, a married man, aged 49 years 1 mo., d. 26 Nov 1791. He was b. in Oct 1742 in Mannington Twp, Salem County. He first married Isabella Avis, by her had 4 children: Elizabeth Murphy, b. 2 May 1765 married to Levi Griffin; Sarah Murphy, single, b. 31 Oct 1767; Rebecca Murphy, b. 11 Nov 1771, married to --- Daugherty; John Murphy, single, b. 31 Jul 1773. Isabella Murphy died in Mar 1782. In Dec 1782 he married the present widow, late Martha White, late widow Burden, maiden name Holms. He was her third husband.
A child of Matthew Gill, Jr., and Elizabeth formerly Taylor d. 8 Feb 1792.
George Helderman, a married man aged 43 years 2 mo 3 weeks 3 days d. 11 Apr 1792. He was born in Europe in the empire of German 16 Jan 1749. 21 Oct 1778 he married his wife, Ann formerly Heins, with her had 5 children: Jacob Helderman, b. 1779; William Helderman, b.

28 Jul 1783; George Helderman, b. 25 Aug 1785; John Adam Helderman, b. 21 Sep 1788; Anna Helderman, b. 5 Aug 1790.

Joseph Shute, a married man aged 58 years 2 mo 4 weeks d. 22 Apr 1792. He was, b. in Woolwich Twp, Gloucester County, state of New Jersey near Racoon Creek 26 Jan 1734. Joseph Shute was married twice; his first wife was Sarah Peteson. With Sarah Peteson, he had 3 children; Samuel Shute, b. ---, lost at sea; Sarah Shute, b. --- single; Ruth Shute, b. 24 Nov 1770 married Jeconia Wood Forrest. Sarah departed 10 Aug 1775. Whereupon on the 31 Jan 1776, he married the present widow Sarah Barber, single. With Sarah, he had 3 children: Hannah Shute, b. 30 Jul 1777; Joseph Shute, b. 4 Jun 1780 and Isaac Shute, b. 15 Aug 1782.

Joseph Smith, d. 12 Sep 1792, little son of Joseph Smith, mariner in Piles Grove, Salem County and his wife Catharine, maiden name Ferrow, b. in Philadelphia 28 Jul 1786. His age was 6 years 1 mo and 2 weeks.

Matthew Gill, Sr. a married man d. 19 Oct 1792. His age was 79 years. He was born in 1713 in Europe in the kingdom of Ireland in Ulster Province in th county of Tyron. In the year 1738 he married his wife, Magdalene, maiden name Halten and with her had 11 children: John Gill, dec'd, b. 1739, married to Silla Patton; Sarah Gill, b. 28 Aug 1742; Magdalene Gill, b. 17 Nov 1744, departed; Cathrine Gill, b. 13 Jan 1746, married to Gerrit Vannemen, decd; Deborah Gill, b. 12 Jan 1748; Maria Gill, b. 16 Mar 1751; Christiana Gill, b. 15 Mar 1753, married to Jeconiah Wood; Matthew Gill, b. 7 Feb 1744, married to Elizabeth Taylor; Josiah Gill, b. 21 Aug 1759, lost at sea; James Gill, b. 3 Oct 1763 married to Maria Dickert; Hannah Gill, b. 1 Dec 1766, dec'd.

Jane Avis, widow of the late George Avis d. 7 Dec 1792, maiden name Angclow, her age 64 years. She was married to her late husband in 1747. On the 19 of Oct 1785 she became a widow. She had 8 children: William Avis, dec'd, b. 17 Aug 1749, married to Ann Rumford; James Avis, 2 Dec 1751 married to Mary Guest; Zacheus Avis, b. Jan 1754 married to Susannah Cashner, dec'd; Joseph Avis, b. 31 Mar 1756 married to Sarah Reily; Hannah Avis, b. 25 Apr 1758, married to Samuel Borden; Rachel Avis, b. 13 Jan 1761, married to Benjamin Johnson; Rebecca Avis, b. 5 Feb 1763 married to Joseph Harker; Jane Avis, b. 31 Mar 1766 married to Martin Kats, Jr.

Sarah Kats, child of Martin and Jane Kats d. 11 Dec 1792.

Agnes Avis, a child of John and Agnes Avis d. 18 Dec 1792.

John Hoffman, widower d. 5 Jan 1793 age 45 years 11 mo 15 days. He married his late wife in 1769 and Mar 10, 1785 became a widower. They had 7 children: Rahel Hoffman, b. 9 Dec 1770; Benjamin Hoffman, b. 9 Feb 1772; Rebecca Hoffman, b. 25 Mar 1774; Amy Hoffman, b. 24 Apr 1776; Lawrence Hoffman, b. 16 Jul 1779; Deborah Hoffman, b. 10 Mar 1782; Elijah Hoffman, b. 28 Jan 1785, d. soon after his mother. John Hoffman was b. 18 Jan 1747 in Piles Grove, Salem County.

Mary VanMemen, d. 14 Apr 1792, aged 69 years 6 mo 3 days, maiden name Halten, widow of Andrew VanMemen who d. 15 Dec 1774. They had 2 sons and 2 daus: Gerrit VanMemen, dec'd, b. --- married to Christine Gill; Andrew VanMemen, b. 31 Jan 1756 married to Catherine Guest; Mary VanMemen, b. 10 Feb 1762, married to John Smith; and a dau dec'd.

Martha Murphy d. 12 May 1792, formerly Holms, a widow aged 56 years. She was born in 1737, was three times married. Her first husband was Jonathan Borden with whom she had 9 children; 2 sons and 1 dau still living and 6 are gone before her. Her second husband was George White with whom she lived only 9 months and had one dau with him. After 12 years of widowhood, she was married to Henry Murphy in Dec 1782. He departed on 25 Nov 1791.

Mary Gill, a child of Matthew and Elizabeth Gill d. 8 Jun 1792.

Rachel Guest, a child of Henry and Jane Guest of Upper Penn's Neck d. 24 Jul 1792.

Joseph Guest, widower, b. 5 Jan 1748, d. 13 Aug 1793 aged 45 years 7 mos 7 days. On 26 Dec 1773 he married Sarah VanMemens, who died 2 Jul 1790. They had 8 children: Mary Guest, b. 24 Oct 1774; William Guest, b. 2 Apr 1777; Christina Guest, b. 8 Dec 1778; John Guest, b. 12 Sep 1780; Elizabeth Guest, b. 7 Mar 1783; Gerret Guest, b. 12 Sep 1784; Sarah Guest, b. 13 Dec 1786 dec'd; Rebecca Guest, b. 7 Feb 1789.

Abraham Smith, son of Joseph and Catherine Smith, b. 2 Jun 1788 Pilesgrove d. 17 Sep 1793.

Gill Wood, son of Jacomiah and Christina Wood, b. 10 Aug 1793, d. 14 Oct 1793.

David Whilly, d. 29 Oct 1793, a married man, farmer of upper Penn's Neck, Salem County. He was twice married, by his first wife had 5 sons and 1 dau who are all alive. Two sons and the dau are married.

Esaias James, son of Kisrael and Elizabeth James d. 7 Dec 1793 aged 17 mos.

Ann Cooper, d. 10 Dec 1793, dau of George and Hannah Cooper, aged 2 years 6 mos.

Margaret Linmyer, wife of Christopher Linmyer d. 11 Feb 1794.
James Hoffman, son of Lawrence and Sarah Hoffman, b. 26 Jan 1794, d. 18 Feb 1794.
--- Williams, wife of Justin Williams of Penn's Neck d. 31 May 1794.
Sarah Kats, dau of Martin and Jane Kats, b. 23 Feb 1771, d. 18 Jul 1794.

BIRTHS AND DEATHS OF WOODBURY MONTHLY MEETING

Anthony Allen of Woodbury, son of Matthew and Martha Allen, b. 11th mo [Jan], 6th da, 1743/4, d. 1st mo, 6th da, 1812 and his wife, Mary, dau of Enoch and Rachel Roberts, b. 8th mo [Oct], 14th da, 1744, d. 2nd mo, 11th da, 1823. Children: Rachel Allen, b. 4th mo, 19th da, 1769, Hannah Allen, b. 8th mo, 23rd da, 1770, d. 10th mo, 9th da, 1789; Mary Allen, b. 3rd mo, 13th da, 1776; Grace Allen, b. 4th mo, 20th da, 1778; Enoch R. Allen, b. 5th mo, 17th da, 1781; Martha Allen, b. 9th mo, 24th da, 1787.

Enoch R. Allen of Woodbury, son of Anthony and Mary Allen, b. 5th mo, 17th da, 1781 and his wife, Beulah, dau of Edward and Hannah Pancoast, b. 3rd mo, 5th da, 1783. Children: Mary R. Allen, b. 3rd mo, 13th da, 1809; Hannah P. Allen, b. 10th mo, 11th da, 1810; Eliza Allen, b. 3rd mo, 14th da, 1813.

William Allen of Greenwich Twp, son of John and Hope Allen, b. 9th mo, 14th da, 1772 and his wife, Rachel, dau of George and Rachel Ward, b. 2nd mo, 15th da, 1769. Children: George Allen, b. 12th mo, 20th da, 1797; Beulah Allen, b. 9th mo, 15th da, 1799; John Allen, b. 12th mo, 12th da, 1801; Mary Allen, b. 5th mo, 26th da, 1802; William Allen, b. 9th mo, 7th da, 1803; Rachel Allen, b. 11th mo, 23rd da, 1805.

William Allen of Greenwich Twp and his wife, Mary, dau of William and Judith Pine, b. 2nd mo, 17th da, 1783. Children: Benjamin Allen, b. 7th mo, 13th da, 1811; Richard Allen, b. 2nd mo, 5th da, 1813; William Allen, twin, b. 7th mo, 29th da, 1815; Mary P. Allen, twin, b. 7th mo, 29th da, 1815, d. 9th mo, 20th da, 1823.

Benajuh Andrews of Deptford Twp, son of Edward and Tabitha Andrews, b. 12th mo, 21st da, 1768 and his wife, Mary, dau of William and Mary Down, b. 6th mo, 26th da, 1771. Children: Benajuh D. Andrews, b. 2nd mo, 4th da, 1801; Josiah Andrews, b. 11th mo, 25th da, 1802; Joel W. Andrews, b. 10th mo, 22nd da, 1804, d. 1st mo, 22nd da, 1808.

Nehemiah Andrews, b. 9th mo, 22nd da, 1785, d. age 13 years, 2 months, 19 days. "Received to be recorded at Preparative Meeting at Woodbury 1st mo, 3rd da, 1822. Recorded the same day."

Isaac Ballinger, son of Amariah and Elizabeth Ballinger, b. 4th mo [Jun], 21st da, 1730, d. 6th mo, 30th da, 1785 and his wife, Patience, dau of Josiah and Ann Albertson, b. 6th mo [Aug], 1736, d. 11th mo, 9th da, 1790.

Isaac Ballenger [Ballinger], son of Thomas and Priscilla Ballenger, b.

10th mo, 18th da, 1770, d. 9th mo, 24th da, 1824 and his wife,
Esther, dau of Thomas and Sarah Stokes, b. 2nd mo, 11th da, 1772.
Children: Maria Ballenger, b. 11th mo, 11th da, 1795; Joseph I.
Ballenger, b. 7th mo, 24th da, 1797; Josiah Ballenger, b. 1st mo, 1st
da, 1799, d. 11th mo, 23rd da, 1799; Richard Ballenger, twin, b. 11th
mo, 6th da, 1800, d. 10th mo, 13th da, 1807; Edward Ballenger, twin,
b. 11th mo, 6th da, 1800; Isaac Ballenger, b. 5th mo, 13th da, 1803;
Thomas Ballenger, b. 12th mo, 21st da, 1804, d. 4th mo, 8th da, 1805;
Sarah Ballenger, b. 1st mo, 24th da, 1806; Jacob Ballenger, b. 9th
mo, 11th da, 1808; Priscilla Ballenger, b. 3rd mo, 31st da, 1810;
Samuel Ballenger, b. 11th mo, 29th da, 1813, d. 11th mo, 30th da,
1813; Elwood Ballenger, b. 5th mo, 11th da, 1816.

William Ballenger [Ballinger] of Deptford Twp, son of John and
Hannah Ballenger, and his wife, Beulah, dau of Isaiah and Abigail
Ward, b. 11th mo, 6th da, 1802. Children: John Ballenger, b. 11th
mo, 28th da, 1825; James W. Ballenger, b. 8th mo, 21st da, 1827;
Isaiah W. Ballenger, b. 8th mo, 9th da, 1829; Mary C. Ballenger, b.
8th mo, 28th da, 1832; William Ballenger, b. 6th mo, 30th da, 1835;
Abigail W. Ballenger, b. 3rd mo, 9th da, 1838; Beulah M. Ballenger, b.
9th mo, 29th da, 1840.

William Beckett of Greenwich Twp, son of Samuel and Hannah
Beckett, b. 6th mo, 1st da, 1770 and his wife, Sarah, dau of
Constantine and Sarah Lord, b. 5th mo, 3rd da, 1766, d. 11th mo,
16th da, 1822.

Rebecca [Alsop] Bell, dau of Othniel and Hannah Alsop, wife of Isaiah
Bell, b. 4th mo, 19th da, 1808.

Joseph Morgan Bennet [Bennett], son of Joseph W. and Mary Bennet,
b. 11th mo, 9th da, 1798.

Asher Brown, son of Samuel and Ann Brown, b. 9th mo, 11th da, 1760
and his wife, Mary, dau of George and Rachel Ward, b. 2nd mo, 12th
da, 1763. Children: David Brown, b. 9th mo, 26th da, 1784; George
Brown, b. 8th mo, 9th da, 1786, d. 6th mo, 1st da, 1803; Samuel
Brown, b. 6th mo, 27th da, 1788; Sarah Brown, b. 7th mo, 17th da,
1790, d. 3rd mo, 14th da, 1793; Ann Brown, b. 9th mo, 8th da, 1792;
Isaac Brown, b. 12th mo, 15th da, 1794, d. 4th mo, 21st da, 1795;
Israel Brown, b. 5th mo, 15th da, 1796; Benjamin Brown, b. 4th mo,
24th da, 1798; Mary C. Brown, b. 4th mo, 27th da, 1802.

David Brown (Elder), d. 5th mo, 11th da, 1816, in his 81st year and his
wife, Susannah. Children: Paul Brown, b. 1st mo, 5th da, 1763; Jesse
Brown, b. 7th mo, 1st da, 1765; David Brown, b. 2nd mo, 2nd da,
1767; Hephsibah [Hepzibah] Brown, b. 11th mo, 15th da, 1769; John

Brown, b. 1st mo, 1st da, 1776; Thomas Brown, b. 9th mo, 17th da, 1778, d. 7th mo, 20th da, 1779.

George Brown of Greenwich Twp, son of James and Catharine Brown, b. 3rd mo, 28th da, 1768 and his wife, Mary, dau of John and Margaret Miller, b. 7th mo, 26th da, 1770, d. 1st mo, 15th da, 1806. Children: John Miller Brown, b. 2nd mo, 21st da, 1793, d. 3rd mo, 8th da, 1793; Margaret Brown, b. 11th mo, 26th da, 1794; James Brown, b. 8th mo, 26th da, 1796; Rebekah Brown, b. 4th mo, 20th da, 1798; Miller Brown, b. 10th mo, 11th da, 1801; Mary Brown, b. 11th mo, 20th da, 1803; Sarah Brown, b. 1st mo, 7th da, 1806.

Jonathan Brown, son of John Brown, b. 7th mo [Sep], 4th da, 1748, d. 7th mo, 4th da, 1824 and his wife, Sarah, dau of Amariah Ballinger, b. 3rd mo, 12th da, 1756. Children: Mary Brown, b. 8th mo, 15th da, 1777, d. 2nd mo, 11th da, 1789; John Brown, b. 3rd mo, 19th da, 1780; Beulah Brown, b. 1st mo, 18th da, 1782, d. 12th mo, 23rd da, 1786; Sarah Brown, b. 12th mo, 7th da, 1784, d. 4th mo, 16th da, 1786; Josiah Brown, b. 1st mo, 25th da, 1787; Charles Brown, b. 7th mo, 22nd da, 1789; Joseph Brown, b. 1st mo, 31st da, 1792; Sarah Brown, twin, 2nd by this name, b. 1st mo, 11th da, 1794; Mary Brown, twin, b. 1st mo, 11th da, 1794; Lydia Brown, b. 10th mo, 25th da, 1797.

Thomas Carpenter of Greenwich Twp, son of Preston and Hannah Carpenter, b. 11th mo, 2nd da, 1752 and his wife, Mary, dau of Edward and Mary Tonkin, b. 9th mo [Nov], 8th da, 1748, d. 8th mo, 5th da, 1822.

Thomas Clark of Greenwich Twp, son of Thomas and Christian Clark, b. 1st mo, 18th da, 1767 and his wife, Achsa, dau of Edward and Hannah Pancoast, b. 1st mo, 26th da, 1767, d. 5th mo, 10th da, 1808. Children: Hannah Clark, b. 10th mo, 18th da, 1787; Thomas P. Clark, b. 5th mo, 17th da, 1789; Mary B. Clark, b. 5th mo, 23rd da, 1791; Beulah Clark, b. 7th mo, 25th da, 1793, d. 6th mo, 7th da, 1816; Achsa [Achsah] Clark, b. 2nd mo, 6th da, 1796; Eliza Clark, b. 5th mo, 2nd da, 1798; Edith Clark, b. 9th mo, 15th da, 1800; Ann Clark, b. 3rd mo, 10th da, 1804.

Hannah Clement, dau of Jacob and Hannah Clement, b. 10th mo, 25th da, 1763, d. 7th mo, 28th da, 1783.

Joseph Clement of Deptford Twp, son of Samuel and Rebecca Clement, b. 2nd mo [Apr], 28th da, 1737, d. 10th mo, 29th da, 1823 and his wife, Ann, dau of John and Ann Brich, b. 3rd mo [May], 28th da, 1738, d. 2nd mo, 15th da, 1814. Children: John Clement, b. 2nd mo, 28th da, 1762, d. 6th mo, 3rd da, 1812; Rebecca Clement, b. 10th mo,

12th da, 1763, d. in childhood; Joseph Clement, b. 10th mo, 13th da, 1765, d. in childhood; James Clement, b. 12th mo, 31st da, 1769, d. 8th mo, 21st da, 1811; Joseph Clement [2nd by this name], b. 8th mo, 15th da, 1772; Ann Clement, b. 3rd mo, 7th da, 1776, d. 11th mo, 8th da, 1814; Hannah Clement, b. 7th mo, 31st da, 1778.

Mark Clement of Deptford Twp, son of Samuel and Elizabeth Clement, b. 7th mo, 22nd da, 1790 and his wife, Rebecca, dau of James and Mary Davis, b. 2nd mo, 21st da, 1791. Children: Mark Clement, b. 8th mo, 5th da, 1813; Jacob Clement, b. 10th mo, 28th da, 1814, d. 4th mo, 5th da, 1818; Mary D. Clement, b. 10th mo, 29th da, 1815; Rebecca Clement, b. 4th mo, 25th da, 1817, d. 9th mo, 17th da, 1824; James D. Clement, b. 9th mo, 7th da, 1818; Isaac Clement, b. 3rd mo, 23rd da, 1820; Joseph Clement, twin, b. 12th mo, 30th da, 1821, d. 5th mo, 8th da, 1822; Benjamin Clement, twin, b. 12th mo, 30th da, 1821; William Clement, b. 3rd mo, 23rd da, 1823; Ann Clement, b. 3rd mo, 25th da, 1825; Joseph T. Clement, b. 10th mo, 25th da, 1826.

Thomas Clement of Deptford Twp, son of Abel and Elizabeth Clement, b. 9th mo, 20th da, 1774, and his wife, Rachel, dau of John and Ann Wood, b. 9th mo, 16th da, 1779, d. 8th mo, 3rd da, 1825. Children: John W. Clement, b. 1st mo, 22nd da, 1801; Sarah W. Clement, b. 1st mo, 11th da, 1803; Ruth Clement, b. 8th mo, 28th da, 1804; Zebedee Clement, b. 6th mo, 4th da, 1806; Charles W. Clement, b. 7th mo, 6th da, 1809; Lettice Clement, b. 10th mo, 5th da, 1810; Chalkley Clement, b. 12th mo, 31st da, 1812; Thomas Clement, b. 4th mo, 28th da, 1815; Rachel Clement, b. 2nd mo, 16th da, 1817; Ann W. Clement, b. 11th mo, 4th da, 1819; Elizabeth Clement, b. 3rd mo, 20th da, 1822.

Benjamin Cloud of Woodbury, b. 4th mo, 8th da, 1778 and his wife, Sarah Cloud, b. 10th mo, 5th da, 1774. Children: Joseph Cloud, b. 7th mo, 5th da, 1801; Adam Cloud, b. 7th mo, 14th da, 1803, d. 10th mo, 12th da, 1803; Lydia Cloud, b. 10th mo, 14th da, 1804; Charles R. Cloud, b. 5th mo, 4th da, 1807; John W. Cloud, b. 6th mo, 10th da, 1809; Hannah W. Cloud, b. 12th mo, 28th da, 1811; Benjamin Cloud, b. 9th mo, 4th da, 1814; Josiah Cloud, b. 10th mo, 19th da, 1817.

John W. Cloud of Deptford Twp, son of Benjamin and Sarah Cloud, b. 6th mo, 10th da, 1809 and his wife, Ann R., dau of Samuel and Margaret Harper, b. 2nd mo, 8th da, 1814.

Josiah W. Cloud of Deptford Twp, son of Benjamin and Sarah Cloud, b. 10th mo, 19th da, 1817 and his wife, Mary T., dau of John and Ann R. Glover, b. 9th mo, 7th da, 1824.

Isaac Collins of Chestnut Ridge, son of Benjamin and Mary Collins, b.

9th mo, [Nov], 17th da, 1742 o.s., d. 4th mo, 21st da, 1826 and his first wife, Sarah, dau of John and Elizabeth Collins, b. 3rd mo, [May], 30th da, 1729 o.s., d. 10th mo, 13th da, 1812. [No issue recorded]

Isaac Collins m. 2nd to Kezia [Kimsey] Chew, widow, dau. of Job and Elizabeth Kimsey, b. 8th mo., 2nd da, 1773. Child of Kezia and her 1st husband: Keziah S. Chew, b. 11th mo, 22nd da, 1808.

John Collins of Deptford Twp and his wife, Charity Collins. Children: John Collins, b. 2nd mo, 13th da, 1789; Elijah Collins, b. 2nd mo, 7th da, 1791; Sybilla Collins, b. 12th mo, 25th da, 1793; Ruth Collins, b. 8th mo, 1st da, 1796; Hannah Collins, b. 1st mo, 15th da, 1799; Aaron Collins, b. 11th mo, 29th da, 1801.

Robert Cook of Greenwich Twp, son of Ebenezer and Elizabeth Cook, b. 8th mo, 29th da, 1756, d. 9th mo, 30th da, 1823 and his wife, Lydia, dau of Abraham and Mary Chattin, b. 4th mo, 29th da, 1752, d. 8th mo, 31st da, 1822. Children: Sibyl Cook, b. 9th mo, 9th da, 1787; Sarah Cook, b. 7th mo, 4th da, 1789; Hannah Cook, b. 5th mo, 5th da, 1792.

Amos Cooper, son of David and Sybil Cooper, b. 10th mo [Dec], 1st da, 1749 and his wife, Sarah, dau of Archibald and Mary Mickle, b. 6th mo, 31st da, 1752, d. 2nd mo, 17th da, 1825. Children: Sybil Cooper, b. 3rd mo, 10th da, 1772; Mary Cooper, b. 8th mo, 26th da, 1776; Sarah Cooper, b. 2nd mo, 10th da, 1778; Hannah Cooper, b. 10th mo, 13th da, 1779; Joseph Cooper, b. 2nd mo, 8th da, 1781, d. 8th mo, 18th da, 1790; Anne Cooper, b. 7th mo, 20th da, 1784; David Cooper, b. 11th mo, 14th da, 1785; Isaac Mickle Cooper, b. 2nd mo, 28th da, 1790; John Cooper, b. 2nd mo, 28th da, 1792; Beulah Cooper, b. 11th mo, 5th da, 1773.

Amos Collins, son of Benjamin and Mary Collins, d. 4th mo, 6th da, 1812 in his 65th year.

David Cooper, son of John and Ann Cooper and father of Amos Cooper above, d. 11th mo, 5th da, 1795 in his 71st year.

Hannah Cooper, dau of John and Ann Cooper, b. 6th mo, 19th da, 1804, d. in 78th year.

David Cooper of Deptford Twp, son of Amos and Sarah Cooper, b. 11th mo, 14th da, 1785 and his wife, Hannah, dau of Thomas and Achsa Clark, b. 10th mo, 18th da, 1787. Children: Achsa [Achsah] Cooper, b. 9th mo, 23rd da, 1808; Lewis Cooper, b. 7th mo, 13th da, 1810; Sarah M. Cooper, b. 2nd mo, 27th da, 1812; Martha Cooper, b. 3rd mo, 3rd da, 1814; Mary Cooper, b. 3rd mo, 14th da, 1816; Redman Cooper, b.

1st mo, 1st da, 1818; David Cooper, b. 11th mo, 23rd da, 1819; Hannah Cooper, b. 11th mo, 28th da, 1821; Edward Cooper, b. 4th mo, 10th da, 1824.

James Cooper, son of John and Ann Cooper, b. 1st mo [Mar], 11th da, 1720, d. 8th mo, 3, 1789 and his wife, Deborah, dau of Richard and Rebecca Matlack, b. 2nd mo [Apr], 18th da, 1729, d. 6th mo, 12th da, 1759. Children: Benjamin Clark Cooper, b. 11th mo [Jan], 15th da, 1748; James Cooper, b. 12th mo [Feb], 3rd da, 1750, d. 11th mo, 17th da, 1753; James Cooper [2nd by this name], b. 2nd mo, 7th da, 1754, d. 9th mo, 1st da, 1819; Rebecca Cooper, b. 10th mo, 11th da, 1756, d. 10th mo, 26th da, 1798.

James Cooper m. second to Mary Jessup, dau of John and Margaret Jessup, d. 2nd mo, 14th da, 1794 in her 57th year. Children: Deborah Cooper, b. 9th mo, 7th da, 1765, d. 3rd mo, 5th da, 1766; Samuel Cooper, b. 1st mo, 1st da, 1767, d. 1st mo, 15th da, 1767; Sarah Cooper, b. 7th mo, 3rd da, 1768, d. 9th mo, 4th da, 1778; William Cooper, b. 9th mo, 24th da, 1770; John Cooper, b. 12th mo, 9th da, 1774; Esther Cooper, b. 10th mo, 28th da, 1777.

Paul Cooper of Deptford Twp, son of David and Sybil Cooper, b. 1st mo, 11th da, 1754 and his first wife, Catharine, dau of Isaac and Anne Smart, b. 8th mo [Oct], 6th da, 1750, d. 10th mo, 13th da, 1781. Child: Catharine Cooper, b. 10th mo, 6th da, 1781.

Paul Cooper m. 2nd to Hannah Branson, dau of John and Sarah Branson, b. 2nd mo, 2nd da, 1763. Child: David B. Cooper, b. 9th mo, 11th da, 1807.

Warner T. Cooper of Deptford Twp, son of William and Hannah Cooper, b. 5th mo, 22nd da, 1813 and his wife, Deborah, dau of David and Ann W. Whitall, b. 9th mo, 16th da, 1824.

William Cooper and his first wife, Ann, dau of Mark and Phebe Miller, b. 3rd mo, 31st da, 1779, d. 4th mo, 29th da, 1800. [No issue recorded]

William Cooper m. second to Sarah, dau of Joseph and Mary Morgan, b. 2nd mo, 12th da, 1774. Children: Mary Cooper, b. 2nd mo, 26th da, 1807; Ann Cooper, b. 9th mo, 19th da, 1808, d. 6th mo, 11th da, 1834; Joseph M. Cooper, twin, b. 6th mo, 8th da, 1810; James Cooper, twin, b. 6th mo, 8th da, 1810; William E. Cooper, b. 4th mo, 11th da, 1812; John Cooper, b. 7th mo, 15th da, 1814.

George Craft of Deptford Twp, son of George and Mary Craft, b. 2nd mo, 27th da, 1767 and his wife, Rebekah, dau of Benjamin and Rebekah Gibbs, b. 9th mo, 29th da, 1766. Children: Beulah Craft, b. 1st mo, 28th da, 1790; Rebekah Craft, b. 7th mo, 11th da, 1792; Aldin

G. Craft, b. 5th mo, 20th da, 1797; George Craft, b. 12th mo, 14th da, 1798; Lydia Craft, b. 8th mo, 30th da, 1800; Mary Ann Craft, b. 8th mo, 3rd da, 1804.

James Davis of Deptford Twp, son of Gabriel and Sarah Davis, b. 7th mo, 8th da, 1764 and his wife, Mary, dau of Thomas and Mary Hackney, b. 5th mo, 11th da, 1769. Children: Rebecca Davis, b. 2nd mo, 21st da, 1791; Samuel Davis, b. 5th mo, 8th da, 1793; Sarah Davis, b. 5th mo, 28th da, 1795; Hannah Davis, b. 2nd mo, 7th da, 1797; Mary Davis, b. 4th mo, 8th da, 1799; James Davis, b. 10th mo, 31st da, 1803; Ann Davis, b. 10th mo, 11th da, 1805; Abigail Davis, b. 8th mo, 15th da, 1808; Gabriel Davis, b. 11th mo, 15th da, 1810.

Joseph Eastlack of Deptford Twp, son of Francis and Phebe Eastlack, b. 7th mo [Sep], 20th da, 1738 o.s. and his wife Hannah, dau of William and Abigail Kaighn, b. 4th mo [Jun], 21st da, 1743 o.s., d. 3rd mo, 31st da, 1813.

Enoch Evens of Greenwich Twp and his wife, Rebecca, b. 4th mo, 7th da, 1787. Children: William Evens, b. 12th mo, 30th da, 1815; Lydia T. Evens, b. 4th mo, 5th da, 1818; Rachel Evens, b. 10th mo, 30th da, 1821; Joseph T. Evens, b. 9th mo, 5th da, 1823.

Jonathan Fisher, son of Jonathan and Mary Fisher, b. 3rd mo [May], 29th da, 1725 and his wife, Hannah, dau of John and Elizabeth Hutchenson, b. 11th mo [Jan], 27th da, 1728, d. 4th mo, 13th da, 1793. Children: Jonathan Fisher, b. 1st mo, 16th da, 1752; Hannah Fisher, b. 11th mo, 15th da, 1753; Sarah Fisher, b. 9th mo, 16th da, 1755; Elizabeth Fisher, b. 1st mo, 23rd da, 1758.

Michael C. Fisher of Gloucester, son of Charles and Ann Fisher, b. 9th mo, 30th da, 1772, and his second wife, Ann, dau of Joseph and Ann [Birch] Clement, b. 3rd mo, 7th da, 1776, d. 11th mo, 8th da, 1814. Children: Rebecca B. Fisher, b. 1st mo, 15th da, 1809; Hannah Ann Fisher, b. 8th mo, 26th da, 1810; Charles Fisher, 11th mo, 25th da, 1812; Sarah Fisher, b. 9th mo, 4th da, 1814, d. 8th mo, 6th da, 1815.

Michael Fisher m. third to Mary, dau of Joseph and Elizabeth Reeves, b. 10th mo, 21st da, 1788. Children: Joseph R. Fisher, b. 3rd mo, 11th da, 1822; William C. Fisher, b. 12th mo, 31st da, 1824; Lydia C. Fisher, b. 4th mo, 25th da, 1826; Mary R. Fisher, b. 4th mo, 26th da, 1830.

Thomas Folwell, b. 4th mo [Jun], 27th da, 1736, d. 1st mo, 6th da, 1787 and his wife, Elizabeth, b. 8th mo [Oct], 11th da, 1738, d. 11th mo, 11th da, 1789. Children: William Folwell, b. 11th mo, 24th da, 1758; Elizabeth Folwell, b. 3rd mo, 23rd da, 1761; Samuel Folwell, b. 6th mo, 22nd da, 1763; Nathan Folwell, b. 3rd mo, 30th da, 1769; John

Folwell, b. 6th mo, 3rd da, 1772; Thomas Folwell, Jr., b. 4th mo, 5th
da, 1774; Mary Folwell, b. 7th mo, 5th da, 1777; Ann Folwell, b. 10th
mo, 30th da, 1779.

Joseph Gibson of Woolwich, son of Joseph and Sarah Gibson, b. 3rd mo
[May], 9th da, 1749, d. 7th mo, 21st da, 1799 and his wife, Sarah, dau
of William and Sarah Haines, b. 1st mo, 28th da, 1756. Children:
Mary Gibson, b. 9th mo, 22nd da, 1779; Sarah Gibson, b. 10th mo,
13th da, 1781; Jacob Gibson, b. 10th mo, 3rd da, 1783, d. 12th mo,
10th da, 1787; Spicer Gibson, b. 12th mo, 7th da, 1785, d. 10th mo,
3rd da, 1802; David Gibson, b. 8th mo, 19th da, 1791, d. 3rd mo, 2nd
da, 1803; Joshua Gibson, b. 5th mo, 21st da, 1793, d. 5th mo, 22nd
da, 1793; Asa Gibson, b. 6th mo, 12th da, 1795; Aaron Gibson, b.
12th mo, 11th da, 1797.

George M. Glover of Woodbury, son of William and Mary Glover, b.
12th mo, 21st da, 1800 and his wife, Beulah, dau of Joseph and Sarah
Glover, b. 7th mo, 2nd da, 1799.

George M. Glover m. second to Elizabeth, dau of James and Hannah
Mickle, b. 6th mo, 14th da, 1794.

William Glover, son of Thomas and Mary Glover, b. 9th mo, 1st da,
1776 and his wife, Mary Mickle, b. 10th mo, 16th da, 1776, d. 2nd
mo, 23rd da, 1825. Children: Geo. Mickle Glover, b. 12th mo, 21st da,
1800; Sarah M. Glover, b. 8th mo, 7th da, 1802; Ann L. Glover, b. 9th
mo, 15th da, 1804; Thomas Glover, b. 9th mo, 15th da, 1806; Hannah
Glover, b. 11th mo, 24th da, 1808; Eliza Glover, b. 4th mo, 17th da,
1812; Sophia Glover, b. 2nd mo, 15th da, 1814; Samuel M. Glover, b.
1st mo, 7th da, 1816; Addeline Glover, b. 5th mo, 21st da, 1817;
Gulielma Glover, b. 10th mo, 30th da, 1819.

Isaac Haines of Greenwich Twp, b. 1st mo, 23rd da, 1792 and his wife,
Hannah P., b. 7th mo, 3rd da, 1795. Children: John Haines, b. 4th
mo, 8th da, 1819; Priscilla P. Haines, b. 11th mo, 21st da, 1821.

Jacob Haines of Greenwich Twp, son of William and Elizabeth Haines,
b. 5th mo, 1st da, 1758, d. 8th mo, 26th da, 1823 and his wife,
Elizabeth, dau of Samuel and Isabel Paul, b. 5th mo, 1st da, 1762, d.
6th mo, 7th da, 1819. Children: Samuel Haines, b. 8th mo, 16th da,
1790, d. 10th mo, 25th da, 1806; Joel Haines, b. 9th mo, 25th da,
1794; Anna Haines, b. 12th mo, 17th da, 1800.

Joel P. Haines of Greenwich Twp, son of Jacob and Elizabeth Haines,
b. 9th mo, 25th da, 1794 and his wife, Hannah. Children: Samuel
Haines, b. 10th mo, 17th da, 1821; Joshua Haines, b. 10th mo, 16th
da, 1823.

William Haines, son of John and Hipparchia Haines, b. 12th mo, 7th da, 1779 and his wife, Ann, dau of William and Ann White, b. 1st mo, 3rd da, 1784. Children: Joshua Haines, b. 1st mo, 31st da, 1804; Ann W. Haines, b. 9th mo, 15th da, 1806; William Haines, b. 3rd mo, 8th da, 1810; Sarah Haines, b. 9th mo, 4th da, 1813; Samuel Haines, b. 9th mo, 27th da, 1816.

Jane M. Harper of Woodbury, dau of Samuel and Margaret Harper, b. 8th mo, 5th da, 1817.

Joshua Henszey [Hensey] of Philadelphia and his wife, Mary. Son: Isaac Henszey [Hensey], b. 1st mo [Mar], 22nd da, 1744.

Aaron Hewes, son of Aaron and Providence Hewes, b. 12th mo [Feb], 26th da, 1743, d. 6th mo, 2nd da, 1789 and his wife, Jane West, b. 3rd mo [May], 10th da, 1746, d. 8th mo, 1st da, 1820.

Providence Hewes, wife of Aaron Hewes, b. 3rd mo [May], 1702, d. 9th mo, 25th da, 1788.

Frances [Paschall] Howell, dau of John and Frances Paschall, widow of John Ladd Howell, b. 10th mo [Dec], 27th da, 1740 o.s., d. 5th mo, 2nd da, 1812.

Joseph Hurst of Gloucester City, Camden Co., moved from near Manchester, England in autumn of 1848, b. 12th mo, 12th da, 1797, d. 6th mo, 23rd da, 1849 and his wife, Mary Hurst, b. 5th mo, 20th da, 1800.

Mark Jenings [Jennings] of Deptford Twp, son of Jacob and Ann Jenings, b. 3rd mo, 17th da, 1786 and his wife, Mary, dau of Richard and Catharine Fleetwood, b. 8th mo, 30th da, 1793. Children: Jacob Jenings, b. 10th mo, 11th da, 1809, d. 8th mo, 3rd da, 1815; Catherine Ann Jenings, b. 4th mo, 9th da, 1812; Mark Jenings, b. 8th mo, 17th da, 1814, d. 11th mo, 13th da, 1821; Mary Jenings, b. 4th mo, 24th da, 1817, d. 8th mo, 26th da, 1817; Richard Jenings, b. 7th mo, 15th da, 1818; Isaac Jenings, b. 1st mo, 21st da, 1820; Jacob M. Jenings, b. 10th mo, 28th da, 1823; Sarah Jenings, b. 6th mo, 21st da, 1826; Job Jenings, b. 5th mo, 7th da, 1828; Jehue Jenings, b. 9th mo, 8th da, 1830; Mary Jane Jenings, b. 1st mo, 14th da, 1833.

John Jessup of Deptford Twp, b. 2nd mo, 23rd da, 1811 and his wife, Elizabeth Jessup, b. 12th mo, 13th da, 1809.

Isaac Jones of Woodbury, son of David and Naomi Jones, d. 7th mo, 19th da, 1803 and his wife, Sarah, dau of Noah and Rebecca Ridgway, b. 6th mo, 4th da, 1760, d. 11th mo, 13th da, 1822. Children: Rebecca Jones, b. 6th mo, 4th da, 1789.

Clement H. Kay and his wife, Edith Kay. Children: Elwood Kay, b. 1st mo, 15th da, 1821; James W. Kay, b. 4th mo, 11th da, 1822. (Acct. rec. from grandfather Isaac Kay on 5th mo, 28th da, 1825, to be recorded. S.M.)

Isaac Kay of Gloucester, son of Joseph and Ann Kay, b. 8th mo, 22nd da, 1765 and his wife, Deborah, dau of William and Deborah Eldridge, b. 1st mo, 19th da, 1770. Children: Hope Kay, b. 11th mo, 6th da, 1789; Deborah E. Kay, b. 4th mo, 21st da, 1792; Joseph Kay, b. 3rd mo, 14th da, 1794; Rebecca Kay, b. 2nd mo, 20th da, 1796, d. 2nd mo, 21st da, 1797; Isaac Kay, b. 3rd mo, 26th da, 1798, d. 9th mo, 29th da, 1799; Ann Kay, b. 2nd mo, 5th da, 1800, d. 6th mo, 21st da, 1800; Clement H. Kay, b. 8th mo, 24th da, 1801; Hannah Kay, b. 3rd mo, 9th da, 1804, d. 8th mo, 17th da, 1804; William E. Kay, b. 8th mo, 18th da, 1805; Sarah Kay, b. 2nd mo, 15th da, 1808.

Martha Kay, dau of Josiah and Martha Kay, b. 3rd mo, 11th da, 1787.

Nathan Keais, b. 11th mo, 10th da, 1781.

John Knight of Upper Greenwich Twp, son of John and Catharine Knight, b. 6th mo, 9th da, 1760 and his first wife, Sarah, dau of Noah and Rebecca Ridgway and relic of Isaac Jones, b. 7th mo, 24th da, 1760, d. 11th mo, 13th da, 1822.

John Knight m. second to Mary, dau of Cabel and Elizabeth Lippincott, b. 11th mo, 27th da, 1768.

Hannah Ladd, widow of John Ladd, b. 3rd mo [Mar], 27th da, 1715 o.s., d. 1st mo, 27th da, 1797.

Samuel Ladd of Deptford Twp, son of Jonathan Ladd, d. 3rd mo, 5th da, 1796 and his wife, Sarah, dau of John and Elizabeth Hambleton, d. 1st mo, 19th da, 1814 in her 81st year. Children: Jonathan Ladd, b. 9th mo, 23rd da, 1755, d. 6th mo, 6th da, 1760; Ann Ladd, b. 7th mo, 11th da, 1757, d. 6th mo, 28th da, 1782; Hannah Ladd, b. 11th mo, 7th da, 1759, d. 11th mo, 2nd da, 1789; Eldad Ladd, b. 6th mo, 2nd da, 1762, d. 8th mo, 11th da, 1776; John Ladd, b. 11th mo, 2nd da, 1764, d. 11th mo, 2nd da, 1765; Deborah Ladd, b. 9th mo, 23rd da, 1766, d. 3rd mo, 3rd da, 1771; Samuel Ladd, b. 11th mo, 10th da, 1771.

Mary Langstaff, widow of Laban Langstaff, b. 9th mo, 2nd da, 1823.

Hannah Leeds, dau of Yemmons and Bridget Gillingham, widow of Daniel Leeds of Deptford Twp, b. 6th mo, 9th da, 1804.

Phebe A. Leeds of Woodbury, dau of Cabel and Lydia Sead and wife of G. Howard Leeds, b. 1st mo, 31st da, 1824.

Samuel B. Lippincott of Gloucester, son of Joshua and Amy Lippincott, b. 8th mo, 16th da, 1784 and his wife, Mary B. [Clark] Lippincott, dau of Thomas and Achsa Clark, b. 5th mo, 23rd da, 1791. Children: Martha D. Lippincott, b. 3rd mo, 20th da, 1810; Bowman Lippincott, b. 4th mo, 13th da, 1813; Thomas Clark Lippincott, b. 3rd mo, 20th da, 1815, d. 2nd mo, 9th da, 1826; Franklin Lippincott, b. 3rd mo, 11th da, 1818; Mary Lippincott, b. 12th mo, 5th da, 1819; Samuel P. Lippincott, b. 1st mo, 28th da, 1826.

William Lippincott, son of Restore Lippincott, b. 10th mo, 15th da, 1755 and his wife, Elizabeth, b. 1753, d. 4th mo, 28th da, 1824. Children: Jacob Lippincott, b. 2nd mo, 18th da, 1775; William Lippincott, b. 12th mo, 18th da, 1776, d. 9th mo, 18th da, 1780; Peter Lippincott, b. 1st mo, 5th da, 1779, d. 2nd mo, 20th da, 1783; Deborah Lippincott, b. 2nd mo, 21st da, 1781; Restore Lippincott, b. 4th mo, 16th da, 1783; William Lippincott (2nd by this name), b. 12th mo, 18th da, 1787, d. 6th mo, 27th da, 1789; Elizabeth Lippincott, b. 11th mo, 20th da, 1789.

Benjamin J. Lord of Deptford Twp, son of Joshua and Sarah Lord, b. 10th mo, 19th da, 1812 and his wife, Mary E., dau of William and Atlantic Thomas, b. 1st mo, 20th da, 1819.

Constantine Lord, son of Edward Lord, d. 5th mo, 29th da, 1790 at age about 55 and his wife, Sarah, dau of Benjamin Albertson, b. 1738, d. 8th mo, 30th da, 1813. Children: Benjamin Lord, b. 4th mo, 23rd da, 1761; Elizabeth Lord, b. 8th mo, 13th da, 1763; Sarah Lord, b. 5th mo, 3rd da, 1766; James Lord, b. 5th mo, 4th da, 1781.

Elizabeth Lord of Deptford Twp, dau of Joshua and Sarah Lord, b. 11th mo, 16th da, 1809.

Hannah Lord, mother of Jehu Lord, d. 12th mo, 25th da, 1801 at age 75 years, 5 months, 10 days. Interred Friends Ground Woodbury on 27th da, 12th mo, 1801.

Jehu Lord, son of Joshua and Hannah Lord, b. 2nd mo, 27th da, 1770 and his wife, Rebecca, dau of Daniel Walton, b. 5th mo, 16th da, 1764. Children: Sarah Lord, b. 12th mo, 31st da, 1792; Hannah Lord, b. 11th mo, 13th da, 1794; Mary Lord, b. 5th mo, 29th da, 1798; Lydia Lord, b. 9th mo, 29th da, 1799.

Joshua Lord of Deptford Twp, son of Joshua and Hannah Lord, b. 4th mo, 21st da, 1766, and his wife, Sarah [Jessup] Lord, b. 9th mo, 29th da, 1771. Children: Joshua Lord, b. 10th mo, 23rd da, 1801, d. 9th mo, 26th da, 1817; James Jessup Lord, b. 7th mo, 27th da, 1803; John Star Lord, b. 6th mo, 10th da, 1805; Mary Lord, b. 8th mo, 9th da, 1807; Elizabeth Lord, b. 11th mo, 16th da, 1809; Benjamin Lord, b. 10th mo, 19th da, 1812; Sarah Lord, b. 2nd mo, 19th da, 1816, d. 9th mo, 22nd da, 1817.

Phineas Lord of Deptford Twp, son of Joshua and Hannah [Enoch] Lord, b. 11th mo [Jan], 21st da, 1749, d. 4th mo, 28th da, 1813 and his wife, Mercy [Gibbs] Lord, dau of Benjamin and Phebe Gibbs, b.

2nd mo, 12th da, 1754.
Hannah Enoch, dau of Thomas and Mary Enoch, mother of Phineas Lord, d. 12th mo, 7th da, 1792.
David Mickle of Clonmell, son of William and Sarah Mickle, b. 3rd mo, 27th da, 1779, d. 6th mo, 25th da, 1819 and his wife, Rachel, dau of Moses and Margaret Wills, b. 6th mo, 24th da, 1777. Children: Sarah L. Mickle, b. 10th mo, 7th da, 1805; Moses Wills Mickle, b. 7th mo, 30th da, 1808; Charles Mickle, b. 5th mo, 14th da, 1812.
Eunice Mickle of Deptford Twp, dau of James and Hannah Mickle, b. 6th mo, 14th da, 1794.
George Mickle of Greenwich Twp, son of William and Sarah Mickle, b. 11th mo, 11th da, 1782 and his wife, Mary, dau of Jonathan and Sarah Brown, b. 1st mo, 11th da, 1794. Children: William Mickle, b. 7th mo, 24th da, 1813; Sarah Mickle, b. 5th mo, 12th da, 1817; Martha Mickle, b. 12th mo, 16th da, 1820; Mary Mickle, b. 3rd mo, 24th da, 1828.
James Mickle of Greenwich Twp, son of William and Sarah Mickle, b. 10th mo [Dec], 26th da, 1747 o.s., d. 10th mo, 26th da, 1815 and his first wife, Lettitia, dau of William and Rachel Wood. Children: Anna Mickle, b. 6th mo, 25th da, 1773, d. 11th mo, 14th da, 1825; Sarah Mickle, b. 2nd mo, 1st da, 1776; Rachel Mickle, b. 6th mo, 25th da, 1777, d. 1779.
James Mickle m. second to Hannah, dau of Joshuah and Hannah Lord, b. 2nd mo, 26th da, 1759. Children: Rebecca Mickle, b. 6th mo, 4th da, 1785; Mary Mickle, b. 10th mo, 20th da, 1786, d. 10th mo, 19th da, 1806; Martha Mickle, b. 1st mo, 18th da, 1788; Hannah Mickle, b. 8th mo, 11th da, 1789; John Mickle, b. 8th mo, 12th da, 1791; Eunice Mickle, twin, b. 6th mo, 14th da, 1794; Elizabeth Mickle, twin, b. 6th mo, 14th da, 1794; James Mickle, Jr., b. 12th mo, 15th da, 1797.
Sarah L. Mickle of Woodbury, dau of David and Rachel Mickle, b. 10th mo, 7th da, 1805.
Samuel Mickle, son of Samuel and Letticia Mickle, b. 7th mo [Sep], 1st da, 1746 o.s., and his wife, Margery, dau of Robert Friend and Hannah Price, b. 2nd mo [Apr], 13th da, 1748 o.s., d. 10th mo, 13th da, 1809 at 1 A.M.
Samuel Mickle of Greenwich Twp, son of William and Sarah Mickle, b. 8th mo, 24th da, 1752, and his first wife, Ann, dau of Joshua and Hannah Lord, b. 2nd mo, 9th da, 1757, d. 9th mo, 2nd da, 1785. Children: Mary Mickle, b. 10th mo, 16th da, 1776, m. William Glover, d. 2nd mo, 23rd da, 1825; Samuel Mickle, b. 12th mo, 4th da, 1780.
Samuel Mickle m. second to Sophia, dau of John [Jonathan] and Sarah

Brown, b. 2nd mo, 1st da, 1753. Children: William Mickle, b. 10th mo, 30th da, 1790; Ann C. Mickle, b. 9th mo, 4th da, 1792; Sarah Mickle, b. 2nd mo, 14th da, 1797.

William Mickle, son of William and Sarah Mickle, b. 2nd mo [Apr], 18th da, 1741, d. 5th mo, 26th da, 1789 and his wife, Sarah, dau of Joshua and Hannah Lord. Children: Joshua Mickle, b. 2nd mo, 14th da, 1773, d. 2nd mo, 4th da, 1791; Hannah Mickle, b. 5th mo, 24th da, 1774, d. 11th mo, 1779; John Mickle, b. 4th mo, 21st da, 1776, d. 11th mo, 1787; David Mickle, twin, b. 3rd mo, 27th da, 1779; William Mickle, twin, b. 3rd mo, 27th da, 1779, d. 9th mo, 1779; William Mickle (2nd by this name), b. 7th mo, 16th da, 1781, d. 11th mo, 1787; George Mickle, b. 11th mo, 11th da, 1782; Sybil Mickle, b. 4th mo, 4th da, 1785.

William Mickle of Deptford Twp, son of George and Mary [Brown] Mickle, b. 7th mo, 24th da, 1813, and his wife, Mary, dau of Joseph and Grace Evans, b. 5th mo, 23rd da, 1823.

Eliz. Knight Newman [Elizabeth Newman Knight], dau of Richard and Ruth Newman, b. 5th mo, 28th da, 1808.

John Packer of Deptford Twp, son of Daniel and Catharine Packer, b. 11th mo, 17th da, 1774 and his wife, Christiannah Dorothy, dau of Laurence and Mary Shuster, b. 10th mo, 31st da, 1778. Children: Jonathan Packer, b. 11th mo, 5th da, 1797; Laurence Packer, b. 11th mo, 30th da, 1799; Esther Packer, b. 2nd mo, 23rd da, 1803; Rhoda Packer, b. 2nd mo, 3rd da, 1806; John Packer, b. 4th mo, 3rd da, 1809; Daniel Packer, b. 6th mo, 19th da, 1812; Christiana Packer, b. 11th mo, 5th da, 1814; Elizabeth Packer, b. 8th mo, 2nd da, 1817.

Jonathan Packer of Deptford Twp, son of John and Christiannah [Dorothy] Packer, b. 11th mo, 5th da, 1797 and his wife, Elizabeth R., dau of Samuel and Deborah Coleman, b. 6th mo, 27th da, 1798.

Samuel Packer, b. 7th mo, 20th da, 1772 and his wife, Sarah Packer, b. 3rd mo, 26th da, 1772. Children: Catharine Packer, b. 1st mo, 10th da, 1793; John Packer, b. 9th mo, 10th da, 1795; Samuel Packer, Jr. b. 4th mo, 28th da, 1798; Ann Packer, b. 1st mo, 5th da, 1801; William P. [Paul] Packer, b. 8th mo, 2nd da, 1803.

Cooper Paul of Greenwich, son of Joshua and Mary Paul, b. 10th mo, 2nd da, 1781, d. 8th mo, 15th da, 1813 and his wife, Sibyl, dau of William and Sarah Mickle, b. 4th mo, 4th da, 1785. Children: George Mickle Paul, b. 4th mo, 13th da, 1804; William Mickle Paul, b. 1st mo, 19th da, 1806; Joshua Paul, b. 11th mo, 16th da, 1807; Charles Paul, b. 8th mo, 28th da, 1809; Hannah Paul, b. 1st mo, 15th da, 1812, d. 8th mo, 23rd da, 1813; Sarah Cooper Paul, b. 1st mo, 18th da, 1814.

George M. Paul of Deptford Twp, son of Cooper and Sibyl Paul, b. 4th mo, 13th da, 1804 and his wife, Mary Ann, dau of Samuel and Sarah Webster, b. 11th mo, 7th da, 1803.

Joshua Paul of Woodbury, son of Cooper and Sibyl Paul, b. 11th mo, 16th da, 1807 and his wife, Lydia C., dau of Michael C. and Mary R. Fisher.

Samuel Paul of Greenwich, b. 1774, d. 1st mo, 17th da, 1823 and his wife, Delia. Children: Harriet Paul, b. 7th mo, 27th da, 1799; Isabella Paul, b. 8th mo, 28th da, 1801; Joel Paul, b. 1st mo, 6th da, 1804; Samuel Paul, b. 2nd mo, 21st da, 1807; Elizabeth Paul, b. 3rd mo, 26th da, 1809, d. 10th mo, 5th da, 1823; Mary Ann Paul, b. 12th mo, 10th da, 1810; David S. Paul, b. 12th mo, 1st da, 1812; Sarah D. Paul, b. 4th mo, 6th da, 1815; Delia Paul, b. 8th mo, 6th da, 1817; Nathan Paul, b. 5th mo, 6th da, 1819.

Mary Pettit, dau of Joseph and Mary Pettit, b. 8th mo, 10th da, 1793.

Jane H. [Sleeper] Pickering, dau of Benjamin H. and Deborah Sleeper, wife of Jonathan Pickering of Woodbury, b. 12th mo, 21st da, 1819.

Rebecca [Scattergood] Pike of Woodbury, dau of Thomas and Sarah Scattergood, widow of Stephen Pike.

Stephen Pike of Woodbury and wife, Rebecca, dau of Thomas and Sarah Scattergood, b. 10th mo, 4th da, 1790. Children: Sarah Pike, b. 9th mo, 27th da, 1820; Mary Pike, b. 10th mo, 19th da, 1822; Thomas Scattergood Pike, b. 9th mo, 25th da, 1824.

William Pine of Greenwich, son of Benjamin and Hannah Pine, b. 3rd mo, 11th da, 1759 and his wife, Judith, dau of Daniel and Hannah Lippincott, b. 1st mo, 24th da, 1763, d. 3rd mo, 8th da, 1823. Children: Mary Pine, b. 2nd mo, 17th da, 1783; Joseph Pine, b. 2nd mo, 1st da, 1787; Benjamin Pine, b. 9th mo, 29th da, 1788; Joshua Pine, b. 1st mo, 14th da, 1791; Hannah Pine, b. 7th mo, 3rd da, 1795; Priscilla Pine, b. 12th mo, 31st da, 1797; Rebecca Pine, b. 10th mo, 10th da, 1799; Samuel Pine, b. 9th mo, 3rd da, 1801.

Beulah [Brown] Reeve, dau of John and Sarah Brown, widow of John Reeve, Jr. b. 9th mo, 4th da, 1807.

Biddle Reeves, son of Biddle Reeves, b. 10th mo, 4th da, 1766 and his wife, Elizabeth, dau of Joseph and Mary Haines, b. 3rd mo, 13th da, 1767, d. 9th mo, 4th da, 1800. Children: Joshua Reeves, b. 1st mo, 24th da, 1794; Biddle Reeves, b. 11th mo, 9th da, 1796, d. 6th mo, 12th da, 1799.

Biddle Reeves, son of Biddle Reeves, b. 10th mo, 4th da, 1766 and his second wife, Elizabeth, dau of Peter and Miriam Ellis, b. 2nd mo, 27th da, 1774. Children: Biddle Reeves (2nd by this name), b. 9th mo,

13th da, 1807, d. 3rd mo, 4th da, 1808; Elizabeth Reeves, b. 7th mo, 6th da, 1809; Biddle Reeves (3rd by this name), b. 5th mo, 14th da, 1814.

Biddle Reeves of Deptford Twp, son of Biddle and Elizabeth [Ellis] Reeves, b. 5th mo, 14th da, 1814 and his wife, Sarah, dau of Paul and Hope Scull, b. 10th mo, 19th da, 1816.

John Reeve, son of Joseph and Eleanor Reeve, b. 5th mo [Jul], 1729, d. 1st mo, 4th da, 1816 and his wife, Jane West-Hewes Reeve.

Joseph Reeves, son of Thomas and Sarah Reeves, b. 4th mo [Jun], 20th da, 1741 and his wife, Elizabeth, dau of Joseph and Sarah Morgan, b. 3rd mo, 17th da, 1752, d. 9th mo, 1797. Children: Hannah Reeves, b. 4th mo, 4th da, 1775; Sarah Reeves, b. 7th mo, 25th da, 1777, d. 3rd mo, 8th da, 1817; Joseph Reeves, b. 1st mo, 9th da, 1780, d. 8th mo, 30th da, 1798; Isaac Reeves, b. 9th mo, 22nd da, 1782; John Reeves, b. 3rd mo, 30th da, 1785, d. 9th mo, 1797; Mary Reeves, b. 10th mo, 21st da, 1788; Samuel Reeves, b. 10th mo, 23rd da, 1790; Benjamin Reeves, b. 1st mo, 6th da, 1795, d. 10th mo, 21st da, 1819.

Sarah [Gill] Reeves, dau of John and Sarah Gill, second wife of Joseph Reeves above, b. 5th mo [Jul], 28th da, 1751.

Thomas Robson, b. 5th mo, 21st da, 1785.

Joseph P. [Powell] Rogers of Deptford Twp, son of Thomas and Sarah Rogers, b. 5th mo, 7th da, 1772 and his wife, Sarah, dau of Abraham and Hannah Inskeep, b. 9th mo, 5th da, 1773. Children: Sarah Ann Rogers, b. 1st mo, 19th da, 1800; Hannah Rogers, b. 6th mo, 18th da, 1801; Abraham Inskeep Rogers, b. 8th mo, 23rd da, 1804; Samuel Rogers, b. 11th mo, 22nd da, 1807; Thomas Rogers, b. 7th mo, 30th da, 1814; Joseph Powell Rogers, b. 8th mo, 10th da, 1816.

Abram P. Rudolph of Woodbury, son of Thomas and Hannah Rudolph, b. 9th mo, 21st da, 1818 and his first wife Elizabeth, dau of Isaiah and Sarah Dillin, b. 11th mo, 6th da, 1811.

Sarah Ann [Dillin] Rudolph, dau of Owen and Julianna Dillin, second wife of Abram P. Rudolph, b. 4th mo, 18th da, 1810.

Benjamin Rulon, son of Henry and Theodosia Rulon, b. 1st mo, 14th da, 1761 and his wife, Sarah, dau of John and Mary West, b. 5th mo, 27th da, 1769. Children: Mary Rulon, b. 9th mo, 24th da, 1797; John Rulon, b. 1st mo, 4th da, 1799.

Clayton Rulon, son of Moses Rulon, b. 3rd mo, 20th da, 1799 and his wife, Priscilla, dau of William and Judith Pine, b. 12th mo, 31st da, 1797, d. 2nd mo, 23rd da, 1824.

Henry Rulon of Woodbury, son of Henry and Theodosia Rulon, b. 2nd mo, 1st da, 1769, d. 7th mo, 21st da, 1815 and his wife, Sibyl, dau of Amos and Sarah Cooper, b. 3rd mo, 20th da, 1774.

Theodosia Rulon, widow of Henry Rulon, d. 2nd mo, 26th da, 1825.

James Saunders of Woodbury, son of Thomas and Rachel Saunders, b. 10th mo, 26th da, 1770 and his wife, Sarah, dau of Samuel and Mary Richards, b. 4th mo, 13th da, 1778. Children: Mary Saunders, b. 10th mo, 17th da, 1799; Isaac Saunders, b. 5th mo, 20th da, 1801; Rachel Saunders, b. 1st mo, 31st da, 1803; Elizabeth Saunders, b. 11th mo, 27th da, 1804; Samuel Richards Saunders, b. 11th mo, 19th da, 1806; Joseph Saunders, b. 9th mo, 24th da, 1808; Sarah Saunders, b. 5th mo, 15th da, 1811, d. 10th mo, 21st da, 1814; James Saunders, b. 3rd mo, 12th da, 1813.

John Saunders and his wife, Elizabeth. Children: Sarah Saunders, b. 9th mo, 28th da, 1770; Deborah Saunders, b. 9th mo, 11th da, 1772; John Saunders, b. 12th mo, 4th da, 1774; Sol. Lippincott Saunders, b. 1st mo, 30th da, 1777; Mary Saunders, b. 3rd mo, 9th da, 1779.

John M. Saunders of Woodbury, son of Thomas and Marsha M. Saunders, b. 7th mo, 10th da, 1812 and his wife, Sarah M., dau of Myles and Beulah Snowdon, b. 10th mo, 10th da, 1821.

Samuel R. Saunders of Deptford Twp, son of James and Sarah Saunders, b. 11th mo, 19th da, 1806 and his wife, Lydia, dau of Benjamin and Sarah Cloud, b. 10th mo, 14th da, 1804.

Thomas Saunders of Deptford Twp, son of John and Elizabeth Saunders, b. 4th mo [Jun], 1st da, 1744, d. 12th mo, 4th da, 1802 and his wife, Rachel, dau of Isaac and Rachel Stephens, b. 2nd mo, 6th da, 1752, d. 8th mo, 3rd da, 1822. Children: James Saunders, b. 10th mo, 26th da, 1770; Edney Saunders [dau], b. 11th mo, 5th da, 1773, d. 1st mo, 22nd da, 1787; Isaac Saunders, b. 4th mo, 26th da, 1775, d. 9th mo, 18th da, 1798; Rebecca Saunders, b. 1st mo, 14th da, 1778; Hannah Saunders, b. 11th mo, 31st da, 1780; Samuel Saunders, b. 10th mo, 1st da, 1782, d. 9th mo, 13th da, 1783; Samuel Saunders [2nd by this name], b. 11th mo, 4th da, 1784; Thomas Saunders, b. 11th mo, 23rd da, 1786, d. 10th mo, 26th da, 1823; Joseph Saunders, b. 7th mo, 13th da, 1789.

Hope [Kay] Scull, dau of Isaac and Deborah Kay, widow of Paul Scull, dec'd, of Woodbury, b. 6th mo, 11th da, 1789.

John Sharp, b. 8th mo [Oct], 26th da, 1734, d. 9th mo, 23rd da, 1813 and his wife, Sarah, dau of Nehemiah and Elizabeth Andrews, b. 2nd mo [Apr], 25th da, 1742, d. 3rd mo, 24th da, 1795. Children: Anthony

Sharp, b. 3rd mo, 23rd da, 1763, d. 9th mo, 18th da, 1793; Nehemiah Sharp, b. 9th mo, 25th da, 1765, d. 9th mo, 28th da, 1793.

Rebecca J. Sheppard of Woodbury, dau of Richard W. and Lydia Sheppard, b. 9th mo, 10th da, 1805.

Stephen Sims [Simms] of Deptford Twp, son of David and Sarah Sims [Simms], b. 12th mo, 25th da, 1765 and his wife, Sarah, dau of John and Sarah Collins-Bales, b. 3rd mo, 17th da, 1759. Children: David Sims [Simms], b. 3rd mo, 5th da, 1801; Sarah Sims [Simms], b. 10th mo, 30th da, 1803.

Daniel Smith, son of John and Mary Smith, b. 4th mo [Jun], 5th da, 1748, d. 4th mo, 17th da, 1808.

Jesse Smith, son of Thomas and Rebecca Smith, b. 8th mo, 1763 and his wife, Mary, dau of Israel and Rebecca Cassell, b. 1st mo, 29th da, 1761, d. 9th mo, 24th da, 1804. Children: Mary Smith, b. 7th mo, 17th da, 1797; Rebecca Smith, b. 5th mo, 4th da, 1799; Elizabeth Smith, b. 12th mo, 22nd da, 1800, d. 9th mo, 22nd da, 1804; Rachel Smith, b. 1st mo, 22nd da, 1802, d. 8th mo, 27th da, 1802.

Beulah [Cooper] Snowdon, dau of Amos and Sarah Cooper, widow of Myles Snowdon, dec'd, of Woodbury, b. 11th mo, 5th da, 1793.

Mary Snowdon of Woodbury, dau of Myles and Beulah [Cooper] Snowdon, b. 4th mo, 30th da, 1818.

William Snowden and his wife, Margaret. Children: Hannah Snowden, b. 1st mo, 3rd da, 1763; John Snowden, b. 11th mo, 29th da, 1766; Lydia Snowden, b. 9th mo, 12th da, 1769.

Carleton P. Stokes of Woodbury, son of Isaac and Lydia Stokes of Cropwell, Burlington Co., b. 7th mo, 12th da, 1810 and his first wife, Lydia, dau of Samuel and Sarah Webster, b. 6th mo, 21st da, 1807.

Elizabeth J. [Morris] Stokes, dau of John and Prudence Morris, second wife of Carleton P. Stokes, b. 12th mo, 2nd da, 1813.

Josiah Stokes of Deptford Twp, son of Thomas and Sarah Stokes, b. 8th mo, 24th da, 1768 and his wife, Hope, dau of Isaac and Mary Borton, b. 1st mo, 30th da, 1772. Children: Mary Stokes, b. 10th mo, 9th da, 1795; Ann Stokes, b. 7th mo, 3rd da, 1797; Sarah Stokes, b. 1st mo, 31st da, 1799; Lydia Stokes, b. 11th mo, 24th da, 1800; Susan Stokes, b. 12th mo, 11th da, 1802; William Stokes, b. 4th mo, 26th da, 1805, d. 7th mo, 26th da, 1806; Josiah Stokes, b. 5th mo, 3rd da, 1807; Hannah Roberts Stokes, b. 4th mo, 26th da, 1811; Isaac Borton Stokes, b. 6th mo, 22nd da, 1814.

John Tatum, son of John and Sarah Tatum, b. 6th mo [Aug], 4th da, 1739, d. 11th mo, 7th da, 1821, and his first wife, Sarah, dau of George and Margaret Ward, b. 7th mo [Sep], 12th da, 1733, d. 8th mo, 26th da, 1778. Children: George Tatum, b. 10th mo, 12th da, 1763, d. 9th mo, 8th da, 1772; Isaac Tatum, b. 2nd mo, 19th da, 1766, d. 10th mo, 13th da, 1766; John Tatum, b. 9th mo, 11th da, 1767; Sarah Tatum, b. 5th mo, 11th da, 1776.

John Tatum m. second to Elizabeth, dau of David and Sybil Cooper, b. 10th mo [Dec], 9th da, 1751, d. 11th mo, 11th da, 1814. Children: Sybil Tatum, b. 8th mo, 20th da, 1781; David Tatum, b. 4th mo, 27th da, 1783; George Tatum, b. 1st mo, 9th da, 1785; Josiah Tatum, b. 11th mo, 1st da, 1790.

John Tatum, Jr. of Deptford Twp, son of John and Sarah Tatum, b. 9th mo, 11th da, 1767, and his first wife, Hannah, dau of William and Grace Rogers, b. 11th mo, 12th da, 1773, d. 10th mo, 26th da, 1819. Children: William R. Tatum, b. 1st mo, 8th da, 1795, d. 9th mo, 23rd da, 1795; Sarah Tatum, b. 8th mo, 13th da, 1796, d. 11th mo, 16th da, 1796; Allen Tatum, b. 9th mo, 20th da, 1797; John Ward Tatum, b. 6th mo, 30th da, 1799; Ann Tatum, b. 3rd mo, 30th da, 1801, d. 5th mo, 29th da, 1801; Mary Tatum, b. 3rd mo, 28th da, 1803; Joseph Tatum, b. 7th mo, 30th da, 1806; William Rogers Tatum, b. 9th mo, 6th da, 1811.

John Tatum, Jr. m. second to Anne, dau of Owen and Sarah Biddle, b. 7th mo, 23rd da, 1780. d. 9th mo, 4th da, 1860. [No issue recorded.]

Joseph Tatum of Deptford Twp, son of John and Hannah Tatum, b. 7th mo, 30th da, 1806 and his wife, Ann dau of William and Sarah Cooper, b. 9th mo, 19th da, 1808.

Josiah Tatum of Deptford Twp, son of John and Elizabeth Tatum, b. 11th mo, 1st da, 1790 and his wife, Rachel, dau of Daniel and Ann Offley, b. 5th mo, 3rd da, 1791. Children: Daniel Offley Tatum, b. 2nd mo, 21st da, 1815; Josiah Tatum, b. 4th mo, 30th da, 1816; Elizabeth Tatum, b. 7th mo, 23rd da, 1817; Ann Tatum, 10th mo, 3rd da, 1818; Edward Tatum, b. 6th mo, 25th da, 1821; John Tatum, b. 1st mo, 19th da, 1823; Charles Tatum, b. 1st mo, 4th da, 1825, d. 1st mo, 15th da, 1825.

Lucy [Middleton] Tatum, dau of Samuel and Sarah Middleton, third wife of Joseph Tatum, b. 8th mo, 31st da, 1813.

William R. Tatum of Deptford Twp, son of John and Hannah Tatum, b. 9th mo, 6th da, 1811 and his wife, Sarah, dau of George and Mary Mickle, b. 5th mo, 12th da, 1817.

Zaccheus Test, son of Benjamin and Sarah Test, b. 9th mo, 23rd da, 1762, and his first wife, Rebekah, dau of Gabriel and Sarah Davis, b. 9th mo, 22nd da, 1758, d. 4th mo, 14th da, 1798. Children: Benjamin Test, b. 11th mo, 7th da, 1783; Isaac B. Test, b. 6th mo, 8th da, 1787;

Samuel Test, b. 1st mo, 3rd da, 1791; Sarah Test, b. 3rd mo, 26th da, 1793; Rebekah Test, b. 4th mo, 16th da, 1796.

Zaccheus Test, son of Benjamin and Sarah Test, and his second wife, Hannah, dau of Joseph and Elizabeth Reeves, b. 4th mo, 4th da, 1775. Son: Joseph R. Test, b. 8th mo, 28th da, 1801.

Hannah Thomson of Woodbury, dau of Peter and Rebecca Owen Thomson, b. 3rd mo, 10th da, 1800.

Amos Thorp of Woodbury, son of Jabez and Hannah Thorp, b. 4th mo, 16th da, 1809 and his wife, Meribuh, dau of Robert and Hannah Warren, b. 3rd mo, 22nd da, 1823.

Joseph Tomlinson of Gloucester Twp, son of Ephraim and Ann Tomlinson, b. 12th mo, 28th da, 1779, d. 10th mo, 1st da, 1805 and his wife, Mary, dau of Benjamin and Ann Cooper, b. 3rd mo, 9th da, 1783. Children: Joseph Tomlinson, b. 2nd mo, 5th da, 1803; Vurner Tomlinson, b. 8th mo, 18th da, 1804.

Samuel Tonkin of Greenwich, son of Edward and Mary Tonkin, b. 3rd mo [May], 24th da, 1736, d. 2nd mo, 24th da, 1821 and his wife, Mary, dau of Preston and Hannah Carpenter, b. 11th mo, 18th da, 1750, d. 10th mo, 30th da, 1821.

Charles Ward of Deptford Twp, son of George and Edith Ward, b. 8th mo, 20th da, 1797, d. 12th mo, 16th da, 1825 and his wife, Eliza, b. 5th mo, 2nd da, 1798. Children: Ann C. Ward, b. 2nd mo, 22nd da, 1822; Achsa E. Ward, b. 7th mo, 13th da, 1824.

David Ward, son of George and Rachel Ward, b. 9th mo, 12th da, 1760, d. 11th mo, 22nd da, 1807 and his wife, Hannah, dau of John and Sarah Brown, b. 11th mo, 13th da, 1762, d. 1st mo, 14th da, 1804. Children: Rachel Ward, b. 1st mo, 26th da, 1789; David Ward, b. 5th mo, 27th da, 1791; Ann Ward, b. 2nd mo, 19th da, 1793, d. 8th mo, 27th da, 1796; Ruth Ward, b. 11th mo, 11th da, 1794; Hannah Ward, b. 2nd mo, 1st da, 1800; John B. Ward, b. 5th mo, 26th da, 1802.

George Ward, dec'd, and his wife, Ann [Branson] Ward, dau of David and Mary Branson, b. 2nd mo [Apr], 5th da, 1747, o.s. Children: George Ward, b. 4th mo, 5th da, 1767; Hannah Ward, no date.

George Ward of Deptford Twp, son of George Ward and his wife, Edith, dau of John and Ann Wood, b. 11th mo, 21st da, 1770. Children: Charles Ward, b. 8th mo, 20th da, 1797; Ann Ward, b. 12th mo, 30th da, 1801; Mary Ward, b. 9th mo, 22nd da, 1805.

Isaiah Ward of Deptford Twp, son of James and Margaret Ward, b. 5th mo, 24th da, 1762 and his wife, Abigail, dau of William and Susanna Tatum, b. 5th mo, 24th da, 1770. Children: James Ward, b. 12th mo, 14th da, 1791; William T. Ward, b. 7th mo, 10th da, 1793; Isaiah

Ward, b. 10th mo, 8th da, 1796, d. 3rd mo, 10th da, 1816; Joseph T. Ward, b. 12th mo, 13th da, 1798; Margaretta Ward, b. 1st mo, 24th da, 1801; Beulah Ward, b. 4th mo, 6th da, 1802; Susanna Ward, b. 4th mo, 30th da, 1805, d. 10th mo, 17th da, 1823; Abigail Ward, b. 12th mo, 25th da, 1810.

Hannah A. Warner of Deptford Twp, dau of Michael C. and Ann Fisher and wife of Henry Warner, b. 8th mo, 26th da, 1815.

Nathan Warrington of Greenwich, b. 10th mo, 3rd da, 1789 and his wife, Priscilla, dau of John Brown, b. 3rd mo, 4th da, 1801. Children: John Brown Warrington, b. 1st mo, 9th da, 1820; Seth Harrison Warrington, b. 8th mo, 3rd da, 1821; Margaret Warrington, b. 7th mo, 14th da, 1823, d. 10th mo, 31st da, 1823; Edward Warrington, b. 12th mo, 6th da, 1824, d. 7th mo, 7th da, 1825.

Samuel Webster, Jr. of Woodbury, son of Samuel and Sarah Webster, b. 3rd mo, 4th da, 1771 and his wife, Sarah, b. 2nd mo, 10th da, 1778. Children: Mary Ann Webster, b. 11th mo, 7th da, 1803; Lydia Webster, b. 6th mo, 21st da, 1807.

Benjamin Whitall, Jr. son of Benjamin and Elizabeth Whitall, b. 4th mo, 8th da, 1772, d. 10th mo, 24th da, 179-, and his wife Hannah, dau of John and Elizabeth Estaugh Mickle, b. 2nd mo, 13th da, 1773. Benjamin Whitall, Jr. was the first husband of Hannah Mickle. [No issue recorded. See Joseph Whitall.]

David Whitall of Deptford Twp, son of Joseph and Hannah Whitall, b. 1st mo, 1st da, 1794 and his first wife, Ann W., dau of Samuel and Ann Stockton, b. 12th mo, 31st da, 1793. Children: William Whitall, b. 2nd mo, 10th da, 1818; Henry Whitall, b. 4th mo, 28th da, 1819; Edith Whitall, b. 10th mo, 14th da, 1820; Hannah Ann Whitall, b. 5th mo, 27th da, 1822; Susan S. Whitall, twin, b. 9th mo, 16th da, 1824; Deborah Whitall, twin, b. 9th mo, 16th da, 1824; Jane Whitall, b. 8th mo, 15th da, 1826; Margaret Whitall, twin, b. 8th mo, 11th da, 1828, d. 10th mo, 7th da, 1828; Mary Whitall, twin, b. 8th mo, 11th da, 1828, d. 10th mo, 21st da, 1828.

David Whitall, m. second to Susan [Stockton] Whitall, dau of Samuel and Ann Stockton.

David Whitall, m. third to Mary [Cooper] Whitall, dau of William and Hannah Cooper, b. 10th mo, 27th da, 1806.

Elizabeth Whitall, b. 12th mo, 11th da, 1808.

James Whitall, father of first named James (below), b. 7th mo [Sep], 4th da, 1717 o.s., d. 9th mo, 29th da, 1808, n.s. and his wife, Ann, dau of John and Ann Cooper, b. 4th mo [Jun], 23rd da, 1716, d. 9th mo, 22nd da, 1797. Child: James Whitall, b. 12th mo [Feb], 22nd da, 1742,

d. 2nd mo, 18th da, 1796.

James Whitall, son of James and Ann Whitall, and his wife, Rebecca, dau of Richard and Mary Matlack, b. 9th mo [Nov], 13th da, 1746, d. 9th mo, 23rd da, 1797. Children: Mary Whitall, b. 9th mo, 26th da, 1764; Deborah Whitall, b. 9th mo, 25th da, 1766; Zatthu Whitall, b. 6th mo, 6th da, 1768; James Whitall, b. 5th mo, 11th da, 1770; Richard Whitall, b. 5th mo, 3rd da, 1772; George Whitall, b. 6th mo, 18th da, 1774, d. 11th mo, 8th da, 1775; George Whitall, [2nd by this name], b. 6th mo, 5th da, 1776; William Whitall, b. 7th mo, 25th da, 1778; Rebecca Whitall, b. 5th mo, 25th da, 1780; Abraham Whitall, b. 3rd mo, 30th da, 1782, d. 4th mo, 1st da, 1782; Jean Whitall, b. 5th mo, 29th da, 1783; Ann Whitall, b. 9th mo, 6th da, 1786, d. 3rd mo, 7th da, 1788.

Job Whitall, son of James and Ann Whitall, b. 1st mo [Mar], 27th da, 1743, d. 9th mo, 11th da, 1797 and his wife, Sarah, b. 5th mo [Jul], 28th da, 1751. Children: David Whitall, b. 8th mo, 29th da, 1771, d. 9th mo, 26th da, 1788; Job Whitall, b. 7th mo, 27th da, 1773, d. 10th mo, 18th da, 1797; Hannah Whitall, b. 9th mo, 26th da, 1775; Sarah Whitall, b. 1st mo, 11th da, 1779, d. 9th mo, 19th da, 1797; John Gill Whitall, 7th mo, 7th da, 1781; Aaron Whitall, b. 5th mo, 27th da, 1783, d. 9th mo, 19th da, 1797; Amy Whitall, b. 3rd mo, 8th da, 1785, d. 3rd mo, 10th da, 1785; Mark Whitall, b. 2nd mo, 23rd da, 1786; Joseph Cooper Whitall, b. 9th mo, 21st da, 1788; Mercy Whitall, b. 8th mo, 17th da, 1790; Charles Whitall, b. 2nd mo, 15th da, 1793.

John S. Whitall, of Woodbury, son of James and Ann Whitall, b. 5th mo, 31st da, 1757 and his wife, Sarah, dau of John and Elizabeth Estaugh Mickle, b. 11th mo, 20th da, 1766. Children: Elizabeth Estaugh Whitall, b. 2nd mo, 10th da, 1789, d. 8th mo, 14th da, 1790; Ann Cooper Whitall, b. 2nd mo, 19th da, 1791; Caroline Whitall, b. 2nd mo, 12th da, 1793, d. 11th mo, 20th da, 1803; Israel Franklin Whitall, b. 2nd mo, 24th da, 1795; Hannah Whitall, b. 3rd mo, 14th da, 1797; James Whitall, b. 9th mo, 4th da, 1799, "Lived 6 hours"; John Mickle Whitall, b. 11th mo, 4th da, 1800; Sarah [Mickle] Whitall, b. 8th mo, 22nd da, 1803; Caroline Whitall, (2nd by this name), b. 1st mo, 27th da, 1806, d. 4th mo, 22nd da, 1814; Elizabeth Whitall, b. 9th mo, 7th da, 1808.

Joseph Whitall, b. 3rd mo, 17th da, 1770 and Hannah [Mickle] Whitall, dau of John and Elizabeth Estaugh Mickle, widow of Benjamin Whitall, Jr. b. 2nd mo, 13th da, 1773. Children: David Whitall, b. 1st mo, 1st da, 1794; Joseph Whitall, Jr. b. 12th mo, 15th da, 1795; Benjamin Whitall, b. 12th mo, 16th da, 1797; Joshua Whitall, b. 11th mo, 2nd da, 1799; Ebenezer Whitall, b. 10th mo, 20th da, 1801; Elizabeth Whitall, b. 10th mo, 11th da, 1803. Joseph Whitall was the second husband of Hannah Mickle Whitall.

William Whitall, of Deptford Twp, son of David and Ann W. Whitall, b. 2nd mo, 10th da, 1818 and his wife, Hannah W., dau of Benjamin and Sarah Cloud, b. 12th mo, 28th da, 1811.

William White, b. 11th mo, 11th da, 1751 o.s. [should be 1st mo, 11th da, 1752 N.S.], and his wife, Ann, b. 8th mo, 31st da, 1759, d. 11th mo, 21st da, 1801. Children: William White, b. 1st mo, 11th da, 1780; Samuel White, b. 10th mo, 1st da, 1781; Ann White, b. 1st mo, 3rd da, 1784; Rebecca White, b. 4th mo, 28th da, 1786; Mary White, b. 3rd mo, 2nd da, 1788; Joseph White, b. 1st mo, 27th da, 1790; Sarah White, b. 1st mo, 29th da, 1792; Isaac White, b. 4th mo, 5th da, 1794; John White, b. 11th mo, 9th da, 1796; Joel White, b. 10th mo, 13th da, 1798.

Jacob Wood, son of Henry and Ruth Wood, b. 7th mo, 29th da, 1758 and his wife, Elizabeth, d. 6th mo, 28th da, 1791.

Elizabeth Wright of Woodbury, dau of Nathan and Mary Wright, b. 9th mo, 16th da, 1825.

Sarah B. [Thomson] Upton, dau of Peter and Rebecca O. Thomson, widow of Smith Upton of Woodbury, b. 1st mo, 1st da, 1797.

FAMILY RELATIONSHIPS FROM WOODBURY MONTHLY MEETING MINUTES

Enoch R. Allen, his wife, Beulah [Pancoast] and their minor children: Mary R., Hannah P., Eliza and Enoch, recorded 8th da, 5th mo, 1817.

Ira Allen, his wife, Catharine [Cooper] and their infant dau, Ann, recorded 12th da, 5th mo, 1807.

Ira Allen, his wife, Catharine [Cooper] and their children: Joseph, Hope and Ira Allen, recorded 5th da, 11th mo, 1818. [Ann, their first child, not listed.]

Mary [Pine] Allen, late of Pilesgrove Monthly Meeting, Salem Co., and her children: Benjamin, William P. and Mary P. Allen, recorded 6th da, 4th mo, 1820.

Jedidiah Allen and his four minor children: Elizabeth, William, Rachel and Jedidiah, recorded 10th da, 5th mo, 1785.

Rachel [Ward] Allen and her minor children: John, Beulah W., Mary, David W. and Charles Allen, recorded 7th da, 8th mo, 1817.

Isaac Andrews died in the spring of 1786, recorded 11th da, 4th mo,

1786.

Josiah Atkinson and his wife, Priscilla, recorded 9th da, 6th mo, 1801.

Priscilla Atkinson, mother of Lydia Atkinson, recorded 12th da, 4th mo, 1803.

Isaac Ballinger died in 1785, recorded 13th da, 9th mo, 1785.

John Ballinger, his wife, Hannah and their three minor children: Sarah, Mary and William, recorded 10th da, 5th mo, 1808.

Joseph Barger, late of Philadelphia, his wife, Mary and their son, William W. [Wood] Barger, recorded 13th da, 12th mo, 1795.

William Bartin [Barten], his wife, Anna, their son, Samuel and their five minor daus, recorded 15th da, 10th mo, 1805.

William Barten and his minor children: Rebecca, Samuel, Ann and Patience, recorded 11th da, 4th mo, 1809.

Nathan Basset, his wife, Sarah, and their children: Hannah, Anna, Elizabeth and Deborah, recorded 10th da, 2nd mo, 1795.

Joseph W. Bennet [Bennett], his wife, Mary, and their minor son, Joseph Morgan Bennet, recorded 10th da, 12th mo, 1799.

Mary Bennet and her daus: Louisa, Mary and Caroline, recorded 6th da, 8th mo, 1818.

Ann Blackwood and her five children: John M., Benjamin W., Abigail, Sarah and Ann, recorded 5th da, 5th mo, 1814.

Francis Boggs, his wife, Ann, and their children: Joseph, Joshua Haines and Mary, recorded 13th da, 5th mo, 1794.

Abraham Borton, his wife, Mary and their three children: Rebecca D., Hannah and Elwood T., recorded 5th da, 5th mo, 1814.

Lydia Borton recorded 8th da, 5th mo, 1820.

Edward Borton, his wife, Mary, and their children: Rebecca, Job and Emeline Borton, recorded 15th da, 5th mo, 1810.

James S., Mary Ann and Edward D. Borton, recorded 25th da, 8th mo, 1823.

Sarah Borton and her minor children: Hannah Ann, Beulah and Miriam, recorded 27th da, 9th mo, 1824.

Thomas Borton, late of Salem Co., his wife, Maria and their minor son, Elwood, recorded 4th da, 4th mo, 1816.

Job, Aron [Aaron] and Elizabeth Borton recorded 26th da, 5th mo, 1823.

Elizabeth Braddock and her four minor children: Samuel, Sarah, Lydia and Thomas, recorded 9th da, 5th mo, 1809.

George Branner, his wife, Sarah and their minor son, George, recorded 7th da, 6th mo, 1821.

Asher Brown, his wife, Mary and their children: David, Samuel, Israel,

Ann, Mary and Benjamin, recorded 10th da, 4th mo, 1804.
David Brown, his wife, Charity, and their minor children: John, Isaac, William, Amos, Abigail and Hannah, recorded 15th da, 5th mo, 1792.
John Brown and his wife, Ruth, recorded 12th da, 5th mo, 1807.
Benjamin Carter, his wife, Rebecca [Fluallen], and their two minor children, Benjamin and Mary, recorded 12th da, 4th mo, 1796.
Kezia Chew, dau of Kezia Collins, recorded 7th da, 11th mo, 1816.
Thomas Clark, his wife, Rachel and their dau, Ann, recorded 6th da, 4th mo, 1820.
Thomas P. [Pancoast] Clark, his wife, Deborah E. [Kay] and their children, Deborah K. and Achsah, recorded 7th da, 5th mo, 1818; Beulah and Anna Clark, recorded 25th da, 7th mo, 1825.
James Clement, father of Abel Clement, recorded 13th da, 5th mo, 1794.
Joseph Clement, father of James Clement, recorded 14th da, 6th mo, 1785.
Joseph Clement, his wife and their three minor children: Aaron, Isaac and Ann, recorded 12th da, 5th mo, 1795.
Samuel Clement, deceased father of adult sons, Able and Joseph Clement, recorded 14th da, 10th mo, 1806.
Benjamin Cloud and his wife, Sarah Cloud recorded 9th da, 6th mo, 1801.
Hannah Cole and her minor dau, Rebecca Enoch Cole, recorded 7th da, 6th mo, 1821.
Richard M. Cole, his wife, Mary and their infant son, William B. Cole, recorded 28th da, 6th mo, 1824.
Robert Cook, his wife, Lydia and their daus: Sybilla [Sibyl], Sarah and Hannah Cook, recorded 13th da, 10th mo, 1807.
James Cooper [son of James and Deborah Cooper] died 1819, recorded 5th da, 8th mo, 1819.
John B. Cooper and his wife, Isabella P. [Paul] Cooper, recorded 30th da, 5th mo, 1825.
Sarah Cooper, late of Doncaster Monthly Meeting in Yorkshire, Great Britain, and her sons: Edmond, Edward, Samuel, Henry and Jackson Cooper, recorded 6th da, 4th mo, 1820.
Jacob Cozens and his minor son, Joshua, recorded 9th da, 3rd mo, 1790.
George Craft, Jr. his wife, Rebecca [Gibbs] Craft and their five children: Beulah, Rebecca, Aden [Aldin G.], George and Lydia, recorded 10th da, 4th mo, 1804.
Gabriel Davis and his wife, Abigail, recorded 11th da, 3rd mo, 1788.

174 EARLY CHURCH RECORDS OF GLOUCESTER COUNTY

Hezekiah Eastlack, unnamed wife, and their minor children, John and Rhoda, recorded 10th da, 4th mo, 1798.

Simeon Eastlack, his wife, Rachel and their children: Amy, Sarah, Elwood, Joseph B., Elizabeth, Lydia S., Hannah and Rachel, recorded 5th da, 7th mo, 1821.

Job Eldridge, his wife, Tacy and their five minor children: Hannah Pancoast Eldridge, William Malander Eldridge, Job and Isaac Kay Eldridge, recorded 12th da, 5th mo, 1807; Deborah M. Eldridge, recorded 4th da, 5th mo, 1815.

William M. Eldridge and his wife, Sarah, recorded 9th da, 5th mo, 1809.

Thomas Enoch, his wife, Mary and their three children: Thomas, Hannah and Elizabeth, recorded 15th da, 4th mo, 1788.

Thomas Enoch, his wife, Mary, and their children: Thomas, Martha and Elizabeth, recorded 9th da, 4th mo, 1799.

Enoch Evins and his wife, Rebecca, recorded 9th da, 6th mo, 1814.

Asa Gibbs, his wife, Sarah and their two minor children, Charles and Edward Gibbs, recorded 9th da, 12th mo, 1806.

Asa Gibbs, dec'd. and his minor orphan children: Charles, Edward, Alice, Aaron, Hannah and Maria Gibbs, recorded 9th da, 4th mo, 1818.

Gideon Gibson, and his two children, Daniel and Gideon, recorded 13th da, 10th mo, 1789.

Sarah Gibson, mother of Spicer Gibson, recorded 9th da, 12th mo, 1800, and minor sons, Mark and Aaron Gibson, recorded 10th da, 5th mo, 1803.

Jacob Glover, his wife, Mary and their minor children: Rachel, Chalkley, Barclay and Caroline, recorded 7th da, 9th mo, 1815.

Mary Harper, late of Montgomery Co., PA., and her minor children: Daniel, Samuel, Martha, Nathan and Margaret, recorded 5th da, 9th mo, 1822.

Benjamin Heritage, Jr., his wife, Sarah and their minor children: Jonathan, William and Sarah, recorded 15th da, 8th mo, 1797.

Sarah Hoffman and her seven minor children: Martha, Job, Isaac, Sarah, Mary, Rebekah and Abigail, recorded 15th da, 5th mo, 1804.

Joseph Jennings, his wife, Sarah, and her minor children: Hannah, Ann, Mary and Charles, recorded 11th da, 6th mo, 1811; Jacob, recorded 6th da, 5th mo, 1813.

Levi Jennings, father of Thomas Jennings, recorded 12th da, 5th mo, 1795.

Richard Johns, his wife, Rachel, and their dau, Sarah Johns, recorded

12th da, 2nd mo, 1793.
Elizabeth Jones, mother of minor children: Arthur, Jacob, Lydia S. and Tacy Jones, recorded 6th da, 6th mo, 1816.
Isaac Cooper Jones, wife Sarah [Ridgway] Jones, and their minor children: Isaac, Rebecca and Beulah Atkinson Jones, recorded 11th da, 5th mo, 1790.
John Jones, his wife, Elizabeth and their four minor children: Arthur, Esther, Jacob and Lydia Jones, recorded 9th da, 7th mo, 1812.
Sarah Keais, and her minor son, William, recorded 11th da, 9th mo, 1792.
William Keais died 1790, recorded 11th da, 8th mo, 1790.
Sarah Kirby, late of Maurice River Monthly Meeting, and her dau, Mercy, recorded 5th da, 12th mo, 1822.
Charles Knight, his wife, Achsah [Clark] and their infant son, Thomas C. Knight, recorded 5th da, 4th mo, 1821.
John Knight of Woodbury, late of Salem Co., wife Sarah [Ridgway-Jones] Knight, dau of Noah and Rebecca Ridgway and widow of Isaac Cooper Jones. Adopted child: Elizabeth [Newman] Knight, natural child of Richard and Ruth Newman, recorded 4th da, 5th mo, 1815.
Thomas Knight, his wife, Mary [Stokes] and their infant son, Josiah Stokes Knight, recorded 9th da, 7th mo, 1818.
Aaron Lippincott, his wife, Mary and their minor children: Mary F., Charles C., Francis D., Samuel C. and Anna Lippincott, recorded 25th da, 4th mo, 1825.
Elizabeth Lippincott and her minor son, Samuel Lippincott, recorded 9th da, 6th mo, 1789.
James Lord and his recently married wife, Hannah Lord, recorded 7th da, 3rd mo, 1816.
Nathan Lord, and his minor son, David, recorded 14th da, 4th mo, 1789.
William Lucas, his wife, Esther and their minor children: Elizabeth and Robert, recorded 10th da 1st mo, 1797; Esther, recorded 13th da, 6th mo, 1797.
Seth Matlack, his wife, Sarah B. and their minor children: Ellwood [Elwood], Emaline, Maria and Beulah, recorded 26th da, 4th mo, 1824.
Ann Mickle and her two minor children, Benjamin and Ann Blackwood, recorded 9th da, 1st mo, 1817.
Samuel Mickle, son of Samuel Mickle, Jr. recorded 9th da, 3rd mo, 1802.

Samuel Mickle, his wife, Susanna and their minor children: Mary Ann, Elizabeth, John Clemson and Samuel Mickle, recorded 9th da, 7th mo, 1812, and Susanna, recorded 4th da, 5th mo, 1815.

Jonathan Morgan, his wife, Elizabeth, and their minor children: David, Jonathan, Isaac and Hannah, recorded 11th da, 4th mo, 1795.

Joseph W. Newbold, late of Upper Springfield, Burlington Co., and his wife Hannah C. Newbold, recorded 8th da, 7th mo, 1819.

Joseph Owen, his wife, Mercy and their two minor children, Benjamin and David, recorded 5th da, 6th mo, 1817, John and Joseph, recorded 27th da, 1st mo, 1823.

Samuel Packer, his wife, Sarah and their minor children: John, Samuel, Ann C., William Paul, Richard and Joel Packer, recorded 22nd da, 10th mo, 1811, James and Sarah Ann, reported 5th da, 4th mo, 1821.

Aaron Pancoast, his wife, Ann [Anna Cooper], their son Aaron Whitall Pancoast, recorded 12th da, 6th mo, 1798.

James Pancoast, his wife, Martha and their three minor children: Hannah A., Sarah and Martha, recorded 14th da, 5th mo, 1811.

Joshua Paul died in 1785, recorded 13th da, 9th mo, 1785.

Amos Peasley, a minister, and his two minor sons, Elijah and Amos, also Esther Peasley and Anna Peasley, recorded 31st da, 10th mo, 1825.

Joseph Pettit, his wife, Sarah, and their six children: Woodnut, David, Jonathan, Thomas, Rachel and Mary, recorded 11th da, 4th mo, 1795.

Hannah Reeve and her two minor children, John and Beulah, recorded 4th da, 8th mo, 1814.

John Reeve, son of John and Beulah [Brown] Reeve, he dec'd, was the grandson of John Reeve, recorded 10th da, 5th mo, 1803.

John Reeve, father of minor son, Miles [Myles], recorded 14th da, 6th mo, 1808.

Clement Reeves, his wife, Sarah, and their minor children: Louisa, Susan, Israel, Mary, Joseph and Ann Reeves, recorded 10th da, 9th mo, 1811, and Sarah B. Reeves, added to record 4th da, 4th mo, 1816.

Rebecca Ridgway died 1808, recorded 12th da, 4th mo, 1808.

Thomasin Robert, two minor daughters: Hester, recorded 11th da, 8th mo, 1792; Unity, recorded 11th da, 5th mo, 1793.

Moses Rulon, his wife, Susannah, and their minor children: Rachel, Clayton, Daniel, Moses, Ephraim, Beulah, Susannah and Mark Townsend Rulon, recorded 13th da, 8th mo, 1811.

Jonathan Rulon, his wife, Mary and their children: Phebe, Mary, Hannah and David, recorded 7th da, 10th mo, 1813.

James Saunders, and his wife, Sarah [Richards], recorded 12th da, 2nd mo, 1799.

Anna Sharp and her children, Elizabeth and Anthony, recorded 13th da, 12th mo, 1796.

Samuel Shute, his wife, Alice and their minor children: Ann Hazeleton, Hariet [Harriet], Charles, Aaron, Samuel and Hiram Shute, recorded 9th da, 7th mo, 1811.

Jacob Smith, his wife, Phebe and their children: Thomas, Jonathan, Randall, Elizabeth, Ann, Israel, William, Samuel Smith, recorded 15th da, 11th mo, 1785.

Jesse Smith, his wife, Mary [Cassell] Smith and her two children by her former husband, William Atkinson Paul and Yeomans [Yemmons] Paul, recorded 13th da, 6th mo, 1797.

Isaac Snowden, his wife, Mary and their minor children: William, Elizabeth and Abigail, recorded 10th da, 4th mo, 1792.

Richard Snowden, his wife, Sarah and their minor children: Mary, Leonard, Rebecca, Elizabeth and Sarah, recorded 12th da, 5th mo, 1789, and Miles [Myles], recorded 14th da, 6th mo, 1808.

William Snowdon [Snowden], his wife, Margaret and their children: John, Mary, Hannah, Lydia, recorded 15th da, 4th mo, 1788.

Isaac Stephens, his wife, Hannah and their four minor children: Ann, Sarah, Isaac and Jacob, recorded 8th da, 2nd mo, 1816, and Harriet, recorded 10th da, 12th mo, 1818.

Aquila [Aquilla] Stokes, his wife, Sarah and their three minor children: Elizabeth, Samuel and Harvey, recorded 9th da, 6th mo, 1814, Henry and William Borton Stokes, recorded 8th da, 5th mo, 1820.

Mary Stratton and her minor sons, Bethuel Stratton, recorded 12th da, 1st mo, 1790, Isaiah and Elias, recorded 15th da, 5th mo, 1792.

Joseph Tantum, his wife, Susanna and their children: Warren, Benjamin T., Abigail R., Thomas H. and George B., recorded 6th da, 5th mo, 1819.

Thomas Tantum, his wife, Susanna and their minor children: Warren, Benjamin T., Abigail R., Thomas H. and George B., recorded 6th da, 5th mo, 1819.

Aaron Thompson, son of Samuel, dec'd, recorded 12th da, 6th mo, 1798.

Aaron Thompson, his wife, Abigail, and their children: Rebecca and Ann, recorded 9th da, 8th mo, 1791, and Deborah, recorded 12th da, 12th mo, 1797.

Thomas Thorn, his wife, Mary [Haines] and their minor children: John, Lydia, Sarah and Mary Ann Thorn, recorded 13th da, 8th mo, 1811.

Mary Tomlinson and her two children, Joseph and Warner, recorded 10th da, 2nd mo, 1807.
George W. Tonkin and his wife, Martha, recorded 6th da, 3rd mo, 1817.
Paul Trosh, his wife, Sybilla and their four minor children: William, James, Jacob and Elizabeth, recorded 9th da, 6th mo, 1801.
George C. Ward, his wife, Deborah and their four minor children: Joshua, Rebekah, Eliza and Mary Ann, recorded 10th da, 7th mo, 1804.
Isaac Ward, his wife, Ann and their children: Rebecca, Elizabeth, Gulielma and Mary, recorded 12th da, 2nd mo, 1788.
Isaiah Ward and his minor son, James Ward, recorded 12th da, 1st mo, 1808.
Mason Ward and his wife, Hannah, recorded 9th da, 4th mo, 1818.
Samuel Webster, his wife, Sarah [Cooper] and their children: Samuel, Josiah, Isaac, Sarah and Hannah, recorded 11th da, 4th mo, 1786.
Amos Willit, his wife, Charity and their six minor children: Edward, John, Isaac, William, Amos and Abigail, recorded 12th da, 5th mo, 1789.
David Wood and his minor dau, Rebecca, recorded 15th da, 10th mo, 1793.
Jeremiah Wood, his wife, Mary [Horner] and their six minor children: Elizabeth, Isaac Horner, Mary, Hannah and Jehu, recorded 12th da, 5th mo, 1801
Lydia Wood and her three minor children: Rachel, William and Sarah, recorded 9th da, 6th mo, 1795.

MARRIAGES AT WOODBURY MONTHLY MEETING

John Sharp, son of Anthony and Mary (Dimock) Sharp of Deptford Twp and Sarah Andrews, dau of Nehemiah and Elizabeth (Lippincott) Andrews of Greenwich Twp, m. 4th mo, 28th da, 1761, at the new meeting house above Raccoon Creek in the Township of Greenwich, having consent of parents.
Richard Hill Morris of the Borough of Chester in Pennsylvania, son of William Morris, late of the city of Philadelphia, dec'd, and Margaret, his wife, and Mary Mifflin, dau of Samuel Mifflin, late of the county of Gloucester, dec'd, and Mary, his wife, m. 3rd mo, 17th da, 1786 at Woodbury, having consent of parents.
Benjamin Carter of Woolwich Twp, son of Nathaniel Carter, dec'd and

Rebeckah Fluallen of the same place, dau of Abraham Fluallen, dec'd, m. 5th mo, 11th da, 1786 at public meeting in Upper Greenwich, having the consent of relations.

Josiah Kay of Woolwich Twp, son of Joseph Kay, dec'd, and Martha Smith, dau of Piley Smith, dec'd, of the same place, m. 5th mo, 11th da, 1786 at public meeting in Upper Greenwich, having consent of relations.

James Wilson of the City of Philadelphia, son of Thomas Wilson of the Borough of Wilmington, County of Newcastle on Delaware and Mary Hinchman, dau of James Hinchman of Deptford Twp, dec'd, m. 10th mo, 20th da, 1786 at Woodbury, parents consenting.

Joseph Estlack [Eastlack] of Deptford Twp, son of Francis Estlack [Eastlack], dec'd, and Hannah Kaighn of the same, dau of William Kaighn, dec'd, m. 2nd mo, 23rd da, 1787 at Woodbury meeting house, having consent of Friends and relations.

Gabriel Davis of Gloucester Twp, son of Gabriel Davis, dec'd, and Abigail Bassett, dau of William Bassett of Pilesgrove Twp, Salem County, m. 1st mo, 18th da, 1788 at Woodbury meeting house, parents consenting.

Jacob Wood of Deptford Twp, son of Henry Wood, dec'd, and Elizabeth Snowden, dau of William Snowden of the same, m. 3rd mo, 14th da, 1788 at Woodbury meeting house, her parents and his mother consenting.

David Ward of Deptford Twp, son of George Ward, dec'd, and Hannah Brown, dau of John Brown, dec'd, of the same, m. 3rd mo, 28th da, 1788 at Woodbury meeting house.

John S. Whitall, son of James Whitall, of Woodbury in Deptford Twp and Sarah Mickle, dau of John Mickle, dec'd, of the same, m. 5th mo, 17th da, 1788 at Woodbury meeting house.

Isaac Mickle of Newton Twp, son of Archibald Mickle, dec'd, of the same and Sarah Wilkins, dau of John Wilkins of Deptford Twp, m. 10th mo, 4th da, 1788 at Woodbury meeting house, with consent of parents.

Benjamin Rulon of Chester Twp, Burlington Co., son of Henry Rulon of Fairfield Twp, Cumberland Co. and Eunice Lord, dau of Joshua Lord, dec'd, of Deptford Twp, m. 4th mo, 17th da, 1789 at Woodbury, with consent of parents.

Caleb Townsend of the Upper Precinct in the County of Cape May, son of Daniel Townsend of the same place and Ann Webster, dau of Samuel Webster of Deptford Twp, m. 9th mo, 18th da, 1789 at Woodbury, having consent of parents.

Jacob Haines of Pilesgrove Twp, Salem Co., son of William Haines, dec'd, and Elizabeth Paul of Greenwich Twp, dau of Samuel Paul, m. 11th mo, 12th da, 1789 at Greenwich Twp, having consent of relations.

James Davis of Deptford Twp, son of Gabriel Davis, dec'd, of Gloucester Twp and Mary Hackney of Deptford Twp, dau of Thomas Hackney of Chester Twp, Burlington Co., m. 11th mo, 13th da, 1789, at Woodbury, having consent of parties concerned.

Samuel Mickle, son of William Mickle of Greenwich Twp, dec'd, and Sophia Brown, dau of John Brown of Deptford Twp, dec'd, m. 11th mo, 27th da, 1789 at Woodbury, having consent of relations.

Robert Hopkins of Philadelphia, son of Thomas Hopkins and Mary Whitall, dau of James Whitall, Jr., of Deptford Twp, m. 3rd da, 18th da, 1791 at Woodbury, having consent of parents.

Marmaduke Wood of Woolwich Twp, son of John Wood, dec'd, and Mary Pancost [Pancoast] of the same place, dau of Aaron Pancest [Pancoast], m. 11th mo, 17th da, 1791 at Upper Greenwich, having consent of relations.

Benjamin Heritage of Deptford Twp, son of Benjamin Heritage and Hannah White of Greenwich Twp, dau of William White, m. 3rd mo, 15th da, 1792, at Upper Greenwich, Greenwich Twp, having consent of parents.

Joseph Whitall, of Deptford Twp, son of Benjamin Whitall, of the same place and Hannah Mickle, dau of John Mickle, dec'd, of the town and twp of Gloucester, m. 10th mo, 12th da, 1792 at Woodbury, having the consent of parents.

Amasa Moore of Evesham Twp, Burlington Co., son of Bethual Moore and Agness French of Greenwich Twp, dau of Samuel French, m. 12th mo, 20th da, 1792 at Greenwich Twp, having consent of relations.

John Reeve of Hopewell Twp, Cumberland Co. and Jane Hewes, widow of Aaron Hewes, late of Deptford Twp, m. 5th mo, 4th da, 1793 at a public meeting at Woodbury, with consent of Friends.

Nathan Folwell of Pilesgrove Twp, Salem Co., son of Thomas Folwell, dec'd and Rebekah Iardall [Iredell] of the same place, dau of Thomas Iardall [Iredell], m. 12th mo, 19th da, 1793 in Greenwich Twp, having consent of relations.

Isaac Tatem Hopper of Philadelphia, a tailor, son of Levi Hopper of Deptford Twp and Sarah Tatum, dau of John Tatum of Deptford Twp, m. 9th mo, 18th da, 1795 at public meeting at Woodbury, having consent of parents.

WOODBURY MONTHLY MEETING 181

Mark Reeve of Philadelphia, merchant, son of Mark Reeve, dec'd, of Fairfield Twp, Cumberland Co. and Hannah Whitall, dau of Job Whitall, of Deptford Twp, m. 10th mo, 23rd da, 1795 at public meeting at Woodbury, having consent of parents and parties concerned.

Henry Rulon of Deptford Twp, son of Henry Rulon of Fairfield Twp, Cumberland Co. and Sybil Cooper, dau of Amos Cooper of Deptford Twp, m. 4th mo, 22nd da, 1796 in a public meeting in Woodbury, having consent of parents.

Benjamin Rulon of Deptford Twp, son of Henry Rulon of Cumberland County and Sarah West of Burlington Co., dau of John West, m. 12th mo, 16th da, 1796 at a public meeting at Woodbury, having consent of parents.

Isaac Gibbs of Woolwich Twp and Mary Holdcraft of Greenwich Twp, widow of William Holdcraft, dec'd, m. 3rd mo, 16th da, 1797 in Greenwich Twp, having consent of Friends.

William Allen, son of John Allen, dec'd, of Evesham Twp, Burlington Co. and Rachel Ward, dau of George Ward, dec'd, of Deptford Twp, m. 3rd mo, 17th da, 1797, at public meeting in Woodbury.

Isaac Cooper Jones of Philadelphia, son of Aquilla Jones and Hannah Ffrith of Woolwich Twp, dau of Azariah Ffrith, dec'd, m. 4th mo, 20th da, 1797 at public meeting in Greenwich Twp, having consent of their relations and Friends.

Jacob Ballenger [Ballinger] of Philadelphia Monthly meeting for the northern district, son of Thomas Ballenger [Ballinger] and Hannah Butlar of Greenwich Twp, dau of John Butlar, dec'd, m. 5th mo, 11th da, 1797 at public meeting in Greenwich Twp, having the consent of relations and Friends.

William Beckett [Becket], son of Samuel Beckett of Woolwich Twp and Sarah Lord, dau of Constantine Lord, dec'd, of Deptford Twp, m. 5th mo, 12th da, 1797 in public meeting at Woodbury, having consent of parents.

Joseph Miller, son of John Miller of Greenwich, Cumberland Co. and Sarah Dawson of Greenwich Twp, Gloucester Co., dau of Frances Dawson, dec'd, m. 3rd mo, 15th da, 1798 in Greenwich Twp, having consent of relations.

Isaac Mickle of Newton Twp, son of Archibald Mickle and his wife, Mary, dec'd, and Mary Matlack of Deptford Twp, dau of Joseph and Hannah Matlack, she dec'd, m. 4th mo, 13th da, 1798 at Woodbury, having consent of parents.

Charles Teas [Tees] of Philadelphia, son of John and Rachel Teas

[Tees] of the same place and Mary Gibson of Woolwich Twp, dau of Joseph and Sarah Gibson, also of Woolwich Twp, m. 5th mo, 17th da, 1798 at Woodbury meeting house, having consent of their parents.

Benajah Andrews, son of Edward and Tabitha Andrews of Deptford Twp and Mary Down, dau of William and Mary Down, he dec'd, of the same place, m. 11th mo, 16th da, 1798, at public meeting in Woodbury, having consent of parents.

Amos Collins of Deptford Twp, son of Benjamin Collins, dec'd and Hannah (Crammer) Mathews, widow of the same place, dau of Stephen Crammer, dec'd, m. 7th mo, 19th da, 1799, at Woodbury meeting House, having consent of parents.

Thomas Thorn, son of Thomas and Abigail Thorn of Waterford Twp and Mary Haines, dau of John and Hepakiah [Hipparchia] Haines of Greenwich Twp, m. 11th mo, 15th da, 1799 in Woodbury, having consent of parents.

William Glover of the town and twp of Gloucester, son of Thomas and Mary Glover of the same place, both dec'd and Mary Mickle of Greenwich Twp, dau of Samuel and Ann Mickle, she dec'd, m. 1st mo, 16th da, 1800 in Greenwich Twp, having consent of parents and guardians.

William Wood of Greenwich Twp, son of Frances Wood, dec'd, and Ann [Platt] Mounc [Mounce], widow of the late John Mounc [Mounce], dec'd, dau of Joseph Platt, dec'd, of the same place, m. 3rd mo, 12th da, 1800 at Greenwich Twp.

Thomas Iredall [Iredell] of Woolwich Twp, son of Thomas and Ann Iredall [Iredell] of the same place and Sibylla Moore of Greenwich Twp, dau of Joshua and Rachel Moore, m. 5th mo, 21st da, 1800, at Mullaca Hill meeting house in Greenwich Twp, with consent of parents.

Zacheus Test of Deptford Twp, son of Benjamin Test and Hannah Reeves, dau of Joseph Reeves of the same place, m. 8th mo, 22nd da, 1800, at Woodbury, having consent of surviving parents.

Joshua Lord of Deptford Twp, son of Joshua, dec'd, and Hannah Lord and Sarah Jessup, dau of John and Elizabeth Jessup, m. 12th mo, 12th da, 1800 at Woodbury, having consent of surviving parents.

Aaron Hewes Middleton of Deptford Twp, son of Abel and Mary Middleton of Burlington County, dec'd, and Deborah Whitall, dau of James and Rebecca Whitall, of Deptford Twp, Gloucester Co., dec'd, m. 5th mo, 15th da, 1801 at Woodbury, having consent of Friends.

Joseph Ogden of Woolwich Twp, son of Samuel and Mary Ogden of Pilesgrove Twp, Salem Co. and Sibyl Tatum, dau of John and

Elizabeth Tatum of Deptford Twp, m. 6th mo, 12th da, 1801 at Woodbury Twp.

Joseph Tomlinson of Gloucester Twp, son of Ephraim and Ann Tomlinson, she dec'd, of the same place and Mary Cooper, dau of Benjamin Clark, dec'd, and Ann Cooper of Waterford Twp, m. 3rd mo, 12th da, 1802 at Woodbury, having consent of surviving parents.

Joseph Reeves of Deptford Twp, widower and Sarah Whitall, of the same place, widow, m. 3rd mo, 19th da, 1802, at public meeting in Woodbury, having consent of Friends.

Samuel Webster of Woodbury Twp, son of Samuel and Sarah Webster of Newton Twp and Sarah Cooper, dau of Amos and Sarah Cooper of Deptford Twp, m. 12th mo, 17th da, 1802 at Woodbury, having consent of parents.

Cooper Paul of Greenwich Twp, son of Joshua and Mary Paul, she dec'd, and Sybil Mickle, dau of William and Sarah Mickle, he dec'd, of Greenwich Twp, m. 1st mo, 13th da, 1803 at Greenwich Twp, having consent of relations.

William Haines of Greenwich Twp, son of John and Heppikiah Haines of the same place and Ann White, dau of William and Ann White, she dec'd, of the same place, m. 3rd mo, 24th da, 1803 at Greenwich Twp, with consent of parents.

Jedidiah Allen, Jr., of Mannington, Salem Co., son of Jedidiah and Ann Allen, she dec'd, of the same place and Lettice Hinchman, dau of James Hinchman of Deptford Twp, m. 11th mo, 25th da, 1803, at Woodbury, having consent of their parents.

Aaron Pancoast of Woolwich Twp, son of Aaron and Hannah Pancoast of the same place and Anne Cooper, dau of Amos and Sarah Cooper of Deptford Twp, m. 3rd mo, 16th da, 1804 at Woodbury, having consent of surviving parents.

Ira Allen of Woodbury, son of John and Hope Allen, he dec'd, and Catharine Cooper, dau of Paul and Catharine Cooper, she dec'd, of Deptford Twp, m. 5th mo, 18th da, 1804, at Woodbury, having consent of surviving parents.

Eliada Paxton, son of Aaron and Leticia Paxton of Solebury Twp, Bucks Co. and Mary Cooper, dau of Amos and Sarah Cooper of Woodbury, m. 11th mo, 13th da, 1804 at Woodbury, having consent of parents.

John Knight of Mannington, Salem Co. and Sarah (Ridgway) Jones, widow of Isaac Jones, late of Deptford Twp, dau of Noah Ridgway of Northampton Twp, Burlington Co., m. 3rd mo, 15th da, 1805 at Woodbury.

William Foster Miller of Mannington, Salem Co., son of Mark and Phebe Miller, he dec'd, of the same place and Esther Cooper of Deptford Twp, dau of James and Mary Cooper, she dec'd, of the same place, m. 3rd mo, 11th da, 1806.

Charles Potts of Woodbury, son of Samuel and Sarah Potts, he dec'd, and Susan Wood, dau of John and Mary Wood, he dec'd, m. 4th mo, 25th da, 1806.

William Sloan of Newton Twp, son of James and Rachel Sloan of the same place and Hannah Clement, dau of Joseph and Ann Clement of Deptford Twp, m. 10th mo, 23rd da, 1806.

Paul Cooper of Deptford Twp, widower, son of David and Sibyl Cooper of the same place, dec'd, and Hannah Knight, widow, dau of John and Sarah Branson, he dec'd, of Newton Twp, m. 11th mo, 13th da, 1806.

Michael C. Fisher of Gloucester Town and Twp, son of Charles and Ann Fisher, she dec'd, and Ann Clement, dau of Joseph and Ann Clement of Deptford Twp, m. 3rd mo, 17th da, 1808.

Enoch R. Allen of Deptford Twp, son of Anthony and Mary Allen and Beulah Pancoast, dau of Edward and Hannah Pancoast of Greenwich Twp, m. 5th mo, 12th da, 1808.

John Jessup, Jr. of Evesham, Burlington Co., son of John and Elizabeth Jessup of Deptford Twp and Sarah Wood, dau of John and Ann Wood of Deptford Twp, m. 2nd mo, 16th da, 1809.

Samuel B. Lippincott of Woolwich Twp, son of Joshua and Amy Lippincott, both dec'd, and Mary B. Clark of Greenwich Twp, dau of Thomas and Achsa Clark, Jr., she dec'd, also of Greenwich Twp, m. 5th mo, 11th da, 1809.

Thomas Saunders of Woodbury, son of Thomas and Rachel Saunders, he dec'd, of Woodbury and Martha Mickle, dau of James and Hannah Mickle, m. 1st mo, 18th da, 1810.

William Allen of Woolwich Twp, son of Enoch and Hannah Allen, she dec'd, of the same place and Mary Pine, dau of William and Judith Pine, m. 3rd mo, 22nd da, 1810.

Mark Clement of East Nottingham, Cecil County, MD., son of Samuel and Elizabeth Clement, dec'd, and Rebecca Davis, dau of James and Mary Davis of Deptford Twp, m. 11th mo, 20th da, 1811.

Enoch Allen of Philadelphia, son of John and Hope Allen, dec'd, and Rachel Ward of Greenwich Twp, dau of David and Hannah Ward, m. 12th mo, 5th da, 1811.

George Mickle of Greenwich Twp, son of William and Sarah Mickle, he dec'd, and Mary Brown, dau of Jonathan and Sarah Brown, m. 10th mo, 15th da, 1812.

Jacob Middleton, Jr., bricklayer, of Philadelphia Co., son of Jacob and Hannah Middleton of Nottingham Twp, Burlington Co. and Sybilla West, dau of John and Elizabeth West of Greenwich Twp, she dec'd, m. 12th mo, 17th da, 1812.

George W. Tonkin of Greenwich Twp, son of Israel and Christiana Tonkin of Burlington Co. and Martha Kay of Greenwich Twp, dau of Josiah and Martha Kay, she dec'd, m. 11th mo, 11th da, 1813.

Samuel Shute of Woolwich Twp, son of Henry and Lydia Shute, she dec'd, and Sibyl Cook, dau of Robert and Lydia Cook of the same place, m. 4th mo, 14th da, 1814.

Joseph Miller of the Town of Greenwich, Cumberland Co., son of John and Margaret Miller of the same place, dec'd, and Mary Allen, Jr., dau of Anthony and Mary Allen, he dec'd, of Woodbury, m. 10th mo, 20th da, 1814.

Isaac Collins of Deptford Twp and Kezia Chew of the same place, m. 12th da, 10th mo, 1814.

Thomas P. Clark of Gloucester Twp, son of Thomas and Achsah Clark of Deptford Twp, she dec'd and Deborah E. Kay, dau of Isaac and Deborah Kay of the town of Gloucester, m. 3rd mo, 16th da, 1815.

Paul Scull of Pilesgrove Twp, Salem Co., son of Gideon and Sarah Scull of Upper Penn's Neck, Salem Co. and Hope Kay, dau of Isaac and Deborah Kay of Gloucester Town, m. 5th mo, 25th da, 1815.

Thomas Knight of Woodbury, son of Thomas and Hannah Knight, he dec'd, of the same place and Mary Stokes, dau of Josiah and Hope Stokes, m. 5th mo, 23rd da, 1816.

Joseph Mickle of Newton, son of Archibald and Mary Mickle, she dec'd, and Ann Blackwood, widow of John Blackwood, m. 11th mo, 21st da, 1816.

Myles Snowdon of Philadelphia, son of Richard and Sarah Snowdon, she dec'd, and Beulah Cooper of Woodbury, dau of Amos and Sarah Cooper, he dec'd, m. 12th mo, 12th da, 1816.

Joseph Saunders of Woodbury, son of Thomas and Rachel Saunders, he dec'd, and Maria Ballenger [Ballinger], dau of Isaac and Esther Ballenger [Ballinger] of Woodbury, m. 11th mo, 20th da, 1817.

Isaac Haines of Greenwich Twp, son of John and Hipparchia Haines and Hannah Pine, dau of William and Judith Pine of the same place, m. 11th mo, 20th da, 1817.

Michael C. Fisher of Deptford Twp, son of Charles and Ann Fisher of the same, dec'd, and Mary Reeves, dau of Joseph and Elizabeth Reeves, dec'd, of same place, m. 2nd mo, 19th da, 1818.

Thomas Wood of Philadelphia, son of William Wood, dec'd, and Catharine Wood and Anna Maria Wood, dau of Marmaduke and Mary Wood of Deptford Twp, m. 9th mo, 17th da, 1818.

Charles Knight of Deptford Twp, son of Thomas and Hannah Knight, he dec'd, and Achsah Clark, dau of Thomas and Achsah Clark, she dec'd, of the same place, m. 3rd mo, 11th da, 1819.

Nathan Warrington of Woolwich Twp, son of John and Mary Warrington, late of Burlington, dec'd, and Priscilla H. Brown, dau of John and Margaret Brown of Greenwich Twp, m. 3rd mo, 11th da, 1819.

Charles Ward, son of George and Edith Ward of Deptford Twp and Eliza Clark, dau of Thomas and Achsah Clark, she dec'd, of the same place, m. 11th mo, 11th da, 1819.

Clement H. Kay, son of Isaac and Deborah Kay of the town of Gloucester and Edith Clark, dau of Thomas and Achsah Clark, she dec'd, m. 3rd mo, 16th da, 1820.

George Branner, Jr., son of George and Sarah Branner of Deptford Twp and Hannah Davis, dau of James and Mary Davis of the same place, m. 10th mo, 17th da, 1821.

David Gill of Pilesgrove Twp, Salem Co., son of John and Susanna Gill, she dec'd, of the same and Rachel Rulon, dau of Moses and Susanna Rulon of Woolwich Twp, m. 12th mo, 13th da, 1821.

Joseph Brown, son of Jonathan and Sarah Brown of Deptford Twp and Margaretta Ward, dau of Isaiah and Abigail Ward of the same, m. 12th mo, 13th da, 1821.

Thomas Knight of Woodbury, Deptford Twp, son of Thomas and Hannah Knight, he dec'd, and Rebecca Andrews, dau of Benajah and Mary Andrews of Woodbury, m. 11th mo, 21st da, 1822.

Clayton Rulon of Woolwich, son of Moses and Susanna Rulon of the same and Priscilla Pine, dau of William and Judith Pine of Woolwich Twp, m. 11th mo, 21st da, 1822.

Daniel Harper, son of George and Mary Harper of Deptford Twp and Sarah Simms, dau of Stephen and Sarah Simms of Deptford Twp, m. 1st mo, 9th da, 1823.

Samuel Bassett, son of Joseph and Mary Bassett of Salem Co. and Mary Ann Craft, dau of George and Rebecca Craft of Gloucester Co., m. 2nd mo, 6th da, 1823.

Joseph Ogden, son of Samuel and Mary Ann Ogden, she dec'd, and Hannah M. Carty, dau of Thomas M. and Elizabeth Carty, she dec'd, m. 2nd mo, 6th da, 1823.

Charles R. Middleton of the Northern Liberties in the County of

Philadelphia, son of Gabriel and Elizabeth Middleton, she dec'd, and
Ann Clark of Gloucester Co., dau of Thomas Clark of Burlington Co.,
m. 11th mo, 6th da, 1823.
Benajah D. Andrews, son of Benajah and Mary Andrews of Deptford
Twp and Sarah Stokes, dau of Josiah and Hope Stokes of the same
place, m. 12th mo, 11th da, 1823.
William Ballenger [Ballinger] of Pilesgrove Twp, Salem Co., son of John
and Hannah Ballenger [Ballinger], he dec'd, and Beulah Ward, dau
of Isaiah and Abigail Ward of Deptford Twp, m. 5th mo, 6th da, 1824.
Benjamin Sheppard of Greenwich, Cumberland Co., son of John and
Mary Sheppard and Mary R. Saunders, dau of James and Sarah
Saunders of Woodbury, m. 5th mo, 6th da, 1824.
John B. Cooper of Deptford Twp, son of William and Hannah Cooper of
the same place, both dec'd, and Isabella Paul, dau of Samuel and
Delia Paul, he dec'd, m. 1st mo, 6th da, 1825.
Howard Abbott of the town of Gloucester, son of Timothy and Rebecca
Abbott of Philadelphia, she dec'd, and Susan Stokes, dau of Josiah
and Hope Stokes of Gloucester Co., m. 4th mo, 7th da, 1825.
John Knight of Greenwich Twp, Gloucester Co. and Mary Lippincott of
the same place, m. 5th mo, 5th da, 1825.

MINUTES OF WOODBURY MONTHLY MEETING

At Woodbury the 11th Day of the 1st Month 1785:

"This being the day fixed by the quarterly meeting for Gloucester and
Salem, to hold the first Monthly Meeting at this place for Woodbury
and Upper Greenwich, after a solemn time of worship in which
several living testimonies were born, Friends proceeded to business.
At a quarterly meeting held at Salem the 15th of the 11th mo. 1784,
Haddonfield in their reports sent up the following minute for the
approbation of this meeting, to wit, This meeting having considered
the several matters proposed by the quarter, respecting the division
thereof, agree to report as our sense, that the Monthly Meeting be
held at Woodbury on ye third day of ye week next following the
second day of each month, to begin at the 11th hour, to be called by
the name of Woodbury Monthly Meeting; the first meeting to be held
in the first month next; and that the meeting of ministers and elders
continue together use heretofore for the present, and be held at
Woodbury on the morning preceding the Monthly Meeting there in

the 3rd, 5th, 9th and 11th months to begin at the 9th hour."

15th da, 2nd mo, 1785. Solomon Lippincott is continued as elder for Upper Greenwich, and David Cooper and James Whitall, Jr. for Woodbury. Isaac Ballinger and James Whitall, Jr. are continued as overseers for Woodbury and Benjamin Horton and David Brown, as overseers for Upper Greenwich. Testimony read against Elizabeth West. Samuel Gibson provides an acknowledgment in writing condemning his disorderly walking.

15th day of 3rd mo, 1785. Friends appointed to attend the ensuing quarterly meeting at Haddonfield: Isaac Ballinger, William Snowden, Jonathan Fisher, James Wood, William White, Samuel Mickle, Jr., Josiah Stratton and Samuel Paul.

12th da, 4th mo, 1785. Abijah Collins dealt with for fighting and neglecting meeting.

10th da, 5th mo, 1785. Jedidiah Allen granted a certificate to Salem Monthly Meeting for himself and his four minor children: Elizabeth, William, Rachel and Jedidiah. Richard Wood, Jr. granted a certificate to Greenwich Monthly Meeting. Peter Wright, an apprentice placed with Aaron Hewes, produced a certificate from Salem Monthly Meeting. Aaron Hewes appointed clerk of the Monthly Meeting.

14th da, 6th mo, 1785. Joseph Clement granted a certificate for his son, James Clement, placed for a time with Jeremiah Paul in Philadelphia. Isaac Taylor granted a certificate to New Garden Monthly Meeting. Anthony Allen produced a certificate for himself, Mary [Roberts], his wife, and five children: Rachel, Hannah, Mary, Grace and Enoch. John Gaunt, an apprentice, produced a certificate. Zaccheus Test produced a certificate for himself, Rebecca [Davis] Test, his wife with their infant child, Benjamin Test. Isaac Andrews dealt with for taking strong drink to excess, which he neglects to condemn.

12th da, 7th mo, 1785. Mary Sparks received into membership. William Cozens dealt with for administering the oath, which he neglects to condemn. William Cozens, Jr. dealt with for fighting, frequenting taverns and places of diversion, which he neglects to condemn.

9th da, 8th mo, 1785. Josiah Holdcraft produced a certificate from Haddonfield Monthly Meeting dated 11th da, 7th mo, 1785.

13th da, 9th mo, 1785. John Tatum and William White appointed as replacements for Isaac Ballinger and Joshua Paul, both dec'd, on the committee for the care of the Black People.

11th da, 10th mo, 1785. William Cozens disowned for administering the oath. Joseph Clement appointed as overseer of Woodbury Preparative Meeting.

15th da, 11th mo, 1785. Jacob Smith granted a certificate to Wrightstown Monthly Meeting for himself, his wife, Phebe and their seven children: Thomas, Jonathan, Randall, Elizabeth, Ann, Israel and William; and also for his son, Samuel Smith, who is placed as an apprentice with Anthony Hartley of Buckingham Monthly Meeting, Buckingham Twp, Bucks Co., PA.

10th da, 1st mo, 1786. Hannah Lord (by Constantine Lord) granted a certificate for her son, Jehu Lord, a minor, to Evesham Monthly Meeting, Burlington County.

14th da, 3rd mo, 1786. Asa Branson granted a certificate to Upper Springfield Monthly Meeting, Burlington Co. Joshua Thompson placed as an apprentice in Greenwich.

11th da, 4th mo, 1786. Isaac Andrews died since last meeting; therefore, testification against him will not be published. Samuel Webster produced a certificate from Haddonfield Monthly Meeting for himself, his wife, Sarah and five children: Samuel, Josiah, Isaac, Sarah and Hannah. Josiah Cozens dealt with for being concerned with horse racing, laying a wager thereon and neglecting meeting, which he neglects to condemn. Mary [Mufflin] Morris granted a certificate to Chester Monthly Meeting on account of marriage.

9th da, 5th mo, 1786. Isaac Ward granted a certificate to marry at Salem Monthly Meeting. Nathan Lord, Jr. granted a certificate to Salem Monthly Meeting. Azubah, Keziah and Sarah Lord granted a certificate to Salem Monthly Meeting. Membership is informed by Horsham Monthly Meeting that Joshua Davis moved into the Woodbury Monthly Meeting area but neglected to request a certificate. Woodbury Monthly Meeting informed by Great Eggharbour Monthly Meeting that Isaac Dole has lived in the Woodbury area for some time.

11th da, 7th mo, 1786. Joseph Cook, late of Chesterfield received into membership.

12th da, 9th mo, 1786. Jacob Cozens, son of Joshua Cozens, granted a certificate to the southern district of Philadelphia Monthly Meeting. Sarah Branson granted a certificate to Springfield Monthly Meeting, Burlington Co.

10th da, 10th mo, 1786. James Wilson produced a certificate of clearance from Philadelphia Monthly Meeting and his father's consent in writing to marry.

12th da, 12th mo, 1786. Mary Wilson granted a certificate to

Philadelphia Monthly Meeting. Sarah Armitt granted a certificate to Bradford Monthly Meeting.

9th da, 1st mo, 1787. Debora Sanders and Solomon Lippincott Saunders granted a certificate to Evesham Monthly Meeting, Burlington Co.

13th da, 2nd mo, 1787. Susannah Ewing granted a certificate to Salem Monthly Meeting. Testification ordered against Elizabeth Leonard for unchaste freedom and going out in marriage. Testimony read against Sarah Paul for the lie offense.

13th da, 3rd mo, 1787. William Down, Jr. spoken with for neglecting meeting and going out in his marriage. David Brown appointed elder. Hannah Albertson granted a certificate to Haddonfield Monthly Meeting. John Albertson, a minor, granted a certificate to Haddonfield Monthly Meeting.

10th da, 4th mo, 1787. Andrew Ridgway produced a certificate from Burlington Monthly Meeting dated 5th da, 3rd mo, 1787. Richard Snowdon [Snowden] produced a certificate for himself, his wife, Sarah, and children: Mary, Leonard and Rebecca from Philadelphia Monthly Meeting for the northern district. Thomas Wilson produced a certificate from Kennet Monthly Meeting. Chattin Zane acknowledges his marriage by a magistrate. James Hinchman dealt with for taking strong drink to excess.

15th da, 5th mo, 1787. William Ridgway and Aquilla Ridgway produced a certificates from Mt. Holly Monthly Meeting, Burlington Co. Testification requested against Abel Nichelson for unchaste freedom before marriage, going out in marriage to his brother's widow, taking strong drink to excess and using profane language.

12th da, 6th mo, 1787. Women's Meeting voted to disown Elizabeth Nicholson. Sarah Saunders granted a certificate to Salem Monthly Meeting.

10th da, 7th mo, 1787. Chattin Zane disowned. Nehemiah Sharp granted a certificate to Philadelphia Monthly Meeting for the northern district.

14th da, 8th mo, 1787. James Clement produced a certificate from Philadelphia Monthly Meeting dated 25th of the 5th mo, 1787.

9th da, 10th mo, 1787. Benjamin Rulon received into membership. Joseph Low, Jr. disowned. Peter Wright granted a certificate to Salem Monthly Meeting. Samuel Webster appointed overseer of Woodbury.

11th da, 12th mo, 1787. Benjamin Rulon granted a certificate to Philadelphia Monthly Meeting. A letter was received from Springfield

Monthly Meeting, Burlington Co., informing the membership of Sarah Harper's unchaste freedom before marriage and accomplishing her marriage by a priest.

15th da, 1st mo, 1788. Thomasin Roberts and her children, Unity and Hester Roberts received into membership. William and Enoch Allen, minors, from Evesham Monthly Meeting, Burlington Co., produced a certificate dated 7th da, 12th mo, 1787.

12th da, 2nd mo, 1788. Aquilla Ridgway granted a certificate to Mt. Holly Monthly Meeting, Burlington Co. Keziah Shreve granted a certificate to Springfield Monthly Meeting, Burlington Co. Joseph Clement granted a certificate for his son, James Clement to Haddonfield Monthly Meeting. Certificate granted for John Folwell who is placed as apprentice with Samuel Biddle in the verge of Philadelphia Monthly Meeting. A certificate was granted to Salem Monthly Meeting for Isaac and Ann Ward and their four children: Rebecca, Elizabeth, Gulielma and Mary.

11th da, 3rd mo, 1788. Gabriel Davis and his wife, Abigail granted a certificate to Evesham Monthly Meeting, Burlington Co. Sarah Ward granted a certificate to Salem Monthly Meeting. John Ellis produced a certificate from Haddonfield Monthly Meeting.

15th da, 4th mo, 1788. William Snowdon granted a certificate for himself, his wife, Margaret, and their children: John, Mary, Hannah and Lydia Snowden to Evesham Monthly Meeting, Burlington Co. Thomas Enoch produced a certificate from Burlington Monthly Meeting dated 7th da, 4th mo, 1788 for himself, his wife, Mary and their three children: Thomas, Hannah and Elizabeth. Asher Brown produced a certificate for himself, his wife, Mary and their two children, David and George from Mt. Holly Monthly Meeting, Burlington Co. Jacob Spicer bequeathed in his will, dated the 10th da, 7th mo, 1779, one and a half acres for a burying ground and meeting house at Mullica's Hill.

13th da, 5th mo, 1788. Aaron Hewes Middleton produced a certificate from Philadelphia Monthly Meeting.

10th da of the 6th mo, 1788. Jonathan Carmalt, Jr. produced a certificate from Philadelphia Monthly Meeting for the northern district.

15th da, 7th mo, 1788. Ann Steward and her dau, Elizabeth granted a certificate to Haddonfield Monthly Meeting.

9th da, 9th mo, 1788. Bridget Steward, a minor, granted a certificate to Chesterfield Monthly Meeting, Burlington Co.

14th da, 10th mo, 1788. Margery Mickle received into membership.

James Cooper, an approved minister requested and received permission to visit the meetings of Friends in the Jersies.

11th da, 11th mo, 1788. Jane Brick granted a certificate to Salem Monthly Meeting. Keziah Howell granted a certificate to Chesterfield Monthly Meeting, Burlington Co. William Wood Wilkins and Benjamin Waite Low granted a certificate to Philadelphia Monthly Meeting.

9th da, 12th mo, 1788. Joseph and Ann Bispham granted a certificate to Mt. Holly Monthly Meeting, Burlington Co. Elizabeth Bispham granted a certificate to Evesham Monthly Meeting, Burlington Co. Sarah Mickle granted a certificate to Haddonfield Monthly Meeting. Joshua Cozens disowned for going out in marriage and neglecting meeting.

13th da, 1st mo, 1789. William Ridgway expressed sorrow for his marriage by a hireling minister. Isaiah Cozens disowned for going out in marriage and neglecting meeting. Sarah Hinchman granted a certificate to Philadelphia Monthly Meeting. Jesse Brown granted a certificate to Salem Monthly Meeting. Edward Andrews dealt with for striking one of his fellow men.

10th da, 2nd mo, 1789. John Collins dealt with for neglecting meeting and going out in marriage. Jonathan Carmalt granted a certificate to the northern district of Philadelphia Monthly Meeting.

14th da, 4th mo, 1789. James Wilkins, a lad, granted a certificate to Philadelphia Monthly Meeting. Nathan Lord granted a certificate to Philadelphia Monthly Meeting for his minor son, David Lord. William Ridgway disowned for going out in marriage.

12th da, 5th mo, 1789. Richard Snowden, his wife, Sarah, and their five minor children: Mary, Leonard, Rebecca, Elizabeth and Sarah, granted a certificate to Haddonfield Monthly Meeting. Andrews Ridgway dealt with for going out in marriage. Aquilla Down dealt with for unchaste freedom with her who is now his wife and going out in marriage.

9th da, 6th mo, 1789. Eunice Rulon granted a certificate to Evesham Monthly Meeting, Burlington Co., on account of marriage. Amos Willit produced a certificate from Evesham Monthly Meeting, Burlington Co., dated 8th day, 5th mo, 1789, for himself, his wife, Charity and their six minor children: Edward, John, Isaac, William, Amos and Abigail. Elizabeth Lippincott and her son, Samuel Lippincott, a minor, produced a certificate from Haddonfield Monthly Meeting, dated 11th day, 5th mo, 1789.

14th da, 7th mo, 1789. Samuel Mickle appointed to replace Aaron

WOODBURY MONTHLY MEETING

Hewes, dec'd, as clerk.

11th da, 8th mo, 1789. Jonathan Cowgill granted a certificate to Salem Monthly Meeting. Mary Duel granted a certificate to Evesham Monthly Meeting, Burlington Co. David Brown is appointed overseer of Upper Greenwich Preparative Meeting in the room of our Friend, William Mickle, late dec'd.

15th da, 9th mo, 1789. Andrews Ridgway disowned for going out in marriage. Elizabeth Folwell granted a certificate to Salem Monthly Meeting for her minor son, Thomas Folwell, Jr.

13th da, 10th mo, 1789. Gideon Gibson produced a certificate from Salem Monthly Meeting for himself and his two children: Daniel and Gideon. Hope Sharp granted a certificate to Haddonfield Monthly Meeting.

10th da, 11th mo, 1789. Josiah Kay granted a certificate to Haddonfield Monthly Meeting. Ann Townsend granted a certificate to the Monthly Meeting for Eggharbour and Cape May. Abigail Swift granted a certificate to Salem Monthly Meeting.

15th da, 12th mo, 1789. Samuel Folwell condemned for going out in marriage and striking one of his fellow men.

12th da, 1st mo, 1790. Joseph Brown, a lad, produced a certificate from Burlington Monthly Meeting dated 7th da, 12th mo, 1789. Mary Stratton granted a certificate to Salem Monthly Meeting for her minor son, Bethuel Stratton. James Whitall, Jr. granted a certificate to Derby [Darby] Monthly Meeting, for his minor son, Richard Whitall. Deborah Middleton granted a certificate to Philadelphia Monthly Meeting for the southern district.

9th da, 2nd mo, 1790. James Clement produced a certificate from Haddonfield Monthly Meeting dated the 8th instant. Elizabeth Haines granted a certificate to Salem Monthly Meeting. Job Brown granted a certificate to marry at Salem Monthly Meeting. John Clement granted a certificate to marry at Derby [Darby] Monthly Meeting.

9th da, 3rd mo, 1790. John Hunt of Evesham Monthly Meeting, Burlington Co., with Elizabeth Collins and Grace Rogers intend to visit families of Friends in Upper Greenwich Twp. Joshua Cozens, a minor, son of Jacob Cozens, granted a certificate to Philadelphia Monthly Meeting.

13th da, 4th mo, 1790. Francis Boggs produced a certificate from Evesham Monthly Meeting, Burlington Co., dated 5th da, 3rd mo, 1790, for himself, his wife, Ann, and their infant son, Joseph. Joseph Gibson charged with imprudent and unseemly conduct with women.

11th da, 5th mo, 1790. Isaac Jones produced a certificate from Haddonfield Monthly Meeting dated 10th da, 5th mo, 1790, for himself, his wife, Sarah [Ridgway] and their three minor children: Isaac, Rebecca and Beulah Atkinson Jones. Reuben Jennings granted a certificate to Haddonfield Monthly Meeting.

15th da, 6th mo, 1790. Ephraim Gardiner produced a certificate from Haddonfield Monthly Meeting dated the 14th instant. Ann Oldcraft granted a certificate to Philadelphia Monthly Meeting northern district.

11th da, 8th mo, 1790. Since the last meeting, William Keais died. Hezekiah Eastlack acknowledged his going out in marriage. Elijah Clark produced a certificate from Burlington Monthly Meeting dated the 2nd instant. Mary Down granted a certificate to Philadelphia Monthly Meeting.

11th da, 9th mo, 1790. Barzillai Zane made no attempt to repent his misconduct; disowned.

12th da, 10th mo, 1790. John Elliot granted a certificate to Salem Monthly Meeting.

9th da, 11th mo, 1790. Joseph Zane, Jr. dealt with for marrying out, his unchaste freedom with her who is now his wife and neglecting meetings, showed no desire to recant his actions; disowned.

14th da, 12th mo, 1790. Joseph Allen, a minor, produced a certificate from Evesham Monthly Meeting, Burlington Co., dated 5th da, 11th mo, 1790. Sibyl Wood granted a certificate to Haddonfield Monthly Meeting.

11th da, 1st mo, 1791. Thomas Wilkins produced a certificate from Greenwich Monthly Meeting dated the 1st da, 12th mo, 1790. Isaac Lanning, a minor, produced a certificate from Evesham Monthly Meeting, Burlington Co., dated the 7th instant.

15th da, 2nd mo, 1791. Samuel Cooper disowned. Elizabeth Lippincott granted a certificate for herself and her minor son, Samuel Lippincott to Philadelphia Monthly Meeting northern district. Mary Mickle, in her minority, granted a certificate to Haddonfield Monthly Meeting.

15th da, 3rd mo, 1791. David Wood was dealt with for neglecting the payment of his just debts. Anthony Sharp granted a certificate to marry at Evesham Monthly Meeting, Burlington Co.

12th da, 4th mo, 1791. Mary Stratton granted a certificate to Salem Monthly Meeting. Samuel Webster granted a certificate to Haddonfield Monthly Meeting for himself, his wife, Sarah and his four children: Josiah, Isaac, Sarah and Hannah, and one for Samuel Webster, Jr. Patience Webster granted a certificate to Haddonfield

Monthly Meeting. John Tatum, a minister, granted a certificate to make a religious visit to families in the verge of Eggharbour and Cape May.

10th da, 5th mo, 1791. Marmaduke Wood of Upper Greenwich received into membership. Jeremiah Wood received into membership. Daniel Smith received into membership. Samuel Inskeep received into membership. Mary Hopkins granted a certificate to Philadelphia Monthly Meeting for the northern district. Reuben Jennings produced a certificate from Haddonfield Monthly Meeting. John Duel, a minor, who was placed as apprentice with John Kille, produced a certificate from Salem Monthly Meeting. Francis Eastlack dealt with for going out in marriage. Nathan Folwell dealt with for gaming or gambling, which he partly justifies based on his winning a sum of money. James Clement granted a certificate to Philadelphia Monthly Meeting for the southern district.

11th da, 6th mo, 1791. Alice Keais granted a certificate to Philadelphia Monthly Meeting.

12th da, 7th mo, 1791. James Wood, Jr. dealt with for going out in marriage; disowned. Robert Zane of Upper Greenwich disowned for marrying his first cousin.

9th da, 8th mo, 1791. Mary Cozens, late Eastlack, disowned for unchaste freedom with the person who is now her husband and going out in marriage. Hannah Lippincott and Hannah French granted a certificate to Evesham Monthly Meeting, Burlington Co. Elizabeth Ridgway granted a certificate to Mt. Holly Monthly Meeting, Burlington Co. Aaron Thompson produced a certificate from Salem Monthly Meeting for himself, his wife, Abigail and their children: Rebecca and Ann. Jehu Lord produced a certificate from Evesham Monthly Meeting, Burlington Co., for himself and his wife, Rebecca.

15th da, 9th mo, 1791. Rachel Hopper received into membership. George Ash West, a minor, who was placed as an apprentice with Thomas West, produced a certificate from Mt. Holly Monthly Meeting, Burlington Co.

11th da, 10th mo, 1791. Mary Sharp granted a certificate to Philadelphia Monthly Meeting. Jeremiah Wood granted a certificate to marry at Haddonfield Monthly Meeting. John Haines dealt with for using profane language and making insulting remarks to his fellow man.

15th da, 11th mo, 1791. Jane Bickham granted a certificate to Evesham Monthly Meeting, Burlington Co. Thomas West produced a certificate from Mt. Holly Monthly Meeting, Burlington Co.

13th day 12th mo, 1791. Azuba Zane disowned for keeping company with a man in a reproachful manner. Elizabeth Perkins granted a certificate to Haddonfield Monthly Meeting. Nathan Basset produced a certificate from Salem Monthly Meeting for himself, his wife, Sarah and their children: Hannah, Elizabeth and Anna. Joseph Kimsey dealt with for using profane language and striking his fellow man. Patience Ballinger left £10 silver to the school fund in her will dated the 11th da, 7th mo, 1790.

4th da, 2nd mo, 1792. Benjamin Cozens, a minor, is placed with a Friend at Philadelphia Monthly Meeting.

3rd da, 3rd mo, 1792. Biddle Reeves received into membership. James Matlack, a minor, was placed as an apprentice with a Friend of the Derby [Darby] Monthly Meeting. Nathan Folwell granted a certificate to Salem Monthly Meeting.

10th da, 4th mo, 1792. Isaac Snowden, his wife, Mary their minor son, William and two minor daus, Elizabeth and Abigail granted a certificate to Evesham Monthly Meeting, Burlington Co. Isaac Nixon, a minor, who had been placed as an apprentice to Aaron Thompson, produced a certificate from Salem Monthly Meeting dated the 27th of the 2nd mo, last.

15th da, 5th mo, 1792. David Brown, his wife, Charity, their minor children: John, Isaac, William and Amos, Abigail and Hannah granted a certificate to Greenwich Monthly Meeting. Biddle Reeves granted a certificate to marry at Burlington Monthly Meeting. Mary Stratton granted a certificate for her two minor sons; Isaiah Stratton to Salem Monthly Meeting, and Elias Stratton to Haddonfield Monthly Meeting. John Knight produced a certificate from Haddonfield Monthly Meeting dated 15th da, 3rd mo last.

12th da, 6th mo, 1792. Rachel Johns and her daughter-in-law, Sarah Johns granted a certificate to Philadelphia Monthly Meeting for the southern district; also, certificates prepared for Benjamin Johns and Richard Johns to the same meeting. George Brown granted a certificate to marry at Greenwich Monthly Meeting. Thomas Wilkins dealt with for going out in marriage.

10th da, 7th mo, 1792. Mary Sparks granted a certificate to Haddonfield Monthly Meeting. Patience Folwell granted a certificate to Burlington Monthly Meeting.

11th da, 8th mo, 1792. Thomas Wilkins disowned for going out in marriage. Thomasin Roberts and her minor daughter, Hester Roberts granted a certificate to Salem Monthly Meeting. James Cooper appointed overseer of the Woodbury Monthly Meeting in the room of our Friend James Whitall, Jr. Josiah Cattle produced a certificate from Evesham Monthly Meeting, Burlington Co., dated 8th da, 6th mo, 1792.

11th da, 9th mo, 1792. Elizabeth Wood granted a certificate to Philadelphia Monthly Meeting for the southern district. Sarah Keais granted a certificate for her minor son, William Keais to Philadelphia Monthly Meeting for the northern district. Samuel Mickle, Jr. and Ann White appointed elders of Upper Greenwich Monthly Meeting. Jacob Cozens dealt with for using abusive and profane language and neglecting meeting.

9th da, 10th mo, 1792. Amos Cooper treated with for committing adultery with a single woman; which sinful conduct he confesses.

13th da, 11th mo, 1792. Isaac Hensey received into membership. Jeremiah Wood granted a certificate to Haddonfield Monthly Meeting. Anthony Sharp granted a certificate for himself, his wife, Anna, and their apprentice lad, Isaac Laning to Philadelphia Monthly Meeting. Elijah Clark dealt with for neglecting meeting and removing from us in a disreputable manner.

11th da, 12th mo, 1792. Hannah Gamble, late Kimmsey, dealt with for unchaste freedom with a person who is now her husband and marrying out of Friends; disowned.

15th da, 1st mo, 1793. Thomas West granted a certificate for himself and his apprentice lad, George Ash West, to Mt. Holly Monthly Meeting, Burlington Co. Elizabeth West granted a certificate to Mt. Holly Monthly Meeting. David Cooper, John Tatum, Job Whitall, John Jessup, David Brown, Samuel Tonkin and Samuel Paul appointed trustees of the of the school fund and David Ward appointed treasurer for the next year. Joseph Pettit produced a certificate from Haddonfield Monthly Meeting for himself, his wife, Sarah and their five minor children: Woodnut, David, Jonathan, Thomas and Rachel.

12th da, 2nd mo, 1793. Levi Jennings, Jr. disowned for removing to Virginia without the advice of Friends and going out in marriage. Rachel Johns, now in Philadelphia, wife of Richard Johns, and their dau Sarah Johns, reported in bad financial trouble. Joseph Clement appointed as elder.

12th da, 3rd mo, 1793. Elijah Clark disowned for removing without advice of Friends and neglecting meeting.

9th da, 4th mo, 1793. Abraham Iredell of Upper Greenwich disowned for going out in marriage and neglecting meeting. Jacob Wood granted a certificate for Henry Wood, a minor, to Philadelphia

Monthly Meeting. Joshuah Oldcraft dealt with for neglecting meeting and for unchaste freedom with the one who is now his wife.

11th da, 5th mo, 1793. Ann Blackwood granted a certificate to Haddonfield Monthly Meeting. Rebecca Mickle, a minor, granted a certificate to Greenwich Monthly Meeting. Unity Robert, a minor, dau of Thomasin Robert, granted a certificate to Burlington. John Reeve produced a certificate to marry from Greenwich Monthly Meeting.

9th da, 7th mo, 1793. Mark Brown disowned for going out in marriage. Ann Folwell, a minor, granted a certificate to Philadelphia Monthly Meeting. Agnes Moore granted a certificate to Evesham Monthly Meeting, Burlington Co.

13th da, 8th mo, 1793. David Brown granted a certificate to Salem Monthly Meeting.

10th da, 9th mo, 1793. John Wilkins of Upper Greenwich, son of Constantine, treated with for accepting a military commission and neglecting meetings. Henry Zane treated with for unchaste freedom with the person who is now his wife and neglecting meeting. Hephzibah [Hepzibah] Brown granted a certificate to Gunpowder Monthly Meeting, Baltimore Co., Maryland. John Reeve produced a certificate from Greenwich Monthly Meeting.

15th da, 10th mo, 1793. David Wood granted a certificate for his minor dau, Rebecca Wood to Philadelphia Monthly Meeting for the southern district. Joseph Matlack, a minor, issued a certificate to Philadelphia Monthly Meeting. William Wood Wilkins produced a certificate from Philadelphia Monthly Meeting. John Elketon stands charged with fathering two bastard children by two women, one of which he has since married.

10th da, 12th mo, 1793. John Tatum, Jr., son of John Tatum, Sr. granted a certificate to marry at Evesham Monthly Meeting, Burlington Co.

14th da, 1st mo, 1794. Extracts of the last annual meeting regarding propriety of dress were read to the effect that the Monthly Meetings may disown our youth or others who depart from the simplicity of dress and copy after the extravagant fashions of the world. John Wilkins, Jr. disowned for accepting a military commission and neglecting meeting. David Brown, Jr. of Upper Greenwich reported for unchaste freedom with the person who is now his wife and neglecting meeting. Gideon Gibson treated with for unchaste freedom with the person who is now his wife.

11th da, 2nd mo, 1794. Sarah Bates received into membership.

11th da, 3rd mo, 1794. Rachel Low, Jr. disowned for being the mother of an illegitimate child. During the 5th month of last year, Jonathan Cowgill produced a certificate from Salem Monthly Meeting dated the 28th da, 1st Mo, 1793.

15th da, 4th mo, 1794. Jonathan Morgan, Jr. treated with for reproachful conduct and being in the company of individuals who removed the property of others.

13th da, 5th mo, 1794. Francis Boggs granted a certificate to Pilesgrove Monthly Meeting, Salem Co., for himself, his wife, Ann and their three minor children: Joseph Boggs, Joshua Haines Boggs and Mary Boggs. James Clement granted a certificate to Haddonfield for his son, Abel Clement. William Wood Wilkins granted a certificate to Philadelphia Monthly Meeting for the southern district. Richard Whitall, produced a certificate from Derby [Darby] Monthly Meeting. Ann Steward and her dau, Elizabeth Steward granted a certificate to Pilesgrove Monthly Meeting, Salem Co. Joseph Ridgway Brown, a minor, produced a certificate from Mt. Holly Monthly Meeting, Burlington Co.

10th da, 6th mo, 1794. Jonathan Cowgill treated with for neglecting meeting and marrying contrary to the good order among Friends; disowned. Paul Cooper appointed an overseer of the Woodbury Preparative Meeting. Henry Rulon produced a certificate from Greenwich Monthly Meeting.

15th da, 7th mo, 1794. Othniel Alsip, a young man from Great Britain with a certificate from that place to Philadelphia Monthly Meeting, has remained in the compass of this meeting for several months due to the prevalence of yellow fever in Philadelphia and now is granted a recommendation from this meeting to that place. Rebecca Folwell granted a certificate to Philadelphia Monthly Meeting.

12th da, 8th mo, 1794. Thomas Saunders granted a certificate for his minor son, Isaac Saunders to Philadelphia Monthly Meeting. James Whitall, Jr. granted a certificate for his son, Zatthu Whitall, to Philadelphia Monthly Meeting.

9th da, 9th mo, 1794. John Tatum, on behalf of George Ward, granted a certificate to marry at Haddonfield Monthly Meeting.

14th da, 10th mo, 1794. Jacob Lippincott disowned for non-payment of just debts and neglecting meeting. John Wood granted a certificate for himself, and his minor nephew, Caleb Wood to Salem Monthly Meeting.

11th da, 11th mo, 1794. Paul Cooper granted a certificate for Enoch Allen, a minor, who is placed as an apprentice to Newberry Smith within the verge of Philadelphia Monthly Meeting for the northern district.

9th da, 12th mo, 1794. Sarah Nicholson granted a certificate to Derby [Darby] Monthly Meeting. Sarah Nicholson, Jr. granted a certificate to Haddonfield Monthly Meeting.

13th da, 1st mo, 1795. William Wood treated with for going out in marriage. John Whitall, treated with for neglecting meeting and being included in a lottery; disowned.

10th da, 2nd mo, 1795. Nathan Bassett granted a certificate to Pilesgrove Monthly Meeting, Salem Co., for himself, his wife and their four minor children: Hannah, Ann, Elizabeth and Deborah.

10th da, 3rd mo, 1795. [Joseph] Ridgway Brown granted a certificate to Mt. Holly Monthly Meeting, Burlington Co. Jonathan Morgan granted a certificate to Pilesgrove Monthly Meeting, Salem Co. Thomas Andrews produced a certificate from Salem Monthly Meeting. Keziah Andrews treated with for falsely accusing Friends and neglecting meeting; disowned. Samuel Down treated with for going out in marriage and neglecting meetings.

11th da, 4th mo, 1795. Joseph Pettit granted a certificate to Pilesgrove Monthly Meeting, Salem Co., for himself, wife and six children: Woodnut, David, Jonathan, Thomas, Rachel and Mary. Lydia Brady, late Wood, treated with for going out in marriage; disowned. Elizabeth Morgan, wife of Jonathan, granted a certificate to Pilesgrove Monthly Meeting, Salem Co., for herself and four minor children: David, Jonathan, Isaac and Hannah. Hannah Fisher granted a certificate to Pilesgrove Monthly Meeting, Salem Co.

12th da, 5th mo, 1795. Samuel Down disowned for accomplishing his marriage out of unity and neglecting meetings. Joseph Clement, by his father, granted a certificate to Derby [Darby] Monthly Meeting, for himself, wife and three minor children: Aaron, Isaac and Ann. Levi Jennings and his son, Thomas Jennings granted a certificate to Haddonfield Monthly Meeting. George Ward, son of George Ward treated with for accomplishing his marriage out of unity before a magistrate.

9th da, 6th mo, 1795. Josiah Dunn, a minor, produced a certificate from Little Egg Harbor Monthly Meeting, Burlington Co. Lydia Wood granted a certificate to Philadelphia Monthly Meeting for the southern district for herself and her three minor children: Rachel, William and Sarah.

11th da, 7th mo, 1795. Samuel Webster, Jr. produced a certificate from Upper Evesham Monthly Meeting, Burlington Co. Levi Hopper requested to be received into membership.

11th da, 8th mo, 1795. Richard Johns granted a certificate to Philadelphia Monthly Meeting for the southern district.

15th da, 9th mo, 1795. Levi Hopper's request to be received into membership was returned for the moment. Isaac Saunders produced a certificate from Philadelphia Monthly Meeting. Benjamin Rulon produced a certificate from Greenwich Monthly Meeting.

13th da, 10th mo, 1795. Mark Reeve produced a certificate to marry from Philadelphia Monthly Meeting. Jonathan Knight granted a certificate to Haddonfield Monthly Meeting.

11th da, 11th mo, 1795. Sarah [Tatum] Hooper granted a certificate to Philadelphia Monthly Meeting on account of marriage.

15th da, 12th mo, 1795. Hannah [Whitall,] Reeve granted a certificate to Philadelphia Monthly Meeting on account of marriage.

12th da, 1st mo, 1796. John Jessup, Joseph Clement, Joseph Reeves, Jonathan Brown, William Lippincott, Samuel Paul and Samuel Tonkin are appointed as Trustees, and David Ward as Treasurer to the School Fund for the coming year.

9th da, 2nd mo, 1796. Joseph Whitall released of the service of preparing certificates of recommendation at his request.

15th da, 3rd mo, 1796. Caleb Pancoast issued a certificate to marry at Pilesgrove Monthly Meeting, Salem Co.

12th da, 4th mo, 1796. William Stratton, a minor, issued a certificate to Pilesgrove Monthly Meeting, Salem Co. Benjamin Carter granted a certificate to Pilesgrove Monthly Meeting, Salem Co., for himself, Rebecca his wife, and their two minor children, Benjamin and Mary. James Jessup treated with for going out in marriage before a magistrate. John Collins treated with for neglecting meeting.

10th da, 5th mo, 1796. Joseph Whitall, appointed as a minister. Samuel Becket appointed as overseer of Greenwich Preparative in the place of David Brown.

14th da, 6th mo, 1796. Thomas Saunders granted a certificate for his son, James to the Philadelphia Monthly Meeting for the southern district. Abigail Deaton treated with for marrying out of Friends. Jonathan Brown appointed an elder. Josiah Cattle treated with for neglecting meeting and removing from us in a disreputable manner, particularly not paying his just creditors; disowned. James Matlack produced a certificate from Derby [Darby] Monthly Meeting.

12th da, 7th mo, 1796. Mary Weathers granted a certificate to Salem Monthly Meeting. Ann Caldwell, late Wood, treated with for going out in marriage.

9th da, 8th mo, 1796. Edward Willits issued a certificate to Haddonfield Monthly Meeting. Isaac Jones granted a certificate to Haddonfield Monthly Meeting for his minor son, Isaac Jones, Jr. Testimony respecting our beloved Friend David Cooper, dec'd, was read and signed. Hester Goslin treated with for going out in marriage; disowned.

13th da, 9th mo, 1796. Keziah Wilson received into membership.

11th da, 10th mo, 1796. David Ward appointed as overseer in the room of Joseph Clement. Aaron Pancoast granted a certificate to marry at Haddonfield Monthly Meeting.

15th da, 11th mo, 1796. William Becket received into membership.

13th da, 12th mo, 1796. Anna Sharp granted a certificate to Philadelphia Monthly Meeting for herself and her minor children, Elizabeth and Anthony. William White granted a certificate to Philadelphia Monthly Meeting for the northern district, for his minor son, William White, Jr.

10th da, 1st mo, 1797. Unity Roberts granted a certificate to Pilesgrove Monthly Meeting, Salem Co. Ann Clement appointed an elder. William Lucas, who is sick and infirm, produced a certificate of recommendation from Philadelphia Monthly Meeting for the northern district, for himself, his wife, Esther and their young children, Elizabeth and Robert.

14th da, 2nd mo, 1797. Sarah Ward granted a certificate to Haddonfield Monthly Meeting. Micajah Clement treated with for going out in marriage; disowned. William Gibson treated with for going out in marriage; disowned.

14th da, 3rd mo, 1797. Sarah Hooton and her minor children [unnamed] granted a certificate to Evesham Monthly Meeting, Burlington Co. Marsha Nicholson granted a certificate to Pilesgrove Monthly Meeting, Salem Co.

11th da, 4th mo, 1797. Ephraim Gardiner requested a certificate to Pilesgrove Monthly Meeting, Salem Co. Nathan Keais, in his minority, granted a certificate to Salem Monthly Meeting. Isaac Ballinger produced a certificate from Haddonfield Monthly Meeting for himself, Esther, his wife and their infant dau, Maria.

9th da, 5th mo, 1797. Ephraim Gardiner withdraws his request for a certificate.

13th da, 6th mo, 1797. Benjamin Whitall, Jr. received into membership. Aaron Pancoast granted a certificate for himself and his son, Aaron Pancoast to Haddonfield Monthly Meeting. Esther Lucas granted a certificate for herself and her three minor children: Elizabeth, Robert and Esther to Haddonfield Monthly Meeting. Jesse Smith produced a certificate from Haddonfield Monthly Meeting for himself, his wife, [Mary Cassell Smith] and her two children by her former husband, William Atkinson Paul and Yeomans Paul.

11th da, 7th mo, 1797. Edith Ward received into membership. Hannah Jones and Hannah Ballinger granted certificates to Philadelphia Monthly Meeting for the northern district. Hannah Cooper, late Pancoast, treated with for unchaste freedom with the person who is now her husband; disowned.

15th da, 8th mo, 1797. Benjamin Heritage, Jr. granted a certificate to Pilesgrove Monthly Meeting, Salem Co., for himself, his wife, Sarah and their three minor children: Jonathan, William and Sarah. Mary Lunback granted a certificate to the Monthly Meeting for Eggharbour and Cape May. James Cooper appointed an elder. Azuba Zane disowned for fornication. Ephraim Rulon, a minor, produced a certificate from Greenwich Monthly Meeting.

12th da, 9th mo, 1797. Samuel Keais, in his minority, granted a certificate to Philadelphia Monthly Meeting for the northern district.

10th da, 10th mo, 1797. Martha Tatum granted a certificate to Haddonfield Monthly Meeting.

12th da, 12th mo, 1797. Aaron Thompson granted a certificate for himself and his dau, Deborah to Derby [Darby] Monthly Meeting. Ann Cooper granted a certificate to Hudson Monthly Meeting.

9th da, 1st mo, 1798. Rebecca Thompson granted a certificate to Derby [Darby] Monthly Meeting. John Tatum, Joseph Clement, John Jessup, Joseph Reeves, David Brown, William White, and Samuel Paul appointed as trustees, and David Ward as treasurer for the coming year.

13th da, 3rd mo, 1798. Hannah Beckett, wife of Samuel Beckett, received into membership. Tacy Eldridge, late Pancoast; disowned for going out in marriage.

10th da, 4th mo, 1798. Hezekiah Estlack [Eastlack] granted a certificate and recommendation for himself, his wife and their two minor children, John and Rhoda, to Pilesgrove Monthly Meeting, Salem Co. William Lippincott granted a letter of recommendation for himself, his wife, Elizabeth, his three minor children: Deborah, Restore and Elizabeth, and for his grown son, Jacob on their removal to Friends residing within the province of Canada. Samuel Becket [Beckett] granted a few lines of recommendation for himself and his wife, Hannah on their removal to Friends in the province of Canada. Amy Cauley granted a certificate to Pilesgrove Monthly Meeting,

Salem Co.

15th da, 5th mo, 1798. Rebecca Cooper granted a certificate to Chesterfield Monthly Meeting, Burlington Co. Anna Hooton granted a certificate to Evesham Monthly Meeting, Burlington Co. Sarah Miller granted a certificate to Greenwich Monthly Meeting. Joseph W. Bennet produced a certificate from Mt. Holly Monthly Meeting, Burlington Co. Jacob French of Upper Greenwich dealt with for going out in marriage before a Justice of the Peace. Joseph Iredell dealt with for fornication with the person who is now his wife.

12th da, 6th mo, 1798. Aaron Thompson, son of Samuel Thompson, dec'd, granted a certificate to Haddonfield Monthly Meeting. Mary Mickle, wife of Isaac Mickle, granted a certificate to Haddonfield Monthly Meeting. Keziah Chew, late Kimsey, treated with for going out in marriage. Aaron Pancoast, his wife, Ann and their son, Aaron produced a certificate from Haddonfield Monthly Meeting. John Zane produced a certificate from Haddonfield Monthly Meeting. Aaron Lippincott, a minor, produced a certificate from Upper Evesham Monthly Meeting, Burlington Co.

10th da, 7th mo, 1798. Jacob French disowned for going out in marriage. Rebecca Test, a minor, granted a certificate to Evesham Monthly Meeting, Burlington Co. Elizabeth Perkins granted a certificate to Pilesgrove Monthly Meeting, Salem Co. Mary [Gibson] Tees [Teas] granted a certificate to Philadelphia for the southern district on account of marriage. William White is appointed overseer for Upper Greenwich Preparative Meeting. Ebenezer Cresson produced a certificate from Chester Monthly Meeting, Burlington Co.

14th da, 8th mo, 1798. Aaron Thompson disowned for joining the militia. Benjamin Wilkins of Greenwich treated with for being concerned with military services.

11th da, 9th mo, 1798. Joanna Wilkins disowned for neglecting meetings. Sarah Sims, late Bates disowned for going out in marriage.

9th da, 10th mo, 1798. John Jessup, Jr. granted a certificate to marry at Evesham Monthly Meeting, Burlington Co. A letter was received from Mt. Holly Monthly Meeting, Burlington Co., stating that William Coat Atkinson hath left them without applying for a certificate.

19th da, 12th mo, 1798. Elizabeth French, late Zane, dealt with for unchaste freedom. Samuel Paul, Jr. treated with for fornication and has since married another person. David Allinson produced a certificate from Evesham Monthly Meeting, Burlington Co. Hannah Ballinger granted a certificate to Haddonfield Monthly Meeting.

15th da, 1st mo, 1799. Hannah Mathews received into membership with Friends.

12th da, 2nd mo, 1799. Stephen Heritage treated with for going out in marriage. George Whitall, treated with for going out in marriage. James Saunders and Sarah, his wife, produced a certificate from Philadelphia Monthly Meeting for the southern district. Our beloved Friend, Gervis Johnson, a minister, on a religious visit from Ireland attended the meeting and produced a certificate from Antrim Monthly Meeting with an endorsement thereon by the Quarterly meeting of ministers an elders for Ulster Province.

12th da, 3rd mo, 1799. Tacy Jennings, late Walton, dealt with for going out in marriage. John Zane treated with for joining the militia and neglecting meetings; disowned.

9th da, 4th mo, 1799. Thomas Enoch granted a certificate to Pilesgrove Monthly Meeting, Salem Co., for himself, his wife, Mary Enoch and their children: Thomas, Martha and Elizabeth Enoch. Mary Smart granted a certificate to Salem Monthly Meeting. Hope Fisher treated with for conduct contrary to her profession; disowned. Samuel Mickle, Jr. appointed overseer for Upper Greenwich in the room of Thomas Enock, who has removed to Salem Co. Enoch Allen produced a certificate from Evesham Monthly Meeting, Burlington Co. Levi Jennings produced a certificate from Haddonfield Monthly Meeting.

14th da, 5th mo, 1799. John Brown of Upper Greenwich treated with for going out in marriage. Charles French of Upper Greenwich treated with for going out in marriage.

11th da, 6th mo, 1799. John Jessup, Jr. granted a certificate to Evesham Monthly Meeting, Burlington Co. Beulah Atkinson, a minor, granted a certificate to Upper Evesham Monthly Meeting, Burlington Co. Francis Eastlack granted a certificate to Pilesgrove Monthly Meeting, Salem Co.

9th da, 7th mo, 1799. Rebecca Swift, late Gibbs, treated with for going out in marriage; disowned.

13th da, 8th mo, 1799. Joseph Allen granted a certificate to Salem Monthly Meeting. Simon Zane, Jr. of Upper Greenwich treated with for fornication.

10th da, 9th mo, 1799. Zaccheus Test granted a certificate for himself and his minor son, Benjamin Test to Philadelphia Monthly Meeting for the northern district. Anne Jess, a minor, granted a certificate to Evesham Monthly Meeting, Burlington Co.

15th da, 10th mo, 1799. Marmaduke Wood treated with for neglecting meeting, neglecting the payment of his just debts and being concerned with horse racing; disowned. Job Gibbs treated with for going out in marriage; disowned.

12th da, 11th mo, 1799. James Pancoast, his wife and his three children: David, Hannah and Sarah, received into membership. Clayton Brown produced a certificate from Upper Evesham Monthly Meeting, Burlington Co. Joseph Stokes produced a certificate from Mt. Holly Monthly Meeting, Burlington Co.

10th da, 12th mo, 1799. Joseph W. Bennet granted a certificate for himself, his wife, Mary and their minor son, Joseph Morgan Bennet. Isaac Nixon granted a certificate to Greenwich Monthly Meeting. William Cooper granted a certificate to marry at Salem Monthly Meeting.

14th da, 1st mo, 1800. Stephen Heritage granted a certificate to Pilesgrove Monthly Meeting, Salem Co. Mary Morton, formerly Zane, treated with for going out in marriage; disowned.

11th da, 2nd mo, 1800. Elizabeth Folwell granted a certificate to Burlington Monthly Meeting.

11th da, 3rd mo, 1800. Ira Allen produced a certificate from Philadelphia Monthly Meeting. William Glover produced a certificate from Haddonfield Monthly Meeting.

15th da, 4th mo, 1800. Enoch Allen granted a certificate to marry at Pilesgrove Monthly Meeting, Salem Co. Mary Thorn granted a certificate to Haddonfield Monthly Meeting. Anna Mickle granted a certificate to Philadelphia Monthly Meeting for the northern district.

13th da, 5th mo, 1800. David Allinson granted a certificate to Burlington Monthly Meeting. William Howey produced a certificate from Pilesgrove Monthly Meeting, Salem Co. Mary Browning, late Paul, treated with for going out in marriage.

10th da, 6th mo, 1800. George Brown granted a certificate to Salem Monthly Meeting for himself, his wife and three children: Margaret, James and Rebecca. Mary Allen, late Enoch, read an acknowledgment of her going out in marriage.

15th da, 7th mo, 1800. Ruth Jess granted a certificate to Evesham Monthly Meeting, Burlington Co.

12th da, 8th mo, 1800. Anthony Allen granted a certificate for his son, Enoch Allen to Salem Monthly Meeting. John Down treated with for paying a military fine and neglecting meetings; disowned. Jacob Haines granted a certificate to Philadelphia Monthly Meeting for the southern district, for himself, his wife, Elizabeth and their two minor sons, Samuel and Joel.

9th da, 9th mo, 1800. John Brown produced a certificate from Upper Evesham Monthly Meeting, Burlington Co. Jacob Iredell produced a

certificate from Haddonfield Monthly Meeting.
11th da, 11th mo, 1800. Thomas Moore granted a certificate to marry at Pilesgrove Monthly Meeting, Salem Co. Ann Pancoast granted a certificate to Haddonfield Monthly Meeting. Ann Mounce received into membership. Joshua Lippincott granted a certificate to marry at Pilesgrove Monthly Meeting, Salem Co.
9th da, 12th mo, 1800. Isaac Collins, Amos Collins and John Collins granted permission to hold a meeting for divine worship in their school house at Chestnut Ridge. Martha Clark Hensly received into membership. Sarah Gibson granted a certificate for her minor son, Spicer Gibson, who is placed as an apprentice with a Friend of Philadelphia Monthly Meeting.
13th da, 1st mo, 1801. Thomas Knight, a minor, produced a certificate from Haddonfield Monthly Meeting dated 8th da, 2nd mo, 1800.
10th da, 2nd mo, 1801. Jehu Lord granted a certificate to London Grove Monthly Meeting, Chester Co., PA, for himself, his wife and their four minor children: Sarah, Hannah, Mary and Lydia. Josiah Dunn granted a certificate to New York Monthly Meeting. Richard Matlack reported for unbecoming conduct.
10th da, 3rd mo, 1801. William Whitall, granted a certificate to Philadelphia Monthly Meeting.
14th da, 4th mo, 1801. Richard Matlack disowned. Ephraim Hermitage disowned for marrying his first cousin.
12th da, 5th mo, 1801. John Nicholson granted a certificate to Derby [Darby] Monthly Meeting. Lindsay Nicholson granted a certificate to Philadelphia Monthly Meeting for the northern district. Benjamin Cloud received into membership. Jeremiah Wood produced a certificate from Haddonfield Monthly Meeting for himself, his wife, Mary and their five minor children: Elizabeth, Isaac Haines, Mary, Hannah and Jehu. David Ward, Jonathan Brown, James Cooper, John Tatum, Jr., Samuel Tonkin, Samuel Paul, William Wood and William Beckett appointed to attend the next quarterly meeting.
9th da, 6th mo, 1801. Benjamin Cloud and his wife, Sarah received into membership. Josiah Atkinson and his wife, Priscilla produced a certificate from Haddonfield Monthly Meeting. Paul Trosh, his wife, Sybilla and their four minor children: William, James, Jacob and Elizabeth produced a certificate from Upper Evesham Monthly Meeting, Burlington Co.
14th da, 7th mo, 1801. Hannah Hooten granted a certificate to Evesham Monthly Meeting, Burlington Co. Hester Roberts granted a certificate to Pilesgrove Monthly Meeting, Salem Co. William and

Lylia Reeve, minors, produced a certificate from Greenwich Monthly Meeting.

11th da, 8th mo, 1801. Rachel Long received into membership. Sybil Ogden granted a certificate to Pilesgrove Monthly Meeting, Salem Co. Joseph Brown dealt with for going out in marriage; disowned. Sarah Driver gone out in marriage. John Tatum, Jr., Isaac Ballinger, Isaac Jones, James Davis, Samuel Tonkin, William Lippincott, Samuel Paul and William Wood appointed to attend the next quarterly meeting.

15th da, 9th mo, 1801. Joseph Powell Rogers, his wife, Sarah [Inskeep] and their minor children, Sarah Ann and Hannah produced a certificate from Haddonfield Monthly Meeting. Elizabeth Whitall gone out in marriage.

13th da, 10th mo, 1802 [1801]. Keziah Long granted a certificate to Philadelphia Monthly Meeting for the northern district.

10th da, 11th mo, 1801. Joseph Stokes granted a certificate to Evesham Monthly Meeting, Burlington Co. Hepsibah [Hepzibah] Kimsey granted a certificate to Pilesgrove Monthly Meeting, Salem Co.

15th da, 12th mo, 1801. George West, a minor, produced a certificate from Mt. Holly Monthly Meeting, Burlington Co. Evan Lewis, Jr. produced a certificate from Radnor Monthly Meeting, near Haverford, PA.

12th da, 1st mo, 1802. James Matlack treated with for going out in marriage; disowned.

9th da, 2nd mo, 1802. John Zane, a minor, granted a certificate to Philadelphia Monthly Meeting for the northern district. Josiah Heritage treated with for going out in marriage; disowned.

9th da, 3rd mo, 1802. Samuel Mickle, son of Samuel Mickle, Jr, produced a certificate. William Down treated with for paying his military fines and neglecting meetings; disowned. William Lippincott appointed overseer of Upper Greenwich Preparative Meeting in place of Samuel Mickle.

13th da, 4th mo, 1802. Hannah Clement produced a certificate from Haddonfield Monthly Meeting. William Glover, his wife, Mary and their child, George granted a certificate to London Grove Monthly Meeting, Chester Co., PA. Josiah Stokes produced a certificate from Upper Evesham Monthly Meeting, Burlington Co., for himself, his wife, Hope and their four children: Mary, Ann, Sarah and Lydia and their apprentice, Martha Hirl. Joseph Lippincott, a minor, produced a certificate from Pilesgrove Monthly Meeting, Salem Co.

11th da, 5th mo, 1802. Hope Allen granted a certificate to Salem Monthly Meeting. Rachel C. Elliott granted a certificate to Philadelphia Monthly Meeting for the northern district. Sarah Gibson produced a certificate from Pilesgrove Monthly Meeting, Salem Co. Paul Troth, his wife, Sybilla, and their four children: William, James, Jacob and Elizabeth granted a certificate to Haddonfield Monthly Meeting.

13th da, 6th mo, 1802. Mary Nicholson treated with for unbecoming conduct; disowned. Rachel Long granted a certificate to Philadelphia Monthly Meeting for the northern district.

13th da, 7th mo, 1802. Josiah Atkinson treated with for unjustifiably contracting debts which he was unable to pay and for moving away in a disreputable manner; disowned. Rachel Long returned the certificate granted last month because her health was poor in Philadelphia. Joseph Tomlinson produced a certificate from Haddonfield Monthly Meeting. Hannah Shute married out of unity; disowned.

10th da, 8th mo, 1802. John Tatum, Jr. appointed overseer of the preparative meeting of Woodbury in the room of James Cooper.

14th da, 9th mo, 1802. Samuel Brown produced a certificate from Upper Evesham Monthly Meeting, Burlington Co. Sarah Sheldon, late Down, gone out in marriage; disowned.

12th da, 10th mo, 1802. Abel Clement, Jr. granted a certificate to marry at Haddonfield Monthly Meeting.

9th da, 11th mo, 1802. Joseph Haines, a minor, granted a certificate to Philadelphia Monthly Meeting.

15th da, 2nd mo, 1803. David Mickle granted a certificate to marry at Burlington Monthly Meeting.

15th da, 3rd mo, 1803. Samuel Holdcraft treated with for paying fines in lieu of personal service in the militia. Elizabeth Jennings, late Fisher, gone out in marriage; disowned.

12th da, 4th mo, 1803. Eran [Aaron] Lewis granted a certificate to Concord Monthly Meeting, Chester Co., PA. Levi Jennings granted a certificate to Pilesgrove Monthly Meeting, Salem Co. Priscilla Atkinson granted a certificate to Haddonfield Monthly Meeting for herself and her daughter, Lydia. Jacob Haines was appointed overseer for Upper Greenwich in place of William White.

10th da, 5th mo, 1803. John Reeve granted a certificate for his minor grandson, John Reeve, son of Beulah Reeve, to Greenwich Monthly Meeting. Sarah Gibson granted a certificate to Pilesgrove Monthly Meeting, Salem Co., for herself and her two minor sons, Mark and

Aaron Gibson. Mary Mickle granted a certificate to Haddonfield Monthly Meeting. James Saunders appointed overseer for Woodbury Monthly Meeting in place of Paul Cooper. Benjamin Lord treated with for going out in marriage and paying military fines.

14th da, 6th mo, 1803. Asa Gibson, a minor, granted a certificate to Salem Monthly Meeting. Jacob Lippincott, Jr. treated with for neglecting meeting and going out in marriage. Enoch Allen produced a certificate from Salem Monthly Meeting dated the 25th da, 4th mo, 1803.

12th da, 7th mo, 1803. Samuel Packer, his wife, Sarah and their four minor children: John, Samuel, Kitturah [Catharine] and Ann received into membership. Mary Hopper, late Saunders; disowned for marrying out of unity.

13th da, 9th mo, 1803. George Whitall, treated with for neglecting the payment of debts, leaving his creditors in a disreputable manner and frequenting places of diversion; disowned.

11th da, 10th mo, 1803. Rebecca Stratton granted a certificate to Upper Evesham Monthly Meeting, Burlington Co. Sybilla Collins, a minor, granted a certificate to Upper Evesham Monthly Meeting, Burlington Co.

13th da, 12th mo, 1803. Clayton Brown granted a certificate to Upper Evesham Monthly Meeting, Burlington Co. Samuel Brown, a minor, granted a certificate to Upper Evesham Monthly Meeting, Burlington Co.

13th da, 3rd mo, 1804. Abel Clement, Jr. granted a certificate to Haddonfield Monthly Meeting. Aaron Pancoast produced a certificate to marry from Pilesgrove Monthly Meeting, Salem Co.

10th da, 4th mo, 1804. William White granted a certificate to Pilesgrove Monthly Meeting, Salem Co., for himself and his six minor children: Rebecca, Mary, Joseph, Isaac, John and Joel, and for his grown son, Samuel. Asher Brown granted a certificate to Miamies [Miami] Monthly Meeting, Warren Co., Ohio, for himself and his four sons: David, Samuel, Israel and Benjamin. Mary Brown, wife of Asher Brown, and their two daughters, Ann and Mary may be included therein. George Craft, Jr. produced a certificate from Burlington Monthly Meeting for himself, his wife, Rebecca [Gibbs] Craft and their five children: Beulah, Rebecca, Aden [Aldin G.], George and Lydia.

15th da, 5th mo, 1804. William Wood, a minor, produced a certificate from Philadelphia Monthly Meeting for the southern district dated 28th da, 3rd mo, 1804. John Ridgway produced a certificate from

Pilesgrove Monthly Meeting, Salem Co., dated 26th da, 4th mo, 1804 for himself and his apprentice lad, Job Kirby. Abel Rulon produced a certificate from Greenwich Monthly Meeting dated 28th da, 3rd mo, 1804. Sarah Hoffman produced a certificate from Pilesgrove Monthly Meeting, Salem Co., for herself and her seven minor children: Martha, Job, Isaac, Sarah, Mary, Rebekah and Abigail.

12th da, 6th mo, 1804. David Tatum granted a certificate to Philadelphia Monthly Meeting for the southern district. William Barton produced a certificate from Haddonfield Monthly Meeting dated 14th da, 5th mo, 1804.

10th da, 7th mo, 1804. Isaac Collins granted a certificate to Haddonfield Monthly Meeting for his minor son, John Collins. Charity Evans, late Collins, treated with for going out in marriage; disowned. George C. Ward granted a certificate to Miamies [Miami] Monthly Meeting, Warren Co., Ohio, for himself, his wife, Deborah and their four minor children: Joshua, Rebekah, Eliza and Mary Ann. Ephraim Rulon stands charged with wrong doing and has abruptly left this place without being treated; disowned.

11th da, 9th mo, 1804. Charles Potts received into membership.

15th da, 1st mo, 1805. Mary Parson granted a certificate to Buckingham Monthly Meeting, Bucks Co., PA. John Knight produced a certificate to marry from Salem Monthly Meeting.

12th da, 3rd mo, 1805. Hope Collins received into membership. Aaron Hewes Middleton treated with for taking strong drink to excess. Thomas Clement produced a certificate from Nottingham Monthly Meeting, Burlington Co., dated the 28th da, 7th mo, 1805.

9th da, 4th mo, 1805. Joseph Powell Rogers granted a certificate to Haddonfield Monthly Meeting for himself, his wife, Sarah and their three minor children: Sarah Ann, Hannah and Abraham.

14th da, 5th mo, 1805. Samuel Packer granted a certificate to Miamies [Miami] Monthly Meeting, Warren Co., in the state of Ohio for himself, his wife, Sarah and their five minor children: Catharine, John, Samuel, Ann and William P. Packer. William Wood granted a certificate to Pilesgrove Monthly Meeting, Salem Co., for himself, his wife, Ann. Our esteemed Friend, Eunid Starr, visiting minister, produced a certificate from Exeter Monthly Meeting, Berks Co., PA, dated the 24th day of the 4th mo, 1805. Sarah [Ridgway-Jones] Knight granted a certificate to Salem Monthly Meeting on account of marriage. Beulah Atkinson granted a certificate to Salem Monthly Meeting. Anne Pancoast granted a certificate to Pilesgrove Monthly Meeting, Salem Co. Sarah Gibson produced a certificate from

Greenwich Monthly Meeting, Salem Co., for herself and her two minor children, Mark and Aaron Gibson.

11th da, 6th mo, 1805. Rebecca West, late Whitall, gone out in marriage; disowned. David Tatum produced a certificate from Philadelphia Monthly Meeting for the southern district dated the 29th da, 5th mo, 1805.

9th da, 7th mo, 1805. Anne Thompson produced a certificate from Greenwich Monthly Meeting. George Brown produced a certificate from Salem Monthly Meeting for himself, his wife, Mary and their five minor children: Margaret, James, Rebecca Miller and Mary Brown.

13th da, 8th mo, 1805. John Hinchman granted a certificate to Upper Evesham Monthly Meeting, Burlington County.

15th da, 10th mo, 1805. Samuel Bartin, son of William Bartin, received into membership. Anna Bartin, wife of William, and their five minor daughters received into membership. Aaron Hewes Middleton treated with for taking strong drink to excess.

12th da, 11th mo, 1805. John Tatum, Jr. appointed elder for Woodbury Monthly Meeting. Susannah Hopper produced a certificate from Wilmington Monthly Meeting, Newcastle Co., Delaware, dated the 10th da, 10th mo, 1805. Charles Knight, a minor, produced a certificate from Haddonfield Monthly Meeting dated the 14th da, 10th mo, 1805. Joseph Hiles, a minor, produced a certificate from Mt. Holly Monthly Meeting, Burlington Co., dated the 10th da, 10th mo, 1805.

10th da, 12th mo, 1805. Gideon Gibson granted a certificate to Pilesgrove Monthly Meeting, Salem Co. Tacy Eldridge married out of unity.

11th da, 2nd mo, 1806. George Tatum granted a certificate to marry at Salem Monthly Meeting. Sarah Dennis received into membership.

11th da, 3rd mo, 1806. Rachel Clement, wife of Thomas Clement, and their two daughters, Sarah and Ruth and their infant son, John, received into membership. Robert Zane, Jr. treated with for neglecting meeting and taking strong drink to excess. Robert Holdcraft of Upper Greenwich treated with for going out in marriage.

15th da, 4th mo, 1806. William Cooper granted a certificate to marry at Darby Monthly Meeting. Thomas Clement granted a certificate to Nottingham Monthly Meeting. Samuel Wood gone out in marriage; disowned. John Brown gone out in marriage; disowned.

13th da, 5th mo, 1806. George Tatum granted a certificate to Pilesgrove Monthly Meeting, Salem Co. Esther Miller and Rebecca

Smith, a minor, granted a certificate to Salem Monthly Meeting. Ann Cooper, Jr. granted a certificate to Upper Evesham Monthly Meeting, Burlington County.

10th da, 6th mo, 1806. Amos Cooper granted a certificate to Philadelphia Monthly Meeting for his minor son, Isaac Mickle Cooper. William Holdcraft of Upper Greenwich treated with for neglecting meetings and going out in marriage; disowned.

15th da, 7th mo, 1806. Priscilla Dilks, later Heritage, gone out in marriage; disowned. Wilkin [William] Zane was charged with neglecting meetings, keeping a disorderly life and conversation, insulting his fellow man with abusive language and going to sea without being treated; disowned.

9th da, 9th mo, 1806. Biddle Reeves granted a certificate to marry at Upper Springfield Monthly Meeting, Burlington County.

14th da, 10th mo, 1806. Isaiah Ward, his wife, Abigail and their minor children: James, William, Isaiah, Joseph, Margaretta, Beulah and Susannah received into membership. Mary Collins received into membership. Able Clement reported an error in the division of land left to himself and his brother, Joseph by their father, Samuel Clement.

9th da, 12th mo, 1806. Mary Carpenter received into membership. Job Kirby granted a certificate to Pilesgrove Monthly Meeting, Salem Co. Robert Cooper treated with for going out in marriage. Asa Gibbs produced a certificate for himself, his wife, Sarah and their two minor children, Charles and Edward Gibbs. Lydia Cook treated with for going out in marriage.

13th da, 1st mo, 1807. John Brown granted a certificate to Haddonfield Monthly Meeting.

10th da, 2nd mo, 1807. David Cooper granted a certificate to marry at Pilesgrove Monthly Meeting, Salem Co. Hannah Sloan granted a certificate to Haddonfield Monthly Meeting. William Paul, a minor, granted a certificate to Philadelphia Monthly Meeting. Mary Tomlinson granted a certificate to Upper Evesham Monthly Meeting, Burlington Co., for herself and her two children, Joseph and Warner. William White, Jr. produced a certificate from Philadelphia Monthly Meeting for the northern district dated 23rd da, 12th mo, 1806.

10th da, 3rd mo, 1807. John Tatum, Jr, Isaac Ballinger and James Saunders appointed as overseers for Woodbury Monthly Meeting. William Lippincott and Jacob Haines appointed as overseers for Upper Greenwich Preparative Meeting. James Saunders appointed as clerk.

14th da, 4th mo, 1807. Elizah Collins granted a certificate to Haddonfield Monthly Meeting. Elizabeth Hooten granted a certificate to Evesham Monthly Meeting, Burlington Co. Joseph P. [Powell] Rogers produced a certificate from Haddonfield Monthly Meeting for himself, his wife, Sarah and their three minor children: Sarah, Hannah and Abraham. Isaac Kay produced a certificate from Haddonfield for himself, his wife, Deborah [Eldridge] and their five minor children: Hope, Deborah, Joseph, Clement and William. Noah Murphy produced a certificate from Salem Monthly Meeting.

12th da, 5th mo, 1807. Ira Allen granted a certificate to Salem Monthly Meeting for himself, his wife, Catharine [Cooper] and their infant dau, Ann. Rebecca Ridgway treated with for going out in marriage, reconciled. Job Eldridge produced a certificate from Pilesgrove Monthly Meeting for himself, his wife, Tacy and their minor children: Hannah Pancoast Eldridge, William Malander Eldridge, Job and Isaac Kay Eldridge. Atlantic Ballinger granted a certificate to Haddonfield Monthly Meeting. Eliza Hinchman, a minor, granted a certificate to Salem Monthly Meeting. Priscilla Hirf gone out in marriage; disowned. Thomas Carpenter produced a certificate from Salem Monthly Meeting. Edward Gibbs produced a certificate from Haddonfield Monthly Meeting. John Brown produced a certificate from Haddonfield for himself and his wife, Ruth.

14th da, 7th mo, 1807. William Pine, his wife, Mary and their minor children: Joseph, Benjamin, Joshua, Hannah, Priscilla, Rebecca and Samuel received into membership. Rebecca Jones, dau of Isaac and Sarah [Ridgway] Jones, granted a certificate to Salem Monthly Meeting.

11th da, 8th mo, 1807. Elizabeth Cowperthwaite [Copperthwaite] granted a certificate to Haddonfield Monthly Meeting.

15th da, 9th mo, 1807. Daniel and Sarah Pillman, minors, produced a certificate from Burlington Monthly Meeting dated 3rd da, 8th mo, 1807.

13th da, 10th mo, 1807. Sybilla [Sibyl], Sarah and Hannah Cook, daus, of Robert and Lydia Cook received into membership.

15th da, 12th mo, 1807. Michael C. Fisher received into membership. George West granted a certificate to Mt. Holly Monthly Meeting, Burlington Co. Noah [Ridgway] Jones, the minor son of Isaac and Sarah [Ridgway] Jones, granted a certificate to Salem Monthly Meeting.

12th da, 1st mo, 1808. Griffith Hinchman, a minor, granted a certificate to Salem Monthly Meeting. Isaiah Ward granted a certificate for his

WOODBURY MONTHLY MEETING

minor son, James Ward to Philadelphia Monthly Meeting for the northern district. Rebecca Ridgway granted a certificate to Salem Monthly Meeting. Mary Hinchman granted a certificate to Derby [Darby] Monthly Meeting, Chester Co., PA.

9th da, 2nd mo, 1808. Beulah Pancoast received into membership. Mary Allen, Jr. granted a certificate to Philadelphia Monthly Meeting for the northern district.

14th da, 3rd mo, 1808. Jonathan Allen, a minor, produced a certificate from Pilesgrove Monthly Meeting, Salem Co. Hannah Mickle, Jr. granted a certificate to Haddonfield Monthly Meeting.

12th da, 4th mo, 1808. The certificate granted to Rebecca Ridgway to the Salem Monthly Meeting was returned because of her death before it could be delivered. Elizabeth Braddick granted a certificate for herself and her four minor children: Samuel, Sarah, Lydia and Thomas to Upper Evesham Monthly Meeting, Burlington Co.

10th da, 5th mo, 1808. Clement Reeves, his wife and their five minor children: Louisa, Susan, Israel, Mary and Joseph received into membership. Samuel Saunders married out of unity. Samuel Clement married out of unity; disowned. John Ballinger produced a certificate from Eggharbour Monthly Meeting for himself, his wife, Hannah and their three minor children: Sarah, Mary and William. Elizabeth Nicholson granted a certificate to Centre Monthly Meeting, New Castle County, PA.

14th da, 6th mo, 1808. John Reeve granted a certificate for William Reeve, a minor, to Chester Monthly Meeting, Burlington Co. Josiah Ward treated with for going out in marriage; disowned. Richard Snowden [Snowdon] produced a certificate from Haddonfield Monthly Meeting for himself and his minor son, Miles [Myles].

12th da, 7th mo, 1808. Joseph Hyle granted a certificate to London Grove Monthly Meeting, Chester Co., PA.

9th da, 8th mo, 1808. Rebecca Cooper treated with for neglecting meetings and attending places of diversion; disowned.

11th da, 10th mo, 1808. Richardson Andrews granted a certificate to Philadelphia Monthly Meeting. Jesse Smith treated with for going in marriage. Anna Shivers treated with for going out in marriage

13th da, 12th mo, 1808. Sarah Wood received into membership. Samuel Lippincott married out of unity. Joseph Barger produced a certificate from Philadelphia Monthly Meeting for the northern district for himself, his wife, Mary and their son, William Wood.

10th da, 1st mo, 1809. Yhamons [Yemmons] Paul, a minor, granted a certificate to Philadelphia Monthly Meeting.

14th da, 2nd mo, 1809. Joseph Reeves, Jr. received into membership. Joseph Clement, Jr. granted a certificate to marry at Chester Monthly Meeting. James Saunders appointed as clerk.

14th da, 3rd mo, 1809. Thomas Clark produced a certificate from Pilesgrove Monthly Meeting, Salem Co., for himself and his seven minor children: Thomas P., Mary B., Beulah, Achsah, Eliza, Edith and Ann Clark. John Knight, a minor, produced a certificate from Haddonfield Monthly Meeting.

11th da, 4th mo, 1809. William Barten granted a certificate to Upper Evesham Monthly Meeting, Burlington Co., for himself and his minor children: Rebecca, Samuel, Ann and Patience. Joseph Reeves, Jr. granted a certificate to marry a Friend of Pilesgrove Monthly Meeting, Salem Co. Sarah [Wood] Jessup produced a certificate from Upper Evesham Monthly Meeting, Burlington County.

9th da, 5th mo, 1809. Samuel B. Lippincott produced a certificate to marry from Pilesgrove Monthly Meeting, Salem Co. James Pancoast produced a certificate from Pilesgrove Monthly Meeting, Salem Co., dated 20th da, 4th mo, 1809, for himself, his wife, Mary and their three minor children: Hannah, Sarah and Martha. William M. Eldridge produced a certificate from Haddonfield Monthly Meeting dated 8th da, 5th mo, 1809 for himself and his wife, Sarah. John Woolley produced a certificate from Upper Springfield, Burlington County. Elizabeth Braddock produced a certificate from Haddonfield Monthly Meeting for herself and her four minor children: Samuel, Sarah, Lydia and Thomas.

13th da, 6th mo, 1809. Joseph Clement, Jr. granted a certificate to Chester Monthly Meeting. John Tatum, John Reeve, Joseph Clement, James Cooper, Phineus Lord, Jacob Haines, David Brown, Samuel Mickle, Jr., William Beckett, Samuel Paul, Joseph Whitall, and William Lippincott appointed as elders.

11th da, 7th mo, 1809. Joseph Reeves, Jr. granted a certificate to Pilesgrove Monthly Meeting, Salem Co. Martha Hoil granted a certificate to Upper Evesham Monthly Meeting, Burlington County. Mary B. Lippincott granted a certificate to Pilesgrove Monthly Meeting, Salem Co. David C. Wood produced a certificate from Greenwich Monthly Meeting dated 27th da, 7th mo, 1809. Richard French produced a certificate from Pilesgrove Monthly Meeting, Salem Co. Isaac Howy produced a certificate from Pilesgrove Monthly Meeting, Salem Co. Elizabeth Haines and Hannah Tatum appointed as elders.

10th da, 10th mo, 1809. Mary Brown produced a certificate from Upper

Evesham Monthly Meeting, Burlington County. Letitia Ware, Mary R. Garigues and John Hunt, on a religious visit, produced certificates from Darby Monthly Meeting.

14th da, 11th mo, 1809. John Tatum, Jr., Isaac Ballinger and James Saunders appointed as overseers for Woodbury Monthly Meeting. Jacob Haines and Josiah Stokes appointed overseers for Upper Greenwich Preparative Meeting.

12th da, 12th mo, 1809. Samuel C. Hopkins produced a certificate from Philadelphia Monthly Meeting for the southern district.

9th da, 1st mo, 1810. Samuel Inskeep treated with for contracting debts beyond his ability to pay and paying some debts in preference to others.

13th da, 2nd mo, 1810. Joseph Lippincott, a minor, granted a certificate to Chester Monthly Meeting. Joseph Jennings, Mark Jennings and Job Jennings produced a certificate from Haddonfield Monthly Meeting. Daniel and Sarah Pittman, minors, returned to their home in the verge of Burlington Monthly Meeting.

13th da, 3rd mo, 1810. John Cooper, Jr. a minor, granted a certificate to Philadelphia Monthly Meeting for the northern district. William Allen produced a certificate to marry from Pilesgrove Monthly Meeting. James Hinchman treated with for going out in marriage.

10th da, 4th mo, 1810. Mary [Horner] Wood granted a certificate to Haddonfield Monthly Meeting for herself and her five children: Elizabeth Wood, Isaac Hornor Wood, Mary Wood, Hannah Wood and Jehu Wood.

15th da, 5th mo, 1810. Martha Pratt, late Heritage, gone out in marriage; disowned. Mary Allen granted a certificate to Pilesgrove Monthly Meeting, Salem Co. Jedidiah T. Allen produced a certificate from Salem Monthly Meeting. Asa Borton, a minor, produced a certificate from Evesham Monthly Meeting, Burlington County. Edward Borton produced a certificate from Upper Evesham Monthly Meeting, Burlington Co., for himself, his wife, Mary and their three minor children: Rebecca, Job and Emeline Borton.

10th da, 6th mo, 1810. Mark Gibson gone out in marriage with a person not in membership.

10th da, 7th mo, 1810. Thomas Clement granted a certificate to Haddonfield Monthly Meeting for himself, his wife, Rachel and their four minor children: John, Ruth, Zebedee and Charles.

14th da, 8th mo, 1810. Jonathan Brown granted a certificate to Pilesgrove Monthly Meeting, Salem Co., for his minor son, Joseph Brown. Benjamin Hinchman, a minor, granted a certificate to Salem

Monthly Meeting.

11th da, 9th mo, 1810. Mary Hilman, late Mary Wood, gone out in marriage; disowned.

9th da, 10th mo, 1810. Mary Moor [Moore], late Mary Brown, gone out in marriage before a magistrate. Charles Hopkins produced a certificate from Haddonfield Monthly Meeting. Thomas Ballinger produced a certificate from Haddonfield Monthly Meeting.

13th da, 11th mo, 1810. Ebenezer Fogg, a minor, produced a certificate from Greenwich Monthly Meeting.

11th da, 12th mo, 1810. John Packer, his wife, Christiana [Christiannah] Dorothy and their five minor children: Jonathan, Lawrence, Esther, Rhoda and John received into membership. Margaret Brown, a minor, granted a certificate to Haddonfield Monthly Meeting.

15th da, 1st mo, 1811. Benjamin Pine granted a certificate to Pilesgrove Monthly Meeting, Salem Co.

12th da, 2nd mo, 1811. Samuel Saunders granted a certificate to Salem Monthly Meeting. Tacy Lippincott gone out in marriage; disowned. Mary Moore granted a certificate to Upper Evesham Monthly Meeting, Burlington Co.

9th da, 4th mo, 1811. Isaac Kay granted a certificate to Philadelphia Monthly Meeting for himself and his family. William M. Eldridge granted a certificate to Philadelphia Monthly Meeting for himself, his wife and their infant son. Noah Murphy granted a certificate to Salem Monthly Meeting. Deborah Brown, late Deborah Middleton gone out in marriage; disowned. Cooper Paul treated with [no reason recorded]. John Woolley acknowledged paying a fine in lieu of military service.

14th da, 5th mo, 1811. Jedidiah Allen, Jr. granted a certificate to marry at Salem Monthly Meeting. James Pancoast granted a certificate to Pilesgrove Monthly Meeting for himself, his wife, Martha and their three minor children: Hannah A., Sarah and Martha.

11th da, 6th mo, 1811. Charles Jennings, minor son of Joseph Jennings, received into membership. Sarah Jennings, wife of Joseph, and their three minor daus, .: Hannah, Ann and Mary, received into membership. Thomas P. [Pancoast] Clark, son of Thomas Clark, granted a certificate to Philadelphia Monthly Meeting. Edward Bradway of Greenwich Monthly Meeting and his wife, Susanna Bradway granted a certificate to perform a religious visit within the compass of this meeting.

9th da, 7th mo, 1811. George Brown gone out in marriage. Samuel

Shute produced a certificate from Pilesgrove Monthly Meeting, Salem Co., for himself, his wife, Alice and their six minor children: Ann Hazleton, Hariet [Harriet], Charles, Aaron, Samuel and Hiram Shute.

13th da, 8th mo, 1811. Benjamin Rulon granted a certificate to Philadelphia Monthly Meeting for the northern district for himself, his wife, Sarah [West] and their two minor children: Mary W. and John W. Rulon. Aaron Gibson, a minor, granted a certificate to Philadelphia Monthly Meeting for the southern district. Jedidiah Allen, Jr. granted a certificate to Philadelphia Monthly Meeting for the southern district. Joseph C. Whitall, granted a certificate to Middletown Monthly Meeting, Bucks County, PA. Ann Rulon granted a certificate to Philadelphia Monthly Meeting for the northern district. Thomas Thorn produced a certificate from Haddonfield Monthly Meeting for himself, his wife, Mary [Haines] and their four minor children: John, Lydia, Sarah and Mary Ann Thorn. Moses Rulon produced a certificate from Greenwich Monthly Meeting for himself, his wife, Susannah and their eight minor children: Rachel, Clayton, Daniel, Moses, Ephraim, Beulah, Susannah and Mark Townsend Rulon.

10th da, 9th mo, 1811. Clement Reeves granted a certificate to Philadelphia Monthly Meeting for himself, his wife, Sarah and their six minor children: Louisa, Susan, Israel, Mary, Joseph and Ann Reeves. Joseph Whitall, granted a certificate to Concord Monthly Meeting for himself and his wife, Hannah [Mickle]. Beulah Warrick, late Beulah Clement, married out of unity; disowned. John Brown produced an acknowledgment of his going out in marriage on the 9th da, 9th mo, 1811.

22nd da, 10th mo, 1811. James Brown, minor son of George Brown, granted a certificate to Philadelphia Monthly Meeting. Isaac Ballinger, William Cooper and James Saunders appointed as overseers for Woodbury and Jacob Haines and William Beckett as overseers for Upper Greenwich. Isaac Mickle Cooper produced a certificate from Philadelphia Monthly Meeting. Samuel Packer produced a certificate from Miami Monthly Meeting in the state of Ohio for himself, his wife, Sarah and their six minor children: John, Samuel, Ann C., William Paul, Richard and Joel Packer.

19th da, 11th mo, 1811. John Brown granted a certificate to Upper Evesham Monthly Meeting, Burlington Co. Grace Fisher granted a certificate to Haddonfield Monthly Meeting. Deborah Bassett granted a certificate to Wilmington Monthly Meeting, Newcastle Co., Delaware.

24th da, 12th mo, 1811. James Holdcraft gone out in marriage.
21st da, 1st mo, 1812. Isaac Harvey produced a certificate. Barnes Crawford produced a certificate from Pilesgrove Monthly Meeting, Salem Co.
18th da, 2nd mo, 1812. Rachel Allen granted a certificate to Philadelphia Monthly Meeting.
24th da, 3rd mo, 1812. Abel Rulon granted a certificate to Pilesgrove Monthly Meeting, Salem Co. Edwin Boggs, a minor, produced a certificate from Pilesgrove Monthly Meeting, Salem Co. The following were appointed as elders: Joseph Clement, James Cooper, John Tatum, William Cooper, Jacob Haines, Samuel Mickle, Jr, David Brown, Thomas Carpenter and William Beckett.
28th da, 4th mo, 1812. Charles Reeve granted a certificate to Greenwich Monthly Meeting. Anna Lippincott, a minor, granted a certificate to Chester Monthly Meeting. Isaac Reeves gone out in marriage with his first cousin.
4th da, 6th mo, 1812. Catharine Vaughn West received into membership. Samuel Paul, Jr. disowned. Samuel B. Lippincott produced a certificate from Philadelphia Monthly Meeting for himself, his wife, Mary B. [Clark] and their infant dau, Martha D. Lippincott. Isaac Kay produced a certificate from Philadelphia Monthly Meeting for himself, his wife, Deborah [Eldridge] and their minor children: Clement H., William E. and Sarah Kay. Sarah Reeves, late Haines gone out in marriage; disowned. Martha Allen granted a certificate to Philadelphia Monthly Meeting for the northern district. Sarah Reeve granted a certificate to Greenwich Monthly Meeting.
9th da, 7th mo, 1812. John Jones produced a certificate from Philadelphia Monthly Meeting for the northern district for himself, his wife, Elizabeth their children: Arthur, Esther, Jacob and Lydia Jones. Samuel Mickle produced a certificate from Sadsbury Monthly Meeting, Lancaster Co., PA, for himself, his wife, Susanna and their four minor children: Mary Ann, Elizabeth, John Clemson and Samuel Mickle.
6th da, 8th mo, 1812. Samuel Paul, Jr., his wife, Delia and their minor children: Harriet, Isabella, Joel, Samuel, Elizabeth and Mary Paul received into membership. William Cooper appointed as clerk and Samuel Webster, Jr. appointed as assistant clerk. Sarah White granted a certificate to Pilesgrove Monthly Meeting, Salem Co.
10th da, 9th mo, 1812. Sybilla West received into membership. Mark Clement produced a certificate from Nottingham Monthly Meeting.
8th da, 10th mo, 1812. Thomas P. Clark produced a certificate from

Philadelphia Monthly Meeting.

5th da, 11th mo, 1812. Barnes Crawford treated with for enlisting as a military soldier; disowned.

10th da, 12th mo, 1812. Alexander Long received into membership. Jacob Middleton produced a certificate to marry from Chesterfield Monthly Meeting, Burlington Co.

4th da, 2nd mo, 1813. Samuel C. Hopkins gone out in marriage; disowned. Asa Gibbs treated with for neglecting to pay his just debts and neglecting meetings; disowned.

4th da, 3rd mo, 1813. John Haines granted a certificate to marry at Salem Monthly Meeting. John G. Whitall, gone out in marriage.

8th da, 4th mo, 1813. Ebenezer Fogg, a minor, granted a certificate to Salem Monthly Meeting. Ann Townsend granted a certificate to Pilesgrove Monthly Meeting, Salem Co. Sarah Test granted a certificate to Salem Monthly Meeting in the state of Ohio.

6th da, 5th mo, 1813. John Wooley granted a certificate to Shrewsbury Monthly Meeting, Monmouth Co. Joseph Jinnings [Jennings] granted a certificate to Haddonfield Monthly Meeting for himself, his wife, Sarah and their four minor children: Hannah, Ann, Charles and Jacob. David C. Wood granted a certificate to Philadelphia Monthly Meeting. Job Brown treated with for administering the oath.

10th da, 6th mo, 1813. Tacy Whitall, late Wood, gone out in marriage; disowned. Sibyl Middleton granted a certificate to Philadelphia Monthly Meeting for the northern district.

8th da, 7th mo, 1813. Thomas Clement granted a certificate to Haddonfield Monthly Meeting for himself, his wife, Rachel [Wood] and their six minor children: John, Ruth, Zebidee [Zebedee], Charles W., Letitia and Chalkley Clement. Lewis Miller produced a certificate from Greenwich Monthly Meeting.

5th da, 8th mo, 1813. Jane Beldon, late Whitall, gone out in marriage; disowned. Benjamin Darlington produced a certificate from Philadelphia Monthly Meeting for the northern district. Sarah Brown, a minor, granted a certificate to Salem Monthly Meeting.

9th da, 9th mo, 1813. Israel F. Whitall, a minor, granted a certificate to Philadelphia Monthly Meeting for the southern district. Isaiah Ward granted a certificate to Philadelphia Monthly Meeting for the northern district.

7th da, 10th mo, 1813. George W. Tomkin received into membership. Samuel Shute granted a certificate to Pilesgrove Monthly Meeting, Salem Co, for himself and his six minor children: Ann Hazelton, Harriett [Harriet], Charles, Aaron, Samuel and Hiram Shute.

Jonathan Rulon produced a certificate from Mauris [Maurice] River Monthly Meeting for himself, his wife, Mary and their four minor children: Phebe, Mary, Hannah and David Rulon. Mary Allen, Jr. produced a certificate from Philadelphia Monthly Meeting for the northern district.

4th da, 11th mo, 1813. Ruth Ward granted a certificate to Philadelphia Monthly Meeting. Martha Allen produced a certificate from Philadelphia Monthly Meeting for the northern district. Ann Jess, a minor, produced a certificate from Greenwich Monthly Meeting. Mary Langstaff produced a certificate from Mauris [Maurice] River Monthly Meeting. George Ward leaves £5 to Woodbury Monthly Meeting in his will.

10th da, 2nd mo, 1814. Jonathan Allen granted a certificate to Pilesgrove Monthly Meeting, Salem Co. Margaret Brown granted a certificate to Philadelphia Monthly Meeting.

10th da, 3rd mo, 1814. Asa Borton granted a certificate to marry at Pilesgrove Monthly Meeting, Salem Co. Joseph Estlack [Eastlack] gone out in marriage; disowned.

7th da, 4th mo, 1814. Josiah Tatum granted a certificate to marry at Philadelphia Monthly Meeting for the southern district. Samuel Shute produced a certificate to marry at Pilesgrove Monthly Meeting, Salem Co.

5th da, 5th mo, 1814. Following members appointed as overseers: Isaac Ballenger [Ballinger], Josiah Stokes and William Cooper for Woodbury, and Jacob Haines and William Haines appointed as overseers for Upper Greenwich. James Ward produced a certificate from Philadelphia Monthly Meeting for the northern district. Abraham Borton produced a certificate from Philadelphia Monthly Meeting for himself, his wife, Mary and their three children: Rebecca D., Hannah and Elwood T. Ann Blackwood produced a certificate from Haddonfield Monthly Meeting for herself and her five children: John M, Benjamin W., Abigail, Sarah and Ann.

9th da, 6th mo, 1814. Aquila [Aquilla] Stokes produced a certificate from Upper Evesham Monthly Meeting, Burlington Co., for himself, his wife, Sarah and their three minor children: Elizabeth, Samuel and Harvey. Thomas Rawlings produced a certificate from Gwynedd Monthly Meeting, Montgomery Co., PA. Enoch Evins [Evens] produced a certificate from Chester Monthly Meeting, Burlington Co., for himself and his wife, Rebecca. Keziah Chew acknowledged her going out in marriage before a justice, accepted.

7th da, 7th mo, 1814. James Haines acknowledged his going out in

WOODBURY MONTHLY MEETING

marriage; accepted.

4th da, 8th mo, 1814. Alexander Long granted a certificate to Philadelphia Monthly Meeting. Sybilla Shute granted a certificate to Pilesgrove Monthly Meeting, Salem Co. Hannah Reeve and her two minor children, John and Beulah, received into membership.

8th da, 9th mo, 1814. Sarah Hazelet acknowledged her going out in marriage; accepted. Sarah Borton produced a certificate from Pilesgrove Monthly Meeting, Salem Co.

6th da, 10th mo, 1814. Joseph Miller produced a certificate to marry from Greenwich Monthly Meeting. Rachel Tatum produced a certificate from Philadelphia Monthly Meeting for the southern district. Joseph Kay produced a certificate from Philadelphia Monthly Meeting. Sarah Gibbs disowned for neglecting meetings.

8th da, 12th mo, 1814. Benjamin Darlington disowned for volunteering for military service.

5th da, 1st mo, 1815. Mary A. Miller granted a certificate to Greenwich Monthly Meeting.

9th da, 2nd mo, 1815. James Ward disowned for volunteering for military service.

9th da, 3rd mo, 1815. Susanna Packer granted a certificate to Upper Evesham Monthly Meeting. Benjamin Shinn produced a certificate from Haddonfield Monthly Meeting. Sarah Hazlet [Hazelet] granted a certificate to Pilesgrove Monthly Meeting.

4th da, 5th mo, 1815. Edwin Boggs, a minor, granted a certificate to Philadelphia Monthly Meeting for the southern district. Job Eldridge granted a certificate to Mt. Holly Monthly Meeting, Burlington Co., for himself and his five minor children: William M., Hannah P., Deborah M., Job and Isaac K. Eldridge. Samuel Mickle, Jr. granted a certificate to Fallow-field in Pennsylvania for himself, his wife, Susanna and their five minor children: Mary Ann, Eliza, John Clemson, Samuel and Susanna. Paul Scull produced a certificate from Pilesgrove Monthly Meeting, Salem Co. Susan Scott treated with for going out in marriage. John Knight produced a certificate from Salem Monthly Meeting for himself, his wife, Sarah [Ridgway-Jones] and their adopted dau, Elizabeth [Newman] Knight. Hannah Clement produced a certificate from Haddonfield Monthly Meeting.

8th da, 6th mo, 1815. Miles [Myles] Snowdon granted a certificate to Philadelphia Monthly Meeting for the northern district. Rebecca Jones produced a certificate from Salem Monthly Meeting.

6th da, 7th mo, 1815. Mary Jennings, wife of Mark Jennings, received into membership. Paul Rawlings disowned. Hope Scull granted a certificate to Pilesgrove Monthly Meeting. Sarah Ballenger [Ballinger] granted a certificate to Evesham Monthly Meeting, Burlington Co.

10th da, 8th mo, 1815. Thomas Rawlings disowned for volunteering for military service.

7th da, 9th mo, 1815. Sarah Brown, a minor, produced a certificate from Salem Monthly Meeting. Jacob Glover produced a certificate from Haddonfield Monthly Meeting for himself, his wife, Mary and their minor children: Rachel, Chalkley, Barclay and Caroline.

5th da, 10th mo, 1815. Ann Jess granted a certificate to Salem Monthly Meeting.

9th da, 11th mo, 1815. Joseph Pine granted a certificate to marry at Salem Monthly Meeting.

7th da, 12th mo, 1815. Joseph Barger granted a certificate to Philadelphia Monthly Meeting for the southern district himself, his wife, Mary and their son, William W. [Wood] Barger. Samuel Ladd treated with for going out in marriage; disowned. John Knight, Jr. married out of unity. Mary Wilson produced a certificate from Philadelphia Monthly Meeting for the northern district.

4th da, 1st mo, 1816. Sarah [Ridgway-Jones] Knight appointed elder. James Lord of Upper Greenwich treated with for going out in marriage; acknowledgment accepted.

8th da, 2nd mo, 1816. Isaac Stephens, his wife, Hannah and their four minor children: Ann, Sarah, Isaac and Jacob received into membership.

7th da, 3rd mo, 1816. Isaac Kay granted a certificate to Philadelphia Monthly Meeting for the northern district for his son, Joseph Kay. John Knight, Jr. acknowledged his going out in marriage; accepted. Hannah Lord acknowledged her going out in marriage to James Lord; accepted. John Brown treated with for going out in marriage; disowned.

4th da, 4th mo, 1816. Clement Reeves granted a certificate to Philadelphia Monthly Meeting for himself, his wife, Sarah and their children: Louisa M., Susan, Israel, Mary, Joseph, Ann and Sarah B. Job Brown treated with for being concerned in wagering and frequenting places of diversion, acknowledgment accepted. Thomas Borton produced a certificate from Pilesgrove Monthly Meeting, Salem Co., for himself, his wife, Maria and their minor son, Elwood. Samuel Saunders produced a certificate from Salem Monthly Meeting.

9th da, 5th mo, 1816. Samuel B. Lippincott granted a certificate to Mt. Holly Monthly Meeting, Burlington Co., for himself, his wife, Mary and their minor children: Martha D., Bowman and Thomas Clark. Joseph Pine granted a certificate to Pilesgrove Monthly Meeting, Salem Co. Rebecca and Sarah Snowdon granted a certificate to Philadelphia Monthly Meeting for the northern district.

6th da, 6th mo, 1816. Elizabeth Jones granted a certificate for her two minor sons, Arthur Jones to Mt. Holly Monthly Meeting, Burlington Co., and Jacob Jones to Upper Evesham Monthly Meeting, Burlington Co. Elizabeth Jones granted a certificate to Mt. Holly Monthly Meeting, Burlington Co., for her two minor daus, Lydia S. and Tacy Jones.

4th da, 7th mo, 1816. Phebe Brown granted a certificate to Pilesgrove Monthly Meeting, Salem Co. Esther Jones granted a certificate to Philadelphia Monthly Meeting for the northern district.

8th da, 8th mo, 1816. Ann Blackwood granted a certificate to Frankford Monthly Meeting in Pennsylvania for her minor son, John Blackwood.

10th da, 10th mo, 1816. Job Jennings granted a certificate to Miamie [Miami] Monthly Meeting in the state of Ohio.

7th da, 11th mo, 1816. Kezia Chew, dau of Kezia Collins, received into membership. Joseph Mickle produced a certificate to marry from Haddonfield Monthly Meeting.

5th da, 12th mo, 1816. Thomas Clark granted a certificate to marry at Salem Monthly Meeting. Miles [Myles] Snowdon produced a certificate to marry from Philadelphia Monthly Meeting on Green Street.

9th da, 1st mo, 1817. Ann Mickle granted a certificate to Haddonfield Monthly Meeting for her two minor children, Benjamin and Ann Blackwood. Richard Snowdon treated with for contracting debts he was unable to pay; disowned.

6th da, 3rd mo, 1817. George W. Tonkin granted a certificate to Haddonfield Monthly Meeting for himself and his wife, Martha. David Whitall, granted a certificate to marry at Upper Springfield Monthly Meeting, Burlington Co. Rachel R. Clark produced a certificate from Salem Monthly Meeting. Beulah Snowdon granted a certificate to Philadelphia Monthly Meeting for the northern district.

6th da, 4th mo, 1817. George Craft granted a certificate to Maurice River Monthly Meeting, for himself, his wife, Rebecca and their three minor children: George, Lydia, and Mary Ann and their majority children, Beulah and Rebecca Craft, Jr.

8th da, 5th mo, 1817. Thomas Knight granted a certificate to Maurice River Monthly Meeting, for himself and his wife, Mary. Enoch R.

Allen granted a certificate to Maurice River Monthly Meeting, for himself and his wife, Beulah [Pancoast] and their minor children: Mary R., Hannah P., Eliza and Enoch. Aaron Gibson produced a certificate from Philadelphia Monthly Meeting for the southern district. Sarah Howly, late Davis, treated with for going out in marriage; disowned. Rebecca Lord, late Brown, treated with for going out in marriage; disowned. Mary Cook, late Hoffman, treated with for going out in marriage; disowned. Rebecca Allen produced a certificate from Salem Monthly Meeting. Elizabeth Walton produced a certificate from Abington Monthly Meeting, Montgomery Co., PA.

5th da, 6th mo, 1817. Charles Haines produced a certificate from Greenwich Monthly Meeting. Samuel B. Lippincott produced a certificate from Mt. Holly Monthly Meeting, Burlington Co., for himself, his wife, Mary and their minor children: Martha D., Bowman and Thomas Clark Lippincott. Mason Ward produced a certificate from Haddonfield Monthly Meeting for himself and his wife, Hannah. Joseph Owen produced a certificate from Salem Monthly Meeting for himself, his wife, Mercy and two minor children, Benjamin and David.

10th da, 7th mo, 1817. James H. Haines of Upper Greenwich treated with for frequenting taverns, taking strong drink to excess and contracting debts contrary to the advice of Friends; disowned. Ann W. Whitall, produced a certificate from Upper Springfield Monthly Meeting, Burlington Co.

7th da, 8th mo, 1817. Rachel Allen granted a certificate to Philadelphia Monthly Meeting on Green Street for her minor children: John, Beulah W., Mary, David W. and Charles Allen. Aaron Lippincott produced a certificate from Pilesgrove Monthly Meeting, Salem Co., for himself and his wife, Mary.

9th da, 10th mo, 1817. Josiah Stokes, Joshua Lord and William Cooper appointed as overseers for Woodbury and John Knight and William Haines for Upper Greenwich. Francis Test, a minor, produced a certificate from Greenwich Monthly Meeting. Margaret Brown produced a certificate from Philadelphia Monthly Meeting.

8th da, 1st mo, 1818. Benjamin Shinn treated with for going out in marriage; acknowledgment accepted.

5th da, 2nd mo, 1818. Samuel Webster appointed as clerk and Isaiah Tatum appointed assistant clerk. Ann Rawlings, late Brown treated with for going out in marriage; disowned. Mary Roberts granted a certificate to Haddonfield Monthly Meeting. Hannah Woodward produced a certificate from Chesterfield Monthly Meeting, Burlington Co. Thomas P. Clark treated with for neglecting meetings and being in the practice of the vain sport of fox chasing, acknowledgment accepted.

9th da, 4th mo, 1818. Edith Weatherby received into membership. Mason Ward granted a certificate to Haddonfield Monthly Meeting for himself and wife, Hannah. James Saunders granted a certificate to Westland Meeting, Washington Co., Pennsylvania, for his son, Isaac. Charles, Edward, Alice, Aaron, Hannah and Maria Gibbs, all minor children of the late Asa Gibbs, granted a certificate to Upper Evesham Monthly Meeting, Burlington Co.

7th da, 5th mo, 1818. Benjamin Shinn granted a certificate to Haddonfield Monthly Meeting. Mark Whitall, treated with for neglecting meetings; disowned. Thomas P. [Pancoast] Clark, his wife, Deborah and their two children, Deborah and Achsah, granted a certificate. Joseph Saunders disowned. Joshua Reeves disowned. William Ward treated with for going out in marriage; disowned. Marie Saunders disowned. Hannah and Mary Ballenger [Ballinger] granted a certificate to Pilesgrove Monthly Meeting, Salem Co. Nathan Warrington produced a certificate from Chester Monthly Meeting.

4th da, 6th mo, 1818. Ann Cox and Priscilla Tomlinson produced a certificate from Haddonfield Monthly Meeting. Rachel Allen produced a certificate from Philadelphia Monthly Meeting for herself and her children: Beulah W., Mary and Charles Allen. Edward Darnel and June Darnel produced a certificate from Evesham Monthly Meeting, Burlington Co.

9th da, 7th mo, 1818. Hannah Collins and Rebecca Allen granted a certificate to Salem Monthly Meeting. Thomas Knight, his wife and their infant son, Josiah Stokes Knight granted a certificate to Maurice River Monthly Meeting. Thomas Tantum produced a certificate from Haddonfield Monthly Meeting for himself, his wife, Susanna and their minor children: Warren, Benjamin, Abigail, Thomas H. and George.

6th da, 8th mo, 1818. William Tatem Ward acknowledged going out in marriage before a magistrate. Samuel Reeves disowned. David Tantum produced a certificate from Haddonfield Monthly Meeting. Mary Bennet produced a certificate from Haddonfield Monthly Meeting for herself and her daus, Louisa, Mary and Caroline.

10th da, 9th mo, 1818. Thomas Wood produced a certificate to marry from Philadelphia Monthly Meeting.. Charles Hopkins acknowledged striking a person in anger; accepted.

8th da, 10th mo, 1818. Deborah Brown acknowledged going out in marriage; accepted.

5th da, 11th mo, 1818. Aaron Gibson, a minor, granted a certificate to Evesham Monthly Meeting, Burlington Co. Ira Allen granted a certificate to Salem Monthly Meeting for himself, his wife, Catharine and their children: Joseph, Hope and Ira Allen.

10th da, 12th mo, 1818. Isaac Stephens granted a certificate to Chesterfield Monthly Meeting, Burlington Co., for himself, his wife, Hannah and their children: Ann, Sarah, Isaac, Jacob and Harriet. Priscilla H. Brown received into membership. Joseph Whitall, produced a certificate from Concord Monthly Meeting, for himself and his wife, Hannah. Edith Weatherby granted a certificate to Chesterfield Monthly Meeting, Burlington Co. Hannah Andrews granted a certificate to Chester Monthly Meeting.

4th da, 2nd mo, 1819. John Sharp granted a certificate to Philadelphia Monthly Meeting for the southern district. John B. Ward, a minor, granted a certificate. Samuel Davis granted a certificate to marry at Abington Monthly Meeting, Montgomery Co., PA. Mary Sharp granted a certificate to Philadelphia Monthly Meeting for the southern district.

4th da, 3rd mo, 1819. Joshua Pine granted a certificate to marry at Haddonfield Monthly Meeting.

8th da, 4th mo, 1819. Anna Maria Wood granted a certificate to Philadelphia Monthly Meeting. Jesse Smith married out of unity.

6th da, 5th mo, 1819. Charles Harmer [Harper] granted a certificate to Greenwich Monthly Meeting. David Cooper granted a certificate to Haddonfield Monthly Meeting for himself, his wife, Hannah [Clark] and their children: Achsah, Lewis, Sarah M., Martha, Mary and Redman. Joseph Tantum granted a certificate to Chesterfield Monthly Meeting, Burlington Co., for himself, his wife, Susanna and their children: Warren, Benjamin T., Abigail R., Thomas H. and George B.

10th da, 6th mo, 1819. Joseph Brown produced a certificate from Philadelphia Monthly Meeting for the southern district. Sarah Hoffman granted a certificate to Philadelphia Monthly Meeting for the northern district. Rebecca Hoffman granted a certificate to Salem Monthly Meeting.

8th da, 7th mo, 1819. Samuel B. Fisher received into membership. Samuel Webster appointed as clerk and Josiah Tatum appointed as assistant clerk. Joseph W. Newbold produced a certificate from Upper Springfield Monthly Meeting, Burlington Co. Hannah C. Newbold, wife of Joseph W. Newbold, produced a certificate from Burlington Monthly Meeting. Mary Smith granted a certificate to

Salem Monthly Meeting. Hannah Clement granted a certificate to Nottingham Monthly Meeting. Edward Darnall [Darnel] gone out in marriage; disowned. David Simms gone out in marriage; disowned. Samuel Packer, Jr. gone out in marriage; disowned.

5th da, 8th mo, 1819. James Lord treated with for taking strong drink to excess, a charge he denies; disowned. James Cooper [son of James and Deborah Cooper] died since our last Monthly Meeting. Mary Matlack, late Davis, gone out in marriage; disowned. Susanna Davis produced a certificate from Abington Monthly Meeting, Montgomery Co., PA. Sarah Wood produced a certificate from Salem Monthly Meeting.

9th da, 9th mo, 1819. Isaac Hoffman, Jr. treated with for seeing one of our members before a magistrate; disowned.

7th da, 10th mo, 1819. Sarah and Abigail Hoffman granted a certificate to Pilesgrove Monthly Meeting, Salem Co.

4th da, 11th mo, 1819. John Miller, Jr. produced a certificate from Greenwich Monthly Meeting. Mary H. Pine produced a certificate from Haddonfield Monthly Meeting.

9th da, 12th mo, 1819. Hannah M. Carty produced a certificate from Burlington Monthly Meeting.

6th da, 1st mo. 1820. Samuel B. Fisher granted a certificate to marry at Salem Monthly Meeting. Joseph Tomlinson, a minor, produced a certificate from Pilesgrove Monthly Meeting, Salem Co. Anna Mickle produced a certificate from Haddonfield Monthly Meeting. Mary Reeves produced a certificate from Short Creek Monthly Meeting [Harrison Co., Ohio].

10th da, 2nd mo, 1820. Charles Whitall, gone out in marriage; acknowledgment accepted. Priscilla Tomlinson granted a certificate to Upper Evesham Monthly Meeting, Burlington Co.

6th da, 4th mo, 1820. Thomas Clark granted a certificate to Burlington Monthly Meeting for himself, his wife, Rachel and their dau, Ann. Sarah Cooper produced a certificate from Doncaster Monthly Meeting in Yorkshire, Great Britain, for herself and her sons: Edmond, Edward, Samuel, Henry and Jackson. This certificate was granted to Russia, but there being no Monthly Meeting of Friends in that place, the certificate was directed to any particular meeting. Sarah and her sons remained in Russia for about a year before coming to this country and settling within the compass of this meeting. Mary Allen produced a certificate from Pilesgrove Monthly Meeting, Salem Co., for herself and her children: Benjamin, William P. and Mary P. Allen. Hope Collins granted a certificate to Pilesgrove Monthly Meeting,

Salem Co. Thomas Clark granted a certificate for himself, his wife, Rachel and their dau, Ann.

4th da, 5th mo, 1820. John Reeve, a minor, granted a certificate to Philadelphia Monthly Meeting for the southern district. Mary Sharp, late Wood, gone out in marriage; disowned. Sarah Ann Rogers granted a certificate to Upper Evesham Monthly Meeting, Burlington Co.

8th da, 5th mo, 1820. Abraham Borton granted a certificate to Haddonfield Monthly Meeting for himself, his wife, Mary and their children: Rebecca D., Hannah, Elwood T. and Lydia. Aquilla Stokes granted a certificate to Philadelphia Monthly Meeting for the northern district for himself, his wife, Sarah and their children: Elizabeth F., Samuel, Henry and William Borton Stokes. Elizabeth S. Walton granted a certificate to Birmingham Monthly Meeting. Eliza H. Fisher produced a certificate from Salem Monthly Meeting. Aaron Dudley and David Dudley, minors, produced a certificate from Pilesgrove Monthly Meeting, Salem Co.

6th da, 7th mo, 1820. Theodosia Wilkins produced a certificate from Haddonfield Monthly Meeting.

10th da, 8th mo, 1820. Allen Tatum produced a certificate from Salem Monthly Meeting.

7th da, 9th mo, 1820. Josiah Stokes, Joshua Lord and Samuel Webster appointed as overseers for Woodbury, and John Knight and William Haines appointed as overseers for Upper Greenwich.

5th da, 10th mo, 1820. Ann Glover produced a certificate from Haddonfield Monthly Meeting. Sibyl C. Rulon granted a certificate to Haddonfield Monthly Meeting.

9th da, 11th mo, 1820. Asa Borton disowned. Jerusha and Catharine V. West granted a certificate to Mt. Holly Monthly Meeting, Burlington Co.

7th da, 12th mo, 1820. Joel Haines granted a certificate to marry at Pilesgrove Monthly Meeting, Salem Co. Richard French granted a certificate to Upper Evesham Monthly Meeting, Burlington Co.

4th da, 1st mo, 1821. Margaret Harker, late Brown, gone out in marriage; disowned.

8th da, 2nd mo, 1821. Clement H. Kay treated with for paying a military fine and frequenting taverns and places of diversion. Elisha Stokes produced a certificate from Haddonfield Monthly Meeting. Aaron Lippincott of Upper Greenwich treated with for striking a person in anger, acknowledgment accepted.

8th da, 3rd mo, 1821. Benjamin Perkins produced a certificate from

Pilesgrove Monthly Meeting, Salem Co.

5th da, 4th mo, 1821. Samuel Packer granted a certificate to Haddonfield Monthly Meeting for himself, his wife, Sarah and their minor children: William P. [Paul], Richard, Joel, James and Sarah Ann. Joseph Brown granted a certificate to Philadelphia Monthly Meeting. Charles Knight granted a certificate to Haddonfield Monthly Meeting for himself, his wife, Achsah [Clark] and their infant son, Thomas C. Knight. Ann C. Packer granted a certificate to Haddonfield Monthly Meeting. Francis Test gone out in marriage; acknowledgment accepted.

10th da, 5th mo, 1821. Joseph P. [Powell] Rogers granted a certificate for himself, his wife, Sarah [Inskeep] and their minor children: Abraham Inskeep, Samuel, Thomas and Joseph Powell Rogers. Joseph I. Ballenger [Ballinger] granted a certificate to Burlington Monthly Meeting. Elizabeth Clement and Hannah I. Rogers granted a certificate to Upper Evesham Monthly Meeting, Burlington Co. Elizabeth Ewen produced a certificate from Salem Monthly Meeting. Richard M. Cole and William S. Cole produced a certificate from Abington Monthly Meeting, Montgomery Co., PA. Joseph Cloud gone out in marriage; disowned.

7th da, 6th mo, 1821. George Branner produced a certificate from Philadelphia Monthly Meeting for the northern district for himself, his wife, Sarah and their minor son, George. Hannah Cole produced a certificate from Abington Monthly Meeting, Montgomery Co., PA, for herself and Rebecca Enoch, a minor. Hannah Haines produced a certificate from Pilesgrove Monthly Meeting, Salem Co. Samuel English produced a certificate from Philadelphia Monthly Meeting for the northern district.

5th da, 7th mo, 1821. Simeon Eastlack produced a certificate from Haddonfield Monthly Meeting for himself, his wife, Rachel and their children: Amy, Sarah, Elwood, Joseph B., Elizabeth, Lydia S., Hannah and Rachel. Hannah Willets granted a certificate to Philadelphia Monthly Meeting on Green Street.

9th da, 8th mo, 1821. Ephraim Rulon and Josiah Hews Middleton, minors, granted a certificate to Burlington Monthly Meeting. John Packer, Jr. gone out in marriage; disowned.

4th da, 10th mo, 1821. Joseph C. Clement, a minor, produced a certificate from a Monthly Meeting of Friends held in New York.

8th da, 11th mo, 1821. Richard M. Cole granted a certificate to marry at London Grove Monthly Meeting. The certificate for Joseph C. Clement was endorsed to Chester Monthly Meeting.

6th da, 12th mo, 1821. David Gill produced a certificate to marry from Pilesgrove Monthly Meeting, Salem Co. Joseph Brown produced a certificate from Philadelphia Monthly Meeting to marry Margaretta Wood.

31st da, 1st mo, 1822. Aaron Dudley, a minor, granted a certificate to Chester Monthly Meeting. Ruth Johnson gone out in marriage; disowned. Margaretta [Wood] Brown granted a certificate to Philadelphia Monthly Meeting on account of marriage.

7th da, 3rd mo, 1822. George Allen of Upper Greenwich gone out in marriage; disowned. Mary B. Cole produced a certificate from London Grove Monthly Meeting.

4th da, 4th mo, 1822. Joseph R. Brown treated with for neglecting meetings and deviating from our profession, particularly in address; disowned. Rachel Gray, late Glover, gone out in marriage; disowned. Harriet Allen gone out in marriage; disowned. Ann Clark produced a certificate from Burlington Monthly Meeting.

9th da, 5th mo, 1822. Samuel English granted a certificate to Philadelphia Monthly Meeting for the northern district. John Tatum granted a certificate to marry at Philadelphia Monthly Meeting. George Mickle and Sarah Webster appointed as elders. Mary Reeves granted a certificate. George Craft granted a certificate to Maurice River Monthly Meeting for himself, his wife, Rebecca [Gibbs] and their children: Mary Ann, Lydia and George Craft, Jr. Clark Cooper produced a certificate from Maurice River Monthly Meeting. David Gill produced a certificate from Pilesgrove Monthly Meeting, Salem Co.

6th da, 6th mo, 1822. Sarah Cooper granted a certificate to Philadelphia Monthly Meeting on Green Street for herself and her children: Edmond, Edward, Samuel, Henry and Jackson. Charles Knight produced a certificate from Haddonfield Monthly Meeting for himself, his wife, Achsah [Clark] and their infant son, Thomas C. Knight.

4th da, 7th mo, 1822. Aron [Aaron] Lippincott of Upper Greenwich treated with for contracting debts beyond his ability to pay. Elizabeth R. Coleman produced a certificate from Chesterfield Monthly Meeting, Burlington Co. Mary Merritt produced a certificate from Mt. Holly Monthly Meeting, Burlington Co.

5th da, 8th mo, 1822. William Wood, a minor, granted a certificate to Philadelphia Monthly Meeting.

5th da, 9th mo, 1822. Anne Tatum produced a certificate from Philadelphia Monthly Meeting. Mary Harper produced a certificate from Abington Monthly Meeting for herself and her minor children: Daniel, Samuel, Martha, Nathan and Margaret. Elizabeth Harper produced a certificate from Abington Monthly Meeting. Joseph Ward treated with for neglecting meetings and going out in marriage; disowned.

7th da, 11th mo, 1822. Albertus Somers received into membership.

5th da, 12th mo, 1822. Albertus Somers granted a certificate to marry at Pilesgrove Monthly Meeting, Salem Co. Sarah Kirby produced a certificate from Maurice River Monthly Meeting for herself and her dau, Mercy.

27th da, 1st mo, 1823. Joseph Ogden produced a certificate to marry from Pilesgrove Monthly Meeting, Salem Co. Samuel Bassett produced a certificate to marry from Salem Monthly Meeting. Job Brown treated with for neglecting meeting. Joseph Owen granted a certificate to Pilesgrove Monthly Meeting, Salem Co., for himself, his wife, Mercy and their minor children: Benjamin, David, John and Joseph.

24th da, 2nd mo, 1823. John Ward Tatum granted a certificate to Wilmington Monthly Meeting, Newcastle Co., Delaware. Dubré Knight produced a certificate from Byberry Monthly Meeting.

31st da, 3rd mo, 1823. Hannah M. Ogden granted a certificate to Pilesgrove Monthly Meeting, Salem Co., on account of marriage. Ann Glover granted a certificate to Haddonfield Monthly Meeting. Daniel P. [Pedrick] Ridgeway [Ridgway], a minor, produced a certificate from Salem Monthly Meeting.

26th da, 5th mo, 1823. John Miller, Jr. granted a certificate to Greenwich Monthly Meeting. Thomas Borton granted a certificate to Pilesgrove Monthly Meeting, Salem Co., for himself, his wife, Maria and their children: Elwood, Job, Aron [Aaron] and Elizabeth. Thomas Carpenter disowned. Elizabeth Coleman granted a certificate to Chesterfield Monthly Meeting, Burlington Co. Mary Ann Bassett granted a certificate to Salem Monthly Meeting. Hannah Somers produced a certificate from Pilesgrove Monthly Meeting, Salem Co. Isaac Saunders produced a certificate from Uwchlan Monthly Meeting [in the Welsh Tract near Chester, Delaware Co., PA].

30th da, 6th mo, 1823. Rebecca Knight disowned. John Reeve, a minor, produced a certificate from Philadelphia Monthly Meeting for the southern district.

28th da, 7th mo, 1823. Job Brown disowned. Thomas Knight disowned. Hannah Wood produced a certificate from Birmingham Monthly Meeting.

25th da, 8th mo, 1823. Edward Borton granted a certificate to Miami Monthly Meeting in Ohio for himself, his wife, Mary and their minor children: Rebecca, Job, Emiline, James S., Mary Ann and Edward D. Borton. Joseph Clement, Jr. produced a certificate from Darby Monthly Meeting.

29th da, 9th mo, 1823. Jonathan Packer granted a certificate from Chesterfield Monthly Meeting, Burlington Co., expressing clearness to marry. Elizabeth Walton produced a certificate from Concord Monthly Meeting.

27th da, 10th mo, 1823. Charles R. Middleton produced a certificate to marry Ann Clark from Philadelphia Monthly Meeting on Green Street. Benjamin Warner and Joseph Cooper, minors, produced a certificate from Salem Monthly Meeting.

24th da, 11th mo, 1823. Joseph Whitall, Jr. granted a certificate to Chester Monthly Meeting. Mary B. Allen granted a certificate to Salem Monthly Meeting. Deborah Cooper produced a certificate from Salem Monthly Meeting. Sarah Maylin received into membership.

29th da, 12th mo, 1823. Isaac Hinchman treated with for administering oaths, which he justifies, and neglecting meeting; disowned. Josiah Stokes, Joshua Lord and Samuel Webster appointed as overseers for Woodbury and John Knight and George Mickle were appointed overseers for Upper Greenwich. Caroline Bennett [Bennet], a minor, granted a certificate to Philadelphia Monthly Meeting. Louisa Bennett [Bennet] granted a certificate to Kennet Monthly Meeting in the town of Kennet Square, Chester Co., PA.

26th da, 1st mo, 1824. Ann C. Middleton granted a certificate to Philadelphia Monthly Meeting on Green Street.

23rd da, 2nd mo, 1824. David Dudley granted a certificate to Haddonfield Monthly Meeting. John Borton Cooper produced a certificate from Salem Monthly Meeting. Sarah [Mickle] Whitall, wife of John S. Whitall, granted a certificate to Philadelphia Monthly Meeting for the northern district for herself and their daus, Hannah M., Sarah M. and Elizabeth.

26th da, 4th mo, 1824. Benjamin Sheppard produced a certificate from Greenwich Monthly Meeting to marry Mary P. Saunders. William Ballenger [Ballinger] produced a certificate from Pilesgrove Monthly Meeting, Salem Co. to marry Beulah Ward. Thomas Clark produced a certificate from Burlington Monthly Meeting for himself, and his wife, Rachel. Seth Matlack produced a certificate from Evesham Monthly Meeting, Burlington Co., for himself, his wife, Sarah B. and their minor children: Ellwood [Elwood], Emaline, Maria and Beulah.

WOODBURY MONTHLY MEETING

31st da, 5th mo, 1824. Joshua Lord and Josiah Stokes appointed as elders. Samuel Packer produced a certificate from Haddonfield Monthly Meeting for himself, his wife, Sarah and their minor children: William P., Richard, Joel, James and Sarah Ann. Howard Abbott produced a certificate from Chesterfield Monthly Meeting, Burlington Co. Susan Scott granted a certificate to Pilesgrove Monthly Meeting, Salem Co. Catharine Packer and Ann C. Packer produced a certificate from Haddonfield Monthly Meeting. Theodosia Rulon produced a certificate from Greenwich Monthly Meeting.

28th da, 6th mo, 1824. Richard M. Cole granted a certificate to Germantown Monthly Meeting, PA., for himself, his wife, Mary and their infant son, William B. Cole. Mary R. Sheppard granted a certificate to Greenwich Monthly Meeting. Beulah W. Ballenger [Ballinger] granted a certificate to Pilesgrove Monthly Meeting, Salem Co. Elizabeth Clement produced a certificate from Haddonfield Monthly Meeting. Mary Darnel and Deborah Darnel produced a certificate from Pilesgrove Monthly Meeting, Salem Co.

26th da, 7th mo, 1824. Francis Test treated with for neglecting meeting; disowned. A letter was received from Westfield Monthly Meeting in Ohio stating that Joseph Brown, a former member of this meeting disowned for going out in marriage, has been reinstated. Beulah W. Allen granted a certificate to Philadelphia Monthly Meeting for the western district.

27th da, 9th mo, 1824. Job Hoffman granted a certificate to Salem Monthly Meeting. Elizabeth R. Packer produced a certificate from Chesterfield Monthly Meeting, Burlington Co. Sarah Borton granted a certificate to Miami Monthly Meeting in Ohio for herself and her minor children: Hannah Ann, Beulah and Miriam. Elizabeth Walton granted a certificate to Philadelphia Monthly Meeting for the western district. Hannah S. Wood granted a certificate to Birmingham Monthly Meeting.

29th da, 11th mo, 1824. Josiah Tatum appointed as clerk in the room of Samuel Webster, who is released by his request. Benjamin Whitall, appointed as assistant clerk. Sibyl C. Rulon produced a certificate from Haddonfield Monthly Meeting.

27th da, 12th mo, 1824. Esther Ballenger [Ballinger] granted a certificate to Burlington Monthly Meeting for herself and her minor children: Sarah S., Jacob and Ellwood [Elwood]. Mary Bennet granted a certificate to Kennet Monthly Meeting in Kennet Square, Chester Co., PA. Elizabeth Cooper produced a certificate from Upper Evesham Monthly Meeting, Burlington Co.

31st da, 1st mo, 1825. Dubré Knight granted a certificate to Indian Spring Monthly Meeting, Montgomery Co., MD.

28th da, 2nd mo, 1825. Moses Rulon, Jr. granted a certificate to marry at Haddonfield Monthly Meeting.

28th da, 3rd mo, 1825. Mary Lippincott produced a certificate from Chester Monthly Meeting. Ann Kirby produced a certificate from Pilesgrove Monthly Meeting, Salem Co. Rachel Allen granted a certificate to Philadelphia Monthly Meeting.

25th da, 4th mo, 1825. William S. Cole granted a certificate to Haddonfield Monthly Meeting. Aaron Lippincott granted a certificate to Farmington Monthly Meeting, [Ontario Co.] New York, for himself, his wife, Mary and his minor children: Mary F., Charles C., Francis D., Samuel C. and Anna Lippincott. Sarah Maylin granted a certificate to Pilesgrove Monthly Meeting, Salem Co. Hannah Cole granted a certificate to Haddonfield Monthly Meeting. Rebecca Enoch, a minor under the care of Hannah Cole, granted a certificate to Upper Springfield Monthly Meeting, Burlington Co.

30th da, 5th mo, 1825. John B. Cooper granted a certificate to Pilesgrove Monthly Meeting, Salem Co., for himself and his wife, Isabella P. Cooper. Susanna Clayton produced a certificate from Philadelphia Monthly Meeting for the southern district. Eleanor Rulon produced a certificate from Haddonfield Monthly Meeting. Rachel Allen, Jr. granted a certificate to Salem Monthly Meeting.

27th da, 6th mo, 1825. John Knight granted a certificate to Farmington Monthly Meeting, [Ontario Co.] New York.

25th da, 7th mo, 1825. Joseph Whitall, Jr. produced a certificate from Chester Monthly Meeting. Deborah E. Clark produced a certificate from Haddonfield Monthly Meeting for herself and her minor children: Deborah K., Achsah, Beulah and Anna Clark.

29th da, 8th mo, 1825. Charles Paul, a minor, granted a certificate to Chester Monthly Meeting.

25th da, 9th mo, 1825. Chalkley Glover gone out in marriage; disowned. Charles W. Knight and Hannah C. Knight, minors, produced a certificate from Chester Monthly Meeting. Hannah Cook granted a certificate to White Water Monthly Meeting, [Wayne Co.] Indiana.

31st da, 10th mo, 1825. Amos Peasley, a minister, produced a certificate from Chesterfield Monthly Meeting, Burlington Co., for himself and his two minor sons, Elijah and Amos, also certificates for Esther Peasley and Anna Peasley.

CONGREGATION OF THE EPISCOPAL CHURCH OF ST. JOHN

Register of marriages, baptisms and deaths of the Congregation of the Episcopal Church of St. John. Established at the head of Timber Creek, Gloucester County, State of New Jersey Nov 1789.

Jacob Sickler and Esther Burrough were married by Rev. Mr. Heath, Rector of the above church.
John Husinger and Elizabeth Sickler were married by Rev. Mr. Heath on 20 Jul 1793.

Anne, the dau of Joseph and Susannah Fleming was bapt. by Rev. Mr. Spraggs, 8 Aug 1789 a little before the establishment of the church.
William, son of John and Hannah Sickler was bapt. in Sep 1789.
William Hugg, son of William Hugg and Anne was bapt. 29 May 1790.
Barberry, dau of George and Mary Blakiney was bapt. 29 May 1790.
Peter Blakiney, son of George and Mary Blakiney and Mary Blakiney, adults, were bapt. 29 May 1790.
George Taylor, son of George and Elizabeth Taylor was bapt. 29 May 1790.
Charity, the dau of John and Margaret --- was bapt. ---.
Catherine, wife of Jacob ---, an adult was bapt. 7 Jan 1791.
Esther Taylor, dau of George and Elizabeth Taylor was bapt. 11 Nov 1792.
The children of William and Elizabeth Beakley were bapt. 23 Jun 1793.
Christopher Sickler, John Ashbrook Sickler and Susanna Sickler, children of John and Hannah Sickler, bapt. 4 May 1794.
Adam Bendler, Anthony Bendler, and Barberry Bendler, children of Jacob and Catherine Bendler, bapt. 16 Nov 1794.
Mary Taylor, dau of George and Elizabeth Taylor was bapt. 17 Jul 1797.
Hannah Taylor, dau of George and Elizabeth Taylor was bapt. 23 Sep 1798.
John Berry, Jr., son of John Berry and his wife was bapt. 31 Oct 1802.
Rebecca Berry and Mary Berry, daus of John Berry and wife were bapt. 31 Oct 1802.

Philip Grimmers's child was buried 1790.
John Pidgeon was buried 1790.
Job Pidgeon, son of the above John Pidgeon was buried 1790/1.
Joseph Canne, son of James and --- was buried 12 Aug 1792.

Patrick McDurmont was buried 23 Sep 1793.
John Laitheart's child was buried 7 Jan 1794.
George Taylor's dau, Esther was buried 1 Jan 1794.
Jacob Phipier, Jr. was buried 15 Sep 1794.
Michael Phipier's child was buried 15 Nov 1794.
William Parker's child was buried 20 Nov 1794.
Doctor James Landorfore was buried 7 Mar 1795.
Adams Batts, son of John Batts was buried 24 Aug 1795.
Jacob Phiper, Sr. was buried 17 Sep 1795.
John Parker, Jr. was buried 1 Jun 1796.
Ann Ginson, wife of Merit Ginson was buried 29 Oct 1797.
George Edwards was buried 9 May 1797.
Thomas Kirkpatrick was buried 19 Jun 1797.
Elizabeth Smith's child was buried 1 Jun 1797.
Samuel Hassled was buried 20 Jan 1798.
Daniel Holland's child was buried 1 Feb 1798.
Daniel Holland's child was buried 13 Feb 1798.
Tabor Wilts and child was buried 18 Jul 1798.
Elmer Hickey was buried 12 Sep 1798.
Tailer Smith, son of James B. Smith was buried 15 Sep 1798.
John Clamor was buried 22 Sep 1798.
William Gibson was buried 23 Sep 1798.
James Smith was buried 26 Sep 1798.
George Fisher, apprentice of Thomas Tomkins was buried 1 Oct 1798.
Adam Ball was buried 1 Oct 1798.
Thomas Sickler, son of John Sickler was buried 2 Feb 1799.
John Smith, son of John Smith, dec'd, was buried 1 Aug 1799.
John Parker, son of John Parker, Sr., dec'd, was buried 11 Aug 1799.
Jeremiah Simes formerly of Delaware State was buried 26 Aug 1799.
Ann Lewrie, dau of J. Lewrie was buried 11 Oct 1799.
Elizabeth Bendellow, dau of Jacob Bendellow and Catherine, was buried 28 Oct 1799.
Elizabeth Olden was buried 20 Jan 1800.
John Bendellow was buried 2 Apr 1800.
Samuel Holland, child of Margret Holland was buried Aug 1800.
Mrs. Sarah Smith, wife of James, b. Smith was buried 12 Aug 1800.
Thomas Nobel was buried 30 Aug 1800.
Barbary Holland, child of Daniel and Rebecca Holland was buried --- 1800.
Ann Barrett, dau of John and Rebecca Barrett was buried -- Jan 1801.
John Landers was buried 1 Mar 1801.

James Hollen, son of Daniel Hollen was buried 6 Sep 1801.
Cabel Kimbel was buried 13 Oct 1808.
Hannah Lewis, dau of James and Ann Lewis was buried 19 --- 1801.
Frederick Shinfell was buried -- Dec 1801.
Joseph Cox, Jr., son of Thomas Cox and his wife was buried 1 Apr 1802.
James B. Smith was buried 2 May 1802.
George Taylor was buried 9 Jan 1802.
Alice Curtis was buried 9 Aug 1802.
George Taylor was buried 26 Aug 1802.
Mary Medowel's child was buried 17 Oct 1802.
Ester Jones, wife of Jonathan Jones was buried 19 Oct 1802.
Elizabeth Coonhoon's child was buried 20 Dec 1802.
John Thomas, Sr. was buried 5 Mar 1803.
--- Ficher was buried 1 Jul 1803.

REGISTER OF ST. MARY'S CHURCH, COLESTOWN, NJ

A regulation made and concluded upon by the Wardens and Vestry of the St. Mary's Church, Colestown in the township of Waterford and County of Gloucester on the 1st da, Sept 1796 for the use of the church and the burying ground.

"Whereas a regulation in the graveyard is ardently to be wished and has long been desired, for the burden has lain heavy on some, this long times who have always been willing to cast in their mite for the support of the above said place to keep it in order, and again there are others that will not help to support the place for say they. We shall be as well off as they, who do support it nor shall we pay more for a grave than they do, therefore concerning the aforesaid plan, the Wardens and Vestry of the church have taken it into consideration, and have set forth this plan to the fellow brethren, far and near.

to all whom it may concern be it know that any one meaning to hold a rite to church and graveyard known by the name of Colestown Church in the township of Waterford, and county of Gloucester to pay a certain sum of money yearly, which shall be on the first Monday in September each year for the support of the church and yard, and in case they do not pay that year nor second year subscription to the Wardens who shall meet on the aforesaid day, for that purposes. Their names shall be erased out of the book. A nonsubscriber notwithstanding what they ..

And it is likewise agreed on by the Wardens and Vestry of the church that all those who will not become subscribers, yearly, for the support of the church and burying ground, (which becomes every good Christian, to help support a place for their dead), Be it known unto them that they shall pay for breaking the ground, for every time they cause it to be broke, which sum shall be from one dollar to four dollars according to their abilities, which to be judged by Joseph Oats, Warden of the Church, or any other that may be appointed for that purpose. Hereafter, shall think fit, which money shall be put into the treasurer's hands for the use of repairs and being free from the sexton's fees. The sexton's fees to be paid besides for his labor.

And thirdly, the Wardens and Vestry, have a serious consideration for the poor who can scarcely provide for the cares of this life, therefore,

ST. MARY'S CHURCH

whey they come to lay their heads in the lap of earth, such shall have free liberty to inter their dead in the above church yard, free from all other expenses but the sexton's fees. Therefore, we who have hereunto set our names do promise to pay, or cause to be paid, the sum assigned against our names by the first Monday in September 1797 and continue it yearly as witness our hands this fifth day of September 1796."

Entered according to order by Command Regacy, Clerk of the Church.

SUBSCRIBERS

Abraham Johnson, 1797, 1798, 1799, 1800; Joseph Johnson, 1797, 1798, dec'd; John Warden; Isaac Warden; Hezekiah Toy, 1797, 1798, 1799, 1800; Philip Terrapin, 1797, 1798; Dorcas Haines, 1797, 1798, dec'd; David Claypole, 1797, 1798; John Fish; Ann Budd, 1797, 1798; William Heulings, 1797, 1798, 1799; Jacob Wishem, 1797, 1798; William Peacock, 1797, 1798; Thomas Quick, 1797, 1798; John Quick, 1797, 1798; Jacob Toy, 1797; Levy Stiles, 1797; --- Quick, 1797, 1798, 1799, 1800; Thomas Hunter, 1797, 1798; George Browning, absent first 2 years, 1799, 1800; John Bispham, 1797, 1798, 1799, 1800; James Stiles (James Stiles paid for his right to be buried in the year 1826); Owen Oster; Samuel Baxter; David Wallace, dec'd; Samuel Oster; Joshua Oster; Mary Thorn; Samuel Taylor, dec'd; Henry Parch; Abraham Browning, 1797, 1798, 1799; Patience Morgan, 1797, dec'd; John Bell, 1797, dec'd; Jacob Streomback, 1797, 1798; James Hunter; George Mintle, 1797; Joseph Githens, 1797; Charles Daniel, 1797, 1798, 1799; John Berry, 1797; Rachel Hannold, 1797; Joseph Whitelock; Samuel Hunt, 1797; Nicholas Stiles, 1797, 1798, dec'd; Thomas Peacock, 1797; James Burden, 1797; Jane Burden, 1797; Elias Firth, 1797, 1798, 1799, 1800; Robert Beck or Peck, 1797, 1798, 1799; George Daniel; Abraham Fish, 1797, 1798; Andrew Toy; Job Archer; William Dodd; Mary Whetstone, 1797, 1798; Hezekiah Ward, 1797; Francis Williamson; Samuel Middleton; John Collins; Amos Owens, 1797, 1798; Benjamin Hollingshead, 1797, 1798, 1799, 1800; Lawrence Vandergrift, 1797; Joseph Stiles, 1797, 1798, 1799; Isaac Stiles, 1797, 1798; William Chambers, 1797; Isaac Fish, 1797, 1798, 1799, 1800; Joseph Armstrong, 1797, 1798, 1799, 1800, dec'd; Michael Korn; John Radderon, 1797; Henry ---; William Clements; John Pike, 1797, 1798; William Leaconey; Sissee Thomas; John Stone, Sr.;

242 EARLY CHURCH RECORDS OF GLOUCESTER COUNTY

William Holmes, Jr.; David Clements; Brazilla Allen, 1797, 1798, 1799; John Wilson, 1797, 1798; John Stiles; Michael Stow, 1797, 1798, 1799; Joseph Heppard, removed; Andrew Mains, 1797, 1798, 1799; Thomas Morris, 1797, 1798; John Chambers, Sr. ; John Chambers, Jr., 1797, 1798, 1799; Thomas Brooks, 1797, 1798; Samuel Jones, 1797, 1798, dec'd; Valentine Bowens; Deborah Kinsey, dec'd, 1797; Elizabeth Wilson, 1797, 1798, dec'd; Ann Jones, 1797; 1798; Hannah Lippincott, 1797, 1798; Mary Wilson, 1797, 1798, 1799; Mary Pearson, 1797; Sarah Pearson, 1797, 1798 [Mary and Sarah Pearson were crossed out on the ledger]; Thomas Hunter, 1797; William Johnson, 1797, 1798; Ann Stiles, 1797, 1798; Thomas Davis, 1797; John Barson 1797; Samuel Wilson, 1797, 1798, 1799, 1800; James Hale, 1797, 1798; Edward Morgan, dec'd; Isaac Brady, 1797; Benjamin Fish; Adam Vennal, 1797, 1798; W. Waters, 1797; William Rudderow, Sr., 1797; Samuel Rudderow, 1797, 1798; Joseph Coles, 1797, 1798, 1799, 1800; William Hunter, 1797, 1798, 1799, 1800, dec'd; Emmanuel Begary, 1797, 1798, 1799, 1800; Abraham Harris, 1797, 1798, 1799, 1800; John Coles; Samuel Slim, 1797, 1798, 1799; Joseph Plum, 1797, 1798, 1799; Joseph Githins, 1797, 1798, 1799, 1800, dec'd; Kendal Coles, Jr.; John Middleton; Frederick Plum, 1797, 1798, 1799; Peter Slim, 1797; Clement Kimsey, 1797, 1798, 1799; John ---, Sr.; 1797, 1798, 1799, 1800; Joseph Newton, 1797, 1798, 1799; Gideon Bates; William Jones; George Grayham, 1797, 1798, 1799; John Holland, 1797; Andrew Crocket, 1797; Thomas McMasters, 1797, 1798, 1799, 1800; John Jonson, 1797; Elijah Toy; John Plum, Jr., 1797, 1798, 1799; Francis French, 1797, 1798; Abraham Stone, 1797; Sarah Stone, 1797; Mary Clements, 1797; Andrew Crocket; Henry Deets, 1797, 1798, dec'd; Richard Leaconey, 1797, 1798, dec'd; William Middleton, 1797, 1798, 1799, dec'd; Thomas Stone; 1797; John Stone, 1797; Elizabeth Anderson; Humphrey Day, 1797, 1798; William Holmes, 1797; 1798; Joseph Dawson, dec'd; James Vaughan; 1797, 1798, dec'd; Isaac Venable, 1797, 1798; William Venable, 1797, 1798; Joseph Pike; David ---; John Leaconey, 1797, 1798, 1799; Thomas Rogers, 1797; John Williamson, dec'd; Amos London, 1797, 1798, 1799; Elizabeth Holmes, 1797, 1798, dec'd; Simon Cliffton, 1797; Samuel Giles, Jr.; Sarah Oster, 1797, 1798.

INDEX

-A-

AARONSON, Aaron, 80; Mary, 80; Rebecca, 80
ABBOT, George, 54; Rebecca, 54; William, 54
ABBOTT, George, 70; Hannah, 100; Howard, 187, 235; Jane, 80; Mary, 70; Rebecca, 54, 187; Samuel, 54, 70; Timothy, 187; William, 54
ADAMES, Hester, 2; James, 2; John, 2; Judedya, 2; Thomas, 2
ADAMS, Abigail, 37; Abraham, 119, 120; Bridget, 119, 120; Deborah, 35; Elizabeth, 34, 35, 37; Esther, 38, 69, 86; Hannah, 37, 69; James, 38, 69, 86; Jedidiah, 38; Jeremiah, 113; John, 34, 35, 37, 93, 99; Mary, 119; Mercy, 99; Priscilla, 120; Ruth, 102; Sarah, 40, 140; Susannah, 34; Thomas, 66, 86, 94
ADAMSON, John, 37, 97
ADDAMS, Judediah, 95
ADKINS, Samuel, 102
ADKINSON, Esther, 106
ADMAN, Esther, 112
AKIRT, Lydia, 140
ALBERSON, Abraham, 112; Ann, 7, 33; Hannah, 7, 68, 88; Joseph, 112; Josiah, 7, 68; Kitturah, 7; Mary, 7; William, 33, 68
ALBERTSON, Abigail, 27; Ann, 19, 27, 42, 43, 44, 45, 51, 55, 63, 64, 76, 78, 82, 150; Benjamin, 42, 160; Casandrew, 7; Cassandra, 78, 90; Caturah, 86; Chalkley, 19; Eleanor, 14, 19, 53, 55, 64; Elizabeth, 7, 32; Esther, 73; Hannah, 14, 19, 53, 76, 91, 190; Isaac, 14, 19, 38, 92; Jane, 77; John, 14, 19, 27, 55, 63, 64, 190; John P., 27; Joshia, 14; Josiah, 7, 14, 19, 27, 42, 43, 44, 45, 51, 53, 55, 63, 76, 78, 82, 86, 150; Kesiah, 50; Ketuah, 19; Keturah, 44; Kezia, 90; Keziah, 115; Mary, 14, 19, 32, 61; Patience, 7, 82, 150; Sarah, 7, 42, 52, 88, 160; Thomas H., 27; William, 73, 88
ALCOTT, Susanna, 71
ALEXANDER, Adam, 57; Hannah, 57; James A., 57; John Adamson, 57
ALLCUTT, Susanna, 72
ALLEN, Ann, 14, 32, 171, 183, 214; Anthony, 150, 184, 185, 188, 206; Benjamin, 90, 150, 171, 229; Beulah, 150, 171, 226; Beulah W., 171, 226, 227, 235; Brazilla, 242; Bridget, 141; Catharine, 171, 214, 228; Charles, 171, 226, 227; David, 60; David W., 171, 226; Deborah, 90; Doni, 139; Eliza, 150, 171, 226; Elizabeth, 37, 171, 188; Enoch, 47, 57, 184, 188, 191, 199, 206, 210, 226; Enoch R., 150, 171, 184, 226; Esther, 38, 69, 86; Gartrew, 92; George, 150, 232; Grace, 53, 150, 188; Hannah, 37, 41, 69, 78, 150, 184, 188; Hannah P., 150, 171, 226; Henry, 37; Hope, 150, 171, 183, 184, 209, 228; Ira, 171,

183, 206, 214, 228; Jedediah, 37, 48; Jedidah, 171; Jedidiah, 14, 183, 188, 218; Jedidiah T., 217; Jeremiah, 141; John, 105, 150, 171, 181, 183, 184, 226; Jonathan, 215, 222; Joseph, 171, 194, 205, 228; Juda, 35; Judiah, 48; Martha, 47, 150, 220, 222; Mary, 3, 35, 72, 75, 111, 150, 171, 184, 185, 188, 206, 215, 217, 222, 226, 227, 229; Mary B., 234; Mary P., 150, 171, 229; Mary R., 150, 171, 226; Matthew, 3, 35, 41, 47, 72, 150; Mercy, 3; Nathaniel, 92; Rachel, 35, 150, 171, 188, 220, 226, 227, 236; Rebecca, 60, 226, 227; Richard, 150; Samuel, 60; Sarah, 92; Thomas, 3; William, 41, 75, 141, 150, 171, 181, 184, 188, 191, 217; William P., 171, 229

ALLIN, Hannah, 35; Juda, 35; Mary, 35; Matthew, 94

ALLINSON, David, 204, 206; Elizabeth, 46; Joseph, 46; Samuel, 46

ALLISON, Joseph, 87; Samuel, 87

ALSIP, Othniel, 199

ALSOP, Hannah, 151; Othniel, 151; Rebecca, 151

AMBLER, Mary, 139

ANDERSON, Elizabeth, 242; Jacob, 145

ANDRES, Elizabeth, 178; Nehemiah, 178; Sarah, 178

ANDREW, Nehemiah, 104

ANDREWS, Abigail, 41, 71, 77; Amy, 65; Ann, 71; Benajah, 182, 186, 187; Benajah D., 187; Benajuh, 150; Benajuh D., 150; Catherine, 85; Ebenezer, 9, 41, 77, 80; Edward, 8, 9, 82, 150, 182, 192; Elizabeth, 8, 9, 30, 80, 85, 165; Esther, 9, 81, 82, 85; Frances, 42; Hannah, 8, 9, 85, 228; Isaac, 8, 9, 42, 86, 102, 171, 188, 189; Jeremiah, 9, 86; Joel W., 150; Joseph, 8; Josiah, 150; Keziah, 200; Lettita, 30; Lettitia, 9; Luke, 8; Lydia, 65; Mary, 9, 30, 80, 150, 186, 187; Nehemiah, 8, 85, 105, 150, 165; Paul, 8; Peter, 80, 81, 82, 85; Peterr, 82; Phebe, 55; Rachel, 8; Rebecca, 186; Richardson, 215; Roger, 41, 65; Samuel, 81; Sarah, 8, 9, 30, 42, 85, 165; Tabitha, 150, 182; Thomas, 41, 71, 77, 80, 85, 200

ANTRIM, Ann, 71; Elizabeth, 40, 76, 83; Frances, 65; Francis, 65; John, 65; Mary, 79

ANTRUM, Ann, 94

APLY, Joseph, 124; Mary, 124

APPLINS, Joseph, 141

APPLY, Mary, 143

ARCHER, Job, 241

ARMITT, Sarah, 190

ARMSTRONG, Deborah, 91; John, 128, 132; Joseph, 241; Phoebe, 126; Sarah, 126, 127, 128, 130, 131, 132, 137, 138, 139; William, 126, 127, 128, 130, 131, 132, 137, 138, 139

ARNEY, Ann, 16; Barclay, 16; Beulah, 16, 32; Charlotte, 16; Daniel, 16; Elizabeth, 16

ARNOLD, Ann, 77

ASHBROOK, Elizabeth, 74, 76; Hannah, 86; Mary, 79, 91

INDEX

ASHEAD, Abel, 14, 57; Amos, 13, 57, 73, 76; Eleanor, 14; John, 13, 73; Lydia, 13, 57; Mary, 14, 32

ASHTON, Mary, 110; Sarah, 39

ATKINS, Jane, 35, 67

ATKINSON, Beulah, 205, 211; Caleb, 53; Charles, 18; Elizabeth, 50; Empson, 53; Esther, 53, 58; Esther Ann, 17; Hannah, 2, 41; James, 2, 33; John, 41, 75; Josiah, 17, 58, 172, 207, 209; Lydia, 17, 172, 209; Pricilla, 17; Priscilla, 172, 207, 209; Rebecca, 72; Ruth, 72; Samuel, 41, 53, 58, 72, 75, 90, 95; Samuel B., 17; Sarah, 53; Thomas B., 17; William Coat, 204

ATTWOOD, Susanna, 92, 111

ATWOOD, Susanna, 89

AUSTIN, Amos, 83, 89; Ann, 42, 44, 45, 51, 68, 76, 78, 82; Caleb, 83; Elizabeth, 38, 69, 70, 75, 77, 80; Esther, 83; Frances, 90; Francis, 34, 38, 65, 68, 71, 73, 77, 78; Hannah, 81, 88; Jonathan, 77; Martha, 90; Mary, 38, 65, 68, 71, 73, 77, 78, 80, 84, 88, 90; Nathan, 83; Sarah, 71, 77, 81, 83, 84; Thomas, 90; William, 73, 78

AVIS, Agnes, 123, 124, 125, 126, 127, 128, 129, 131, 132, 133, 134, 135, 136, 145, 147; Ann, 130, 133, 134, 135, 137, 140; Anna, 131, 135; Anny, 133; Catherine, 130; Charles, 132; Christiana, 141; Christina, 137; Christine, 126, 130; Elizabeth, 126, 129, 142; George, 123, 124, 125, 126, 127, 128, 129, 130, 131, 132, 136, 137, 145, 147; Hannah, 126, 128, 136, 137, 139, 147; Isabella, 141, 146; James, 126, 127, 128, 129, 130, 131, 132, 133, 134, 135, 136, 137, 138, 139, 141, 147; Jane, 123, 124, 125, 126, 127, 128, 129, 130, 131, 132, 134, 135, 137, 138, 140, 147; Jane Ann, 135; Jesse, 133; John, 123, 124, 125, 126, 127, 128, 129, 131, 132, 133, 134, 135, 136, 137, 138, 145, 147; Joseph, 131, 134, 137, 140; Lylla, 131; Martha, 131; Mary, 126, 127, 128, 129, 130, 131, 132, 133, 134, 135, 136, 137, 138, 141; Nathan, 140; Rachel, 147; Rebecca, 129, 131, 145, 147; Samuel, 136; Sarah, 124, 131, 132, 134, 137, 147; Sarah Agnes, 124, 137, 138; Sarah Agness, 123; Susanna, 129, 131, 134, 136, 146; William, 128, 130, 131, 133, 135, 137, 140, 147; Zacchaeus, 136; Zacheus, 139, 146, 147; Zachreus, 134; Zekias, 129, 131

AVISE, Agnes, 122; Ann, 121, 122; George, 118, 119, 120, 121, 122, 123; Hannah, 120; James, 118, 145; Jane, 118, 119, 120; John, 122, 123; Joseph, 119; Mary, 145; Rachel, 121; Rebecca, 121, 145; William, 118, 145; Zaccheus, 118

-B-

BACKHOUSE, Sarah, 79

BACON, Elizabeth, 49

BADCOCK, Sarah, 114

BALES, John, 166; Sarah, 166
BALL, Adam, 238
BALLANGER, Henry, 97; Josiah, 95
BALLENGER, Abigail W., 151; Amariah, 75; Beulah, 151; Beulah M., 151; Beulah W., 235; Edward, 151; Ellwood, 235; Elwood, 151; Esther, 150, 185, 235; Hannah, 151, 187, 227; Isaac, 150, 151, 185, 222; Isaiah w., 151; Jacob, 181, 235; James W., 151; John, 151, 187; Joseph I., 151, 231; Joshua, 108; Josiah, 151; Maria, 151, 185; Mary C., 151; Priscilla, 150, 151; Rebekah, 104; Richard, 151; Samuel, 151; Sarah, 151, 224; Sarah S., 235; Thomas, 75, 102, 150, 151, 181; William, 151, 187, 234
BALLINGER, Amariah, 41, 44, 47, 67, 74, 79, 81, 87, 150, 152; Atlantic, 214; Elizabeth, 44, 57, 67, 73, 74, 77, 79, 80, 81, 83, 87, 150; Esther, 202; George, 74; Hannah, 172, 203, 204, 215; Henry, 38, 67, 95; Isaac, 55, 81, 150, 172, 188, 202, 208, 213, 217, 219; John, 80, 91, 172, 215; Joshua, 73; Margaret, 49, 50, 81; Maria, 185, 202; Mary, 38, 41, 47, 67, 70, 74, 86, 172, 215; Patience, 150, 196; Priscilla, 55, 57, 58; Sarah, 41, 57, 74, 152, 172, 215; Susanna, 83; Thomas, 55, 57, 58, 73, 77, 79, 80, 83, 94, 218; William, 172, 187, 215
BANNISTER, Mary, 139
BANNISTON, Elizabeth, 140

BARBER, Aquila, 125; Daniel, 113; Joseph, 172; Mary, 172; Rebecca, 137; Sarah, 125, 139, 147; William Wood, 172
BARDEN, Samuel, 139
BARGER, Joseph, 215, 224; Mary, 215, 224; William W., 224; William Wood, 215
BARKER, Ann, 65; Sarah, 140
BARNARD, Mary, 36, 76
BARNES, Rachel, 88; Sarah, 103
BARNS, Andrew, 140
BARR, Rebecca, 70
BARRETT, Ann, 238; John, 238; Rebecca, 238
BARSON, John, 242
BARTEN, Ann, 172, 216; Patience, 172, 216; Rebecca, 172, 216; Samuel, 172, 216; William, 216
BARTIN, Anna, 172, 212; Samuel, 172, 212; William, 172, 212
BARTON, Amy, 17, 18, 20, 57; Ann, 17, 71, 75, 77, 78; Benjamin, 20; Beulah, 17; David, 17, 20; Edward, 71, 75; Elizabeth, 17, 18, 20, 48, 51, 57, 69, 76; Hannah, 17, 20, 22, 62; John, 17, 18, 20, 22, 33, 46, 48, 51, 57, 60, 62, 69, 75, 78, 87, 104; Joseph, 20; Joshua, 20; Margret, 101; Mary, 17, 72; Meriba, 17; Meribah, 60; Nathaniel, 20, 22, 23, 48, 62; Rachel, 20, 22, 23, 62; Rebecca, 17, 22, 60, 62; Samuel, 17; Sarah, 20, 23, 62; Thomas, 71; William, 211
BASSET, Anna, 172, 196; Daniel, 78; Deborah, 172; Elizabeth,

172, 196; Hannah, 172, 196; Mary, 78; Nathan, 172, 196; Sarah, 172, 196

BASSETT, Abigail, 179; Ann, 200; Daniel, 15, 32, 59; David, 59; David Smith, 15; Deborah, 200, 219; Ebenezer Milton, 16; Elizabeth, 16, 200; Hannah, 16, 200; Joseph, 186; Josiah, 15, 32; Mark, 16; Mary, 15, 32, 50, 59, 109, 186; Mary Ann, 233; Nathan, 200; Ruth, 15, 32; Ruth Ann, 16; Samuel, 186, 233; William, 50, 179

BATE, Abigail, 33; Elizabeth, 81; Esther, 72; Joseph, 35; Mary, 41, 83; Rebecca, 111; Sarah, 34, 67, 71; Thomas, 111; William, 33, 34, 69, 82, 83

BATES, Abigail, 74; Ann, 15, 52, 92; Azra, 88; Benjamin, 90; Elizabeth, 15, 32, 49, 52, 76, 78, 90; Gideon, 242; Hannah, 111; Hezekiah, 15; Hope, 15, 32; John, 11; Joseph, 74, 76, 78, 79; Marcy, 11; Martha, 10, 11, 31, 76; Mary, 15, 49, 74; Mercy, 74, 79; Phebe, 10; Rebecca, 11, 15, 32, 86, 89; Samuel, 15, 32; Sarah, 15, 32, 91, 198, 204; Thomas, 79, 89; Will, 93; William, 10, 15, 49, 52, 86, 89

BATES-WARD, Abigail, 82

BATTIN, Sarah, 51

BATTS, Adams, 238; John, 238

BAUER, Anna, 136, 142

BAXTER, Samuel, 241

BEAKES, Nathan, 81; Ruth, 69, 71, 81; Sarah, 69; Stacy, 98; William, 69, 81

BEAKLEY, Elizabeth, 237; William, 237

BEAKS, Nathan, 71, 101; William, 71

BECK, Robert, 241

BECKET, Peter, 86; Samuel, 201, 203; Sarah, 86; William, 202

BECKETT, Elizabeth, 87; Hannah, 151, 203; Peter, 87; Samuel, 181, 203; Sarah, 151; William, 151, 181, 207, 216, 219, 220

BEGARY, Emmanuel, 242

BELDON, Jane, 221

BELGES, Maudland, 65

BELL, Isaiah, 151; John, 241; Rebecca, 151

BELLAS, Joseph, 114

BELLES, Joseph, 114

BELTON, Jonathan, 110; Mary, 112

BENBOW, Gersham, 97

BENDELLOW, Catherine, 238; Elizabeth, 238; Jacob, 238; John, 238

BENNET, Caroline, 172, 227; Joseph Morgan, 151, 172, 206; Joseph W., 151, 172, 204, 206; Louisa, 172, 227; Margaret, 43, 46; Mary, 151, 172, 206, 227, 235

BENNETT, Alexander, 39; Caroline, 21, 234; John, 56; Joseph Morgan, 151; Joseph W., 20, 56; Louisa, 234; Louise, 21; Margaret, 39; Martha R., 21; Mary, 20, 21; Ruth, 56; Sarah, 39

BERRY, John, 237, 241; Mary, 237; Rebecca, 237

BEWLY, Mongo, 99

BICKHAM, Jane, 195; Martin, 80; Mary, 5, 79, 104; Rebecca, 69; Richard, 5, 79; Sarah, 5, 49, 79, 80

BICKMAN, Hannah, 70; Richard, 67; Sarah, 47, 51; Thomas, 67

BIDDLE, Anne, 167; Owen, 167; Samuel, 191; Sarah, 47, 167

BIDGOOD, Esther, 103; Richard, 70, 100

BIRCH, Ann, 152, 155; Dorothy, 110; John, 152

BIRCHAM, Mary, 78

BISHOP, Elizabeth, 39, 42, 68, 81; Hannah, 81, 83, 84; Isaac, 55; Job, 55; Mary, 55; Thomas, 39, 68, 71

BISPHAM, Ann, 192; Atlantic, 83; Benjamin, 79; Elizabeth, 81, 192; John, 241; Joseph, 79, 81, 192; Joshua, 83; Mary, 83; Sarah, 79

BLACK, Ann, 46; Mary, 46; William, 46

BLACKWOOD, Abigail, 62, 172, 222; Ann, 21, 28, 62, 63, 64, 172, 175, 185, 198, 222, 225; Benjamin, 28, 175; Benjamin W., 63, 172, 222; Elizabeth, 61; Elizabeth M., 21; John, 21, 28, 62, 63, 64, 185, 225; John M., 172, 222; Mary Ann, 28; Newton, 62; Sarah, 172, 222

BLACKWWOD, Ann, 61

BLAKEMAN, Andrew, 111

BLAKINEY, Barberry, 237; George, 237; Mary, 237; Peter, 237

BLISS, Elizabeth, 79; George, 79

BOCHLER, Ann, 134; Anna, 135; Anna Catharine, 144; Francis, 132, 133, 134, 135, 136, 140, 141, 144

BOGGS, Ann, 172, 193, 199; Edwin, 220, 223; Francis, 53, 172, 193, 199; James, 53; Joseph, 24, 172, 193, 199; Joshua Haines, 172, 199; Mary, 172, 199; Sarah, 53

BOHLER, Ann, 133, 134; Anna, 134

BOLGES, Maudland, 94

BORDEN, Amie, 68; Anny, 70; Hannah, 147; Jonathan, 148; Martha, 148; Mary, 48; Samuel, 147

BORTON, Aaron, 233; Abigail, 56, 86; Abraham, 222, 230; Amy, 27; Ann, 34, 61, 69, 77; Arron, 172; Asa, 222, 230; Benjamin, 59; Bethuel, 59; Beulah, 172, 235; Charity, 59; David, 25, 33, 60; Deborah, 82; Deborah A., 25; Edward, 172, 217, 234; Edward D., 172, 234; Elizabeth, 25, 62, 64, 67, 69, 172, 233; Elizabeth T., 25; Elwood, 172, 224, 233; Elwood T., 222, 230; Emeline, 172, 217; Emiline, 234; Esther, 36, 37, 62, 67, 68, 73; Hannah, 33, 60, 67, 81, 84, 222, 230, 235; Hannah Ann, 172, 235; Hester, 82; Hope, 166; Isaac, 43, 166; James S., 172, 234; Job, 172, 217, 233, 234; John, 34, 43, 60, 61, 64, 65, 67, 69, 73, 78, 99, 100, 105; Joseph, 62; Joshua, 86; Lydia, 172, 230; Maria, 172, 224, 233; Martha, 25; Mary, 34, 38, 55, 65, 68, 71, 73, 77, 78, 81, 84, 92, 166, 172, 217, 222, 230, 234; Mary Ann,

172, 234; Mary H., 25; Miriam, 172, 235; Nathaniel, 27, 59; Obadiah, 78, 84, 99; Rachel, 59; Rebecca, 61, 64, 172, 217, 234; Rebecca D., 222, 230; Sarah, 172, 223, 235; Thomas, 172, 224, 233; William, 69, 73, 82, 86
BOSTON, Mary, 90
BOURTON, John, 95
BOWENS, Valentine, 242
BOWN, Samuel, 100
BOWNE, Mary, 78
BOYES, Sarah, 35
BOYOCELIUS, Paul Daniel, 116, 120
BRACKNEY, Frances, 42; John, 42, 83; Mathias, 42, 83
BRADDICK, Elizabeth, 215; Lydia, 215; Samuel, 215; Sarah, 215; Thomas, 215
BRADDOCK, Abigail, 56; Elizabeth, 79, 172, 216; Lydia, 172, 216; Reuben, 56; Robert, 79, 90; Samuel, 172, 216; Sarah, 172, 216; Thomas, 172, 216
BRADOCK, Robert, 36
BRADWAY, Edward, 218; Mary, 36, 64, 69; Susanna, 218
BRADY, Isaac, 242; Lydia, 200
BRAGG, Roger, 99
BRAMEN, Robert, 114
BRANDETH, Mary, 77; Sarah, 76, 77
BRANDICK, Sarah, 80
BRANDMILLER, John, 119
BRANDRETH, Mary, 75
BRANNER, George, 172, 186, 231; Sarah, 172, 186, 231
BRANSON, Ann, 46, 87, 168; Asa, 189; David, 21, 42, 45, 46, 48, 54, 87; Hannah, 54, 155, 184; John, 42, 54, 155, 184; Jonathan, 87; Mary, 42, 45, 46, 48, 54, 87; Rachel, 45; Rebecca, 45; Sarah, 54, 75, 155, 184, 189; Susanna, 54; Susannah, 21
BRANT, Hannah, 141; Robert, 141; Sarah, 141
BRAZINGTON, Lydia, 28; Samuel, 28
BREACH, Ann, 111; Simon, 36, 79, 109
BRIAND, Thomas, 110
BRIARLY, Ann, 123; John, 123, 124, 125; Lydia, 125; Mary, 123, 124, 125; Sarah, 124
BRICK, Abigail, 57; Ann, 57, 84; Ann Mariah, 26; Benjamin H., 26; Charles F., 26; Charlotte, 26; Elizabeth, 26, 51; Harriet, 26; James, 192; John, 57, 84; John Hartley, 26; Mariah, 26; Mercy H., 26; Rebecca, 26; Samuel, 26; William, 26
BRIGGS, Elizabeth, 75; John, 67; Lydia, 67; Rachel, 69; Sarah, 67, 70
BRIGHT, Martha, 114
BRINN, Amey, 111
BRODER, Joshua, 139
BROOKS, Thomas, 242
BROWN, Abigail, 173, 196; Abraham, 36; Amos, 173, 196; Ann, 51, 151, 173, 210, 226; Asher, 51, 151, 172, 191, 210; Beluah, 51; Benjamin, 151, 173, 210; Benjamin Hartley, 21; Beulah, 8, 152, 163; Catharine, 152; Charity, 173, 196; Charles, 152; Chatfield, 85; Clayton, 206, 210; David, 8, 11, 151, 172, 173,

188, 190, 191, 193, 196, 197, 198, 201, 203, 210, 216, 220; Davis, 32; Deborah, 218, 227; Ebenezer, 47, 49, 72, 102, 103; Edmund, 21; Elisha, 21; Elizabeth, 47, 49; Esther, 47; Ezra, 21; Frances, 8; George, 151, 152, 191, 196, 206, 212, 218; Hannah, 8, 30, 168, 173, 179, 196; Hannah H., 21; Hephsibah, 151; Hephzibah, 198; Hepsibah, 11; Hepzibah, 151; Isaac, 151, 173, 196; Israel, 151, 172, 210; James, 8, 85, 152, 206, 212, 219; Jesse, 151, 192; Jessey, 11; Joan, 76; Job, 193, 221, 224, 233; John, 8, 11, 12, 30, 41, 59, 75, 85, 152, 161, 163, 168, 169, 173, 179, 180, 186, 196, 205, 206, 213, 214, 219, 224; John Miller, 152; Jonathan, 8, 12, 41, 59, 152, 161, 184, 186, 201, 207, 217; Joseph, 64, 152, 186, 193, 208, 217, 228, 231, 232, 235; Joseph R., 232; Joseph Ridgway, 199, 200; Josiah, 152; Kezia, 8, 90; Launcelot, 76; Lydia, 152; Margaret, 152, 186, 206, 212, 218, 222, 226; Mark, 198; Martha, 21; Martha H., 21; Mary, 8, 12, 21, 151, 152, 161, 162, 172, 173, 184, 191, 210, 212, 216, 218; Mary C., 151; Mary Hartley, 21; Miller, 152; Nathaniel, 78; Paul, 11, 151; Phebe, 41, 85, 225; Priscilla, 169; Priscilla H., 186, 228; Providence, 54; Prudence, 57; Rebecca, 21, 59, 61, 206, 226; Rebecca Miller, 212; Rebekah, 152; Ruth, 173, 214;
Samuel, 21, 51, 59, 61, 151, 172, 209, 210; Samuel Emlen, 21; Sarah, 8, 30, 49, 59, 151, 152, 161, 162, 163, 168, 184, 186, 221, 224; Sophia, 8, 161, 180; Susannah, 151; Thomas, 8, 152; Thomas Chalkley, 21; William, 173, 196; Zephaniah, 8

BROWNE, Abraham, 37; Ebenezer, 45; Elizabeth, 45; Mary, 37; Samuel, 45

BROWNING, Abraham, 241; Elizabeth, 52, 112; George, 241; Joseph, 52, 79, 90, 92; Mary, 206; Sarah, 52

BRYANT, Hannah, 137; John, 113

BRYERLY, John, 143

BUCKKEN, Mary, 67

BUCKLEY, Richard, 111; Sarah, 54; Sarah Powell, 54; William, 54

BUDD, Ann, 241; Deborah, 72; Rebekah, 102; Thomas, 72

BUFFIN, Ann, 51

BULL, Thomas, 64

BULLOCK, Edward, 28; Hannah, 28; Mary, 45, 46, 48, 54; Rebecca, 28

BUNTING, Silence, 73, 76

BURDEN, Hannah, 128, 133; John, 133; Martha, 146; Samuel, 128; Sarah, 133

BURDNE, James, 241; Jane, 241

BURDSALL, Mary, 78

BURNE, Abigail, 113; Mary, 113

BURNELL, Mary, 88

BUROUGH, John, 107

BURR, Ann, 16; Elizabeth, 39, 40, 80; Henry, 39, 40, 80; Isaiah, 16; Jane, 80; Joseph, 55,

57, 80; Marmaduke, 55; Martha, 40; Mary, 72, 86; Rachel, 55, 57; Rebecca, 39, 70
BURROUGH, Aaron, 19; Abel, 13, 32; Abigail, 7, 84; Ann, 6, 7, 27, 45, 49, 74, 78, 83, 84, 85; Bathsheba, 7, 45; Benjamin, 7, 27; Deborah, 46, 90; Eber, 32; Enoch, 30, 78, 79, 90; Esther, 7, 237; Gideon, 7; Hanah, 6; Hannah, 6, 7, 27, 29, 46, 50, 51, 55, 66, 67, 70, 74, 79, 82; Isaac, 24, 46, 74, 92; Jacob, 79; John, 7, 42, 67, 79, 81, 85; Joseph, 7, 19, 26, 49, 54, 62, 82; Josiah, 7, 82; Kezia, 19, 26, 54, 62; Lydia, 13, 19; Martha, 7, 19, 26, 62; Mary, 7, 24, 30, 42, 64, 78; Phebe, 7, 42, 78, 81, 82; Rachel, 7, 19, 30, 55, 58; Samuel, 6, 7, 13, 29, 32, 45, 49, 66, 67, 70, 74, 78, 79, 83, 84, 85; Sarah, 6, 13, 66, 74, 76, 81
BURROUGHS, Abigail, 53, 57; Bathsheba, 85; Hannah, 81; Jacob, 81; John, 98; Mary, 38, 46; Samuel, 81, 85
BURROWS, Hannah, 35; Samuel, 35
BUTCHER, Ann, 71, 75, 78; Esther, 81, 82, 85; Frances, 65; Francis, 65; John, 34; Joseph, 76; Josh, 105; Mary, 23, 77; Mercy, 77, 86; Morris, 23; Patience, 85; Phebe, 86, 105; Pheby, 102; Prudence, 55; Samuel, 23, 73, 76, 77, 85, 86, 101, 102, 104, 105; Sarah, 77; Silence, 73, 76
BUTLAR, Hannah, 181
BUTLER, Elizabeth, 50; John, 50; Mercy, 82; Patience, 82; Samuel, 82
BUZBY, Edward, 34; Hannah, 83; Isaac, 45; Jabes, 62; John, 69, 83, 91; Joseph, 81; Lydia, 72, 77, 78, 83, 84; Margaret, 45, 81; Mary, 69, 73, 81; Nicholas, 69, 73; Sarah, 62, 73; Thomas, 45, 62, 81

-C-

CABNER, Susanna, 139; William, 140
CALDWELL, Ann, 201; Jane, 89
CALHOON, Hugh, 133; Judith, 133; Peter, 133
CALHOONS, Elizabeth, 135; Hugh, 135; Judith, 135
CANNE, James, 237; Joseph, 237
CARBRET, Sarah, 39
CARLISLE, Mary, 38, 66
CARMALT, Jonathan, 191, 192
CARPENTEER, Mary, 213
CARPENTER, Hannah, 152, 168; Mary, 152, 168; Preston, 152, 168; Thomas, 152, 214, 220, 233
CARR, Catharine, 57; Job, 57; Milisent, 57
CARSON, Mary, 88; Peter, 88
CARTER, Benjamin, 173, 178, 201; Mary, 173, 201; Nathaniel, 178; Rebecca, 173, 201
CARTY, Elizabeth, 186; Hannah M., 186, 229; Owen, 114; Thomas M., 186
CARVER, Mary, 68
CASSELL, Daniel, 127; Israel, 56, 166; Mary, 166, 177; Rebecca, 56, 166; Sarah, 127
CATHCART, William, 81
CATHRALL, Benjamin, 47; Ed-

ward, 47; Rachel, 47
CATTELL, Hannah, 72; Jonas, 72; Mary, 72
CATTLE, James, 89; Jonas, 68; Josiah, 201; Mary, 70
CAULEY, Amy, 203
CAVEY, Ann, 134
CHALTON, Abraham, 98
CHAMBERS, John, 94, 95, 242; William, 241
CHAMBLES, Isaac, 134; Regina, 134; William, 134
CHAMPION, Ann, 90; Benjamin, 77; Deborah, 53; Elizabeth, 39, 46, 48, 51, 78; John, 88; Mary, 77, 78, 85, 110; Nathaniel, 77, 78, 85, 95; Robert, 88; Sarah, 53, 88, 114; Thomas, 53, 85
CHATFIELD, Phebe, 41, 85
CHATTEN, Abraham, 92; Josiah, 92
CHATTIN, Abisha, 5; Abraham, 4, 5, 65, 74, 75, 80, 87, 89, 90, 105, 154; Ann, 5; Frances, 92; Francis, 5; Grace, 4, 74, 75, 80, 87; James, 5; John, 4, 114; Josiah, 5; Lydia, 154; Malachi, 5; Malichi, 29; Mary, 5, 47, 50, 74, 85, 154; Miron, 90; Nickson, 4; Nixon, 106, 107; Sarah, 5, 80
CHEASMAN, Mary, 42; Thomas, 42
CHEESEMAN, Benjamin, 91; Martha, 92; Naomi, 53, 110; Thomas, 110
CHEESMAN, Deborah, 112; Litesha, 114; Mary, 83; Richard, 112; Sarah, 84, 91; Thomas, 83, 84; Uriah, 114
CHEEVES, Abigail, 92
CHERRINGTON, Clement, 82; Mary, 82
CHESTER, Eleanor, 91, 115; Ellena, 110
CHEW, Ann, 37; Hannah, 64, 66, 86, 111; Heziah, 86; Jeremiah, 86; John, 113; Kezia, 154, 173, 185, 225; Keziah, 204, 222; Keziah S., 154; Michael, 111; Richard, 70
CHILD, James, 89
CHRISTIAN, Margaret, 38, 95
CHRISTY, James, 140, 145; Sarah, 145; Thomas, 145
CHURCH, Samuel, 113
CLAMOR, John, 238
CLARK, Achsa, 152, 154, 159, 184; Achsah, 152, 173, 175, 185, 186, 216, 227, 231, 236; Ann, 152, 173, 187, 216, 229, 230, 232, 234; Anna, 27, 173, 236; Benjamin, 67; Beulah, 152, 173, 216, 236; Christian, 152; Deborah, 27, 53, 85, 227; Deborah E., 173, 236; Deborah K., 173, 236; Edith, 152, 186, 216; Elijah, 194, 197; Eliza, 152, 186, 216; Hannah, 152, 154, 228; Joseph, 96; Mary, 39, 67, 68, 96, 140; Mary B., 152, 159, 184, 216, 220; Meribah, 99; Phillis, 85; Rachel, 79, 173, 229, 230, 234; Rachel R., 225; Richard, 68; Thomas, 27, 39, 69, 152, 154, 159, 173, 184, 185, 186, 187, 216, 218, 225, 229, 230, 234; Thomas P., 152, 185, 216, 220; Thomas Pancoast, 173, 218, 227; Thomas R., 226; William, 39, 67, 68, 85, 92, 96
CLARKE, Ann, 41, 44; Elizabeth, 40, 92; John, 72; Mary, 38;

INDEX

Sarah, 38; William, 33, 38
CLAYPOLE, David, 241
CLAYTON, Susanna, 236
CLEMENCE, James, 35; Mercy, 35
CLEMENT, Aaron, 18, 173, 200; Abel, 153, 173, 199, 209, 210; Able, 173, 213; Ann, 40, 68, 77, 83, 84, 152, 153, 155, 173, 184, 200, 202; Ann Harrison, 56; Ann W., 153; Benjamin, 153; Beulah, 27, 52, 54, 56, 219; Chalkley, 153, 221; Charles, 153, 217; Charles W., 221; Elizabeth, 18, 48, 153, 184, 231, 235; Esther, 91; Hannah, 152, 153, 184, 208, 223, 229; Hannah I., 231; Isaac, 173, 200; Jacob, 40, 48, 68, 76, 77, 114, 152, 153; James, 153, 173, 188, 190, 191, 193, 195, 199; James D., 153; John, 32, 48, 152, 184, 193, 212, 217, 221; John W., 153; Joseph, 152, 153, 155, 173, 184, 188, 189, 191, 197, 200, 201, 202, 203, 213, 216, 220, 234; Joseph C., 231; Joseph T., 153; Judah, 91; Letitia, 221; Lettice, 153; Mark, 153, 184; Mary, 18, 63, 112, 220; Mary D., 153; Mercy, 74, 79; Micajah, 202; Mickle, 18; Rachel, 45, 153, 212, 217, 221; Rebecah, 52; Rebecca, 42, 56, 76, 85, 152, 153; Ruth, 27, 45, 53, 153, 212, 217, 221; Samuel, 27, 42, 45, 52, 53, 54, 56, 63, 76, 77, 83, 85, 104, 152, 153, 173, 184, 213, 215; Sarah, 18, 32, 68, 76, 212; Sarah W., 153; Thomas, 112, 153, 211, 212, 217, 221; William, 153;
Zebedee, 153, 217; Zebidee, 221
CLEMENTS, Abel, 18, 58; David, 242; Elizabeth, 58; Hannah Mickle, 18; Keziah, 18; Mary, 242; Rebecca, 26; Samuel, 26; William, 241
CLIFFTON, Mary, 59; Nathan, 59; Rebecca, 59; Simeon, 242
CLIFTON, Henry, 35; Hugh, 95, 96; Susanna, 139
CLOUD, Adam, 153; Ann R., 153; Benjamin, 153, 165, 171, 173, 207; Charles R., 153; Hannah W., 153, 171; John W., 153; Joseph, 153, 231; Josiah, 153; Lydia, 153, 165; Sarah, 153, 165, 171, 173, 207
COATE, Hannah, 45, 49, 76, 77, 79
COATES, Rachel, 55
COATS, Rachel, 57
COBB, Catherine, 116, 117; Samuel, 116, 117; William, 117
COCK, John, 65; Lydia, 112; Peter, 113
CODERRY, Anne, 110; Ruth, 110; William, 110
COFFEE, James, 66
COFFIN, Jacob, 66; Sarah, 73
COLE, Elizabeth, 55; Hannah, 115, 173, 231, 236; Job, 55; Joseph, 75; Mary, 75, 173, 235; Mary B., 232; Rachel, 55, 57; Rebecca Enoch, 173; Richard M., 173, 231, 235; Susanne, 57; William B., 173, 235; William S., 231, 236
COLEMAN, Deborah, 162; Elizabeth, 233; Elizabeth R., 162, 232; Samuel, 162
COLEMONS, Sarah, 110

COLES, Elizabeth, 62, 66, 84; Hannah, 28, 92; Job, 62, 84; John, 242; Joseph, 242; Kendal, 28, 242; Martha, 43, 53; Mary, 11, 31, 43, 69, 70, 82; Patience, 55, 84; Samuel, 11, 31, 43, 69, 70, 82; Sarah, 28; Sarah T., 62

COLLINS, Aaron, 154; Abijah, 188; Amos, 154, 182, 207; Benjamin, 153, 154, 182; Catharine, 67; Charity, 154, 211; Edward, 113; Elijah, 154; Elizabeth, 36, 42, 76, 79, 154, 193; Elizah, 214; Frances, 33, 36; Francis, 76; Hannah, 47, 154, 227; Hope, 211, 229; Isaac, 153, 154, 185, 207, 211; Job, 20; John, 42, 71, 79, 154, 192, 201, 207, 211, 241; Joseph, 67; Katherine, 67; Kezia, 154, 173, 225; Kimsey, 154; Mary, 153, 154, 213; Priscilla, 33, 38, 42, 48, 52, 65; Rebecca, 76, 85; Rosanna, 47; Ruth, 71, 75, 154; Samuel, 47, 77; Sarah, 20, 33, 36, 78, 154, 166; Susanna, 71, 113; Sybella, 91; Sybilla, 154, 210

COMBE, Mary, 78

COMBLE, Mary, 85

COMLEY, Asanath, 60; Isaac, 60

CONARRO, Elizabeth, 91

CONNARO, Darling, 81; Deliverance, 81; Mary, 51, 53, 81

CONNOLLY, Dorothy, 114

CONORO, Rebeckah, 105

COOK, Amos, 154; David, 154; Ebenezer, 79, 154; Elizabeth, 154; Hannah, 154, 173, 214, 236; John, 65; Joseph, 189; Lydia, 154, 173, 185, 213, 214; Mary, 226; Robert, 154, 173, 185, 214; Sarah, 154, 173, 214; Sibyl, 154, 185; Sybilla, 173, 214

COONHOON, Elizabeth, 239

COOPER, Abigail, 16, 57, 59, 105, 112; Abigail Matlack, 17; Abigail Stokes, 16; Achsa, 154; Achsah, 154, 228; Alexander, 17; Alfred, 24; Amos, 6, 12, 38, 46, 154, 165, 166, 181, 183, 185, 197, 213; Ann, 4, 6, 41, 43, 44, 45, 49, 56, 72, 148, 154, 155, 167, 168, 169, 183, 203, 213; Anna, 17, 176; Anna F., 17; Anne, 154, 183; Benjamin, 15, 19, 27, 63, 65, 89, 168; Benjamin Clark, 6, 155, 183; Benjamin Clarke, 46; Beulah, 154, 166, 185; Cadwalder, 16, 32; Caroline, 17, 26; Catharine, 155, 171, 183, 214; Charles Morris, 24; Charlottee Louisa, 24; Clark, 232; Daniel, 16, 34, 44, 51, 65; David, 4, 6, 38, 46, 49, 50, 87, 107, 154, 155, 167, 184, 188, 197, 202, 213, 228; David B., 155; Deborah, 6, 29, 46, 155, 173, 229, 234; Deliverance, 87; Edmond, 173, 229, 232; Edward, 155, 173, 229, 232; Elizabeth, 4, 6, 15, 17, 19, 24, 26, 27, 29, 36, 45, 50, 63, 235; Elizabeth Brown, 17; Esther, 6, 155, 184; Franklin, 16, 32; George, 16, 148; Griffith, 26; Hanna, 79; Hannah, 4, 12, 36, 39, 45, 49, 66, 70, 72, 73, 75, 76, 77, 79, 81, 84, 101, 103, 148, 154, 155, 169, 187, 203, 228, 82; Hannah W., 24;

Henry, 173, 229, 232; Isaac, 45, 49, 76, 77, 79, 97; Isaac Mickle, 154, 213, 219; Isabella P., 236; Isabella Paul, 173; Jackson, 173, 229, 232; Jacob S., 16; James, 4, 6, 26, 29, 41, 44, 46, 76, 155, 173, 184, 192, 196, 203, 207, 209, 216, 220, 229; James B., 26; John, 4, 6, 24, 29, 41, 44, 51, 72, 75, 76, 94, 154, 155, 169, 217; John B., 173, 187, 236; John Borton, 234; Joseph, 4, 12, 24, 29, 33, 36, 54, 65, 66, 71, 94, 96, 97, 98, 100, 101, 103, 154, 234; Joseph Buckley, 24; Joseph Ellis, 16; Joseph M., 155; Joshua, 4, 16, 51; Lewis, 154, 228; Lydia, 4, 29, 36, 65, 66, 76; Margaret, 33, 34; Margret, 4; Mark, 155; Marmaduke, 49; Martha, 6, 46, 87, 154, 228; Mary, 4, 6, 12, 17, 29, 36, 42, 43, 44, 45, 49, 51, 57, 64, 69, 71, 77, 154, 155, 168, 169, 183, 184, 228; Mary H., 26; Mary Volans, 17; Paul, 6, 155, 183, 199, 210; Peter, 184; Phebe, 155; Providence, 54; Prudence, 15, 19, 57; Prudia, 61; Rebecca, 6, 15, 155, 204, 215; Rebecca M., 63; Rebecca W., 27; Redman, 154, 228; Richard M., 17; Richard Matlack, 57; Robert, 86, 213; Samuel, 6, 15, 19, 29, 54, 57, 61, 75, 155, 173, 194, 229, 232; Samuel C., 24; Samuel Willis, 24; Sarah, 4, 6, 12, 41, 51, 61, 65, 66, 88, 154, 155, 166, 167, 173, 178, 183, 185, 229, 232; Sarah Ann, 16; Sarah Buckley, 24; Sarah M., 154, 228; Sarah Ward, 58; Sarah West, 17; Sibyl, 165, 184; Sybil, 6, 12, 29, 38, 46, 49, 154, 155, 167, 181; Sybill, 50; Thomas, 86; Thomas H., 26; Warner T., 155; William, 4, 6, 15, 16, 29, 33, 34, 36, 44, 56, 57, 58, 64, 69, 88, 93, 99, 105, 155, 167, 169, 187, 206, 212, 219, 220, 222, 226; William Daniel, 17; William E., 155; William M., 17

COPELAND, Mary, 56
COPERTHWAITE, Hugh, 100
COPPER, Joseph, 97
COPPERTWAITE, John, 94; Sarah, 94
CORBET, Sarah, 85
CORBETT, Mary, 81, 82
CORBUT, Sarah, 80
CORE, Enoch, 36, 68, 70; Hannah, 68, 77, 80; Mary, 36, 68, 74, 79, 81; Sarah, 68, 70
CORNELIUSIN, Catharine, 139
CORSON, Priscilla, 55, 57, 58
COUSINS, Dorothy, 40, 41, 43; George, 106; Jacob, 75; Sarah, 75
COWGILL, Isaac, 69, 104; Jonathan, 193, 199; Joseph, 77, 107; Mary, 78; Nehemiah, 89, 105; Rachel, 98, 102; Ralph, 100, 104; Thomas, 105
COWPERTHWAITE, Elizabeth, 56, 214; John, 40, 50; Mary, 81; Phebe, 81; Rachel, 50; Sarah, 40; Thomas, 81, 91
COWPERWAITE, Job, 48; John, 71; Mary, 48; Thomas, 48
COX, Amelia, 60; Ann, 227; Hannah, 90; Israel, 60; Joseph, 239;

Thomas, 239
COZEN, George, 91; Samuel, 91
COZENS, Benjamin, 10, 196; Daniel, 10; Dorothy, 40, 41, 43; Eliat, 10; Elizabeth, 10, 31, 85, 87; George, 78, 110; Hannah, 10, 91; Isaiah, 192; Jacob, 10, 31, 75, 85, 87, 91, 173, 189, 193, 197; John, 10, 31; Joshua, 10, 92, 173, 189, 192, 193; Josiah, 189; Mary, 10, 31, 195; Samuel, 10, 31, 91; Sarah, 10, 75, 86, 87; William, 78, 188
CRAFT, Aden, 210; Aden (Aldin G.), 173; Aldin G., 155, 210; Beulah, 155, 173, 210, 225; George, 155, 173, 186, 210, 225, 232; Lydia, 155, 173, 210, 225, 232; Mary, 155; Mary Ann, 155, 186, 225, 232; Rebecca, 173, 186, 210, 225, 232; Rebekah, 155
CRAIG, Annah, 44; Elizabeth, 44, 81; John, 44, 81; Mary, 81
CRAIGE, Elizabeth, 42; John, 42
CRAMMER, Hannah, 182; Stephen, 182
CRAWFORD, Andrew, 140, 146; Ann, 146; Barnes, 146, 220, 221; James, 146
CREESEY, Comfort, 111; Eunice, 111
CRESSEON, Joshua, 61; Mary, 61; Samuel, 61
CRESSON, Caleb, 45; Ebenezer, 204; Elizabeth M., 21; James, 45; John Arnett, 21; John B., 21; Joshua, 21, 45; Mary, 21; Mary Ann, 21; Samuel, 21; Samuel Emlen, 21; Sarah, 45; Sarah Emlen, 21

CRIPPS, Grace, 69; Hannah, 83; John, 69, 72; Mary, 72; Nathaniel, 69
CRIPS, Mary, 99
CRISPIN, Silas, 107
CRISPON, Benjamin, 107; Martha, 107; Rebekah, 107
CROCKET, Andrew, 242
CROSBY, Elizabeth, 97; John, 68; Mary, 68; Nathan, 68
CUMMINGS, Thomas, 81
CURRY, Ann, 141
CURTIS, Alice, 239; Jane, 68, 70; Mary, 36, 74, 111; Sarah, 64
CUSTOM, Mary, 74
CUSTOMS, Mary, 36

-D-

DAIS, Sarah, 226
DALBOW, Mary, 122
DANIEL, Charles, 241; George, 241
DARBE, James, 100
DARLING, Ann, 65
DARLINGTON, Benjamin, 221, 223
DARNALL, Edward, 229
DARNEL, Deborah, 235; Edward, 227; June, 227; Mary, 235
DARNELL, Edward, 81; Hannah, 81, 84; John, 81, 84; Lewis, 84
DARNELLY, John, 67
DAROLING, Anne, 95
DAUGHTERY, Rebecca, 146
DAVIS, Abigail, 173, 191; Amie, 54; Amy, 41, 45, 47, 50; Benjamin, 11; David, 11, 19, 31, 40, 41, 43, 53, 54, 70, 74; Dorothy, 41, 43; Elizabeth, 26; Esther, 89, 104; Gabriel, 51, 74, 155, 167, 173, 179, 180, 191; Han-

INDEX

nah, 155, 186; James, 153, 155, 180, 184, 186, 208; Jane, 74; Jonathan, 74; Joseph, 26, 53; Joshua, 189; Lydia, 26; Martha, 11, 19, 31, 53, 54; Mary, 41, 53, 153, 155, 184, 186, 229; Rachel, 30; Rebecca, 51, 153, 155, 184, 188; Rebekah, 167; Samuel, 155, 228; Sarah, 40, 48, 51, 53, 155, 167; Susanna, 229; Thomas, 97, 242

DAWSON, Frances, 181; Joseph, 242; Sarah, 181

DAY, Humphrey, 242; Nancy, 19, 59; Rebecca, 19; Samuel, 19, 59; Samuel Munson, 19; Sarah, 19, 63; Stephen M., 59; Stephen Munson, 19, 63

DEATON, Abigail, 201

DEBZEL, James, 75

DECOW, Eber, 74; Elizabeth, 72; Isaac, 72; Jacob, 72; Mary, 102; Sarah, 105

DEETS, Henry, 242

DELAFOSSE, Hope, 67, 68, 70

DELAP, Elizabeth, 85; Nathan, 85

DELZEL, Elizabeth, 105; James, 75

DENIS, Thomas, 95

DENNIS, Hannah, 37; John, 88, 102; Jonathan, 37; Mary, 36, 113; Rachel, 37; Ruth, 74, 87, 102; Samuel, 65, 74, 102; Sarah, 65, 212; Thomas, 93, 97; William, 88

DENT, Ann, 40; Hannah, 71, 99, 100

DEVALL, Ann, 111, 112

DICKERT, Maria, 147

DICKEY, Jane, 141

DICKINSON, Joseph, 98, 99

DILKE, James, 65

DILKS, John, 111; Priscilla, 213

DILLIN, Elizabeth, 164; Isaiah, 164; Julianna, 164; Owen, 164; Sarah, 164

DIMMICK, Mary, 39

DIMOCK, Mary, 85, 178

DOBBINS, Joseph, 103

DODD, William, 241

DOLE, Isaac, 189; John, 65; Joseph, 65; Mary, 65

DOLE-GRISCOM, Sarah, 38

DORSEY, Daniel, 124, 143; Elizabeth, 124

DOWN, Aquilla, 192; John, 92, 206; Mary, 150, 182, 194; Robert, 74, 90, 104; Samuel, 200; Sarah, 209; William, 150, 182, 190, 208

DRIVE, Phebe, 85

DRIVER, Jane, 81; Mary, 78; Phebe, 39; Samuel, 39, 78, 81; Sarah, 81, 208

DRUETT, Hannah, 68

DUBREE, Mary, 53

DUBURY, James, 110

DUDLEY, Aaron, 230, 232; David, 230, 234; Frances, 82; Francis, 70; Rachel, 82

DUEL, John, 195; Mary, 193

DUELL, Elizabeth, 56; Hannah, 56; John, 56

DUGDALE, Benjamin, 25, 60; Hannah, 25; James, 25; Samuel, 25; Sarah, 25, 60; Thomas, 25, 60

DUNN, Josiah, 200, 207; Sarah, 51, 110

-E-

EAGERTON, Thomas, 72
EARL, Mary, 102; William, 72
EARYRE, Richard, 38; Thomas, 38
EASBY, Daniel, 129; Diana, 131; William, 129, 131
EASLACK, Elizabeth, 23; Hannah, 23; Samuel, 23
EASTLACK, Amy, 22, 174, 231; Charles H., 23; Elizabeth, 22, 75, 78, 85, 231; Elwood, 22, 174, 231; Francis, 85, 155, 195, 205; Hannah, 22, 59, 61, 155, 174, 231; Hepzibeth, 64; Hezekiah, 174, 194; Isaac Glover, 23; Jemaima, 39; John, 67, 112, 174; Joseph, 123, 155; Joseph B., 22, 174, 231; Lydia S., 22, 174, 231; Mary, 195; Mary Dorcas, 123; Phebe, 29, 85, 155; Rachel, 22, 174, 231; Reston, 91; Rhoda, 174; Samuel, 22, 59, 61, 111; Sarah, 22, 67, 174, 231; Simeon, 22, 59, 174, 231; William, 123
EASTLACKE, Sarah, 111
EASTLAK, Francis, 34; Hepzibah, 34
EASTLAKE, Elizabeth, 67; Francis, 34, 39; Jemima, 34
EASTLOCK, Reston, 91
EAYRE, Grace, 53
EBERHARDT, N. H., 122; Nic. Henry, 121; Sarah, 122
EDGERTON, Joseph, 103, 104; Samuel, 58; Tabitha, 58; Thomas, 39, 48, 92; William, 48, 58
EDWARDS, Dorothy, 113; George, 238

EGERTON, Thomas, 70
EGGINGTON, Elizabeth, 33
ELDRDIGE, Hannah Pancoast, 214; Isaac Kay, 214; Job, 214; Tacy, 212, 214; William Malander, 214
ELDRIDGE, Abraham, 83; Deborah, 62, 159, 214, 220; Deborah M., 174, 223; Esther, 83; Hannah P., 223; Hannah Pancoast, 174; Isaac K., 223; Isaac Kay, 174; James, 83; Job, 62, 174, 223; Rachel, 77; Rebecca, 75; Sarah, 174, 216; Susannah, 114; Tacy, 62, 174, 203; William, 159; William M., 216, 218, 223; William Malander, 174
ELFIRTH, Allen, 60; Jeremiah, 60; Mary, 60
ELFORTH, Jeremiah, 28
ELIS, Jacob, 78; Sarah, 78; Simeon, 78
ELKENTON, Elizabeth, 40; Joseph, 40; Mary, 40
ELKETON, John, 198
ELKINGTON, Elizabeth, 73, 79, 80; Mary, 74, 79, 83
ELKINTON, Amy, 76; Elizabeth, 73, 76, 77, 83; Joseph, 73, 76, 83; Mary, 76, 84
ELLENTON, Jamimah, 90
ELLIOT, Ann, 145; John, 194; Thomas, 145
ELLIOTT, Rachel C., 209
ELLIS, Abigail, 82; Ann, 81; Benjamin, 91; Cartharine, 88; Cassandra, 81; Elizabeth, 163; Hannah, 53, 75; Isaac, 19, 50, 108; Jacob, 90; John, 191; Jonathan, 71, 83; Joseph, 77, 82, 83; Josiah, 81; Martha, 50;

Mary, 19, 23, 50, 80, 82, 83, 88;
Miriam, 163; Peter, 163; Priscilla, 77; Sarah, 67, 69, 71, 74, 83, 91, 113; Simeon, 2, 23, 34, 67, 69, 71, 88, 91, 108; Simon, 93; Thomas, 34, 67, 74, 90, 91, 93; William, 88
ELLIS-WARRINGTON, Hannah, 49
ELLISON, Anna, 114
ELWELL, Daniel, 102, 105; David, 73
ELWELL-ASHBROOK, Mary, 41, 47
EMLEN, Sarah, 45
ENGLE, Hannah, 72, 83, 102; Hannah B., 63; Jane, 69, 78, 84; Joane, 35; Job, 63; John, 68, 69, 71, 72, 73, 77, 80, 89; Joseph, 55, 84; Mary, 44, 46, 48, 55, 68, 69, 71, 72, 73, 77, 78, 80, 86; Obadiah, 55, 84; Rachel, 84; Robert, 35, 84; Sarah, 63
ENGLISH, Isabel, 48; John, 115; Mary, 113; Samuel, 231, 232
ENGWINE, John, 51; Rebecca, 51
ENOCH, Elizabeth, 174, 191, 205; Hannah, 160, 161, 174, 191; Martha, 174, 205; Mary, 161, 174, 191, 205, 206; Phineas, 161; Rebecca, 231, 236; Thomas, 161, 174, 191, 205
ERSAN, Julius, 80
ERVAN, Julius, 80
ERWIN, Dorcas, 38, 66, 70; Elizabeth, 69; John, 94; Margret, 94; Mills, 69; Patience, 110
ESTAUGH, Elizabeth, 94; James, 38, 81; John, 35, 52, 93, 94, 96; Mary, 38, 81
ESTAUGH HOPKINS, Elizabeth, 5; John, 5
ESTLACK, Ann, 6; Diana, 123; Diane, 124, 125, 126; Dinah, 129; Elizabeth, 6; Frances, 6; Francis, 179; George, 27; Hezebiah, 27; Hezekiah, 203; Isaiah, 27; John, 129, 203; Joseph, 6, 132, 137, 140, 179, 222; Margaret, 27; Margarett H., 27; Mary, 6, 123; Mary Diana, 132, 137, 138; Phebe, 6; Rebecca, 126, 145; Restore, 6; Rhoda, 203; Samuel, 6, 126; Sarah, 6, 124, 137; Thomas, 123, 137, 140; William, 123, 124, 125, 126, 129, 132, 137, 138, 144
ESTLAKE, Francis, 1; George, 1; Hepezebeth, 1; Jeremiah, 1; Joseph, 1; Mary, 1; Meriam, 1; Ruth, 1; Sarah, 1
EVANS, Abel, 77; Abigail, 28, 64; Agnes, 85; Beulah, 42, 52, 54, 56; Caleb, 82; Charity, 211; Charles, 28; Elizabeth, 72, 108; Esther, 41, 53, 58, 72, 77, 82; Grace, 162; Hapizah, 64; Jacob, 64, 77, 82; Jane, 80; Jemima, 83; John, 42, 80, 98; Jonathan, 64; Joseph, 162; Josiah, 28; Mary, 64, 77; Rebecca, 82, 83; Ruth, 42, 77, 80; Thomas, 28, 41, 72, 77, 82, 83, 103; William, 63
EVENS, Ann, 18; Deborah, 50; Elizabeth, 3, 37, 48, 97; Elizabth, 37; Enoch, 155; Esther, 41, 75; Hepzibah, 50; James, 18; Jane, 3, 37; John,

50, 52, 59; Joseph T., 155;
Joshua, 41, 48, 52, 58; Josiah,
18; Julius, 50, 51; Lydia T., 155;
Nathan, 59; Priscilla, 48, 52, 58;
Rachel, 52, 155; Rebecca, 18,
41, 48, 59, 155; Ruth, 50;
Samuel, 18; Sarah, 51; Syllania,
59; Thomas, 3, 37, 41, 48, 75,
79, 98, 100, 101; William, 3, 37,
155
EVES, Anna, 70, 73, 79, 80;
John, 80, 95; Mary, 69, 71, 80;
Robert, 72; Samuel, 80; Sarah,
74; Thomas, 35, 71, 72
EVESHAM, Mary, 69; Thomas,
69
EVINS, Beulah, 83; Enoch, 174,
222; John, 83; Rebecca, 174,
222
EWEN, Elizabeth, 231
EWING, Susannah, 190
EYRES, Hannah, 84; Mary, 78;
Priscilla, 79; Richard, 78;
Thomas, 78, 79, 84

-F-

FAIRLAMB, Mary, 87
FAIRLANE, Catherine, 48, 49
FARRON, Abraham, 140
FAWCETT, Walter, 71
FEARNE, Elizabeth, 33; Joshua,
33; Robert, 33; Sarah, 64, 66
FERN, Elizabeth, 36; John, 36
FERROW, Catharine, 147
FFRITH, Azariah, 181; Hannah,
181
FICHER, ---, 239
FIELD, Elizabeth, 66, 67, 70
FIRMAN, Rachel, 36, 37
FIRTH, Elias, 241
FISH, Abrahm, 241; Benjamin,
242; Diana, 112; Elias, 114;
Isaac, 241; John, 241; Michael,
112; Susannah, 114
FISHER, Ann, 155, 169, 184,
185; Charles, 155, 184, 185;
Eliza H., 230; Elizabeth, 52,
155; George, 238; Grace, 107,
219; Hannah, 86, 155, 200;
Hannah A., 169; Hannah Ann,
155; Hope, 205; John, 76, 78;
Jonathan, 52, 78, 86, 155, 188;
Joseph R., 155; Lydia C., 155,
163; Mary, 78, 155; Mary R.,
155, 163; Michael, 155; Michael
C., 155, 163, 169, 184, 185, 214;
Rebecca B., 155; Samuel, 58;
Samuel B., 228, 229; Sarah, 58,
155; William, 58; William C.,
155
FLAMINGTON, Elizabeth, 68
FLANINGHAM, George, 112
FLEETWOOD, Catharine, 158;
Mary, 158; Richard, 158
FLEMING, Anne, 237; Joseph,
237; Susannah, 237
FLEWELLING, Ruth, 92
FLORA, Rhoda, 137, 139; Rothe,
136
FLUALLEN, Abraham, 179;
Rebecca, 173; Rebeckah, 179
FOGG, Charles, 52; Ebenezer,
218, 221; Sarah, 52
FOLWELL, Ann, 156, 198;
Elizabeth, 50, 155, 193, 206;
John, 156, 191; Mary, 156;
Nathan, 155, 180, 195, 196;
Patience, 196; Rebecca, 199;
Samuel, 155, 193; Thomas, 50,
155, 156, 180, 193; William, 155
FOREST, Walter, 33
FORREST, Jeconia Wood, 147;

Ruth, 147
FORRESTER, Alexander, 146; Catharine, 146; Maria, 146
FORRISTER, Alexander, 140
FORSTER, Abigail, 5; Amie, 5, 6, 68; Elizabeth, 5; Hannah, 5, 6; Josiah, 5, 6, 68, 108; Lidya, 5; Martha, 5; Mary, 5, 84; Phebe, 5; Rebecca, 6, 71; Rebeckah, 5; Sarah, 5; William, 5, 6, 68, 84
FORTINES, David, 90
FORTNER, Daniel, 74
FOSTER, Amie, 39; Anny, 70; Elizabeth, 80; Hannah, 70, 77, 80; Josiah, 39, 70; Rebecca, 29, 39; Sarah, 77; William, 77, 80
FOWLER, Elizabeth, 132; Hannah, 104; Jacob, 132; John, 132; Josiah, 102, 108
FOX, Ann, 133; Jacob, 133, 135, 140; Lydia, 133, 135; Sarah, 135
FRANCKLEN, Henry, 99
FRANCKS, Joseph, 96
FRANKLIN, Sarah, 125, 143; William, 125
FRENCH, Abigail, 57, 84; Agness, 180; Ann, 83, 84; Bathsheba, 90; Charles, 40, 83, 84, 87, 205; Eleanor, 40; Elizabeth, 204; Francis, 242; Hannah, 195; Jacob, 87, 204; Jane, 35, 67; Jemimiah, 89; John, 67; Jonathan, 74; Mary, 69, 70, 72, 73, 74; Richard, 74, 216, 230; Robert, 72; Sarah, 180; Thomas, 35, 67, 70, 72, 90
FRENTCH, Joseph, 3; Mary, 3; Thomas, 3
FRIEND, Margery, 161; Robert, 161
FRITZ RANDLE, Jane, 37

FRYER, Anthony, 95

-G-

GABITAS, Deborah, 40, 71
GAGARD, Sarah, 110
GAMBEL, Luther, 134, 135, 137, 140; Mary, 134, 135, 137; Sarah, 134; William, 135
GAMBLE, Hannah, 197
GAMBOLD, Ann, 119; Eleanor, 119; Ernest, 119, 120
GANDY, Elias, 113
GARDINER, Catharine, 85; Ephraim, 194, 202; James, 85; Joseph, 85
GARIGUES, Mary R., 217
GARRISON, Sarah, 141
GARWOOD, Ann, 112; Daniel, 71; Elizabeth, 44, 67, 68, 74, 81; Jane, 67, 90; John, 68, 76; Margaret, 70, 71, 76; Samuel, 97; Thomas, 67, 70, 71, 76, 112; William, 67
GASHELL, Samuel, 91
GASKILL, Benjamin, 82
GAUNT, Daniel, 58; Jane, 52, 58, 87; John, 52, 58, 87, 188
GAVE, Richard, 93
GERRARD, Margaret, 80; Robert, 80
GIBBS, Aaron, 174, 227; Alice, 174, 227; Asa, 174, 213, 221, 227; Benjamin, 46, 155; Burrough, 10; Charles, 174, 213, 227; Edward, 50, 174, 213, 214, 227; Elijah, 10, 31; Enoch, 10; Hannah, 10, 174, 227; Isaac, 82, 181; Job, 205; John, 42, 50; Joshua, 82; Marcy, 46; Maria, 174, 227; Mary, 46; Mercy, 160; Obadiah, 70; Phebe, 10, 46;

Rachel, 79; Rebecca, 205, 210, 232; Rebekah, 155; Richard, 10, 42; Sarah, 10, 174, 213, 223; Solomon, 10

GIBSON, Aaron, 156, 210, 212, 219, 226, 228; Ann, 8, 38; Asa, 156, 210; Daniel, 174, 193; David, 156; Elizabeth, 5; Gideon, 8, 174, 193, 198, 212; Jacob, 156; James, 8; Jedidiah, 219; John, 95; Joseph, 5, 8, 38, 46, 76, 86, 101, 156, 182, 193; Joshua, 8, 156; Luke, 38; Mark, 174, 212, 217; Mary, 156, 182, 204, 209; Rebeckah, 5; Samuel, 188; Sarah, 5, 8, 46, 156, 174, 182, 207, 209, 211; Spicer, 156, 174, 207; Thomas, 38; William, 202, 238

GILCOTT, Esther, 113

GILES, Samuel, 242

GILL, Amie, 14, 54; Amy, 9, 12, 30, 45, 47; Ann, 14; Ann Smith, 27; Anna, 27, 62; Benjamin, 135; Catharine, 138, 139; Catherine, 117, 137; Cathrine, 147; Charlotte, 27; Christiana, 118, 147; Christina, 139; Christine, 148; David, 9, 21, 186, 232; Deborah, 117, 124, 127, 137, 138, 147; Elizabeth, 9, 54, 134, 135, 137, 146, 147, 148; George, 54; Hannah, 9, 11, 30, 40, 44, 122, 143, 147; James, 121, 147; Jeremiah, 54; John, 9, 12, 14, 15, 21, 27, 30, 37, 40, 41, 44, 45, 47, 50, 54, 62, 78, 86, 104, 142, 143, 164, 186; John S., 27; Joseph, 147; Josiah, 120, 134, 147; Magd., 138; Magdalena, 118, 119, 120, 121, 132, 134, 136, 137, 143; Magdalene, 116, 117, 118, 122, 147; Marcia, 54; Marcy, 9, 30; Maria, 147; Mary, 9, 15, 40, 41, 44, 50, 78, 118, 121, 126, 128, 129, 131, 136, 137, 143, 148; Matthew, 116, 117, 118, 119, 120, 121, 122, 134, 135, 137, 143, 146, 147, 148; Polly, 130, 132; Rebecca Maryan, 27; Sally, 126; Sarah, 12, 27, 45, 123, 126, 127, 128, 130, 134, 137, 146, 147, 164; Silla, 147; Susanah, 33; Susanna, 186; Susannah, 21; Thomas, 11; William, 126

GILLINGHAM, Bridget, 159; Yemmons, 159

GILLS, Amy, 50; John, 50

GINSON, Ann, 238; Merit, 238

GITHENS, John, 14; Joseph, 241; Mary, 14, 58; Rebecca, 32; Rebeckah, 14; Sarah, 14; Thomas, 14, 58

GITHINS, Joseph, 242

GLOVER, Addaline, 25; Addeline, 156; Ann, 25, 26, 230, 233; Ann L., 156; Ann R., 153; Anna, 20; Arthur, 20; Barclay, 174, 224; Beulah, 20, 156; Caroline, 174, 224; Catharine Ridgway, 26; Chalkley, 174, 224, 236; Eleanor, 24, 61; Eliza, 25, 156; Elizabeth, 19, 20, 23, 26, 61, 156; Ephraim Inskip, 26; George, 208; George M., 156; George Mickle, 25, 156; Gulielma, 156; Gulilimor Maria, 25; Hannah, 24, 25, 61; Isaac, 9, 19, 23, 61; Jacob, 54, 61, 174, 224; James, 26; John, 9, 19, 20, 51, 53, 54, 56, 79, 87, 153; John A.,

INDEX

26; John Duell, 19; John Inskip, 26; John T., 26; John Thorne, 26; Joseph, 20, 56, 156; Joseph Davis, 26; Lydia, 26; Maria Wood, 26; Mary, 9, 19, 20, 25, 50, 51, 53, 54, 56, 61, 87, 156, 161, 174, 182, 208, 224; Mary T., 20, 153; Mary Thorne, 26; Phebe, 19, 23, 61; Potter, 53; Rachel, 51, 174, 224, 232; Richard, 79; Samuel, 24, 53, 61, 62; Samuel M., 156; Sarah, 9, 20, 25, 156; Sarah B., 61; Sarah M., 156; Sophia, 25, 156; Susannah Mickle, 25; Thomas, 9, 25, 50, 87, 156, 182; William, 9, 25, 156, 161, 182, 206, 208
GOLDIN, David, 139
GOODBODY, Ann, 43, 82
GOSLIN, Hester, 202
GOSLING, John, 115
GOTTSHALK, Matthew, 117
GOULDY, Hannah, 27; William, 27
GRACEBURY, Ann, 117; Mary, 117; William, 117
GRASEBERRY, Beulah, 59; Elizabeth, 92
GRASLY, Thomas, 97
GRAY, Ann, 6, 45, 49, 66, 74, 78, 83, 84, 85; Joanna, 6, 66; John, 113; Rachel, 232; Richard, 6, 66
GRAYHAM, George, 242
GREASLY, Thomas, 97
GREEN, John, 74, 112
GREGORY, Joseph, 113; Mary Ann, 82, 113
GRESLYE, Thomas, 96
GRIFFIN, Elizabeth, 146; Hannah, 143; Levi, 146
GRIFFITH, Elizabeth, 126; Hannah, 126; John, 126
GRIMMERS, Philip, 237
GRISCOM, Andrew, 71, 103; David, 9, 10, 30; Deborah, 9, 10, 30, 40, 52, 71; Hannah, 10, 48; Joseph, 9; Sarah, 9, 10, 30, 48, 53; Tobias, 40, 71, 93; William, 9, 10, 31, 40, 48, 52, 102, 103
GRISSCOM, Joseph, 30
GUEST, Andrew, 130, 132; Benjamin, 119, 142; Catharine, 138; Catherine, 118, 124, 125, 130, 132, 137, 148; Cathrine, 139; Christiana, 119, 120, 121, 127, 146; Christina, 116, 117, 118, 122, 124, 132, 133, 134, 135, 136, 137, 138, 148; Christine, 126, 128, 129, 130, 131, 132, 134; Elizabeth, 131, 137, 143, 148; Gerret, 148; Gerrit, 132; Hannah, 122, 142; Henry, 126, 127, 128, 129, 130, 132, 133, 134, 136, 139, 143, 148; Isaac, 116; James, 127; Jane, 125, 126, 127, 128, 129, 130, 132, 134, 136, 138, 139, 143, 148; John, 130, 148; Jonathan, 126; Joseph, 117, 126, 127, 130, 132, 134, 137, 139, 145, 146, 148; Mary, 118, 126, 127, 137, 139, 141, 145, 148; Nathaniel, 117, 142; Rachel, 134, 148; Rebecca, 148; Robert, 132; Samuel, 130; Sarah, 120, 126, 130, 131, 132, 134, 138, 143, 145, 146, 148; William, 116, 117, 118, 119, 120, 121, 122, 123, 124, 125, 126, 127, 128, 129, 130, 131, 136, 137, 138, 140, 142, 144, 148
GURNELL, Mary, 66, 71, 75

-H-

HA, John, 94
HACKMAN, Amy, 48
HACKNEY, Agnes, 38, 66, 70, 71, 72, 83; Joseph, 82; Mary, 155, 180; Rebecca, 74, 82; Sarah, 65; Thomas, 65, 74, 82, 90, 155, 180; William, 65
HADDON, Elizabeth, 35; John, 35; Sarah, 40
HAINES, Abel, 23; Abraham, 38, 60, 74, 79, 80, 82, 83, 106; Agnes, 82; Albert, 22; Amos, 51, 53, 60, 70, 81; Ann, 53, 57, 76, 90; Ann W., 158; Bathsheba, 23; Benjamin, 60, 62, 79; Benjamin M., 26; Caleb, 89, 105; Charles, 22, 226; Corlile, 106; Darling, 51; Deborah, 90; Deliverance, 60; Dorcas, 241; Eliza, 22, 23; Elizabeth, 57, 60, 62, 63, 69, 70, 105, 108, 156, 163, 193, 206, 216; Elizabeth M., 26; Ephraim, 84; Esther, 36, 37, 41, 67, 68, 72, 74, 77, 82, 83, 89; Ezekial, 106; Grace, 79, 80, 82, 83; Hannah, 81, 156, 231; Hannah P., 156; Hepakiah (Hipparchia), 182; Heppikiah, 183; Hipparchia, 156, 185; Hugh, 106; Isaac, 83, 156, 185; Jacob, 23, 45, 156, 180, 206, 209, 213, 216, 217, 219, 220, 222; James, 222; James H., 226; Jane, 97, 98; Job, 77, 109; Joel, 206, 230; Joel P., 156; John, 7, 36, 37, 47, 58, 62, 63, 66, 67, 68, 76, 83, 93, 95, 97, 104, 108, 156, 182, 183, 185, 195, 221; Jonathan, 69, 73, 74, 77; Joseph, 23, 90, 163, 209; Joshua, 58, 106, 156, 158; Josiah, 40; Kezia, 26; Lydia, 45; Margaret, 45, 66, 81; Martha, 40, 69; Martha B., 26; Mary, 22, 36, 38, 41, 51, 53, 58, 60, 66, 69, 71, 72, 73, 74, 75, 77, 80, 84, 87, 163, 177, 182, 219; Nancy, 23; Nathan, 71, 77, 81, 83, 84; Nathaniel, 108; Nehemiah, 76, 81; Patience, 105; Phebe, 7, 42, 67, 81, 82; Priscilla P., 156; Rachel, 38; Rachel M., 23; Rebecca, 41, 67; Reuben, 63; Richard, 38, 66, 84, 90, 106; Ruben, 108; Ruth, 89; Samuel, 23, 45, 71, 156, 158, 206; Sarah, 46, 47, 51, 71, 77, 81, 83, 84, 87, 91, 156, 158, 220; Thomas, 53, 69, 70; William, 46, 47, 57, 71, 77, 87, 104, 108, 156, 180, 183, 222, 226, 230
HAINS, Jacob, 85; John, 96; Josiah, 96; Lydia, 100; Rebecca, 66; Samuel, 85; Sarah, 98
HALE, James, 242
HALL, Hannah, 78; Martha, 66
HALLET, Richard, 100
HALTEN, Christiana, 146; Magdalene, 147
HAMBILTON, Sarah, 48
HAMBLETON, Elizabeth, 159; John, 159; Sarah, 50, 159
HAMILTON, Sarah, 91
HAMMACK, Esther, 77; George, 76; Samuel, 76, 77
HAMPTON, John, 111, 112; Margaret, 113; Rose, 112; William, 113
HANCOCK, Ann, 1, 37, 40, 76; Elizabeth, 1, 36, 75, 79; Hannah, 1, 35, 37, 73; John, 66, 71,

75, 88; Joseph, 108; Margaret, 70, 71, 76; Mary, 1, 38, 65, 66, 67, 69, 71, 75, 88; Rachel, 35, 36, 37; Sarah, 1, 37; Susannah, 66, 71; Timothy, 1, 35, 36, 37, 66
HANES, Isaac, 94; John, 94
HANK, John, 98, 99
HANKE, Elizabeth, 37; William, 37
HANKS, Elizabth, 37
HANNA, Peter, 56; Samuel, 56
HANNAY, Peter, 56; Samuel, 56
HANNOLD, Rachel, 241
HARDING, Mary, 38, 67
HARKER, Daniel, 140; John, 141; Joseph, 147; Margaret, 230; Rebecca, 147; Samuel, 141; Sarah, 141
HARLAN, Hannah, 51; Joel, 51; Joshua, 51
HARMER, Charles, 228
HARPER, Ann R., 153; Charles, 228; Daniel, 174, 186, 233; Elizabeth, 233; George, 186; Jane M., 158; Margaret, 153, 158, 174; Martha, 174, 233; Mary, 174, 186, 232; Nathan, 174, 233; Samuel, 153, 158, 174, 233; Sarah, 191
HARRIOTT, Sarah, 40, 41
HARRIS, Abraham, 242
HARRISON, Abigail, 73; Ann, 40, 68, 77; Joseph, 87; Mary, 40, 87; Samuel, 65; Sarah, 65, 112; William, 65
HARRISON-CLEMENT, Ann, 79, 81
HARTLEY, Anthony, 189; Benjamin, 21, 59; Mary, 21, 59; Rebecca, 89

HARTLY, Bathsheba, 43; Rebecca, 43; Roger, 43
HARTMAN, Sarah, 74
HARVEY, Isaac, 220; John, 64; Peter, 64; Sarah, 64
HASKER, Elizabeth, 35, 64; Mercy, 35, 69, 73, 77; Sarah, 64; William, 35, 64
HASSLED, Samuel, 238
HATKINSON, John, 81
HAYES, James, 113
HAYNS, Anna, 139
HAZELET, Sarah, 223
HAZLET, Sarah, 223
HEATH, Rev., 237
HEDGER, Deborah, 69; John, 69; Meribah, 69
HEDGERS, Deborah, 82
HEINS, Ann, 146
HELDERMAN, Ann, 129, 133, 138, 143, 146; Anna, 131, 147; Charlotte, 129; George, 129, 131, 133, 135, 136, 138, 139, 143, 146, 147; Jacob, 129, 146; John Adam, 147; William, 131, 146
HELMS, Andrew, 90
HENRY, William, 137
HENSEY, Isaac, 158, 197; Joshua, 158; Mary, 158
HENSLY, Martha Clark, 207
HENSON, John, 48; Tabitha, 48
HENSZEY, Joshua, 158
HEPPARD, Joseph; Sarah, 91
HERITAGE, Benjamin, 41, 74, 174, 180, 203; Hannah, 7, 30, 37, 41, 52, 69, 78; John, 36, 69, 89, 103, 106; Jonathan, 174, 203; Joseph, 7, 30, 34, 37, 41, 69, 78, 102, 106; Josiah, 208; Martha, 217; Mary, 7, 33, 34,

36, 37, 38, 39, 40, 41, 44, 50, 67, 68, 69; Priscilla, 213; Richard, 3, 7, 33, 34, 36, 69, 93; Sarah, 7, 69, 102, 174, 203; Stephen, 205, 206; William, 174, 203
HERMITAGE, Ephraim, 207
HEULINGS, Jacob, 108; William, 241
HEUSTIS, John, 90; Joseph, 82; Sarah, 82
HEW, Martha, 114
HEWES, Aaron, 158, 180, 188; Caleb, 82; Jane, 158, 180; Mary, 82; Providence, 158; William, 82
HEWETS, Samuel, 142
HEWIT, Susanna, 78
HEWLINGS, Rebecca, 47
HEWS, Aaron, 193
HICKEY, Elmer, 238
HIGBEE, Mary, 91
HIGBY, John, 72
HIGGINS, Patience, 134
HILES, Joseph, 212
HILL, John, 66
HILLMAN, Abel, 23, 62; Abigail, 44, 45, 50, 86; Aquilla Shinn, 25; Daniel, 21, 23, 25, 44, 45, 50, 61, 62, 74, 76; Daniel Ellis, 25; Elizabeth, 45, 47, 74, 76, 81; Esther, 25; James, 21, 47; Joel, 114; John, 76, 81; Joshua B., 23; Martha, 21, 23, 61, 62; Martha E., 23; Mary, 21, 47; Mary Ann, 25; Rachel, 23; Rebecca, 23; Richard J., 23; Samuel Stokes, 25; Sarah, 23; Sarah H., 23
HILMAN, Mary, 218
HINCHMAN, Abigail, 110; Amy, 41, 43, 49; Ann, 40, 79, 81, 90; Benjamin, 217; Eliza, 214; Elizabeth, 79; Griffith, 214; Hannah, 40, 73; Hipparchia, 47; Isaac, 234; Jacob, 73; James, 47, 49, 51, 79, 179, 183, 190, 217; John, 40, 73, 79, 81, 212; Joseph, 41, 79; Laetitia, 84; Letitia, 84; Lettice, 183; Littia, 110; Mary, 179, 215; Sarah, 40, 47, 49, 51, 79, 192, 234; Thomas, 78
HIRF, Priscilla, 214
HODGES, Jane, 110
HODGKINS, Hannah, 65
HODSON, Abigail, 27; Abigail C., 63; Mary, 63; Thomas, 27, 63
HOEL, Isaac, 110
HOFFMAN, Abigail, 174, 211, 229; Abraham, 118; Amy, 148; Ann, 124, 137, 140, 146; Benjamin, 121, 148; Catharine, 142; Catherine, 116, 117, 118, 119; Deborah, 116, 131, 148; Elias, 144; Elijah, 133, 148; Elizabeth, 117, 119, 120; Evie, 127; Frederick, 117, 118, 119; Isaac, 174, 211, 229; Jacob, 129; James, 121, 137, 149; Jesse, 126; Job, 174, 211, 235; John, 117, 118, 119, 120, 125, 127, 129, 131, 133, 136, 141, 144, 147, 148; John Lawrence, 132, 133, 138; Laurence, 116, 122, 136; Lawrence, 120, 121, 124, 125, 126, 127, 128, 129, 132, 137, 138, 144, 148, 149; Margaret, 120; Martha, 174, 211; Mary, 116, 117, 119, 174, 211, 226; Matthew, 117; Nicholas, 142; Peter, 116, 117; Rachel, 125, 137, 141; Rahel, 148;

Rebecca, 120, 136, 148, 228;
Rebekah, 174, 211; Samuel,
117; Sarah, 120, 121, 122, 124,
125, 126, 127, 128, 129, 131,
133, 136, 137, 138, 140, 141,
149, 174, 211, 228, 229; Sarah
Chrisitina, 133; Sarah Christina, 133, 138, 144; Uri, 122;
Urie, 142
HOFFMANN, Sarah, 132
HOIL, Martha, 216
HOLDCRAFT, James, 220;
Josiah, 188; Mary, 181; Samuel, 209; William, 181, 213
HOLLAND, Barbary, 238; Daniel, 238; John, 242; Margret, 238; Rebecca, 238; Samuel, 238
HOLLEN, Daniel, 239; James, 239
HOLLINGHAM, Isaac, 65; Katherine, 65
HOLLINGHEAD, John, 97
HOLLINGSHEAD, Agnes, 38, 66, 70, 71, 72, 83; Benjamin, 241; Edmund, 72; Edward, 89, 104; Eleanor, 61; Elizabeth, 91; Grace, 38, 79, 80, 82, 83; Hugh, 70; Hugh F., 61; John, 34, 38, 66, 70, 71, 72, 83, 98; Joseph, 103; Mary, 71; William, 34
HOLLINGSHEAD-ELLIS, Mary, 87
HOLLOWAY, Elizabeth, 96; George, 84; Isaac, 84; John, 64; Sarah, 105; Tobias, 105, 111
HOLLOWELL, Elizabeth, 97; John, 96, 97
HOLLSTEIN, Lawrence, 142, 143; Margaretha, 142
HOLMES, Elizabeth, 242; William, 242

HOLMS, Martha, 146, 148
HOLOWELL, John, 96
HOLSTEIN, Andrew, 120; Ann, 122, 125, 127, 144; Anna, 137; Catherine, 122; Hannah, 121, 145; James, 127; John, 141; Joseph, 125; Lawrence, 118, 120, 121, 122, 125, 127, 141, 144, 145; Margaret, 118, 120, 121, 141; Margareth, 144; Mary, 141; Sarah, 120; Susanna, 118, 137, 144; William, 140
HOLSTINE, John, 118; Lawrence, 117, 118, 119; Margaret, 118, 119, 136; Mary, 117; William, 119
HOLTEN, Christina, 143
HOLTON, Anna, 130; Christiana, 138; Christina, 133, 135, 136, 144; Christine, 124, 127, 129, 130, 132, 138; Christopher, 132, 144; James, 124, 127, 129, 132, 133, 144; John, 130, 133, 136; Mary, 127; Richard, 124, 137
HOMAN, Andrew, 113; Mary, 113
HOMES, Martha, 135
HOOPER, Ann, 70
HOOTEN, Ann, 15, 68, 82; Benjamin, 49; Elizabeth, 15, 49, 52, 82, 214; Hannah, 207; John, 48, 49; Roger, 68; Samuel, 15, 57, 82; Sarah, 48, 49; Thomas, 68, 74, 88
HOOTON, Aaron, 13, 24; Alexander, 24; Ann, 24, 43, 48, 63, 85; Anna, 204; Benjamin, 24; Constantine, 48; Elisha, 24, 57, 13; Elizabeth, 13, 24, 71; Esther, 13, 24, 57; Hannah, 24, 63; Isaac, 24; John, 85; Martha,

13, 24; Mary, 43, 67, 69, 71; Samuel, 13, 24, 43; Sarah, 85, 202; Thomas, 41, 67, 69, 71, 99, 100, 101; William, 13, 24, 63, 69
HOPEWELL, Christian, 75; Elizabeth, 75; John, 70, 90; Joseph, 70, 100; Nathaniel, 75; Sarah, 100
HOPKINS, Ann, 5, 12, 24, 51, 55, 62, 63; Benjamin, 12, 40, 55; Charles, 218, 227; Ebenezer, 5, 12, 29, 31, 40, 43, 45, 51, 55, 71, 85; Elizabeth, 12, 23; Elizabeth Estaugh, 43; Elizabeth Lord, 25; Elizabeth S., 59; Griffith M., 24; Haddon, 5; Hannah W., 24; Isaac, 12; James, 23, 52, 59; John Estaugh, 25, 56, 85; Josiah, 12; Mary, 5, 12, 45, 195; Mary Ann, 24, 28, 63; Rebecca, 23, 59; Rebecca M., 24; Robert, 180; Samuel, 12; Samuel C., 217, 221; Sarah, 5, 12, 24, 27, 40, 43, 45, 52, 55, 56, 62, 85; Thomas, 180; William E., 24, 27, 62, 63; William Estaugh, 56; William O., 28
HOPPER, Elizabeth, 9, 67; Isaac Tatem, 180; John, 9, 67, 71, 112; Levi, 180, 200, 201; Mary, 9, 86, 210; Rachel, 195; Samuel, 9, 71, 86; Sarah, 201; Susannah, 212
HORNER, Azubah, 89; Deliverance, 71; Elizabeth, 54, 57, 64; George, 64; Isaac, 23, 54, 57, 82; Jacob, 81, 82, 89, 97; Kay, 54; Letitia, 79; Malachi, 64; Mary, 54, 81, 82, 178, 217; Rachel, 23, 57

HORNERE, John, 89; Mary, 89
HORTON, Benjamin, 188
HOULINGS, Jacob, 94
HOWEL, John, 102
HOWELL, Frances, 158; Jacob, 71; John, 71; John Ladd, 158; Keziah, 192; Mary, 71, 101; Rebecca, 77, 140
HOWEY, William, 206
HOWLAND, Elizabeth, 37
HOWLY, Sarah, 226
HOWY, Isaac, 216
HUBER, Mary, 146
HUDDLESTON, Katherine, 67
HUDSON, Elizabeth, 39, 40; John, 68; Mary, 37, 68, 71, 75, 78; Thomas, 73; William, 37, 68
HUESTES, Joseph, 90; Sarah, 90
HUESTIS, Jonathan, 75, 77; Joseph, 77; Katherine, 75; Mary, 75, 77
HUGESTES, John, 90
HUGG, Ann, 65, 89; Anne, 237; Gabriel, 110; John, 33, 37, 38, 65, 79, 98; Joseph, 88; Priscilla, 38, 65, 79, 114; Rebeckah, 107; Samuel, 79; William, 112, 237
HUGHES, Caleb, 82; Dorcas, 90; John, 108; Mary, 82; William, 82
HUGHET, Amy, 77
HULINGS, William, 104
HULL, Henry, 61
HULLINGS, Abigail, 92
HULTON, Susannah, 92
HUMPHREY, Joshua, 101
HUMPHREYS, Increase, 108; Josa, 108; Mary, 36, 74
HUNT, Abigail, 82; Elizabeth, 77; Esther, 57; Hope, 49; John, 193, 217; Martha, 49; Robert,

49, 77, 82, 88, 100; Samuel, 241; Sarah, 65; William, 94, 96
HUNTER, James, 241; Thomas, 241, 242; William, 242
HURL, Martha, 208
HURST, Joseph, 158; Mary, 158
HUSINGER, John, 237
HUSTED, Jonathan, 107
HUTCHENSON, Elizabeth, 155; Hannah, 155; John, 155
HUTCHESON, Hannah, 86
HUTCHINSON, Elizabeth, 78, 89; Ezekiel, 114; Hannah, 78; John, 78, 89
HUTTON, Ann, 3; John, 3; Mary, 3; Thomas, 3; William, 3
HYLE, Joseph, 215

-I-

IARDALL, Rebekah, 180; Thomas, 180
IBBS, Elizabeth, 66
INGELDEW, Blackston, 111
INGLE, John, 36, 97; Robert, 68, 97
INSKEEP, Abraham, 164; Anne, 115; Hannah, 164; Samuel, 195, 217; Sarah, 115, 164, 208, 231
INSKIP, Abraham, 43; Ann, 26; John, 26; Sarah, 43, 52, 55, 56
IREDALE, Sarah, 80
IREDALL, Ann, 182; Thomas, 182
IREDELL, Abraham, 45, 73, 197; Jacob, 206; Jonathan, 45; Joseph, 204; Rebekah, 180; Thomas, 180
IRELAND, Joseph, 110
IRWIN, Dorcas, 69; Edward, 110
IVES, Elizabeth, 45, 47, 49, 72; Susannah, 66; William, 101

IZARD, Catherine, 116; Gabriel, 116; Martha, 116

-J-

JACK, Anna Catharine, 144
JACOBS, Israel, 60; John, 60
JAMES, Elizabeth, 135, 137, 145, 148; Esaias, 148; Israel, 133, 135, 137, 145; Joseph, 135; Kisrael, 148; Rebecca, 133, 145
JEFFERIES, Constantine, 85; John, 85
JEFFERYS, John, 77
JEFFREYS, John, 77
JEFFRIES, Constantine, 82; John, 82, 89; Letitia, 82, 89
JENINGS, Ann, 57; Catherine Ann, 158; Isaac, 158; Jacob, 158; Jacob M., 158; Jehue, 158; Job, 158; Mark, 158; Mary Jane, 158; Richard, 158; Sarah, 158
JENNINGS, Ann, 26, 113, 158, 174, 218, 221; Barclay, 26; Charles, 26, 174, 218, 221; Deborah, 46, 74; Elizabeth, 75, 209; Hannah, 26, 174, 218, 221; Isaac, 43, 51, 74, 75, 79, 85, 113; Jacob, 26, 43, 51, 85, 158, 174, 221; Jacob H., 26; Job, 217, 225; Joseph, 26, 174, 217, 218; Judith, 74, 75, 79; Keturah, 26; Kezia, 26; Levi, 57, 174, 197, 200, 205, 209; Margaret, 26; Mark, 158, 217, 223; Mary, 26, 158, 174, 218, 223; May, 26; Reuben, 194, 195; Sarah, 26, 57, 112, 174, 218, 221; Tacy, 205; Thomas, 69, 174, 200
JERDALL, Sarah, 103

JESS, Ann, 222, 224; Anne, 205; Ruth, 206
JESSOP, Jane, 98; John, 71, 98
JESSUP, Elizabeth, 158, 182, 184; James, 11, 201; John, 11, 12, 42, 44, 155, 158, 182, 184, 197, 201, 203, 204, 205; Margaret, 42, 44, 90, 155; Mary, 6, 42, 155; Sarah, 12, 160, 182, 216
JINNINGS, Joseph, 221
JOHN, Ann, 19; Rachel, 19
JOHNS, Benjamin, 196; Rachel, 174, 196, 197; Richard, 174, 196, 197, 201; Sarah, 174, 196, 197
JOHNSON, Abrahm, 241; Benjamin, 131, 132, 135, 144, 147; Elizabeth, 135; Gervis, 205; Jesse, 131, 144; Joseph, 80, 241; Mary, 71, 86; Rachel, 131, 132, 135, 144, 147; Ruth, 232; William, 242
JOHNSTON, Benjamin, 130; Jane, 130; Paul, 99; Rachel, 130
JOLLY, Archibald, 112
JONES, Abraham, 117; Amy, 27; Andrew, 120; Ann, 120, 242; Aquilla, 45, 49, 181; Arthur, 175, 220, 225; Beulah, 27, 28; Beulah Atkinson, 175, 194; David, 158; Eliza, 27; Elizabeth, 120, 175, 220, 225; Ester, 239; Esther, 55, 175, 220, 225; Francis, 97; Griffith, 45; Guila, 117; Hannah, 203; Henry, 53, 110; Hugh, 55; Isaac, 27, 28, 53, 158, 175, 183, 194, 202, 208, 214; Isaac Cooper, 175, 181; Jacob, 120, 175, 220, 225; Jane, 74; John, 110, 175, 220; Jonah, 116; Jonathan, 239; Joseph, 27, 116, 118, 120; Lydia, 175, 220; Lydia S., 175, 225; Margaret, 116, 118, 120; Mary, 49, 68, 120; Mary H., 28; Naomi, 53, 158; Noah, 214; Rebecca, 28, 49, 117, 158, 175, 194, 214, 223; Robert, 68, 88; Samuel, 120, 242; Sarah, 27, 55, 88, 118, 158, 175, 183, 194, 214; Tacy, 175, 225; William, 242
JONSON, John, 242
JORDAN, John, 135; Mary, 135; William, 135
JORDON, Pharaby, 28; Richard, 28

-K-

KAIGHIN, Joseph, 103
KAIGHN, Abigail, 155; Ann, 18, 22; Charity, 18; Charles, 15; Elizabeth, 15, 18, 22, 33, 56, 68; Elizabeth C., 27; Hannah, 18, 22, 25, 56, 60, 155, 179; Hannah Mickel, 15; Isaac, 18; James, 18, 22, 25, 56, 60; John, 15, 18, 22, 110; John B., 22; John M., 27, 63; Joseph, 15, 27, 32, 55, 63, 81, 89; Joseph Mickle, 27; Mary, 15, 18, 22, 33, 81; Prudence, 15, 55; Rachel, 22; Rebecca, 22; Rebecca W., 27; Sarah, 15, 18, 27, 63; Sarah M., 27; William, 15, 112, 155, 179
KATS, Ann, 123, 124; Anna, 127, 143; Anna Maria, 141; Anne, 120, 121, 122, 142; Barbara, 119; Catherine, 122; Dorothea, 121, 142; Elizabeth, 128; Jacob, 119, 120, 142; Jaen, 137; Jane, 134, 138, 147, 149; John, 123;

Mananna, 128; Margaret, 120; Marianna, 120, 139; Martin, 119, 120, 121, 122, 123, 124, 127, 128, 132, 134, 135, 136, 137, 138, 139, 140, 141, 142, 143, 147, 149; Mary, 119; Michael, 119; Peter, 127; Rosine, 119; Sarah, 124, 134, 137, 147, 149
KAY, Ann, 48, 54, 159; Ann T., 60; Benjamin, 2; Clement, 214; Clement H., 158, 159, 186, 220; Clement K., 230; Deborah, 159, 165, 186, 214, 220; Deborah E., 159, 173, 185; Edith, 158; Elizabeth, 2, 3, 36, 54, 57, 60, 82, 94; Elwood, 158; Francis, 2, 89; Garvis, 69; Gervias, 88; Hannah, 24, 54, 56, 159; Hope, 159, 165, 185, 214; Isaac, 2, 24, 54, 56, 82, 91, 113, 158, 159, 165, 185, 186, 214, 218, 220, 224; James, 90; James W., 158; John, 2, 3, 36, 69, 88, 93; Joseph, 2, 3, 48, 54, 88, 159, 179, 214, 223, 224; Joshua, 3; Josiah, 2, 54, 60, 90, 103, 159, 179, 185, 193; Martha, 159, 185; Mary Ann, 54, 82; Rebekah, 2; Samuel, 3; Samuell, 2; Sarah, 2, 48, 69, 85, 88, 159, 220; William, 214; William E., 159, 220
KAYS, Alice, 31
KEAIS, Alice, 195; Francis, 31; Nathan, 159, 202; Samuel, 203; Sarah, 175, 197; William, 47, 175, 194
KEASIS, Alice, 12; Frances, 12; Samuel, 12; Sarah, 12; William, 12

KEEN, Abraham, 117; Catherine, 116, 117, 118; Eric, 116, 117, 118; Errick, 143; John, 116, 117; Mary, 116, 143; Rachel, 116; Thomas, 118
KELLY, Abraham, 107; Rachel, 107
KELSON, Joanna, 66
KEMBLE, Anna, 48; Elizabeth, 42, 76
KEMJSTOOP, C. O., 121; C. Otto, 120
KEMP, Andrew, 117; Jane, 117; Paul, 117
KENDALL, Mary, 70
KENT, William, 111
KEY, Sarah, 49
KIDD, Benjamin, 96
KILLE, John, 195
KIMBEL, Cabel, 239
KIMBLE, Mary, 89
KIMMSEY, Hannah, 197
KIMSEY, Clement, 242; Elizabeth, 154; Hepsibah, 208; Job, 85, 154; Joseph, 196; Kezia, 154; Keziah, 204; Sarah, 72; Thomas, 73, 85
KINSEY, Deborah, 242; Thomas, 91
KIRBY, Amos, 57; Ann, 57, 236; Job, 211, 213; Mercy, 175, 233; Sarah, 175, 233
KIRKPATRICK, Thomas, 238
KITTS, Felix, 141; Jane, 141; Robert, 141
KNIGHT, Achsah, 175, 231, 232; Anna, 48; Beulah, 17, 22, 60; Charles, 175, 186, 212, 231, 232; Charles W., 236; Dubre, 233, 236; Elizabeth, 17, 33, 60; Elizabeth Newman, 162, 175,

223; Hannah, 184, 185, 186;
Hannah C., 236; Isaac, 68;
Isabella, 52, 54, 56; John, 106,
183, 187, 196, 211, 216, 223,
224, 226, 230, 234, 236;
Jonathan, 17, 52, 54, 55, 56, 85,
91, 201; Joseph, 97; Josiah
Stokes, 175, 227; Mary, 68, 175,
225; Rebecca, 233; Samuel, 17;
Sarah, 17, 22, 55, 85, 175, 211,
223, 224; Thomas, 54, 85, 175,
185, 186, 207, 225, 227, 233;
Thomas C., 175, 231, 232; William, 17, 22, 33, 52, 60
KOHL, Ann, 123, 124, 129, 130,
135, 138, 142, 146; Anna, 137;
Anne, 128; Jacob, 142; John,
123, 124, 128, 129, 142, 146;
Kesiah, 124
KORN, Michael, 241
KRAIGHN, Joseph, 38; Sarah, 38

-L-

LADD, Ann, 5, 12, 159;
Catharine, 74; Deborah, 12, 31,
76, 159; Eldad, 12, 31, 159;
Elizabeth, 5; Hannah, 12, 48,
159; John, 12, 33, 39, 65, 67,
70, 159; Jonathan, 5, 12, 31, 67,
159; Katherine, 70; Mary, 39,
69, 74, 76, 78, 111; Samuel, 12,
48, 65, 74, 76, 78, 91, 159, 224,
50; Sarah, 12, 48, 50, 65, 67, 70,
159
LAITHEART, John, 238
LAMB, Jacob, 13; Sarah, 13
LANDERS, John, 238
LANDORFORE, James, 238
LANGSTAFF, Laban, 58, 159;
Mary, 58, 159, 222; Samuel, 58
LANGSTON, Deborah, 72;
Sarah, 36
LANING, Isaac, 197
LANNING, Isaac, 194
LATZ, Mary, 118; Michael, 118
LAUTEBACH, Ann, 138
LAUTERBACH, Adam, 119; Ann,
129, 130, 132, 134, 135, 137,
139, 141; Anna, 144; Catherine,
118; Conrad, 119, 140, 141, 145;
Elizabeth, 119, 130, 135, 137,
138, 145; Emmie, 129; Henry,
134; Martha, 130; Mary, 141;
Mathas, 130; Mathias, 119, 129,
132, 134, 135, 141, 144;
Patience, 134, 137, 138; Peter,
118, 141; Widow, 136
LAWRENCE, Mary, 78, 83
LAWSON, Mary, 38, 81
LAWTON, John, 80
LEACONEY, John, 242; Richard,
242; William, 241
LEE, Mary, 41, 72, 73
LEEDS, Daniel, 159; Deborah,
114; G. Howard, 159; Hannah,
159; Phebe A., 159; Rebecca, 53
LENDELL, John, 67
LENTS, Michael, 76
LEONARD, Elizabeth, 190
LETCHWORTH, Diana, 53;
John, 53; William, 53
LEVIS, Samuel, 145
LEWDEN, Hannah, 97; Rebeckah, 107
LEWDON, Joseph, 77
LEWIS, Aaron, 209; Ann, 239;
Eran, 209; Evan, 208; Hannah,
239; James, 239; Tacy, 92
LEWRIE, Ann, 238; J., 238
LINCH, Michael, 106
LINDSAY, Rachel, 87
LINDSEY, Ezekiel, 78; Rachel,

91
LINMEIN, Susana, 127
LINMEIR, Andrew, 131; Christopher, 131; Rebecca, 131; Susanna, 130, 131
LINMEYER, Alexander, 121, 137; Andrew, 121, 123, 136, 139; Christine, 126; Christopher, 134; Elizabeth, 121, 123; George, 134; James, 126; Lawrence, 123; Nicholas, 126, 136; Rebecca, 134; Susanna, 136, 137, 138
LINMIER, Andrew, 127, 128, 130, 131; Christopher, 130; Elizabeth, 130; Rebecca, 130; Susan, 127; Susana, 128; Susanna, 130, 131
LINMYER, Anne, 142; Catharine, 143; Christopher, 139, 141, 142, 143, 149; Margaret, 149; Rebecca, 143
LINMYRE, Christopher, 142; George, 142
LIPPANCOTT, Samuel, 98
LIPPENCOAT, Elizabeth, 142; Hannah, 140; Samuel, 142
LIPPENCOTT, Samuel, 102; Thomas, 99
LIPPINCOAT, Hannah, 139
LIPPINCOTT, Aaron, 75, 79, 175, 204, 226, 230, 232, 236; Abel, 83; Abigail, 70, 108; Abraham, 20, 21, 59; Amy, 159, 184; Ann, 29; Anna, 51, 73, 79, 175, 220, 236; Anne, 54; Barzilla, 9, 30; Benjamin, 22; Bowman, 159, 225, 226; Cabel, 9; Caleb, 44, 48, 50, 51, 54, 58, 80; Charles C., 175, 236; Daniel, 10, 91, 92, 163; Deborah, 49, 160, 203; Deliverance, 87; Elizabeth, 10, 32, 55, 74, 78, 79, 80, 83, 85, 86, 87, 103, 136, 160, 175, 178, 192, 194, 203; Esther, 22, 74; Ezekial, 82; Francis D., 175, 236; Franklin, 160; Freedom, 10, 31, 36, 72, 74, 75, 78, 80, 82, 83, 87, 101; Grace, 9; Hannah, 28, 32, 46, 47, 50, 52, 56, 58, 75, 83, 163, 195, 242; Hope, 28, 40, 70, 72, 75, 89; Isaac, 72, 83; Jacob, 10, 72, 76, 79, 82, 85, 106, 160, 199, 203, 210; James, 73, 79; Jesse, 25; John, 9, 70, 73, 78, 82, 83; John Haines, 25; Joseph, 22, 54, 72, 208, 217; Joseph H., 25; Joshua, 10, 20, 82, 85, 159, 184, 207; Judith, 36, 41, 72, 75, 83, 163; Keturah, 25; Lydia, 22; Martha, 9, 10, 31, 40, 46, 72; Martha D., 159, 220, 225, 226; Mary, 9, 20, 25, 30, 36, 41, 43, 44, 46, 48, 49, 50, 51, 63, 67, 69, 70, 71, 72, 74, 75, 78, 82, 83, 85, 86, 107, 160, 175, 187, 224, 226, 236; Mary B., 159, 216, 220; Mary F., 175, 236; Nathan, 20, 21, 22, 63, 78, 101, 103; Nathaniel, 9, 28, 44, 46, 48, 71, 82, 86; Patience, 41; Peter, 160; Preston, 50; Priscilla, 59; Rachel, 22, 44, 56; Remberance(Rememberance), 111; Restore, 79, 87, 106, 107, 160, 203; Samuel, 40, 50, 58, 59, 70, 72, 74, 75, 101, 107, 108, 175, 192, 194, 215; Samuel B., 159, 184, 216, 220, 224, 226; Samuel C., 175, 236; Samuel P., 160; Sarah, 10, 20, 21, 22, 46, 47, 51, 63, 86, 87; Sarah Ann, 20, 28;

Solomon, 10, 31, 75, 86, 87, 104, 188; Stacy, 20, 28; Tacy, 218; Thomas, 36, 41, 71, 72, 74, 75; Thomas Clark, 159, 225, 226; Wallace, 20, 28; William, 50, 87, 160, 201, 203, 208, 213, 216

LIPPINOCTT, Aaron, 80; Anna, 80; James, 80

LLOYD, Abigail, 131, 132, 133, 135; Bateman, 119, 121, 131, 132, 133, 135, 136, 146; Beekman, 118; Benjamin, 122; Charles, 118; Daniel, 133, 134, 144; Harriet Lydia, 131; Isaac, 121, 134; Jacob, 121, 146; Jaconias, 121; John, 122, 125, 136, 142, 144, 146; Lafford, 132; Lefferts Ware, 135; Lydia, 118, 119, 121, 133, 136, 143; Mary, 136, 144, 146; Obadiah, 118, 119, 120, 121, 122, 123, 124, 125, 136, 137, 138, 145; Polly, 122; Rebecca, 118, 119, 121, 122, 123, 124, 125, 134, 136, 137, 138, 144, 145; Samuel, 119, 133, 144; Sarah, 118, 133, 134, 144, 145; Wood, 122

LOCK, Beata, 113; John, 116; Peter, 116; Priscilla, 116; Rebecca, 116

LODGE, Robert, 105

LONDON, Amos, 242

LONG, Alexander, 221, 223; Keziah, 208; Rachel, 208, 209

LORD, Abigail, 5, 73, 86; Abraham, 5; Alice, 65; Ann, 11, 29, 47, 79; Azubah, 189; Benjamin, 4, 29, 160, 210; Benjamin J., 160; Caleb, 29; Constantine, 42, 151, 160, 181, 189; David, 175, 192; Edmond, 4, 42, 89, 111; Edward, 160; Elizabeth, 3, 4, 5, 29, 40, 42, 44, 64, 69, 73, 160; Eunice, 4, 11, 84, 179; Hannah, 11, 46, 47, 52, 72, 160, 161, 162, 175, 182, 189, 207, 224; Hope, 4, 29; Isaac, 5; Isabel, 4, 28; James, 4, 11, 29, 31, 33, 40, 64, 79, 94, 160, 175, 224, 229; Jehu, 11, 160, 189, 195, 207; John, 2, 4, 66, 80; Jonathan, 4, 29; Josa, 108; Joseph, 91, 115; Joshua, 2, 3, 4, 11, 28, 29, 31, 33, 44, 46, 47, 52, 64, 73, 76, 84, 96, 98, 102, 160, 162, 179, 182, 226, 230, 234, 235; Joshuah, 161; Keziah, 189; Lydia, 207; Mary, 2, 4, 70, 77, 80, 82, 89, 160, 207; Mary E., 160; Mercy, 160; Nathan, 80, 175, 189, 192; Phebe, 160; Phineas, 29, 46, 160; Phinehas, 4, 11; Phineus, 216; Rachel, 5; Rebecca, 160, 195, 226; Robert, 5, 69, 73, 98; Samuel, 77, 82; Samuell, 5; Sarah, 2, 3, 4, 5, 11, 28, 29, 40, 43, 44, 45, 46, 50, 55, 71, 76, 77, 84, 85, 151, 160, 162, 181, 189, 207

LOVETT, Ann, 14; William, 14

LOW, Benjamin Waite, 192; Joseph, 80, 89, 94, 190; Martha, 89; Rachel, 199; Sarah, 37

LOWLANDER, Abraham, 117; Elizabeth, 117

LUCAS, Elizabeth, 175, 202; Esther, 175, 202, 203; Mary, 114; Robert, 175, 202; William, 175, 202

LUNBACK, Mary, 203

LYNMEYER, Ann, 116, 117, 118,

INDEX 275

121; Chistina, 117; Christopher, 116, 117, 118; Nicholas, 118; Sarah, 116
LYNMIER, Andrew, 125; Ann, 125

-M-
MACBLOCK, William, 94
MACCLOCK, William, 93, 94
MCCOLLOCH, John, 115
MCCORMICK, Patrick, 144, 145; Rosanna, 144
MCCRAIG, John, 145
MCDURMONT, Patrick, 238
MACKENNY, Mary, 114
MACKINTOSH, Margaret, 111
MCMASTERS, Thomas, 242
MADDOCK, Rachel, 106
MAGLOUGHIN, Margaret, 113
MAINS, Andrew, 242
MALSON, Catharine, 112
MANNERY, Rachel, 114
MAPES, Joseph, 88; Mary, 88
MARKS, Sarah, 35, 36
MARRIOTT, Sarah, 40, 41
MASON, Anna, 48; Grace, 76, 107; Hannah, 16; Isaac, 78; James, 16, 72, 77, 78, 83, 84, 95; John, 65, 67, 84; Lydia, 72, 77, 78, 83, 84; Martha, 48; Mary, 72; Rebecca, 16, 77; Sarah, 65, 73; Solomon, 48
MATHEWS, Hannah, 182, 204
MATLACK, Abigail, 44, 57, 73; Achsah, 75; Ann, 41, 71; Anna, 78, 82; Bathsheba, 82; Benjamin, 24, 78, 91; Beulah, 175, 234; Caleb, 92; Daniel, 61; Deborah, 41, 46, 76, 155; Eleanor, 24; Elizabeth, 92; Ellwood, 175, 234; Emaline,

175, 234; Esther, 74; George, 74, 88; Hannah, 71, 78, 92, 181; Hannah Ann, 24; Isaac, 90, 111; James, 196, 208; Jane, 92; Jeremiah, 90; John, 41, 72, 73, 74, 78, 82, 88, 89, 92, 111, 112; Joseph, 67, 75, 86, 97, 181, 198; Kezia, 41, 74; Laetitia, 73; Lydia, 92; Maria, 175, 234; Mary, 38, 41, 43, 44, 65, 66, 67, 69, 72, 73, 74, 75, 77, 86, 170, 181, 229; Priscilla, 72; Rachel, 71; Rebecca, 41, 155; Rebekah, 43; Richard, 17, 41, 43, 44, 75, 76, 86, 105, 155, 170, 207; Sabilla, 106; Samuel, 24, 61; Samuel Glover, 24; Sarah, 24, 52, 61, 66, 75; Sarah B., 175, 234; Sarah S., 24; Seth, 61, 175, 234; Stacy, 24, 61; Sybil, 38, 46, 49; Sybill, 50; Tacy, 92; Thomas, 71; Timothy, 38, 40, 69, 72, 73, 75, 97, 105, 106; William, 38, 41, 65, 66, 67, 69, 71, 75, 77
MATLOCK, Richard, 66
MATSON, Catharine, 112
MATTLACK, Timothy, 99
MAXELL, John, 101
MAXFIELD, John, 71
MAYFIELD, Elizabeth, 92
MAYHAM, Sarah, 33
MAYHEM, Sarah, 36
MAYLIN, Salem, 236; Sarah, 234
MEDCALF, Hannah, 112; Jacob, 96; Mary, 76, 78
MEDCALFE, Dorothy, 65; Mary, 65; Matthew, 65
MEDOWEL, Mary, 239
MEORAIG, John, 143; Mary, 143
MERRITT, Mary, 232

METCALF, Mary, 74
MICHNER, John, 105; Sarah, 105
MICKEL, Daniel, 88; Hannah, 88
MICKELL, James, 111
MICKLE, Andrew Ehrmstrong, 16; Ann, 28, 161, 175, 182, 225; Ann Blackwood, 225; Ann C., 162; Anna, 161, 206, 229; Archabald, 30; Archibald, 3, 9, 13, 16, 32, 35, 36, 37, 38, 46, 64, 65, 67, 78, 154, 179, 181, 185; Benjamin, 64, 225; Benjamin Whitale, 28; Benjamin Whitall, 16; Charles, 161; Daniel, 37; David, 161, 162, 209; Deborah, 13, 32; Eliza, 223; Elizabeth, 9, 13, 75, 78, 156, 176, 220; Elizabeth Estaugh, 169, 170; Eunice, 161; Geeorge, 184; George, 161, 162, 167, 232, 234; Hannah, 13, 15, 32, 39, 55, 58, 60, 61, 70, 73, 156, 161, 162, 180, 184, 215, 219; Hepanah, 60; Iaac, 204; Isaac, 9, 16, 64, 179, 181; Isaac P., 28; Isabel, 35, 36; Jack, 92; James, 20, 52, 56, 60, 86, 156, 161, 184; John, 32, 35, 39, 43, 70, 73, 78, 103, 162, 169, 170, 179, 180; John Clemenson, 220; John Clemson, 176, 223; John W., 16; Joseph, 9, 13, 15, 16, 18, 46, 55, 58, 61, 67, 75, 185, 225; Joshua, 162; Keziah, 13, 58; Leticia, 78; Letitia, 56, 161; Lydia, 13, 32; Margery, 161, 191; Martha, 13, 61, 161, 184; Mary, 9, 13, 16, 28, 30, 32, 38, 46, 64, 111, 154, 161, 167, 181, 182, 185, 194, 204, 210; Mary Ann, 176, 220, 223; Moses Wills, 161; Pricilla, 13; Rachel, 65, 161; Rebecca, 161, 198; Samuel, 9, 36, 47, 73, 78, 161, 175, 176, 180, 182, 188, 192, 197, 205, 208, 216, 220, 223; Sarah, 9, 13, 15, 16, 20, 37, 38, 43, 46, 47, 52, 55, 56, 64, 65, 67, 75, 85, 86, 89, 154, 161, 162, 179, 183, 184, 192, 234; Sarah L., 161; Sophia, 161; Susanna, 176, 220, 223; Sybil, 162, 183; William, 39, 43, 46, 47, 52, 70, 85, 86, 161, 162, 180, 183, 184, 193

MIDDLETON, Aaron Hewes, 182, 191, 211, 212; Ann C., 234; Charles R., 186; Charles T., 234; Deborah, 78, 79, 193, 218; Elizabeth, 75, 187; Gabriel, 187; Guili, 53; Hannah, 88, 89, 185; Hudson, 75, 83; Hugh, 90; Jacob, 185, 221; John, 88, 242; Josiah Hews, 231; Lusy, 167; Mary, 73, 75, 78, 83, 182; Samuel, 167, 241; Sarah, 51, 75, 76, 77, 80, 88, 167; Sibyl, 221; Thomas, 73, 75, 76, 78, 79, 80, 83, 88; William, 75, 76, 77, 80, 89, 242

MIDDLETOWN, Thomas, 73

MIFFLIN, Edward, 9, 30, 42; John, 44; Mary, 9, 44, 178; Samuel, 9, 30, 42, 44, 178

MILBAN, John, 107

MILBORN, Elizabeth, 107; John, 107

MILLER, Ebenezer, 42, 44, 86; Elizabeth, 109; Esther, 212; Grace, 65; John, 42, 65, 73, 152, 181, 185, 229, 233; Joseph, 181, 185, 223; Lewis, 221; Margaret,

152, 185; Mark, 44, 86, 184; Mary, 31, 65, 73, 152; Mary A., 223; Michael, 73; Phebe, 184; Sarah, 44, 204; William, 77, 108; William Foster, 184
MILLERN, Elizabeth, 107; John, 107
MILLES, Sarah, 78
MILLS, Elizabeth, 74, 88, 89; Francis, 74; Grace, 65, 74, 75, 80, 87; John, 65; Mary, 65, 74
MINTLE, George, 241
MITCHEL, Henry, 146; Ida, 146; William, 146
MITCHNER, John, 74
MONTGOMERY, William, 82
MOOR, Mary, 218
MOORE, Agnes, 198; Allen, 60; Amasa, 180; Benjamin, 73, 79, 84, 89, 112; Bethual, 180; Bethuel, 60; John, 84; Joseph, 23; Joshua, 182; Keturah, 79; Martha, 60; Mary, 23, 218; Nancy, 23; Rachel, 182; Samuel, 89; Sarah, 73, 78; Sibylla, 182; Thomas, 104, 207
MORAN, Henry, 114
MORE, Benjamin, 71; Joseph, 84, 101; Mary, 84; Patience, 84
MORGAN, Agnes, 85; Agnis, 7; Alexander, 66, 72, 75, 77, 81, 82, 83, 84, 103; Ann, 56; Daniel, 69; David, 176, 200; Edward, 242; Elizabeth, 7, 47, 66, 87, 164, 176, 200; Griffin, 7; Griffith, 56, 66, 85; Hannah, 7, 72, 75, 77, 81, 82, 84, 176, 200; Isaac, 176, 200; Jonathan, 52, 176, 199, 200; Joseph, 7, 8, 47, 49, 56, 75, 83, 84, 85, 87, 89, 103, 155, 164; Lydia, 81; Mary, 8, 49, 52, 56, 72, 155; Patience, 241; Rebecca, 56; Sarah, 8, 47, 49, 82, 155, 164
MORRIS, Anthony, 87; Elizabeth J., 166; Israel, 87; James, 88; John, 166; Margaret, 178; Mary, 189; Prudence, 166; Rachel, 89; Richard Hill, 178; Thomas, 242; William, 178
MORTON, Mary, 206; Samuel, 112
MOSS, Ann, 100
MOUNC, John, 182
MOUNCE, Ann, 207
MUFFLIN, Mary, 189
MULICKA, Catherine, 117; Eric, 117; John, 117
MUNCE, Ann, 182
MURPHY, Elizabeth, 121, 146; Henry, 121, 122, 124, 125, 135, 137, 138, 141, 146, 148; Isabel, 121, 122, 124, 125; Isabella, 141, 146; John, 125, 146; Margareth, 141; Martha, 135, 137, 138, 146, 148; Noah, 214, 218; Rebecca, 124, 146; Sarah, 122, 141, 146
MUSGROVE, Mary, 70

-N-

NEALE, Hugh, 114
NEGRO, Andrew, 136, 138; Christiana, 136; Flora, 124, 136; Quamim, 138; Quamini, 134, 140; Rhoda, 124; Susanna, 136, 140; Susannah, 134; William, 134
NEILL, Hugh, 114
NEISSER, George, 121; Theodore, 121
NELSON, Susanna, 64

NEWBERRY, Hasker, 69; Marcy, 71; Mercy, 69, 73, 77, 82; William, 69, 73, 77
NEWBIE, Hannah, 88
NEWBOLD, Barzillai, 70; Clayton, 84; Hannah C., 176, 228; John, 82; Joseph W., 176, 228; Michael, 82, 84
NEWBOULD, Sarah, 100
NEWBURY, Edward, 35; Hannah, 35; Henry, 35; Mercy, 86; Stephen, 35; William, 35
NEWBY, Edward, 64, 66; Elizabeth, 2, 37; Hannah, 2, 33, 43, 64, 66; Mark, 64, 93; Marke, 2; Stephen, 2
NEWMAN, Eliz. Knight, 162; Richard, 162, 175; Ruth, 162, 175
NEWTON, Joseph, 242
NICHELSON, Abel, 190
NICHOLSON, Abel, 19, 22, 25, 60, 63, 91; Abigail, 44, 45, 50, 74; Ann, 84; Anne, 34; Elizabeth, 190, 215; George, 65; Hannah, 66, 75, 76, 77; Isaac, 19, 22; Isaac W., 22; Jane, 80; John, 207; Joseph, 22, 34, 66, 75, 77, 87, 91; Lindsay, 207; Mark, 87; Marsha, 202; Mary, 19, 22, 60, 209; Nehemiah, 114; Priscilla, 22; Prisilla, 22; Rachel, 87; Rebecca, 19, 25, 60; Ruth, 42, 50, 80; Samuel, 19, 34, 44, 66, 74, 75, 76, 77, 80; Sarah, 44, 74, 76, 200; Zebedea, 22
NICHOLSON-EVANS, Ruth, 45
NICKLES, Hannah, 15; John, 15
NIGHTINGALE, Thomas, 114
NIXON, Isaac, 196, 206; Thomas, 65, 94

NOAH, Isaac, 142; Michael, 142, 143; Sarah, 137, 138, 142, 143, 145
NOBEL, Thomas, 238
NOBLE, Joseph, 76; Lydia, 62, 107; Samuel, 62, 76
NORBURY, Thomas, 103
NORCROSS, Frances, 79; John, 79; Mary, 79
NORRIS, Elizabeth, 43, 113
NYBERG, Laurence, 117; Lawrence, 118

-O-

OATS, Joseph, 240
OFFLEY, Ann, 167; Daniel, 167
OGBORNE, Jane, 68, 70; Mary, 68, 69, 71, 72, 73, 77, 81; Samuel, 68, 70
OGBURN, Mary, 36
OGDEN, Hannah M., 233; Joseph, 182, 186, 233; Mary, 182; Mary Ann, 186; Samuel, 182, 186; Sybil, 208
OLDCRAFT, Ann, 194; Joshuah, 198
OLDEN, Elizabeth, 238
ORIN, Mary, 81
OSBORNE, Mary, 82
OSGDEN, Rebecca, 89
OSTER, Joshua, 241; Owen, 241; Samuel, 241; Sarah, 242
OWEN, Benjamin, 176, 226, 233; David, 176, 226, 233; Humphrey, 92; John, 176, 233; Joseph, 176, 226, 233; Mercy, 176, 226, 233; Rebecca, 82, 168; Rowland, 102; Rowlon, 100
OWENS, Amos, 241; Rebecca, 41, 48, 83

-P-

PACKER, Ann, 162, 210, 211;
Ann C., 176, 219, 231, 235;
Catharine, 162, 210, 211;
Catherine, 235; Christiana, 162,
218; Christiannah Dorothy, 162;
Christinnah Dorothy, 218;
Daniel, 162; Elizabeth, 162;
Elizabeth R., 162, 235; Esther,
162, 218; Jacob, 231; James,
231, 235; Joel, 176, 219, 231,
235; John, 162, 176, 210, 211,
218, 219; Jonathan, 162, 218,
234; Kitturah, 210; Laurence,
162; Lawrence, 218; Paul, 176;
Rhoda, 162, 218; Richard, 176,
219, 231, 235; Samuel, 162, 176,
210, 211, 219, 229, 231, 235;
Sarah, 162, 176, 210, 211, 219,
231, 235; Sarah Ann, 231, 235;
Susanna, 223; William, 176;
William P., 211, 235; William
Paul, 162, 219, 231
PAINE, Elizabeth, 65, 69, 86;
Sarah, 71
PAINTER, John, 84
PANCOAST, Aaron, 56, 176, 180,
183, 202, 204, 210; Aaron
Whitall, 176; Ann, 176, 204,
207; Anne, 211; Benjamin, 79;
Beulah, 150, 171, 184, 215, 226;
Caleb, 201; David, 206; Edward,
150, 152, 184; Hannah, 150,
152, 183, 184, 203, 206, 216;
Hannah A., 176, 218; James,
176, 206, 216, 218; Martha, 176,
216, 218; Mary, 56, 180, 216;
Sarah, 79, 176, 206, 216, 218;
Tacy, 203; William, 56
PARCH, Henry, 241
PARKER, Ann, 35; John, 238;
Joseph, 39, 69; Mary, 98;
Meribah, 39, 69; Rebecca, 43;
Samuel, 108; William, 238
PARROT, Elizabeth, 42
PARROTT, Elizabeth, 44, 81
PARSON, Mary, 211
PARSONS, Anna, 121
PARVIN, Ketherine, 103;
Thomas, 102
PASCHALL, Frances, 158; John,
158
PATRICK, Hannah, 100
PATTON, Silla, 147
PAUL, Ann, 48; Anna, 156; Charles, 236; Charles Paul, 162;
Cooper, 162, 163, 183, 218;
David S., 163; Deborah, 49;
Delia, 163, 187, 220; Elizabeth,
156, 163, 180, 220; George M.,
163; George Mickle, 162; Hannah, 162; Harriet, 163, 220;
Isabel, 48, 156; Isabella, 163,
187, 220; Jeremiah, 188; Joel,
11, 156, 163, 220; Joshua, 49,
162, 163, 176, 183, 188; Josiah,
56; Lydia C., 163; Mary, 56,
162, 183, 220; Mary Ann, 163;
Nathan, 49, 163; Philip, 94;
Samuel, 11, 48, 156, 163, 180,
187, 188, 197, 201, 203, 204,
207, 208, 216, 220; Sarah, 190;
Sarah Cooper, 162; Sarah D.,
163; Sibyl, 162, 163; William
Atkinson, 177, 203; William
Mickle, 162; Yemmons, 215;
Yeomans, 177, 203
PAXTON, Aaron, 183; Eliada,
183; Leticia, 183
PEACOCK, Dinah, 90; Elizabeth,
83; John, 83, 90; Thomas, 241;
William, 241

PEARCE, Levi, 111
PEARSON, Mary, 242; Sarah, 242
PEASLEY, Amos, 176, 236; Anna, 176, 236; Elijah, 236; Esther, 176, 236
PECK, Robert, 241
PEDRIC, Thomas, 69
PEDRICK, Philip, 47, 70; Sarah, 47
PERKINS, Abigail, 66; Benjamin, 230; Elizabeth, 196, 204; Lydia, 68
PETERSEN, Christina, 116; Jeremiah, 116; Laurence, 116; Luke, 116; Magdalene, 117; Susannah, 116; Zachariah, 117
PETESON, Sarah, 147
PETIT, Ann, 24; Jonathan, 24; Sarah, 24
PETTIT, David, 176, 197, 200; Jonathan, 176, 197, 200; Joseph, 163, 176, 197, 200; Mary, 163, 176, 200; Rachel, 176, 197, 200; Sarah, 176, 197; Thomas, 176, 197, 200; Woodnut, 176, 197, 200
PHILLIPS, Elizabeth, 83; Peter, 83; Sarah, 89
PHILPOT, Elizabeth, 116; Nicholas, 116
PHIPIER, Jacob, 238; Michael, 238
PICKERING, Jane H., 163; Jonathan, 163
PIDEGON, Job, 237; John, 237
PIERSON, Gebulon, 143; Mary, 127; Sarah, 127; Zebulon, 127
PIKE, John, 241; Joseph, 242; Mary, 163; Rebecca, 163; Sarah, 163; Stephen, 163

PILGRIM, Thomas, 93
PILLMAN, Daniel, 214; Sarah, 214
PIMM, Elizabeth, 67; John, 67, 89
PINE, Ann, 19, 55; Benjamin, 58, 85, 163, 214, 218; Elizabeth, 38; Hannah, 58, 85, 163, 185, 214; John, 55; Joseph, 163, 214, 224, 225; Joshua, 62, 214, 228; Judith, 62, 150, 163, 164, 184, 185, 186; Mary, 58, 85, 150, 163, 171, 184, 214; Mary H., 229; Priscilla, 58, 163, 164, 186, 214; Rachel, 55, 58; Rebecca, 163, 214; Samuel, 163, 214; William, 62, 150, 163, 164, 184, 185, 186, 214
PINYARD, John, 78, 86, 108; Martha, 86; William, 74
PITTMAN, Daniel, 217; Sarah, 217
PLATT, Ann, 182; Joseph, 86; William, 86
PLUM, Frederick, 242; John, 242; Joseph, 242
POLYRLAEUS, J. C., 117
POND, Robert, 99; Sarah, 99
POTS, Sarah, 99
POTTER, Guila, 57; Guili, 53; James, 53, 57; Thomas Middleton, 53, 57
POTTS, Charles, 184, 211; Samuel, 184; Sarah, 184; Thomas, 69
POULSON, Bridget, 141
POWEL, Robert, 102
POWELL, Sarah, 111
POWELL-NEWBOLD, Elizabeth, 72
POWELL-SATTERTHWAITE,

Rebecca, 80
POYRALAEUS, John C., 116
PRATT, Martha, 217
PREDRICK, Thomas, 98
PRESTON, John, 111; Mary, 50
PRICE, David, 69, 70; Grace, 99; Hannah, 161; Mary, 91; Sarah, 78; William, 78
PRICKETT, Brizallah, 81; Brizzallah, 84; Elizabeth, 83; Ellington, 66; Hannah, 81, 83, 84; Jacob, 81, 83, 84; Josiah, 50; Rosanna, 84; Sarah, 50; Zachariah, 66; Zachary, 66
PRITCHETT, John, 90
PRYOR, Hannah, 53; Mary, 53; Thomas, 53
PULLEN, John, 114

-Q-

QUAMINE, Andrew, 135
QUAMINI, William, 145
QUICK, John, 241; Thomas, 241

-R-

RADDERON, John, 241
RAKESTRAW, Elizabeth, 66; Grace, 66, 67; Hannah, 56, 72, 83; Mary, 72, 75; Sarah, 66; Thomas, 66, 72, 75; William, 66
RAPER, Abigail, 66; Thomas, 66
RATHMELL, John, 38
RAWLE, Francis, 99
RAWLINGS, Ann, 226; Paul, 223; Thomas, 222, 224
RAWLINS, John, 116; Margaret, 116
RAYNOLD, John, 140
RAYNOLDS, Ann, 146; John, 146
REAPER, Joshua, 66
REDMAN, Alexander, 57; Andrew, 91; Elizabeth, 23; Elizabeth Estaugh, 23; Hannah, 11, 31, 44, 57; James H., 23; John, 11, 44; John E., 11; Joseph, 11, 31; Joseph Swatt, 23; Marcy, 11, 31; Mary, 11, 44, 54, 86, 91; Rebecca, 11, 19, 23, 54, 57, 58, 59; Rebecca Hopkins, 23; Sarah, 11, 19, 31, 40, 41, 59; Sarah Hopkins, 23; Thomas, 11, 19, 23, 31, 40, 41, 44, 54, 57, 58, 59, 86, 101, 106, 107; White, 54
REEVE, Ann, 176; Benjamin, 57; Beulah, 163, 176, 209, 223; Charles, 220; Clement, 176; Eleanor, 164; Elizabeth, 51; Hannah, 176, 201, 223; Israel, 176; Jane, 164; John, 51, 164, 176, 180, 198, 209, 215, 216, 223, 230, 233; Joseph, 164, 176; Joshua, 57; Louisa, 176; Lylia, 208; Mark, 181, 201; Mary, 176; Miles, 176; Rachel, 57; Sarah, 176; Sarah B., 176; Susan, 176; William, 207
REEVES, Ann, 219, 224; Benjamin, 164; Biddle, 163, 164, 196, 213; Clement, 63, 215, 219, 224; Elizabeth, 155, 163, 164, 168, 185; Hannah, 164, 168, 182; Henry, 62; Isaac, 164, 220; Israel, 215, 219, 224; John, 164; Joseph, 47, 87, 155, 168, 182, 183, 185, 201, 203, 215, 216, 219, 224, 227; Joseph T., 168; Joshua, 163; Louisa, 215, 219; Louisa M., 224; Mary, 155, 164, 185, 215, 219, 224, 229, 232; Rachel, 62; Samuel, 164, 227; Sarah, 47, 63, 164, 219, 220,

224; Sarah B., 224; Susan, 63, 215, 219, 224; Thomas, 47, 87, 164; William, 216; Zachariah, 62
REILY, Sarah, 147
REINKE, A., 119; Abraham, 116, 117, 118
REITZ, Matthew, 118
RICHARD, Mary, 68
RICHARDS, Mary, 165; Samuel, 165; Sarah, 165, 177
RICHARDSON, Ann, 6; Edward, 6, 68, 82; Elizabeth, 62; Francis, 65; Jesse, 6; Jonah, 6; Jonath, 29; Martha, 6; Mary, 6, 37, 68, 82; Rachel, 76, 110; Ruth, 6, 29; Tabitha, 6, 82; Thomas, 62; William, 62
RICHMAN, Jacob, 112
RIDGEWAY, Daniel P., 233
RIDGWAY, Abigail, 70; Andrew, 190; Andrews, 192, 193; Aquilla, 190, 191; Catharine, 85; Daniel P., 233; Elizabeth, 195; John, 210; Noah, 53, 158, 175, 183; Rebecca, 53, 158, 175, 176, 215; Richard, 70; Sarah, 158, 175, 183, 194, 214; William, 190, 192
RIDGWAY-JONES, Sarah, 211, 223, 224
RIGGS, George, 33; Lydea, 33; Lydia, 36, 65, 66
RIGHT, Rachell, 95; Sarah, 70
RILEY, Sarah, 140
RILLINGS, Walter, 71
RISDON, Ann, 78; George, 78; John, 78
RITEZ, Magadalena, 142; Matthew, 142
ROBERSON, Mary, 73
ROBERT, Hester, 176; Thomasin, 176, 198; Unit, 198;
Unity, 176
ROBERTS, Daniel, 7, 52; Deborah, 83; Elizabeth, 79, 91; Enoch, 60, 87, 90, 150; Hannah, 7, 35, 52, 79; Hester, 191, 196, 207; Jacob, 7, 52; John, 35, 36, 55, 60, 73, 74, 76, 79, 83, 94; Joseph, 57; Joshua, 55, 73; Mary, 30, 35, 52, 69, 71, 72, 74, 76, 79, 83, 150, 188, 226; Phebe, 55, 60; Rachel, 140, 150; Samuel, 87; Sarah, 35, 36, 68, 70; Susanne, 57; Thomasin, 191, 196; Unit, 191; Unity, 202; William, 57
ROBERTSON, James, 112
ROBESON, Sarah, 57
ROBINSON, Elizabeth, 71; Thomas, 37, 93
ROBSON, Elizabeth, 71; Thomas, 80, 164
RODGERS, Nicholas, 42; Thomas, 42
ROGERS, Abraham, 211, 214; Abraham Inskeep, 231; Abraham J., 18; Ann, 76, 89; Esther, 83; Grace, 53, 193; Hannah, 18, 208, 211, 214; Joseph, 18; Joseph Powell, 164, 208, 211, 214, 231; Prudence, 55, 76; Samuel, 164, 231; Sarah, 18, 164, 208, 211, 214, 231; Sarah Ann, 18, 164, 208, 211, 230; Thomas, 164, 231, 242; William, 53, 76, 81, 89, 167
ROSS, Isaiah, 111
ROTHMALL, Mary, 96
ROW, David, 113
ROWAND, Amy, 18; Barton, 18; Charles, 18; Elizabeth, 18; Joseph, 18, 57; Mary, 18;

INDEX

Rachel, 18, 57; Robert, 18, 57; Samuel, 18; William Donaldson, 18
ROWELL, John, 75
ROWEN, John, 75
ROWLAND, Hannah, 114; Sarah, 52
RUDDEROW, Samuel, 242; Sarah, 74, 83; William, 242
RUDOLPH, Abram P., 164; Elizabeth, 164; Hannah, 164; Thomas, 164
RULON, Abel, 211, 220; Ann, 219; Benjamin, 164, 179, 181, 190, 201, 219; Beulah, 176, 219; Clayton, 164, 176, 186, 219; Daniel, 176, 219; David, 176, 222; Eleanor, 236; Ephraim, 176, 211, 219, 231; Eunice, 192; Hannah, 176, 222; Henry, 164, 165, 179, 181, 199; John, 164; John W., 219; Jonathan, 176, 222; Mark Townsend, 176, 219; Mary, 164, 176, 222; Mary W., 219; Moses, 64, 164, 176, 186, 219, 236; Phebe, 176, 222; Priscilla, 164; Rachel, 176, 186, 219; Sarah, 164, 219; Sibyl, 165; Sibyl C., 230, 235; Susanna, 64, 186; Susannah, 176, 219; Theodosia, 164, 165, 235
RUMPERT, Ann, 140
RUNDT, Chas. Godfrey, 121
RUTTER, Catherine, 135; Elizabeth, 135
RYLINS, Walter, 71

-S-

SAINT, Deborah, 75; Elizabeth, 92
SALES, Alice, 65

SALSBURY, Elizabeth, 128; Hannah, 127, 128, 129, 130, 132, 138, 140; John, 127, 128, 129, 130, 132, 139; Joseph, 127; Mary, 132, 145; Samuel, 130
SANDERS, Debora, 190; John, 91; Sarah, 91; William, 142
SATTERTHWAIT, David, 82; Mary, 82; William, 82
SATTERTHWAITE, Jane, 87; Richard, 80
SATTERWAITE, Jane, 52
SAUL, Joseph, 104, 105, 106
SAUNDERS, Deborah, 55, 165; Edney, 165; Elizabeth, 55, 86, 165; Hannah, 165; Isaac, 165, 199, 201, 227, 233; James, 165, 177, 187, 201, 205, 210, 213, 216, 217, 219, 227; John, 55, 69, 72, 86, 165; John M., 165; Joseph, 165, 185, 227; Lydia, 165; Marie, 227; Marsha M., 165; Mary, 165, 210; Mary P., 234; Mary R., 187; Rachel, 165, 184, 185; Rebecca, 165; Samuel, 215, 218, 224; Samuel R., 165; Samuel Richards, 165; Sarah, 165, 177, 187, 190, 205; Sarah M., 165; Sol. Lippincott, 165; Solomon Lippincott, 190; Thomas, 165, 184, 185, 199, 201
SAXBY, Esther, 3
SCATTERGOOD, Aaron, 91; Elizabeth, 46; Rebecca, 91, 163; Sarah, 163; Thomas, 163
SCHNELL, Leonhard, 116
SCOTT, Job, 141; Susan, 223, 235
SCULL, Abel, 114; Daniel, 114; Gideon, 185; Hope, 164, 165, 223; Paul, 164, 165, 185, 223;

284 EARLY CHURCH RECORDS OF GLOUCESTER COUNTY

Philip, 112; Sarah, 164, 185
SEAD, Caleb, 159; Phebe A., 159
SEALLES, Allis, 33
SEAMAN, Rachel, 98
SEATON, Jane, 100, 101
SEERS, Jacob, 140
SEIDEL, An. Nathaniel, 137; Ann Johanna, 123; Nathaniel, 123
SEILLES, Alice, 33
SELLES, Alice, 65
SHAKLE, Thomas, 33
SHARP, Amos, 90; Ann, 69, 90, 105; Anna, 177, 197, 202; Anthony, 2, 7, 14, 30, 39, 85, 177, 178, 194, 197, 202; Elijah, 89; Elizabeth, 1, 2, 3, 7, 14, 28, 30, 38, 64, 65, 69, 86, 113, 177, 202; Esther, 76, 77; Hannah, 2, 35, 66, 73, 86; Hope, 193; Hosea, 7, 30; Hugh, 35, 90; Isabel, 144; Jemaima, 39; Jeremiah, 2; John, 1, 2, 3, 7, 14, 37, 38, 65, 69, 85, 86, 90, 97, 143, 165, 178, 228; Joseph, 1; Judith, 98; Katharine, 28; Katherine, 1; Martha, 1, 28; Mary, 1, 7, 14, 30, 72, 73, 76, 77, 80, 84, 85, 89, 101, 110, 178, 195, 228, 230; Nehemiah, 14, 166, 190; Samuel, 1, 2, 3, 66, 69, 72, 84, 97, 105, 113; Sarah, 1, 2, 14, 28, 64, 66, 81, 84, 165; Silvester, 74; Thomas, 1, 2, 3, 28, 38, 64, 65, 66, 96, 103; William, 2, 35, 39, 65, 71, 73, 74, 76, 77, 80, 81, 83, 84, 88, 100
SHARPE, John, 95; William, 34
SHARPLESS, Daniel, 63; Enos, 63; Hannah, 63
SHELDON, Sarah, 209
SHEPPARD, Benjamin, 187, 234; John, 187; Lydia, 166; Mary, 187; Mary R., 235; Rebecca J., 166; Richard W., 166
SHINFELL, Frederick, 239
SHINN, Azariah, 51, 92; Benjamin, 223, 226, 227; David, 63; Grace, 63; Hannah, 41, 54, 56; Jacob, 56, 75; James, 48; John, 75; Mary, 68, 75, 80; Peter, 63; Sarah, 51, 92; Zilphah, 48
SHIRBE, Joseph, 124; Ruth, 124; Sarah, 124
SHIVER, Samuel, 96
SHIVERS, Amy, 46, 57, 87; Anna, 215; Hannah, 112; John, 46, 87, 112; Mary, 46, 50, 111
SHORES, Mary, 79, 109; Rachel, 78
SHREVE, Amos, 83; Keziah, 191; Mary, 58, 83
SHRIVE, Hannah, 78
SHRIVERS, Ann, 88; Hannah, 88, 111; Joshia, 88
SHRIVES, Abigail, 92; Ann, 92; Joseph, 92
SHUSTER, Christiannah Dorothy, 162; Laurence, 162; Mary, 162
SHUTE, Aaron, 177, 219, 221; Alice, 177, 219; Ann, 119, 120, 121, 142; Ann Hazeleton, 177; Ann Hazelton, 221; Ann Hazleton, 219; Anne, 121; Annie, 119; Catherine Elizabeth, 135; Charles, 177, 219, 221; Deborah, 123, 137; Diana, 121, 143; Elisha, 132; George, 119, 143; Hannah, 123, 125, 128, 147, 209; Hannah Lydia, 134, 137; Hariet, 219; Harriet, 177; Harriett, 221; Henry, 122, 123,

125, 126, 128, 129, 131, 132, 135, 136, 143, 185; Hiram, 177, 219, 221; Isaac, 122, 123, 124, 125, 126, 127, 131, 136, 137, 146, 147; Issac, 125; Ivy, 137; John, 131; Joseph, 120, 123, 125, 126, 127, 128, 129, 131, 132, 135, 136, 137, 138, 139, 143, 147; Joseph Uriel, 124, 142; Levi, 123, 146; Lydia, 122, 123, 125, 126, 128, 129, 131, 134, 135, 136, 185; Mary, 140, 146; Nathan, 128; Obadiah, 136; Rebecca, 129, 136; Ruth, 137, 147; Samuel, 126, 147, 177, 185, 218, 219, 221, 222; Sarah, 123, 124, 125, 126, 127, 128, 129, 131, 132, 135, 136, 138, 143, 144, 146, 147; Susan, 126, 127; Susanna, 122, 123, 124, 127, 133, 137, 140, 146; Susannah, 91; Susanne, 125; Sybilla, 223; Thomas, 122, 125, 132, 134, 136, 144; William, 119, 120, 121, 122, 123, 125, 129, 140, 142, 144, 146; William Henry, 134

SHUTES, Isaac, 138; Sarah, 138, 139; Susanna, 138; Thomas, 138, 139

SHUW, Ann, 37

SICKLER, Christopher, 237; Elizabeth, 237; Hannah, 237; Jacob, 237; John, 237, 238; John Ashbrook, 237; Susanna, 237; Thomas, 238; William, 237

SIDDON, Ezekiel, 37, 64, 68; Jane, 37, 65, 72, 108; John, 64; Sarah, 68

SIDDONS, Hannah, 97; Henry, 113; Job, 61, 75; Josiah, 61; Mary, 89; Rachel, 61

SILVER, Aaron, 78; Abel, 55; Abraham, 55; Anna, 108; Archibald, 78; Hope, 55; Mary, 78

SIMES, Jeremiah, 238

SIMMS, David, 229; Sarah, 186; Stephen, 186

SIMON, Rachel, 35

SIMS, David, 166; Sarah, 166, 204; Stephen, 166

SLEEPER, Benjamin H., 163; Deborah, 163; Jane H., 163; John, 81

SLIM, Peter, 242; Samuel, 242

SLOAN, Amos Haines, 22; Andrew, 89; Ann Brick, 21; Ann Eliza, 21; Beulah, 22; Edwin, 17; Elizabeth, 43, 52, 87; Elizabeth Haines, 17; Hannah, 21, 213; James, 16, 17, 22, 42, 43, 45, 57, 59, 107, 184; James Clements, 21; Jeremiah Haines, 17; John, 16, 22, 60; Joseph, 16, 17; Marmaduke, 17; Mary, 16, 17, 42, 43, 45, 49, 57, 89; Rachel, 16, 17, 22, 32, 57, 59, 184; Rachel Clement, 17; Rebecca, 21; Richard, 22; Ruth, 16, 59; Samuel, 16, 32; Sarah, 42, 54; Sarah Knight, 22; William, 16, 17, 21, 184; William West, 21

SLOANE, James, 60; Rachel, 60

SLOCUM, Hannah, 36; Nathaniel, 36; Sarah, 36, 69

SMALLWOOD, Isaac, 133, 138; Mary, 47

SMART, Anne, 155; Catharine, 155; Isaac, 155

SMITH, Abraham, 136, 148; Ann, 143, 177, 189; Catharine, 147;

Catherine, 136, 148; Cathrine, 138; Daniel, 91, 166; Deborah, 47; Elizabeth, 38, 43, 166, 177, 189, 238; Francis, 100, 102, 103; Frederic, 131; Frederick, 122, 123, 124, 125, 126, 127, 128, 129, 130, 132, 139, 140; Isaac, 43, 85, 113; Israel, 177, 189; Jacob, 177, 189; James, 4, 29, 67, 68, 238; James B., 238, 239; Jane, 4, 68, 88; Jesse, 56, 166, 177, 203, 215, 228; John, 68, 166, 238; Jonathan, 143, 177, 189; Joseph, 136, 147, 148; Joyce, 37; Martha, 179; Mary, 14, 43, 85, 140, 148, 166, 177, 228; Mary Cassell, 203; Phebe, 177, 189; Rachel, 166; Randall, 177, 189; Rebecca, 56, 74, 166, 213; Ruth, 4; Samuel, 177, 189; Sarah, 123, 124, 238; Tailer, 238; Thomas, 37, 38, 56, 93, 166, 177, 189; William, 110, 177, 189

SNAGG, Margareth, 141; Thomas, 141

SNOWDEN, Abigail, 177, 196; Elizabeth, 8, 14, 32, 177, 179, 192, 196; Hannah, 177; Isaac, 177, 196; Isaac Ballenger, 8; Isaac Ballinger, 50; Jane, 49; John, 14, 32, 80, 81, 177; Leonard, 14, 49, 177, 192; Lydia, 177; Margaret, 8, 49, 50, 177; Mary, 8, 14, 177, 192, 196; Rebecca, 14, 177, 192; Richard, 14, 49, 177, 192, 215; Ruth, 80; Sarah, 8, 14, 49, 80, 81, 177, 192; William, 8, 49, 50, 81, 177, 179, 188, 196

SNOWDON, Beulah, 165, 166, 225; Hannah, 166, 191; John, 166, 191; Leonard, 190; Lydia, 166, 191; Margaret, 166, 191; Mary, 166, 190, 191; Miles, 223, 225; Myles, 165, 166, 185; Rebecca, 190, 225; Richard, 185, 190, 225; Sarah, 185, 190, 225; Sarah M., 165; William, 166, 191

SOMERS, Albertus, 233; Hannah, 65, 233; John, 65

SOMMERS, Job, 111

SOUTHERLIN, Thomas, 106

SOUTHWICK, Josiah, 36

SPARKS, Mary, 122, 123, 124, 125, 132, 133, 136, 138, 188, 196

SPENCE, John, 110

SPENCER, Hannah, 81

SPIAROW, Sarah, 141

SPICER, Esther, 3, 34, 64, 93; Jacob, 76, 106, 107, 191; Martha, 64; Samuel, 34, 64; Samuell, 93; Sarah, 34; Thomas, 76, 106

STACY, Rebecca, 68; Ruth, 69, 71, 81

STACY-BEAKES, Ruth, 72

STARR, Eunid, 211; James, 44; John, 84; Moses, 44, 84

STAUGH, James, 102

STEELMAN, Anne, 120; Charles, 120; Elias, 110; Rebecca, 120

STEP, Martin, 135; Susanna, 135; Ursula, 135

STEPHENS, Ann, 177, 224, 228; Elizabeth, 80; Hannah, 177, 224, 228; Harriet, 177, 228; Isaac, 86, 98, 99, 100, 101, 165, 177, 224, 228; Issac, 224; Jacob, 177, 224, 228; James, 103;

INDEX

Rachel, 86, 165; Robert, 40, 80, 81, 97, 100, 103; Samuel, 99; Sarah, 39, 70, 177, 224, 228
STEVENS, Henry, 90; Susannah, 92
STEVENSON, Jennings, 52; Sarah, 52
STEWARD, Ann, 191, 199; Bridget, 191; Elizabeth, 191, 199
STEWART, James, 47; John, 47, 52; Mary, 47, 52
STILES, Ann, 242; Hannah, 29, 50, 51, 87; Isaac, 51, 241; James, 241; John, 242; Joseph, 241; Levy, 241; Mary, 87; Nicholas, 241; Robert, 50, 51, 74, 83, 87; Sarah, 74, 83
STOAKES, Elizabeth, 87; Joseph, 83; Joshua, 87; Judith, 83; Thomas, 43
STOAKS, Joseph, 83; Mary, 83
STOCKDELL, Ann, 76; Jarvis, 72; Mary, 72; Rachel, 48, 72, 86, 87
STOCKEL, Hannah, 68
STOCKTON, Abigail, 70; Ann, 169; Mary, 68; Samuel, 169; Susan, 169
STOGDALE, Mary, 102
STOKES, Abigail, 51; Abraham, 13, 32; Altlantick, 19; Ammy, 8; Amy, 19, 20, 30, 43, 48, 49; Ann, 90, 166, 208; Aquila, 19; Aquilla, 177, 222, 230; Atlantick, 33; Benjamin, 13, 78; Braddock, 56; Carleton, 166; Deliverance, 71, 81; Elisha, 20, 230; Elizabeth, 8, 13, 56, 177, 222; Elizabeth F., 230; Elizabeth J., 166; Esther, 13, 19, 20, 25, 55, 61, 151; Hannah, 8, 13, 52; Hannah Roberts, 166; Harvey, 177, 222; Henry, 177, 230; Hezekiah, 20; Hope, 19, 61, 166, 185, 187, 208; Isaac, 19, 166; Isaac Borton, 166; Jacob, 8, 51, 77; John, 8, 90; Joseph, 8, 13, 36, 40, 41, 72, 73, 75, 76, 84, 206, 208; Joshua, 8, 13, 19, 20, 30, 41, 43, 48, 49; Josiah, 13, 166, 185, 187, 208, 217, 222, 226, 230, 234, 235; Judith, 41, 72, 75, 84; Kezia, 13, 79; Lydia, 45, 71, 166, 208; Martha, 20, 47, 72; Mary, 36, 49, 56, 76, 84, 175, 185, 208; Mary Ann, 20; Priscilla, 19; Rachel, 8, 19, 33, 40, 48, 50, 71, 73, 79; Rebecca, 73; Rosanna, 77, 47; Samuel, 8, 19, 25, 40, 49, 61, 73, 177, 222, 230; Sarah, 13, 52, 55, 56, 73, 78, 151, 166, 177, 187, 208, 222, 230; Susan, 166, 187; Thomas, 8, 13, 36, 40, 41, 43, 52, 55, 56, 65, 71, 73, 76, 77, 79, 151, 166; William, 13, 166; William Borton, 177, 230
STONE, Abraham, 242; John, 241, 242; Mary, 104; Sarah, 242; Thomas, 242
STORY, Hannah, 91
STOULKS(STOKES), Thomas, 95
STOW, Michael, 242
STRAITEN, George, 129; Immanuel, 129, 130; Sarah, 130; Sarah Shute, 129
STRATEN, Emanuel, 35; Mark, 37; William, 35, 37
STRATON, Emmanuel, 37; John,

105

STRATTEN, Immanuel, 144; Sarah, 144

STRATTON, Aaron, 15; Abigail, 15; Ann, 40, 76, 89, 90, 91, 128; Benjamin, 133; Bethuel, 177, 193; Charles, 15, 60; Daniel, 15, 89, 104; David, 40, 84; Elias, 177, 196; Elizabeth, 15; Emanuel, 73; Enoch, 76, 109; George, 15; Hannah, 73; Immanuel, 128, 133, 136; Isaac, 91; Isaiah, 177, 196; John, 89, 104; Joshua, 15; Josiah, 15, 188; Mark, 40, 76; Martha, 73; Mary, 15, 84, 177, 193, 194, 196; Michael, 15, 60; Rebecca, 210; Rhoda, 15, 60; Sarah, 128, 136; Sarah Shute, 133; Susannah, 84; William, 201

STREOMBACK, Jacob, 241

STRETCH, Deborah, 47; Joseph, 47, 87; Joshua, 47, 49, 87; Lydia, 49

SUNDERLAND, Thomas, 70

SWAIN, John, 69

SWAINE, Elizabeth, 81; John, 81; Mary, 81

SWETT, Benjamin, 56; Joseph Cooper, 56; Mary, 56

SWIFT, Abigail, 193; Rebecca, 205

-T-

TABER, Elizabeth, 113

TANNER, John, 71, 72

TANTUM, Abigail, 227; Abigail R., 177, 228; Benjamin, 227; Benjamin T., 177, 228; David, 227; George, 227; George B., 177, 228; Joseph, 177, 228; Susanna, 177, 227, 228; Thomas, 177, 227; Thomas H., 177, 227, 228; Warren, 177, 227, 228

TATUM, Abigail, 168; Allen, 167, 230; Ann, 167; Anne, 167, 232; Charles, 167; David, 211, 212; Edward, 167; Elizabeth, 167, 183; George, 10, 31, 167, 212; Hannah, 167, 216; Isaac, 10, 31, 167; Isaiah, 226; John, 10, 43, 50, 166, 167, 180, 182, 188, 195, 197, 198, 199, 203, 207, 208, 209, 212, 213, 216, 217, 220, 232; John Ward, 167; Joseph, 167; Josiah, 167, 222, 228, 235; Ludy, 167; Martha, 203; Mary, 167; Rachel, 167, 223; Sarah, 10, 31, 43, 50, 166, 167, 180, 201; Sibyl, 182; Susanna, 168; William, 168; William R., 167; William Rogers, 167

TAYLOR, Ann, 106; Dorcas, 133, 145; Elizabeth, 146, 147, 237; Esther, 237, 238; George, 237, 238, 239; Hannah, 66, 67, 70, 74, 79, 81, 237; Isaac, 145, 188; Jacob, 71, 106; Jane, 137, 138, 139; John, 70; Samuel, 241

TEAS, Charles, 181; John, 181; Rachel, 181

TEES, Mary, 204

TERRAPIN, Philip, 241

TEST, Benjamin, 49, 51, 167, 168, 182, 188, 205; Elizabeth, 49; Francis, 49, 226, 231, 235; Hannah, 168; Isaac B., 167; Rebecca, 188, 204; Rebekah, 167, 168; Samuel, 168; Sarah, 51, 167, 168, 221; Zaccheus, 51, 167, 168, 188, 205; Zacheus,

INDEX

182
TEW, Samuel, 113
THACARA, Benjamin, 64; Hepzibeth, 64; Thomas, 64
THACHERA, Thomas, 34
THACKARA, Benjamin, 69; Elizabeth, 87; Hannah, 66; James, 87; Mary, 68; Sarah, 67; Stephen, 87
THACKERA, Richard, 3; Thomas, 3
THACKERELL, Hannah, 91
THACKERY, Elizabeth, 49, 91; Hannah, 43; James, 49; Joseph, 43, 88, 90; Stephen, 43, 49; Thomas, 91
THACKRA, Esther, 93; Thomas, 93
THACKREA, Esther, 35; Francis, 1; Hannah, 34; Hepzabeth, 1; Thomas, 1, 34, 35; Thomas A., 1
THACKRY, Elizabeth, 52; James, 52; Stephen, 52
THOMAS, Atlantic, 160; Grace, 84; Hannah, 78; James, 142; Jesse, 86; John, 86, 239; Jonathan, 113; Mary E., 160; Philip, 78, 84; Prudence, 90; Sissee, 241; William, 160
THOMPSON, Aaron, 177, 195, 196, 203, 204; Abigail, 177, 195; Ann, 54, 177, 195; Anne, 212; Deborah, 177, 203; Edward, 50, 52; Elizabeth, 50; James, 87; Joshua, 189; Peter, 50, 52; Rebecca, 177, 195, 203; Samuel, 87, 177, 204; Sarah, 145
THOMSON, Elizabeth, 50; Hannah, 168; Peter, 50, 168, 171; Rebecca, 168; Rebecca O., 171;
Sarah B., 171
THORN, Abigail, 182; John, 78, 105, 177, 219; Joseph, 78; Letitia, 79, 84; Lydia, 177, 219; Mary, 78, 177, 206, 219, 241; Mary Ann, 177, 219; Sarah, 79, 177, 219; Thomas, 79, 84, 110, 177, 182, 219
THORNBROUGH, Thomas, 95
THORNBURY, Thomas, 99
THORNE, Abigail, 13, 20, 23, 53, 57, 59, 60; Ann, 13, 40, 60, 79; Benjamin, 13; Chalkley, 20; Charles Haines, 20; Clayton, 20; Elizabeth, 20, 23; Esther, 63; Hannah, 24, 84; Hannah D., 24; Isaac, 13, 23, 57; Isaac H., 23; James, 26; Job, 20; John, 13, 26, 40, 53, 79; Joseph, 13, 63; Josiah, 63; Laetitia, 84; Mary, 13, 51, 53, 54, 56, 79, 87; Mary H., 20, 63; Rachel, 23; Richard, 23; Samuel, 13, 20, 63; Samuel Collins, 20; Sarah, 20, 63; Sarah Ann, 23; Sarah S., 20; Thomas, 13, 20, 23, 24, 40, 53, 57, 59, 60, 84; William, 13, 20, 24
THORP, Amos, 168; Hannah, 168; Jabez, 168; Meribugh, 168
TILL, John, 88; Margaret, 88
TILTON, Esther, 34, 64
TIMES, Mary, 34, 36
TINDAL, Benjamin, 103, 104; Joseph, 103
TINDALL, Dorcas, 38, 66, 70; Elizabeth, 38, 94; Isabel, 65; Joseph, 38, 66, 70, 94; Mary, 66, 80, 94; Ruth, 65, 74, 111; Thomas, 65
TINDEL, William, 139
TINDLE, Dorcas, 69; Joseph, 69;

Sarah, 69
TOMES, Samuel, 33
TOMKIN, George W., 221
TOMKINS, Thomas, 238
TOMLINS, Eleanor, 53
TOMLINSON, Ann, 12, 59, 168, 183; Benjamin, 13; Catherine, 12, 48, 49; Daniel, 83, 92; Eleanor, 14, 55; Elenor, 45; Elizabeth, 8, 12, 39, 55, 71, 72, 80, 84; Ephraim, 8, 12, 30, 39, 59, 80, 85, 98, 108, 168, 183; Isaac, 87; James, 12, 32; John, 14, 30, 45, 87, 101; Joseph, 8, 13, 30, 39, 47, 48, 49, 69, 71, 72, 87, 100, 101, 105, 168, 178, 183, 209, 213, 229; Lydia, 12, 31, 47, 87; Margaret, 71; Mary, 8, 69, 72, 85, 87, 178, 213; Othnial, 105; Priscilla, 227, 229; Rebecca, 83, 89; Samuel, 7, 48, 49, 83; Sarah, 8, 12, 31, 59, 80, 85; Vurner, 168; Warner, 178, 213; William, 83, 99
TONKIN, Christiana, 185; Edward, 152, 168; George W., 178, 185, 225; Israel, 185; Martha, 178, 225; Mary, 152, 168; Samuel, 168, 197, 201, 207, 208
TOWNSEND, Abigail, 112; Ann, 193, 221; Caleb, 179; Daniel, 179; Elizabeth, 64; Isaac, 44, 86; John, 64; Richard, 64; Ruddock, 112; Sarah, 44
TOY, Andrew, 241; Elijah, 242; Hezekiah, 241; Jacob, 241
TROSH, Elizabeth, 178, 207; Jacob, 178, 207; James, 178, 207; Paul, 178, 207; Sybilla, 178, 207; William, 178, 207
TROTH, Deborah, 82; Elizabeth, 21, 25, 60, 66, 67, 70, 209; Esther, 21; Jacob, 21, 25, 60, 209; James, 21, 209; Jane, 67, 90; Joseph, 21; Joseph Nicholson, 25; Mary, 21, 60, 66; Mary H., 25; Paul, 21, 25, 60, 61, 82, 209; Paul Hillman, 25; Rebecca, 25, 70; Sabyllah, 21; Sybilla, 209; William, 21, 66, 67, 70, 82, 90, 209
TURNER, George, 84; Jane, 41, 73, 78, 84; John, 41, 69, 73, 77, 78, 84; Mary, 41, 77; Robert, 113; Sarah, 78
TUSSY, Cathrine, 141; Elizabeth, 142; Stephen, 141, 142
TYLER, Edward, 108; Elizabeth, 48; Mary, 77; Rachel, 57; Rebecca, 54
TYLEY, Anna, 114; Elizabeth, 114
TYLY, Mary, 112
TYSON, Ann, 97; Derrick, 68; Isaac, 62; Jesse, 62; Margaret, 62

-U-
UPTON, Sarah B., 171

-V-
VAN NEMEN, Andrew, 138
VANDERGRIFT, Lawrence, 241
VANEMAN, Andrew, 125, 126, 127, 128, 129, 130, 131, 134, 136, 137; Catherine, 127, 128, 129, 130, 131, 134; Christine, 130; Daniel, 132; Ebenezer, 129; Elizabeth, 127; Garrit, 127; Gerrit, 127, 128, 129, 130; Margaret, 128; Mary, 125, 126, 127, 128, 130, 137; Peter, 127, 129,

INDEX

130, 132; Rebecca, 127, 129, 130, 132; Susan, 127
VANERMAN, Gerrit, 126, 136; Mary, 125; Sarah, 136
VANMEMAN, Andrew, 139
VANMEMEN, Andrew, 148; Catherine, 148; Christine, 148; Gerrit, 139, 148; Mary, 148; Sarah, 139
VANMEMENS, Gerret, 137; Sarah, 148
VANNEMAN, Andrew, 122, 123; Catherine, 119, 134; Daniel, 119; David, 120; Isaac, 117; John, 117; Margaret, 120; Mary, 117, 122, 123, 138; Mehetabel, 120; Peter, 119, 142; Samuel, 119; Sarah, 119
VANNEMEN, Cathrine, 147; Gerrit, 147; Sarah, 146
VANNEMENS, Andrew, 139, 143; Catharine, 144; Catherine, 143; Elizabeth, 143; Gerret, 138; Gerrit, 143; John, 144; Mary, 143; Peter, 143, 144; Rebecca, 143, 144
VANNERMAN, Andrew, 123, 124; Mary, 123
VAUGHAN, James, 242
VENABLE, Isaac, 242; William, 242
VENICOMB, Anna, 44, 51; Anne, 54; Frances, 44; Mary, 68; Rachel, 44, 68, 84; Sarah, 42, 85; William, 68
VENNAL, Adam, 242
VICKERS, Ann, 48; Anna, 48; Peter, 48
VINECOMB, Francis, 56; Rachel, 56; William, 56
VINNEMAN, Deborah, 49

VINSON, Rachel, 97

-W-

WADE, John, 117, 118; Lydia, 47; Mary, 47, 52
WAITE, Benjamin, 80; Jane, 80; Rachel, 80
WALKER, Dane, 128; John, 128, 139; Mary, 34, 128
WALL, Martha, 98
WALLACE, David, 241
WALLIS, William, 114
WALMSLEY, Abigail, 61; Jopseh, 61; William, 61
WALTON, Elizabeth, 226, 234, 235; Elizabeth S., 230; Rebecca, 160; Tacy, 205
WARD, Aaron, 17; Abigail, 151, 168, 169, 186, 187, 213; Achsa E., 168; Alexander, 22; Ann, 168, 178, 191; Ann C., 168; Beulah, 151, 169, 187, 213, 234; Charles, 168, 186; David, 114, 168, 179, 184, 197, 201, 202, 203, 207; Deborah, 178, 211; Edith, 168, 186, 203; Eliza, 168, 178, 211; Elizabeth, 178, 191; George, 16, 39, 46, 50, 51, 66, 76, 78, 84, 87, 88, 92, 150, 151, 166, 168, 179, 181, 186, 199, 200, 222; George C., 55, 178, 211; George M., 17; Guilielma, 191; Gulielma, 178; Habbakuk, 72; Hannah, 16, 17, 22, 39, 62, 67, 73, 168, 178, 184, 226, 227; Hezekiah, 241; Isaac, 17, 55, 178, 189, 191; Isaiah, 151, 168, 178, 186, 187, 213, 214, 221; James, 39, 114, 168, 178, 213, 215, 222, 223; John, 16, 22, 62, 73; John B., 22, 168, 228;

Joseph, 213, 233; Joseph T., 169; Joshua, 178, 211; Josiah, 50, 90, 115, 215; Kesiah, 50; Lettitia, 16; Lydia, 22; Mann, 22; Margaret, 46, 166, 168; Margaretta, 169, 186, 213; Martha, 77; Mary, 51, 73, 84, 151, 178, 191; Mary Ann, 178, 211; Mary C., 22; Mason, 16, 22, 62, 178, 226, 227; Moses, 39, 68; Phillis, 85; Phyllis, 68; Rachel, 16, 17, 51, 92, 150, 151, 168, 171, 181, 184; Rebecca, 55, 178, 191; Rebekah, 178, 211; Richard Jordan, 17; Rosanna, 111; Ruth, 168, 222; Samuel, 116; Sarah, 16, 43, 116, 166, 191, 202; Seth Samuel, 116; Susanna, 169; Susannah, 114, 213; Thomas H., 22; William, 70, 73, 110, 213, 227; William T., 168; William Tatem, 227
WARDELL, Eliakim, 68; Lydia, 68
WARDEN, Isaac, 241; John, 241
WARDER, Mary Anne, 110
WARE, Azariah, 51; David, 51; Hope, 92; John, 51, 91; Letitia, 217
WARNER, Agnes, 18; Amos, 18; Benjamin, 234; Francis, 18; Hannah A., 169; Henry, 169; Lydia, 18; Mary, 18; Samuel, 18
WARREN, Hannah, 168; Isaac, 72; Meribugh, 168; Robert, 168
WARRICK, Beulah, 219
WARRINGTON, Abraham, 52; Edward, 169; Elizabeth, 42, 75, 76, 77, 81; Hannah, 39, 53, 76, 81; Henry, 38, 39, 42, 68, 75, 76, 77, 80, 81; John, 68, 75, 186; Margaret, 169; Mary, 52, 77, 186; Nathan, 169, 186, 227; Priscilla, 169; Rachel, 42; Sarah, 81; Seth Harrison, 169; Thomas, 52, 76
WARWICK, Anthony, 59; Elizabeth, 59
WATERS, Mary, 140; W., 242
WATSON, Esther, 114; Samuel, 114
WATTINILE, J., 137
WATTS, Isabella, 64; Sarah, 37, 64, 65, 67
WAYATT, Bartholomew, 39
WEATHERS, Mary, 201
WEATHRBY, Edith, 228
WEAVER, Thomas, 92
WEBB, John, 50
WEBSTER, Ann, 14, 179; Beulah, 18; Elizabeth, 14, 18, 25, 52; Hannah, 14, 63, 178, 189, 194; Hannah Willis, 25; Isaac, 14, 25, 178, 189, 194; Jacob, 14, 32; James G., 18; Joseph, 25; Joshua Evens, 18; Josiah, 14, 18, 32, 58, 59, 178, 189, 194; Katherine, 80; Lydia, 166, 169; Marmaduke, 18, 25; Mary Ann, 163, 169; Newton, 62; Patience, 14, 58, 194; Priscilla, 18; Samuel, 14, 18, 25, 42, 52, 58, 59, 63, 163, 166, 169, 178, 179, 183, 189, 190, 194, 200, 220, 226, 228, 230, 234, 235; Sarah, 14, 25, 42, 52, 58, 59, 62, 63, 85, 163, 166, 169, 178, 183, 189, 194, 232; Sarah Ann, 25; Thomas, 14, 42, 80, 85, 105
WEISNER, Catherine, 123; Jacob, 123; Mary, 123

INDEX

WEITZEL, Anna Maria, 141; Conrad, 141; Jacob, 141
WEIZEL, Mary, 139
WELLS, Edward, 44; Hope, 40; William, 44
WENZEL, Anna Maria, 141
WEST, Catharine V., 230; Catharine Vaughn, 220; Charles, 77, 78, 79; Elizabeth, 185, 188, 197; George, 208; George Ash, 195, 197; James, 77; Jane, 158; Jerusha, 230; John, 164, 181, 185; Mary, 44, 51, 108, 164; Rebecca, 212; Sarah, 164, 181, 219; Sybilla, 185, 220; Thomas, 78, 195, 197
WEST-HEWES, Jane, 164
WETHERBY, Edith, 227
WETHERILL, Ann, 112
WEVER, Edward, 98
WHETSTONE, Mary, 241
WHILLY, Ann, 145; David, 148
WHITAKER, Margaret, 42, 44, 71
WHITAL, Ann, 43; James, 43
WHITALL, Aaron, 170; Abraham, 10, 31, 170; Amy, 170; Ann, 12, 45, 169, 170; Ann Cooper, 170; Ann W., 155, 169, 171, 226; Benjamin, 169, 170, 180, 202, 235; Caroline, 170; Charles, 170, 229; David, 12, 155, 169, 170, 171, 225; Deborah, 10, 155, 169, 170, 182; Ebenezer, 171; Edith, 169; Elizabeth, 169, 171, 208, 234; Elizabeth Estaugh, 170; George, 10, 31, 170, 205, 210; Hannah, 12, 65, 66, 86, 169, 170, 181, 201, 219, 228; Hannah Ann, 169; Hannah M., 234; Hannah Mickle, 171; Hannah W., 171; Henry, 169; Israel F., 221; Israel Franklin, 170; James, 10, 12, 45, 65, 66, 72, 86, 169, 170, 179, 180, 182, 188, 193, 197, 199; Jane, 72, 169, 221; Jean, 170; Job, 12, 45, 65, 72, 170, 181, 197; John, 12, 66, 200; John G., 221; John Gill, 12, 170; John Mickle, 170; John S., 170, 179, 234; Joseph, 169, 170, 171, 180, 201, 216, 219, 228, 234, 236; Joseph C., 219; Joseph Cooper, 170; Joshua, 170; Lathia, 10; Margaret, 169; Mark, 170, 227; Mary, 10, 65, 70, 72, 73, 74, 75, 80, 169, 170, 180; Rebecca, 10, 170, 182, 212; Richard, 10, 170, 193, 199; Sarah, 12, 66, 80, 81, 170, 183, 234; Sarah M., 234; Sarah Mickle, 170; Susan, 169; Tacy, 221; William, 10, 169, 170, 171, 207; Zatthu, 170, 199
WHITE, Ann, 158, 171, 183, 197; Ann W., 171; Catharine, 28; David, 171; George, 148; Hannah, 180; Isaac, 171, 210; Jane, 67; Joel, 171, 210; John, 171, 210; Joseph, 40, 72, 171; Joshia, 11; Josiah, 39, 71; Martha, 103, 146, 148; Mary, 210; Peter, 39, 70; Rebecca, 11, 57, 171, 210; Rebeckah, 105; Samuel, 171, 210; Sarah, 40, 171, 220; William, 40, 48, 86, 158, 171, 180, 183, 188, 202, 203, 204, 210, 213
WHITEALL, Hannah, 4, 37, 97; James, 4, 37, 102; Jane, 4, 68; Job, 4, 29, 37; John, 34;

Thomas, 88
WHITELOCK, Joseph, 241
WHITLACK, Joan, 76
WHITTAKER, Margaret, 44
WHITTALL, Ann Cooper, 170
WHITTEN, Grace, 69
WICKERS, Elizabeth, 64
WICKWARD, Samuel, 73, 104; Sarah, 73; William, 65, 73
WICKWARE, Sarah, 67
WILCOX, Elizabeth, 99; Joseph, 80
WILKENS, Alice, 90; Thomas, 90
WILKINS, Amos, 91, 102; Ann, 14, 48; Benjamin, 14, 204; Constantine, 14, 32, 48, 85, 198; Elizabeth, 58, 69, 72, 86; Hannah, 66, 80, 88; Isaac, 79; Jacob, 26, 63, 83; James, 14, 84, 192; Joanna, 14, 85, 204; John, 14, 48, 70, 84, 86, 88, 179, 198; Joseph, 74; Martha, 78; Mary, 66, 72, 74, 75, 79, 81; Mary C., 26; Rachel, 51, 70; Rebecca, 26, 65, 74, 82, 83; Samuel L., 26; Samuel T., 63; Sarah, 58, 74, 83, 86, 179; Sarah Ann, 26; Susanna, 65, 66; Susannah, 67, 68, 70, 72; Theodosia, 230; Theoscia, 63; Thomas, 14, 65, 66, 68, 69, 70, 72, 74, 79, 80, 81, 83, 85, 98, 194, 196; William, 58, 67, 78, 81, 83, 86, 96; William Wood, 192, 198, 199
WILLARD, Henry, 67, 112; Judith, 67; Thomas, 34, 67, 93
WILLET, Richard, 107
WILLETS, Hannah, 231; Jeremiah, 63; Job, 27, 63; Judith, 28; Mary, 27, 63; Nathan L., 27; Sarah, 44; Sarah A., 27
WILLETTS, Jeremiah, 28; Jeremiah L., 27
WILLIAMS, Agnes, 135, 145; Elizabeth, 113; Isaac, 76, 106; John, 135; Judah, 95; Justice, 135, 145; Justin, 149; Sarah, 88
WILLIAMSON, Francis, 241; John, 242
WILLIS, Esther, 73
WILLIT, Abigail, 178, 192; Amos, 178, 192; Charity, 178, 192; Edward, 178, 192; Isaac, 178, 192; John, 178, 192; William, 178, 192
WILLITS, Edward, 202; Mercy, 64; Pheby, 98
WILLS, Aaron, 42; Abigail, 108; Amey, 50; Amy, 15; Ann, 67; Daniel, 42, 68, 77; Deborah, 78; Elizabeth, 15, 42, 68, 74, 77, 78, 79, 80, 87, 97; Hannah, 50; Hope, 67, 68, 70, 72, 75; Jacob, 76; James, 68, 76; Joab, 15, 47, 50; John, 67, 68, 70, 108; Margaret, 161; Micajah, 47; Moses, 161; Rachel, 161; Rebecca, 47, 49, 83; Sarah, 44, 76, 84, 108
WILLS-TOMLINSON, Rebecca, 86
WILLSHIRE, John, 113
WILSON, Elizabeth, 242; James, 179, 189; John, 242; Keziah, 202; Mary, 189, 224, 242; Samuel, 242; Thomas, 179, 190
WILTS, Tabor, 238
WILTSE, Mary, 141
WILTSHIRE, John, 113
WINN, Elizabeth, 1, 3; John, 1
WISEMAN, John, 116
WISHEM, Jacob, 241

INDEX

WITTERS, Mary, 82
WOOD, Abigail, 70, 88; Alice, 65, 69, 70, 72, 80; Allis, 1; Ann, 86, 153, 184, 201, 211; Anna Maia, 228; Anna Maria, 186; Benjamin, 36, 75, 110, 126; Beulah, 27; Caleb, 199; Catharine, 62, 140, 142; Catherine, 125, 186; Christiana, 126, 147; Christina, 132, 133, 136, 137, 148; Christine, 125, 128, 129, 130, 131, 143; Constantine, 1, 69, 70, 72, 80, 98; David, 178, 194, 198; David C., 216, 221; Elizabeth, 42, 75, 171, 178, 197, 207, 217; Frances, 182; Francis, 80; George, 43; Gill, 148; Hannah, 5, 34, 36, 49, 50, 53, 66, 70, 75, 77, 178, 207, 217, 233; Hannah Ann, 62; Hannah S., 235; Harriet Smith, 132; Henery, 2; Henrey, 1; Henry, 1, 5, 36, 65, 66, 74, 76, 87, 93, 94, 95, 106, 171, 179, 197; I., 134; Isaac Haines, 207; Isaac Horner, 178; Isaac Hornor, 217; Jachomia, 125, 126, 130, 131, 132, 133, 136, 143; Jachomiah, 125, 134, 138, 139; Jackoniah, 121; Jacob, 171, 179, 197; Jacomiah, 148; Jaconias, 121, 133; James, 5, 27, 53, 62, 72, 80, 83, 86, 188, 195; Jeconiah, 147; Jehu, 54, 178, 207, 217; Jeremiah, 2, 54, 142, 178, 195, 197, 207; Joanna, 69, 85, 98; Jochamia, 128, 129, 136, 142; Jochomiah, 142; John, 1, 2, 5, 65, 70, 72, 74, 80, 87, 93, 98, 128, 153, 180, 184, 199; Jonathan, 5, 33, 93; Joseph, 75; Judith, 67; Kay, 75; Latitia, 86;
Letitia, 56, 82, 89, 161; Lydia, 178, 200; Margaret, 43; Margaretta, 232; Marmaduke, 180, 186, 195, 205; Mary, 1, 5, 54, 67, 70, 72, 74, 75, 79, 80, 125, 178, 184, 186, 207, 217, 218, 230; Mary Gill, 129, 143; Rachel, 48, 86, 87, 153, 161, 178, 200, 221; Rebecca, 27, 86, 178, 198; Rebeka, 2; Richard, 27, 49, 53, 76, 188; Ruth, 27, 62, 87, 92, 171; Samuel, 136, 212; Sarah, 5, 33, 43, 70, 86, 87, 130, 178, 184, 200, 215, 216, 229; Sibyl, 194; Susan, 184; Tacy, 221; Thomas, 186, 227; Widow, 136; William, 48, 50, 62, 72, 86, 87, 161, 178, 182, 186, 200, 207, 208, 210, 211, 232; Zacheus, 143
WOOD-COLE, Mary, 44, 86
WOOD-COLES, Mary, 43
WOODATH, Sarah, 110
WOODS, Abygall, 35; Alice, 33; Elizabeth, 35; Hannah, 34; Henry, 34; John, 33; Judeth, 34; Mary, 39; Rachell, 33; Sarah, 33, 65, 67, 70
WOODWARD, Elizabeth, 77, 107; Hannah, 226; Joseph, 77
WOOLEY, John, 218, 221; Mary, 35
WOOLLEY, John, 216; Mary, 35
WOOLMAN, Abner, 80; Elizabeth, 80; Patience, 84; Samuel, 80
WOOLMAN-PAINE, Elizabeth, 77
WOOLSTON, Elizabeth, 42, 77
WOOTEN, Esther, 32
WRIGHT, Amos, 46; Ann, 46;

Benjamin, 95; Elizabeth, 39, 68,
80, 171; Hannah, 68; John, 39;
Joshua, 68, 80, 82, 96, 98, 106;
Mary, 82, 171; Nathan, 171;
Peter, 188, 190; Rachel, 40, 65,
73, 79; Rebecca, 68; Sarah, 39,
43, 46, 47, 52, 70, 85, 86, 141;
Thomas, 46, 68
WYAT, Elizabeth, 98
WYATT, Bartholomew, 39;
Sarah, 39
WYETH, Sarah, 95
WYRON, Grace, 66

-Y-

YOUNG, Joseph, 78; Mary, 74;
Phebe, 78

-Z-

ZANE, Azuba, 196, 203; Barzillai,
194; Chattin, 190; Ebenezer,
43; Elizabeth, 79, 204; El-
nathan, 43; Esther, 85; Grace,
67, 69, 70, 98; Henry, 198;
Jane, 74, 85; John, 204, 205,
208; Joseph, 194; Margaret, 66;
Mary, 47, 50, 85, 87, 206;
Merion, 69; Nathaniel, 67;
Rachel, 80; Robert, 47, 50, 74,
79, 80, 85, 87, 195, 212;
Simeon, 85; Simon, 205; Wilkin,
213; William, 47, 213
ZANES, Elizabeth Hillman, 23;
James, 23; Mary, 23; Sarah, 23;
Simeon Ellis, 23; William, 23

Other Heritage Books by Charlotte Meldrum:

Abstracts of Bucks County, Pennsylvania Land Records, 1684-1723

Early Church Records of Burlington County, New Jersey Volumes 1-3

Early Church Records of Chester County, Pennsylvania, Volume 2
Charlotte Meldrum and Martha Reamy

Early Church Records of Gloucester County, New Jersey

Early Church Records of Salem County, New Jersey

Early Records of Cumberland County, New Jersey

Johnston County, North Carolina Marriages, 1764-1867

Marriages and Deaths of Montgomery County, Pennsylvania, 1685-1800